Architecting Fail-Safe Supply Networks

Shabnam Rezapour, Ph.D.

Enterprise and Logistics Engineering
Florida International University, Miami, Florida, USA

Amirhossein Khosrojerdi, Ph.D.

Risk and Portfolio Analytics, Credit and Decision Management
Discover Financial Services, Chicago, Illinois, USA

Golnoosh Rasoulifar, Ph.D.

Postdoctoral Research Fellow
Mewbourne School of Petroleum Engineering
University of Oklahoma, Norman, Oklahoma, USA

Janet K. Allen, Ph.D.

James and Mary Moore Professor
School of Industrial and Systems Engineering
University of Oklahoma, Norman, Oklahoma, USA

Jitesh H. Panchal, Ph.D.

School of Mechanical Engineering
Purdue University, West Lafayette, Indiana, USA

Ramakrishnan S. Srinivasan, Ph.D.

Principal Scientist
TCS Digital Manufacturing and Operations Innovation Program
Tata Consultancy Services, Milford, Ohio, USA

Jeffrey D. Tew, Ph.D.

Chief Scientist and Director
TCS Digital Manufacturing and Operations Innovation Program and
TCS Cincinnati Lab, Tata Consultancy Services
Milford, Ohio, USA

Farrokh Mistree, Ph.D.

L.A. Comp Professor
School of Aerospace and Mechanical Engineering
University of Oklahoma, Norman, Oklahoma, USA

CRC Press
Taylor & Francis Group
Boca Raton London New York

CRC Press is an imprint of the
Taylor & Francis Group, an **informa** business

A SCIENCE PUBLISHERS BOOK

CRC Press
Taylor & Francis Group
6000 Broken Sound Parkway NW, Suite 300
Boca Raton, FL 33487-2742

First issued in paperback 2020

ISBN-13: 978-1-4822-2118-3 (hbk)
ISBN-13: 978-0-367-65896-0 (pbk)

Library of Congress Cataloging-in-Publication Data

Names: Allen, Janet K., author.
Title: Architecting fail-safe supply networks / Janet K. Allen [and seven others].
Description: Boca Raton, FL : CRC Press, [2018] | Includes bibliographical references and index.
Identifiers: LCCN 2018022524 | ISBN 9781138504264 (hardback)
Subjects: LCSH: Business logistics. | Materials management.
Classification: LCC HD38.5 .A566 2018 | DDC 658.7--dc23
LC record available at https://lccn.loc.gov/2018022524

Visit the Taylor & Francis Web site at
http://www.taylorandfrancis.com

and the CRC Press Web site at
http://www.crcpress.com

Foreword

Volatility and risk to business have increased with the complexity of today's global supply chain networks. This is why the proposition of "Fail-Safe Supply Networks" becomes promising. This book is the outcome of a collaboration between TCS Research & Innovation, University of Oklahoma, and Purdue University. I congratulate the authors of this monograph for exploring this subject at depth and providing a framework that can be applied across multiple industries.

The authors establish a framework called Fail-Safe Networks, containing five different components: reliability, flexibility, robustness, structural controllability, and resilience. They take a bold stand contrary to current thinking as embodied in the supply network literature: *disruption management decisions made in the strategic network design level are not independent from variation management decisions made in operational flow planning.* These interactions necessitate managing disruptions and variations concurrently in supply networks.

In this monograph, the authors examine the management of risks along the variation-disruption spectrum in simple as well as convoluted supply networks, using the components of the Fail-Safe framework. They present detailed mathematical models and numerical analysis of results for each component in the framework. They also investigate how risk management decisions made to handle variations and disruptions mutually affect each other, and explore the interactions existing between these two groups of risk management decisions. In closing, the authors apply the framework to other networks such as electric grids and transportation arteries, as well as emerging networks like the Internet of Things (IoT). Technological advances catalyze the formation and growth of networks in various domains, and generalizing the Fail-Safe framework will facilitate risk management in these networks as well.

There is a wide variety of supply network risk management theories. What distinguishes this book is that the approach is holistic, considering both variations and disruptions in supply and demand. It brings together a wealth of research in optimization and uncertainty modeling within the domain. The body of work of Professors Allen and Mistree, and their associates in systems research is well recognized. Dr. Jeff Tew and his team at TCS Innovation Labs bring a real world perspective to the models. I strongly recommended this book to network researchers in general and the Supply Chain Management community in particular.

K. Ananth Krishnan
Executive Vice President and Chief Technology Officer
Tata Consultancy Services

Preface

Networks are ubiquitous—from transportation networks to social networks. Supply networks play an essential role within the economy and within the life of every human being. The networks are increasing in sophistication with advancing technologies such as Mobility, Big Data, Social Media, Cloud Computing, and Artificial Intelligence. These technologies are extending the reach of networks while simultaneously accelerating their real-time capabilities. With increasing complexity and technical sophistication, there is a need to design fail-safe supply networks to mitigate the impact of variations and disruptions on people and corporations.

In this monograph we propose an integrated approach for designing fail-safe supply networks, in the face of both supply and demand risks, and how the impacts are propagated across various levels in the network, drawing upon the concepts of reliability, robustness, flexibility, resilience, and structural controllability. This is achieved by (1) developing a network structure that mitigates the impact of disruptions that distort the network and (2) planning a flow through the network to neutralize the impact of variations. Contrary to current thinking as embodied in the supply network literature, decisions made to manage disruptions are not independent of decisions made to manage variations.

The primary audience of this book includes graduate students in industrial engineering, operations research, and supply chain management, and practicing engineers and managers seeking to improve their supply operations. This monograph comprises ten chapters. We recommend reading Chapters 1 and 10 initially to establish context for what is included in this monograph. While we recommend reading the remaining chapters sequentially, each chapter is self-contained, and can be read independently in any sequence.

In closing, we observe that the material in this monograph is anchored in the doctoral dissertations of Shabnam Rezapour and Amirhossein Khosrojerdi whom we were privileged to mentor at the University of Oklahoma, Norman, USA. Their work was supported by the University of

Oklahoma LA Comp Chair and the John and Mary Moore Chair accounts, Grant NSF ECCS 1128826, and Tata Consultancy Services, India. We much appreciate the guidance provided by Vijay Primlani and the staff of CRC Press to create this monograph.

All of the authors are grateful for the sustained support and encouragement from their families throughout the process of writing this book.

Janet K. Allen and Farrokh Mistree

May 11, 2018

Contents

CHAPTER 1

Conception of Fail-Safe Supply Networks

A network is a set of interconnected entities. Networks permeate many aspects of human endeavor, as evidenced by the structures in education, society, and business, with technological advances catalyzing an unprecedented level of connectivity and dynamic flow. The central problem we address in this monograph is network failure precipitated by various types of risks. To assist in exploring and solving this problem, we focus specifically on supply networks, and recommend architecting **Fail-Safe Supply Networks**. We investigate two main types of risks that threaten supply networks, namely variations and disruptions and explain at a high level the elements of Fail-safe supply networks: reliability, robustness, resilience, flexibility, and structural controllability. Finally, we provide an overview of the following chapters, wherein we describe each of these elements, culminating with our thoughts on how these models can extend beyond supply networks.

1.1 Introduction: Networks and the Power of Connections

Many scientists consider the cell to be the fundamental building block of life. Human brain cells are connected by structures called synapses; there are between 50 trillion and 100 trillion synapses in the average human brain. In neuroscience, the term *livewiring* refers to the process of constant modification to the synaptic connections, a process that is essential to the remarkable adaptability of the brain (Eagleman 2015). Similarly, an individual has many abilities; as individuals form family bonds and wider social ties, their physical, mental and monetary capacities also increase. In the same way, the utility of a single medical diagnostic machine is small compared to one that is connected to several databases and physicians, as these connections facilitate the accuracy and rapidity of diagnoses (Ramo

2016). Likewise, a single computer is quite powerful in terms of data storage and computational speed. In contrast, the internet is a collection of interlinked computers, storing several petabytes of data within approximately 75 million servers, and data generated by user interactions are shared between servers through various communication links (Shroff 2013). The above examples demonstrate the power of connections and networks.

A network is a set of interconnected entities. A city with various neighborhoods and schools connected by roads is an example of a physical network. Facebook, by contrast, is a virtual network of social connections. From early examples such as the Roman aqueducts and the trade routes of the Indus Valley civilization, networks have been an integral part of most human activities, and with the passage of time, have grown in strength and scope. For instance, today's transportation networks span the globe, and communication networks extend into space. The formation and growth of a network expands the role and scope of each entity within the network, as highlighted in the opening examples.

In business, the supplier's role extending to the supplier's supplier and the customer's role extending to the customer's customer illustrate this phenomenon. This structural expansion presents the need for a clear understanding of the requirements and capabilities of key entities. Network influences such as inter-customer connections, direct supplier to customer connections, and innovation in one industry generating opportunities in others, are transforming traditional business models. The ubiquity of networks has shortened distances, compressed time and spawned innovations. Tata Consultancy Services (TCS), a global leader in digital solutions, has identified the Digital Five Forces: Mobility & Pervasive Computing, Big Data & Analytics, Social Media, Cloud Computing and Artificial Intelligence & Robotics (Krishnan 2017). These technologies facilitate, enable, and expand networks, catalyzing an unprecedented level of connectivity. With the explosive growth of networks, comes the associated need to avoid network failures, where the network does not perform as expected. Consequently, we address network failure as the central problem in this monograph. To assist in exploring and solving this problem, we focus on one type of network, namely the supply network.

1.1.1 Supply Networks

Supply networks are engines of economic development. Most products, ranging from a carton of milk to the latest laptop, are produced through the collaborative effort of many enterprises which form a network. This network that extends from the supplier to the end consumer is called the supply network. The various participants, through their facilities and processes, add value to the product as it passes through the network.

Each facility forms a *node* in the supply network and the path taken by the product between two facilities is called a link. A *supply chain* is a simple iteration of the supply network, depicted in Figure 1-1. In this figure, each rectangular box represents a facility such as a supplier factory, warehouse, manufacturing plant, distribution center or a retail store. The arrows indicate connections or links between facilities. The number of serial facilities indicates the depth (d) of the supply chain, with each facility representing a stage, echelon or tier.

The more generic form of a *supply network* is depicted in Figure 1-2. In addition to depth, the supply network also has a breadth dimension (b), which indicates the number of facilities in each level. The supply network also has a more complex structure, in terms of the number and arrangement of the facilities, as well as the connections between them. For instance, there can exist alternate paths between two facilities, or the same facility could connect to two other facilities through different paths. It is worth noting that the actual locations of the facilities in a supply network are often spread across the globe. This supply network concept applies to services as well as products.

A supply network contains a number of flows: *material flows, information flows* and *financial flows* as shown in Figures 1-1 and 1-2 (Tang and Nurmaya Musa 2011). Material flow refers to the movement of raw materials, sub-assemblies and final products within and between facilities; typically, material flows from the supplier to the customer, or upstream to downstream in network terms. Information flow is normally bi-directional and includes demands, purchase orders, inventory status and similar data elements. Financial flows refer to payments, credit terms, contracts and other flows related to money; generally, financial flows take place moving from downstream to upstream. Customers place demands on the distributors and retailers and these demands are fulfilled by a flow of materials from the suppliers to the manufacturers and then to the distributors. The Supply Chain Operations Reference (SCOR) Model

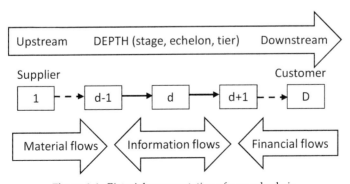

Figure 1-1. Pictorial representation of a supply chain.

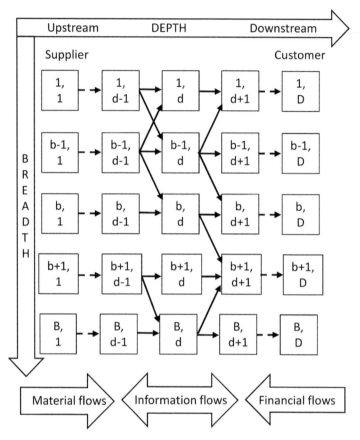

Figure 1-2. Pictorial representation of a supply network.

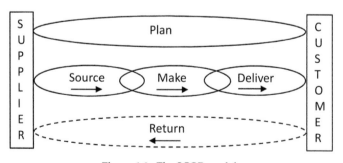

Figure 1-3. The SCOR model.

abstracts the processes at these facilities (Lockamy III and McCormack 2004; Bolstorff and Rosenbaum 2011) as shown in Figure 1-3. The SCOR model provides a unified structure that connects process models, best practices, performance metrics and people skills. For our purposes, we focus on the processes defined in the SCOR model: Plan, Source, Make, Deliver and Return. These processes are interlinked to facilitate bi-directional flows from the supplier's supplier to the customer's customer.

The SCOR model contains processes at four levels. Level 1 includes the top-level processes, namely, Plan, Source, Make, Deliver and Return; these processes establish the scope and parameters of the supply network. In Level 2, the Level 1 processes are further sub-categorized based on the planning and execution configurations. Level 3 comprises process element level detail; for example, transactions and metrics. Level 4 consists of specific company-level tasks. We limit our attention to the processes in Level 1, as these are the core processes for any supply network.

- **Plan:** Encompasses all planning processes focused on synchronizing and optimizing activities across the entire supply network. The key is to balance aggregate demand and supply, including available resources.

- **Source:** Contains processes that procure goods (raw materials, components and finished goods) and services to meet real or anticipated demand; these processes include vendor certification, supplier agreements, inventory management, delivery scheduling, quality control and payment authorization.

- **Make:** Consists of processes that transform materials into a finished product, or create the means for providing services, to meet planned or actual demand. These processes include manufacturing, testing, packaging, storing and releasing the product, as well as managing equipment, facilities, and transportation.

- **Deliver:** Comprises processes that provide services and finished goods to meet planned or actual demand; these processes typically include transportation, order management, warehousing, distribution management, invoicing and import/export requirements.

- **Return:** Includes processes connected to the reverse flow of defective, warranted, or excess products from the customer; these processes include inspection, maintenance, repair, disposition and warranty management. The Return process is an instance of materials flowing from downstream to upstream.

While the SCOR model contains the generic structure of any supply network, depending on the product or service and the type of industry, several derivative structures are possible which manifest as different types of supply networks. For example, an automobile manufacturer has several suppliers, usually in multiple tiers, supplying thousands of different parts to a comparatively limited number of manufacturing plants, where the final products are assembled and sent to distributors. Hur et al. (2004) estimate that 65% of the value added to an automobile is derived from the suppliers. Thus, the automotive supply network is very deep, Source-intensive, and has a converging structure. By contrast, a semiconductor chip manufacturer uses a limited number of raw materials, and in a series of complex manufacturing steps, produces a wide variety of end products. Hur et al. (2004) estimate that more than 50% of the value added in a semiconductor device is attributed to the manufacturing processes, making the semiconductor supply network Make-intensive. This supply network is also deep (though the depth is less than that of an automotive network) and has a diverging structure as the finished products are shipped worldwide.

A retailer's supply network is different from the automotive and semiconductor networks in that it does not usually contain any Make processes, but is heavily focused on Source and Deliver processes for numerous products. These products are typically supplied by Consumer Packaged Goods (CPG) manufacturers, who have extensive supply chains of their own. Since the products must be delivered to retail stores spread across the map, the retail supply network is shallow (limited depth or number of tiers), but has significant breadth. Other supply network structures, for pharmaceutical, textile, and oil & gas companies, are described by Ivanov and Sokolov (2010). While the aforementioned supply networks belong to commercial companies intent on making a profit, there are also other supply networks that are not motivated by profit. The most common examples of the latter are humanitarian supply networks that bring relief supplies and trained professionals to the sites and victims of a disaster (Cozzolino 2012).

In many of these supply networks, both commercial and humanitarian, the primary objective is to satisfy the demands or needs of customers. There could be secondary objectives like maximizing profit or minimizing carbon footprint; however, maximizing demand satisfaction is of paramount importance and most other metrics have a subtle association to satisfy customer demand. Demand in a supply network could be either the orders from an end consumer of the products, such as in a retail store, or the demand from another supply network, such as the orders placed by a retailer on a CPG manufacturer. Some important attributes of demand are:

- Product
- Quantity
- Due date

The Plan activity in the SCOR model balances the supply (of raw materials and components) and the capacity (of resources) with the demand for the end product. The resources include manufacturing resources (for example, machinery and labor) in the manufacturing facilities as well as transport resources (for example, number and maximum volume or weight of trucks) to move material between facilities in the network. If all the flows in the supply network are well coordinated, the supply and capacity are well balanced with the demand; the demand is fulfilled and the customer is satisfied. Any deviation from this balance means unfulfilled demand and consequently, an unsatisfied customer.

Planning is inherently complex, with various sources of complexity: the intricate, static structure of the supply network, the dynamic flows within and between facilities and uncertain events, both internal and external. The complexity also comes into play when the plans are executed. Such widespread complexity leads to a propensity for failures that could occur in the facilities or links of the supply network and impair the network's performance as measured by various metrics related to customer satisfaction. In addition to customer satisfaction metrics, other metrics like cost can also be used to gauge the degree of success or failure of the network. An important customer satisfaction metric is *service level* which has other variants such as *fill rate* and *response delay* (Kleijnen and Smits 2003); a high service level implies a high level of customer satisfaction. There are several examples which underscore the importance ascribed to satisfying customer demand in speedy and timely fashion, exemplifying the service level concept. Amazon is a leader in same day delivery and Barnes & Noble has also partnered with Google to deliver books in specific U.S. locales the same day they were ordered online (Kellogg 2014). Buffalo Wild Wings announced a limited time offer which guaranteed that customers who order from their Fast Break lunch menu would have their food served within 15 minutes or the meal would be free of charge (Taylor 2016). Kroger, a leading retailer, introduced new technology to shorten check out times (Coolidge 2013). Four leading airlines, Delta, Southwest, American, and United are in continuous and fierce competition to differentiate themselves based on their percentage of on-time arrivals (Lazare 2017).

Nevertheless, high service level achieved at high cost is undesirable. In commercial supply networks, increasing cost will reduce profit, while in humanitarian networks, the high cost translates to limited resources, which means providing less relief. Therefore, plans which optimize multiple objectives are generated, for example those which minimize cost and maximize service level. However, even as the most optimal plans are executed, supply network failures are inevitable, due to various risks. Hendricks and Singhal (2005) quantify the negative impacts of supply network failures thus: 33–40% lower stock returns, 107% drop in operating income, 11% increase in cost and 7% lower sales growth. Such far reaching consequences warrant the development of a comprehensive architecture to safeguard the supply network against failures. In the next section, we review the challenges faced by supply networks first at a general level and then at a specific level in various industries.

1.2 Challenges Facing Supply Networks and the Importance of Risk Management

Many adverse circumstances imperil today's supply networks. A few of these challenges are universal: dwindling resources, escalating raw material prices, rising global population and increasing pollution. In this section, we present an overview of the main challenges relevant to supply networks and identify the challenges that are endemic to specific industries. These problems can originate from within or from outside the supply network.

Increasing complexity due to globalization of the supply network: The footprint of any present-day supply network is truly global, with consumers, suppliers, manufacturing and storage facilities spread across the world. This dispersion makes the network structure very complex and allows for the possibility that a disruption in one region of the globe can have ripple effects with the potential to impact multiple partners (Baghalian et al. 2013).

Multiple channels of fulfillment: Most retailers (e.g., Walmart, Target, Macy's) and some manufacturers (e.g., Apple, Dell, Nike) offer many channels to satisfy customer demand. From the traditional brick-and-mortar stores to online portals, various channels create multiple demand streams. Capturing, fulfilling and shaping these demands constitute a major supply chain challenge (Agatz et al. 2008).

Shortening product life cycles: In some industries like high-tech and fashion retail, product life-cycles are continually shrinking; this mandates that the design to production to consumer window be correspondingly short, making the supply network more vulnerable to risk events (Christopher and Lee 2004).

Increasing customer expectations: Recent advancements such as social networks, better quality products (e.g., Blu-ray vs. DVD) and speedy online fulfillment have increased customer expectations. Today's customer expects the delivery of high-quality products cheaper and faster than ever before.

Volatile demand signals: Demands in most industries are subject to high variability, including seasonality (Christopher and Lee 2004). Since demands drive the supply network, these changes must be monitored closely and the supply network operations adjusted accordingly.

High capital investment drives expectation for high capacity utilization: Certain manufacturing industries like semiconductors use capital intensive equipment (Hur et al. 2004). This expense motivates the manufacturers to keep this equipment in operation with as little downtime as possible to increase the return on investment.

Variable supplier commitments and delivery: Suppliers play an integral role in supply networks. Each supplier receives orders from its downstream facility, like a manufacturer. The supplier may not be able to meet the quantity, quality or due date specifications of the order (Christopher and Lee 2004). This impact cascades downstream, ultimately affecting the end customer.

Escalating costs: inventory, transportation, penalties: Significant cost escalation can affect competitiveness and profits. Costs across the supply network, for inventory, transportation, and penalties, must be closely monitored to ensure successful operations (Baghalian et al. 2013).

Complex and sluggish planning processes, needing frequent manual corrections: In most industries supply plans are generated using Advanced Planning Systems (APS) tools. However, these tools have complex data processes and take a long time to run. The resulting plan is obsolete due to changes that occurred in the interim period. The planners must then spend significant amounts of time repairing the plan.

Lack of coordination between various facilities of the supply network: Most facilities of a supply network are subject to variability; it is therefore imperative that the operations of various facilities be closely coordinated (Baghalian et al. 2013). In practice however, such coordination is difficult to achieve. For example, the automotive industry supply network consists of several tiers of suppliers, each with their own databases and planning systems. The geographical spread of supply networks, adds to the challenge.

Focus on Lean and Just-in-Time (JIT) reduces the margin of error: In the past decades, many companies have adopted policies like JIT and Lean Manufacturing focused on reducing costs and increasing efficiency. However, these policies reduce redundant safeguards such as safety stock and multiple suppliers and in so doing, diminish the margin of error in dealing with disruptions (Radjou et al. 2002).

Latency of information flow and lack of real-time visibility: Having access to real-time information would be a great asset in dealing with supply network risks (Christopher and Lee 2004). However, most information flows are subject to delays causing a lack of real-time visibility.

Extracting knowledge or insight from data: In industries like retail, there are many types of data such as POS or point-of-sale data. Similarly, there is an explosion of data from other sources like social media, company reports, and emails. However, companies are not able to exploit these sources for improved network management (Culnan et al. 2010).

Stringent regulatory compliances: Market drivers emerging from sustainability initiatives and pressures from downstream customers, along with complex regulatory requirements, have driven companies to demand more detailed information from manufacturers and suppliers (Wang et al. 2011). Multiple consequences confront companies that fail to adhere to the regulations: from regulatory fines to real impact on the business that could mean reduced market access and position, lower customer satisfaction, and significant operational losses.

Natural disasters: The effects of natural disasters on one far-flung facility in a supply network can cascade through the network causing a failure to fulfill the end-customer demand (Baghalian et al. 2013). For example, following the earthquake and tsunami on 11 March 2011 in Japan, the Toyota Motor Company suffered a production loss of about 140,000 automobiles when it stopped production in twelve assembly plants to allow workers time to repair production facilities and care for their families in the disaster's aftermath (Elkins 2011).

Lack of standard methods and frameworks for risk management: Risk management in supply networks is recognized as a critical requirement. However, paradoxically, investments in risk management are low, compounded by a paucity of standard methods and frameworks (Sodhi and Tang 2012).

In Table 1.1, we list the above challenges faced in supply networks across various industries and identify the specific challenges that we address in this monograph. This list is by no means exhaustive; it is intended to highlight the variety of challenges and the multiple sources of risk that confront supply networks.

The various factors/challenges we describe above lead to *uncertain events* that influence the different processes in the supply network. *Risk* ensues when these uncertainties influence the objectives of the supply network, causing deviations from the expected outcomes (Taylor 2014). In other words, supply network risk is the potential of *failure* or loss due to uncertain events. The loss can emerge either due to the negative impact of the uncertain events, or not acting to take advantage of an opportunity created by the events. The former is known as negative risk and the latter is known as positive risk (Project Management Institute 2013). We do not differentiate between these two types but instead refer to a generic risk,

Table 1-1. Typical challenges faced by supply networks across different industries.

Challenges/Needs/ Priorities	Addressed in Monograph	Industry				
		Hitech	Auto-motive	Manu-facturing	CPG	Retail
Increasing complexity due to globalization of the supply network	Yes-SN structure	x	x	x		
Multiple channels of fulfillment	No	x			x	x
Shortening product life-cycles	No	x	x	x	x	x
Increasing customer expectations	Yes	x	x			x
Volatile demand signals	Yes-demand variation	x	x			x
High capital investment drives expectation for high capacity utilization	No	x	x	x	x	
Variable supplier commitments and delivery	Yes-supply variation	x	x	x		
Escalating costs: inventory, transportation, penalties	Yes-cost optimization		x	x	x	x
Complex and sluggish planning processes, needing frequent manual corrections	No	x	x	x	x	x
Lack of coordination between various facilities of the supply network	Yes	x	x			
Focus on Lean and JIT reduces the margin of error	Yes-safety stock	x	x	x	x	
Latency of information flow and lack of real-time visibility	No		x	x		x
Extracting knowledge or insight from data	Yes	x			x	x
Stringent regulatory compliances	No	x	x	x	x	
Natural disasters	Yes	x	x	x	x	x
Lack of standard methods and frameworks for risk management	Yes	x	x	x	x	x

determined by probability of the uncertain event and its potential impact. The above challenges and the resulting risks engender a need for methods and guidelines to address network risk management. We introduce our architecture for *Fail-safe networks* in the next section.

1.3 An Architecture for Fail-safe Networks

The central problem that we address in this monograph is the failure of supply networks, which necessitates risk management. Several researchers like Handfield et al. (2007) and Wu (2009) emphasize the importance of risk management. Furthermore, some authors like Sodhi and Tang (2012), and Vecchi and Vallisi (2015) consider risk management in supply networks to be a nascent research area. In order to solve this problem, we propose architecting fail-safe supply networks, or in other words, creating an architecture for risk management in supply networks.

Traditionally, architecture has been associated with buildings and construction. However, today architecture is applied to a number of systems such as software, computer hardware, and networks. We adopt the definition proposed by Perry and Wolf (1992): an architecture consists of "elements, form, and rationale". The *elements* are all the different components and connectors that make up the architecture. The *form* expresses the relationships between elements along with associated properties and weights. The *rationale* encapsulates the underlying justification, assumptions and constraints for selecting the appropriate elements and form to satisfy user requirements. Putting these pieces together, an architecture is a high-level model of the organization of components in a system and provides a number of views to satisfy different user requirements.

In the context of an architecture for Fail-safe networks, the elements, form and rationale furnish answers to the *what, how* and *why* questions respectively, for network risk management. Starting with the elements, we identify five different components or methods for risk management as shown in Figure 1-4, namely, reliability, robustness, structural controllability, flexibility and resilience. The connector is the supply chain or supply network, as it contains the variables used in the methods. We express the form of our architecture as mathematical constructs that capture the weights and relationships between the different elements. The elements and their inter-relationships are captured using properties like cost and service level. We use the business need of managing the type(s) of risk to guide the selection of elements and form, along with user assumptions and system constraints, establishing the rationale of the architecture. We summarize the constituents of this architecture and our interpretation in Table 1-2, which represents a single view catering to

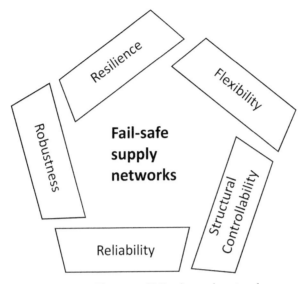

Figure 1-4. Elements of fail-safe supply networks.

Table 1-2. Summary of architecture for fail-safe networks.

Architecture Constituents	Interpretation for fail-safe networks
Elements	**What?**
Components	Methods of network risk management (refer Figure 1-4)
Connectors	The media that link the selected components, typically the supply network
Form	**How?**
Component weights	Relative importance of the selected components
Properties	Attributes of the elements used to form the relationship, e.g., Cost
Relationship	Links within and between components, expressed as a mathematical construct
Rationale	**Why?**
Motivation	The underlying reason to use this model, driven by user requirements
Assumptions	Generalizations or simplifications used to guide the selection of elements and form
Constraints	Upper and lower limits on performance, utilization, etc.
Interpretation	Understanding of the solution; may provide motivation for further study

multiple users. In the next section, we examine the different types of risks and the elements of the fail-safe architecture for supply networks.

1.3.1 *Variations and Disruptions in Supply Networks*

Uncertain events in the supply network give rise to risk (the potential for failure) which could have an impact on the performance of the network. For our purposes, we classify risks depending on the magnitude of impact (Figure 1-5), as variations which are low impact and disruptions which are high impact. *Variations* are minor deviations from the plan that occur during execution. Such variations can emerge either on the supply side or the demand side (upstream or downstream) of the supply network. Examples of supply variations include quality issues in raw materials and scrap in production processes. Jiang (2015) identifies six sources of variation in manufacturing, abbreviated as 5M1E: materials, methods, manpower, machines, measurements, and environment. Most manufacturing processes move gradually from an "in-control" state to an "out-of-control" state; parts produced in this latter state do not meet design specifications and are scrapped (Sana 2010). Demand side variations include fluctuations in order quantities or due dates. *Disruptions* are rare and unanticipated events that have impacts large enough to distort the structure of a supply network by rendering some of its facilities or connecting links inoperative. This distortion affects the network's ability to satisfy customer demand by hampering the normal flow of materials and information; this, in turn, leads to customer dissatisfaction in the short term, and potential damage to brand reputation compounded by the loss of customers in the long term. Disruptions can have natural or man made causes. Some examples of disruptions are: cell phone manufacturer Ericsson reported a quarterly loss of 400 million Euros due to the ripple effects from a fire at one of its supplier plants caused by a lightning strike in March 2000 (Sodhi and Tang 2012); west coast ports in the U.S. were shut down in September–October 2002 for 11 days, leading to losses across many industries estimated at two billion dollars per day (Hall 2004).

1.3.2 *Elements of the Fail-safe Networks Architecture*

Within the Fail-Safe Supply Networks architecture, we propose elements or methods of risk management for different types of risks along the variation-disruption spectrum. Each of these elements has varied definitions in the literature. To level-set the terminology, we will present our definitions and provide references to similar definitions. For variation management, we propose reliability as the preferred risk management method. Variation management is essential, as an unchecked variation can morph into a disruption over time. For example, an overheating motor

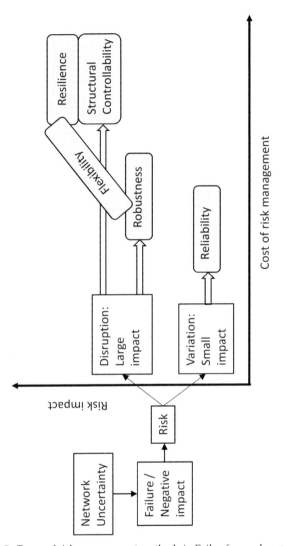

Figure 1-5. Types of risk management methods in Fail-safe supply networks.

in a manufacturing equipment could lead to increased vibrations which can cause a deterioration in surface finish (variation). If the problem is not detected and corrected, over time it could lead to a breakdown of the equipment, thus disrupting the manufacturing facility. Radjou et al. (2002) present an example from a global apparel supply network, where a minor variation in a thread manufacturing machine in Asia snowballs through successive downstream stages and leads to a major delivery delay of a popular model for a European clothing manufacturer, resulting in significant monetary loss.

The generic definition of the "reliability" of a system is its ability to function under normal operating conditions for a certain period (Rausand and Høyland 2004), within specified performance limits (Kapur and Pecht 2014). Stapelberg (2009) indicates that users can identify a lower performance limit, an upper performance limit or both (upper and lower) performance limits. Since the function of a supply network is to fulfill customer demands, the reliability of supply networks is the capability of a company to balance demand and supply quantities. However, from a practical standpoint, this balance is not easily achieved or maintained because both demand and supply processes contain variations. These variations are random and can be modeled as probability distributions based on historical data. We define reliability as the ability of the supply network to meet customer demands in the presence of variations.

In Figure 1-6, the supply network has a nominal performance P_0 which is steady and unchanging, as shown by the solid line. Performance is measured through relevant metrics like demand satisfaction, profit, or capacity utilization. However, since variations are inevitable and their impacts are low, there are small fluctuations in performance around the nominal value. The performance limits for reliability are specified around the nominal performance subject to variations. Typically, these low impact variations are known or can be calculated from historical data. One example is where a supplier's delivery times or quantities have small, known variations. In a supply network, buffering is a typical method for managing variations and ensuring reliability. Hence, in the above example, the manufacturing plant maintains a safety stock of components, which can be used to compensate for the supplier's shortcomings, while maintaining required production levels to satisfy customer demand.

Since the impact of a variation is low, variation management *via* reliability is a relatively low-cost approach. As the magnitude of impact increases and becomes a disruption, other risk management methods are required. These include robustness and resilience, which in turn leverage flexibility and structural controllability. Each of these methods comes at a higher cost as shown in Figure 1-5. A disruption can occur at any facility or lane of the supply network. Flexibility is a supply network's ability to respond to disruptions without excessive time, cost or reduction in service level (Sánchez and Pérez 2005). There are two dimensions of flexibility: *flexibility level* representing robustness, and *flexibility speed* representing resilience. In other words, robustness is defined as the ability of the supply network to maintain an acceptable level of performance when a disruption occurs and resilience is a measure of how quickly the supply network returns to an acceptable level of performance after a disruption,

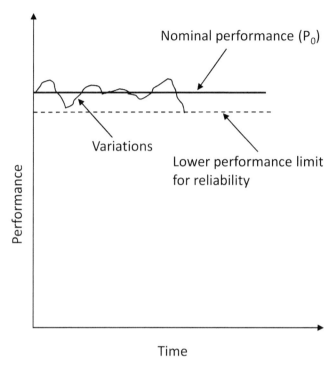

Figure 1-6. Variation and reliability in supply networks.

reflecting the network's capacity to survive, adapt and grow (Ponomarov and Holcomb 2009).

When a disruption occurs, the supply network is no longer operating under normal conditions and the magnitude of the risk's impact is high enough for the performance to deteriorate beyond the bounds of reliability (shown at point A, Figure 1-7). Continuing with the example of the supplier: there could be a fire at the supplier's facility, which shuts down its production completely. This type of risk is a disruption, which requires additional protections and design features to keep the network performance within an acceptable limit. The key for this additional protection lies in increasing the flexibility level or robustness of the supply network. Examples include having a flexible supplier base and flexible transport modes. Thus, when the primary supplier fails, the plan can be adjusted and the required components can be sourced from the secondary supplier. There can be some loss of performance; for instance, the lead time for the secondary supplier could be a slightly longer one, but using this option keeps the performance within acceptable limits. We formally define robustness as the ability of the supply network to withstand the negative impacts of disruptions and maintain an acceptable level of performance, P_a (Figure 1-7).

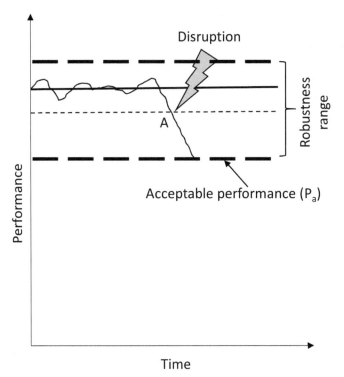

Figure 1-7. Disruption and robustness in supply networks.

Other authors propose similar definitions. Vlajic et al. (2012) characterize robustness as "the degree to which a supply chain shows an acceptable performance ... during and after an unexpected event," and introduce the idea of a "robustness range" with the acceptable performance of Figure 1-7 forming the lower limit of the range. Wieland and Wallenburg (2012) describe an important feature of robustness: "the ability to resist change *without adapting its initial stable configuration.*"

As the impact of a disruption increases, the performance deteriorates correspondingly and outstrips the protection provided by robustness (shown at point B in Figure 1-8). For the above supplier problem, the geographical regions where the primary and secondary suppliers are located could be incapacitated by a hurricane; this impact could shut down all pre-designed supply options, dismantle the structure of the supply network, disrupt the manufacturing operations due to lack of components, and ultimately affect customer demand fulfillment. Furthermore, due to the network connectivity, a disruption at a specific facility can have repercussions beyond that facility, affecting the performance of downstream or upstream facilities as well (Munoz and

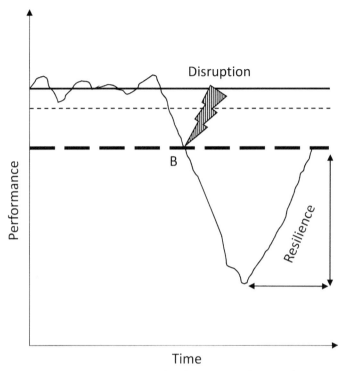

Figure 1-8. Disruption and resilience in supply networks.

Dunbar 2015). Resilience—which includes aspects of flexibility and structural controllability—is the appropriate method of risk management to employ when facing such disruptions. In this case, resilience could involve a dynamic and flexible reconfiguration of the structure of the supply network such as including a spot-buy supplier in the network. This recovery action can often be a lengthy process. Resilience is a measure of how quickly the acceptable performance level can be reached, or the flexibility speed, as shown in Figure 1-8. According to Vecchi and Vallisi (2015) developing resilience in supply networks is among the greatest challenges for a company. The concept of resilience has been studied in various contexts including ecology, materials, and psychology, but the central idea is the return to a stable state after the occurrence of a disruption (Soni et al. 2014). Researchers like Bruneau et al. (2003) and Barroso et al. (2015) refer to the resilience triangle and use the area of the triangle as a measure of resilience. Other authors like Wood et al. (1992) measure resilience as the slope of the recovery curve. We prefer the latter interpretation as it aligns closely with our view of resilience as flexibility *speed*.

1.3.3 Form and Rationale of the Fail-safe Networks Architecture

The preceding sections described the two different types of risk, and the five different elements of the Fail-safe networks architecture. In this section, we will review the rationale and form of the architecture. The form or relationship and weighted properties of the elements are expressed through appropriate mathematical constructs. We use two main constructs in this monograph, namely, optimization, and compromise decision-support. The rationale is driven by the business user requirements, namely to protect the network from different types of risk. This means that the selection of the risk management elements depends on the types of risk that confront the network. For example, protecting the network from variations prompts the user to select reliability, while protecting the network from disruptions drives the user to select robustness and resilience. The rationale also includes the constraints for the mathematical problem, as well as the interpretation of the solution obtained. In the next section, we describe the layout of the monograph and provide a brief description of each chapter.

1.4 Organization of the Monograph

This monograph comprises of ten chapters (Figure 1-9). While we recommend reading the chapters sequentially, each chapter is self-contained and chapters can be read independently or in any preferred sequence. Following this introductory chapter, we have divided Chapters 2–8 into two major parts: variation management and disruption management.

- Variation management: Chapters 2, 3, 4, and 5
- Disruption management: Chapters 6, 7, and 8

We bring together the themes of variation and disruption management in Chapters 9 and 10.

- Combined variation and disruption management: Chapter 9
- Emerging technologies and extension to other networks: Chapter 10

In Chapters 2–9, we revisit the architecture of Fail-safe supply networks, and include a summary with the elements, form and rationale relevant to the type of risks and network being addressed. In the narrative within each chapter, we intertwine the views of the business user and the mathematical modeler in architecting Fail-safe networks.

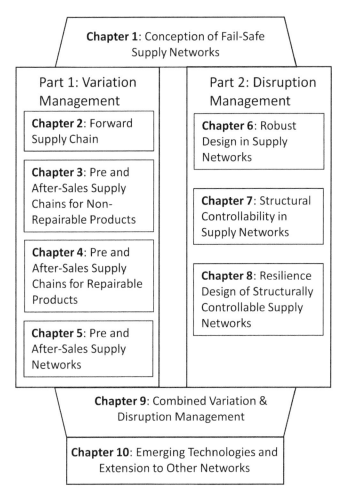

Figure 1-9. Organization of the monograph.

1.4.1 Variation Management: Forward Supply Chain, Concurrent Forward and After-Sales Supply Networks for Non-Repairable and Repairable Products

We focus on variation management in Chapters 2, 3, 4, and 5. In Chapter 2, we revisit the importance of variation management in supply networks and explore the available literature on the subject. We then mathematically formulate and solve the mathematical model for reliability, considering the forward flow of material in a three-echelon supply chain; we also take into account supply-side variations and their propagated effects on the final supply quantities of the supply chain in addition to demand-side variations. In Chapter 3, we address the problem of concurrent flow planning in the forward and after-sales supply chains of *non-repairable products* in the presence of variations in both demand and supply. Where the forward supply chain manufactures and supplies the original products to the market, the after-sales supply chain provides the spare parts needed to satisfy after-sales demands. The profits of the after-sales business are approximately double that of the initial product, making after-sales service an important portion of the economy (Kim et al. 2007). In Chapter 4, we explain how the approach developed in Chapter 3 can be refined and applied to the complicated network of companies providing both pre- and after-sales services for customers of their *repairable products*; that is, where the manufacturer provides a warranty for the product, which in turn produces another stream of revenue. Based on the estimate of Gaiardelli et al. (2007), after-sales services in the consumer electronic devices, power tools, vacuum cleaners and personal computer industries generate an annual income of around $6–$8 billion in the United States. Between 40 to 50 percent of the total revenue generated in European automobile markets is related to after-sales services provided by automobile companies (Bohmann et al. 2003). However, considering after-sales markets makes the mathematical model of the bidirectional network much more complicated. To illustrate, these companies not only include a forward supply network producing and shipping products to customers, but they also include an after-sales supply network that deal with replacing and repairing defective products which have been returned within the warranty period. In other words, we include the *Return* process of the SCOR model in the mathematical formulation. In Chapter 5 we describe an approach that extends the models in Chapters 3 and 4, by adding the breadth dimension to the supply chain, thus transforming it into a supply network. The key difference is that there are multiple facilities in each echelon. We take into account the interactions between the forward network, the after-sales network and the repair sections; then we develop a model to select variation management decisions for multiple sections of the network.

1.4.2 Disruption Management using Robustness, Structural Controllability, and Resilience

In Chapters 6, 7, and 8, we shift our focus to disruption management. As mentioned above, disruptions distort the supply network structure, which can have deleterious effects on the network if improperly managed. Applying a robust design to supply networks is one approach to disruption management. A robust supply network is capable of mitigating impacts on its performance due to disruptions and variations, thereby reducing its performance drop. In Chapter 6, following a literature review on disruption management, we introduce robust supply network design and explain the different steps of modeling, solution and computational results. In Chapter 7, we discuss another method used for disruption management—namely structural controllability—which provides the capability of having access to all markets and customers by so-called driver facilities that help to decrease the recovery time and manage disruptions in supply networks. We explain the graph based foundations for structural controllability and its implementation for an example network. In Chapter 8, we concentrate on the speed of recovery from a disruption, and the related method of resilience. Soni et al. (2014) highlight the lack of awareness about resilience and how to incorporate it into the supply network; they also point out that research focusing on the resilience of supply networks is limited. We detail the formulation of a mathematical model for designing resilient supply networks that incorporate structural controllability as well.

1.4.3 Concurrent Management of Variations and Disruptions

In Chapter 9, we discuss the culmination of the above methods. We begin by reiterating the difference between variations and disruptions and provide a detailed literature survey of both these types of risks in supply networks and the associated decision-making approaches. In any real-world scenario, a supply network would be affected by various kinds of risks. Hence, we focus on the problem of designing supply networks for concurrent variation and disruption management, namely fail-safe supply networks. In other words, a fail-safe supply network is designed to handle both (1) variations modifying its planned flow and (2) disruptions distorting its network structure. We demonstrate the design of fail-safe networks and explore the correlations between the different risk management methods using an integrated mathematical model; this method reveals important insights for architecting fail-safe supply networks.

1.4.4 Extensions of Fail-Safe Networks

The management of risks and the avoidance of failures are essential and continuous actions taken to protect against the variations and disruptions that threaten all networks. The applicability of the techniques presented in this monograph extends beyond the domain of supply networks and into fail-safe networks in other industries. In Chapter 10, we explore such applications and discuss the implications in selected areas such as infrastructure and power networks. Furthermore, sweeping winds of technological advances are reshaping the networks landscape. With emerging technologies, such as the Digital Five Forces (Krishnan 2017), it is becoming easier to acquire and distribute information through web-based and mobile platforms. In the concluding chapter, we discuss ways to leverage these new technologies to implement fail-safe supply networks.

1.5 Definitions of Terms Used

Since we have used several technical terms throughout the monograph, we provide a list of such terms and their definitions below.

1. **Supply Network:** A supply network is a set of enterprises (facilities) that are linked together to produce a set of products or to provide a set of services. A supply network plan is developed to match supply and demand across the network.

2. **Risk:** Risk originates from an uncertain event and represents the potential of failure in a supply network.

   - Uncertain event: An event whose outcome is not clear or fixed; in doubt or not certain.

   - Risk is the potential of failure or loss stemming from an uncertain event and leading to an undesirable impact on the performance of a supply network. Typically, this performance is assessed in terms of an output of the network that is measured by metrics such as throughput, profit, cost and inventory. Users establish nominal values for such metrics.

   - Drop in performance will be used to denote the deviation of the metric of interest from the nominal value, due to risk.

3. **Variation:** Variation is a minor fluctuation that affects the execution of the supply network plan adversely and has a low impact on network performance.

4. **Disruption:** A disruption is an unexpected event that is large enough to distort the structure of a supply network and has a high impact on network performance.

5. **Fail-Safe Supply Network:** A fail-safe supply network is one that is designed to cope with disruptions and variations and to have business continuity at an acceptable level under all conditions.

6. **Reliable Flow Planning in a Supply Network:** Reliable flow planning is capable of neutralizing upstream and downstream variations to preserve the desired service level.

7. **Robust Supply Network:** A robust supply network is capable of mitigating the impacts disruptions and variations have on its

performance, reducing the drop in performance and maintaining an acceptable level of performance.

8. **Resilient Supply Network:** A resilient supply network is capable of rapidly absorbing, adapting to, or recovering from disrupting circumstances and returning to an acceptable level of performance.

9. **Structurally Controllable Supply Network:** A structurally controllable supply network is one that is designed to have access to the entirety of its facilities via driver facilities (or controllers).

10. **Flexible Facilities:** Flexible facilities have flexible processing capacity, that is, an increase or decrease in throughput is feasible in a flexible facility.

11. **Flexible Capacity:** The flexible capacity is the extent to which a flexible facility is designed to increase or decrease its processing capacity as needed.

12. **Flexibility Level:** Flexibility level is an indicator showing how much the throughput can be increased when extra capacity is needed.

13. **Flexibility Speed:** Flexibility speed is an indicator showing how fast the facility can increase or decrease its capacity.

14. **Strategic Decisions:** Long-term decisions determining the number, location, capacity of facilities and transportation lanes in a supply network.

15. **Operational Decisions/Flow Planning:** Short term decisions dealing with production and transportation planning in a supply network's facilities and transportation lanes.

16. **Recovery Strategies:** Recovery strategies refer to both a fail-safe supply network's preparation for unforeseen risks to continued operations (pre-disruption strategies) and to specific actions taken to recover operations after the occurrence of a disruption (post-disruption strategies).

1.6 Closing Remarks

Our motivation in developing this monograph springs from our recognition that the greatest opportunities, as well as the most demanding challenges confronting businesses and societies, are due to the ubiquity of networks. Connections between entities, amplified by current and evolving technologies, facilitate interactions between the members, promote values and innovations, but also propagate failures and epidemics. To focus our discussion, we concentrate on one type of network that drives the flow of various goods and services: the supply network. The need to protect supply networks from failures is paramount and this need is the central issue we address in this monograph. Failures in supply networks eventuate from two kinds of risks: low impact risks or variations and high impact risks or disruptions. The solution we propose is an architecture for *Fail-safe networks* and we examine the different facets of this architecture—with emphasis on the business need and corresponding mathematical models—in the forthcoming chapters. We conclude by asserting that the framework and techniques in this monograph are applicable beyond the supply chain domain for architecting fail safe networks in other industries. In Chapter 2, we begin by investigating the simplest combination of risk type and network structure namely, variation management in a supply chain.

References

Agatz, N. a. H., Fleischmann, M. and Van Nunen, J. a. E. E. 2008. E-fulfillment and multi-channel distribution—A review. European Journal of Operational Research 187(2): 339–356.

Baghalian, A., Rezapour, S. and Farahani, R. Z. 2013. Robust supply chain network design with service level against disruptions and demand uncertainties: A real-life case. European Journal of Operational Research 227(1): 199–215.

Barroso, A. P., Machado, V. H., Carvalho, H. and Machado, V. C. 2015. Quantifying the supply chain resilience. *In*: Tozan, H. and Erturk, A. (eds.). Applications of Contemporary Management Approaches in Supply Chains. Rijeka: InTech.

Bohmann, E., Rosenberg, J. and Stenbrink, P. 2003. Overhauling European auto distribution. McKinsey Quarterly 1: 134–142.

Bolstorff, P. and Rosenbaum, R. 2011. Supply Chain Excellence - A Handbook for Dramatic Improvement Using the SCOR Model (3rd Edition). AMACOM – Book Division of American Management Association.

Bruneau, M., Chang, S. E., Eguchi, R. T., Lee, G. C., O'Rourke, T. D., Reinhorn, A. M., Shinozuka, M., Tierney, K., Wallace, W. A. and Von Winterfeldt, D. 2003. A framework to quantitatively assess and enhance the seismic resilience of communities. Earthquake Spectra 19(4): 733–752.

Christopher, M. and Lee, H. 2004. Mitigating supply chain risk through improved confidence. International Journal of Physical Distribution & Logistics Management 34(5): 388–396.

Coolidge, A. 2013. New Technology Helps Kroger Speed Up Checkout Times 2013 [cited June 13 2017]. Available from https://www.usatoday.com/story/money/business/2013/06/20/new-technology-helps-kroger-speed-up-checkout-times/2443975/.

Cozzolino, A. 2012. Humanitarian logistics and supply chain management. *In*: Humanitarian Logistics: Cross-Sector Cooperation in Disaster Relief Management. Berlin, Heidelberg: Springer.

Culnan, M. J., Mchugh, P. J. and Zubillaga, J. I. 2010. How large US companies can use Twitter and other social media to gain business value. MIS Quarterly Executive 9(4): 243–259.

Eagleman, D. 2015. The Brain: The Story of You. New York: Pantheon Books.

Elkins, C. 2011. Toyota Delays Japan Launch 2011 [cited June 13 2017]. Available from http://www.djournal.com/news/toyota-delays-japan-launch/article_7b4483f4-56f8-57b3-b309-ce6cb4a12962.html.

Gaiardelli, P., Saccani, N. and Songini, L. 2007. Performance measurement of the after-sales service network—Evidence from the automotive industry. Computers in Industry 58(7): 698–708.

Hall, P. V. 2004. We'd have to sink the ships: Impact studies and the 2002 West Coast port lockout. Economic Development Quarterly 18(4): 354–367.

Handfield, R. B., Blackhurst, J., Elkins, D. and Craighead, C. W. 2007. A framework for reducing the impact of disruptions to the supply chain: Observations from multiple executives. *In*: Handfield, R.B. and McCormack, K. (eds.). Supply Chain Risk Management: Minimizing Disruption in Global Sourcing. Boca Raton, FL: Taylor and Francis.

Hendricks, K. B. and Singhal, V. R. 2005. An empirical analysis of the effect of supply chain disruptions on long-run stock price performance and equity risk of the firm. Production and Operations Management 14(1): 35–52.

Hur, D., Hartley, J. L. and Hahn, C. K. 2004. An exploration of supply chain structure in Korean companies. International Journal of Logistics Research and Applications 7(2): 151–164.

Ivanov, D. and Sokolov, B. 2010. Adaptive Supply Chain Management. London: Springer.

Jiang, R. 2015. Introduction to Quality and Reliability Engineering: Berlin Heidelberg. Springer.

Kapur, K. C. and Pecht, M. 2014. Reliability Engineering. Hoboken, NJ: John Wiley & Sons, Inc.

Kellogg, C. 2014. Google and Barnes & Noble take on Amazon's same-day Delivery 2014 [cited June 13 2017]. Available from http://www.latimes.com/books/jacketcopy/la-et-jc-google-barnes-noble-same-day-delivery-20140807-story.html.

Kim, S.-H., Cohen, M. A. and Netessine, S. 2007. Performance contracting in after-sales service supply chains. Management Science 53(12): 1843–1858.

Kleijnen, J. P. C. and Smits, M. T. 2003. Performance metrics in supply chain management. (Author Abstract). Journal of the Operational Research Society 54(5): 507.

Krishnan, K. A. 2017. Digitally reimagining mobility. *In*: Tandon, M. C. and Ghosh, P. (eds.). Mobility Engineering: Proceedings of CAETS 2015 Convocation on Pathways to Sustainability. Singapore: Springer.

Lazare, L. 2017. United Airlines, American Airlines in Heated on-Time Arrival Fight 2017 [cited June 13 2017]. Available from http://www.bizjournals.com/chicago/news/2017/04/05/united-airlines-american-airlines-on-time-arrivals.html.

Lockamy Iii, A. and Mccormack, K. 2004. Linking SCOR planning practices to supply chain performance an exploratory study. International Journal of Operations & Production Management 24(12): 1192–1218.

Munoz, A. and Dunbar, M. 2015. On the quantification of operational supply chain resilience. International Journal of Production Research 53(22): 6736–6751.

Perry, D. E. and Wolf, A. L. 1992. Foundations for the study of software architecture. ACM SIGSOFT Software Engineering Notes 4(17): 40–52.

Ponomarov, S. and Holcomb, M. 2009. Understanding the concept of supply chain resilience. International Journal of Logistics Management 20(1): 124–143.

Project Management Institute. 2013. A guide to the Project Management Body of Knowledge (PMBOK guide), fifth edition. Edited by I. Project Management. 5th ed., PMBOK guide. Newtown Square, Pa.: Projet Management Institute.

Radjou, N., Orloy, L. M. and Nakashima, T. 2002. Adapting to supply network change. Cambridge, MA: Forrester Research Inc.

Ramo, J. C. 2016. The Seventh Sense: Power, Fortune, and Survival in the Age of Networks. New York. Little, Brown and Company.

Rausand, M. and Høyland, A. 2004. System Reliability Theory : Models, Statistical Methods, and Applications. 2nd ed. Hoboken, NJ. Wiley-Interscience.

Sana, S. S. 2010. An economic production lot size model in an imperfect production system. European Journal of Operational Research 201(1): 158–170.

Sánchez, M. A. and Pérez, M. P. 2005. Supply chain flexibility and firm performance: a conceptual model and empirical study in the automotive industry. International Journal of Operations & Production Management 25: 681–700.

Shroff, G. 2013. The Intelligent Web: Search, Smart Algorithms, and Big Data. Oxford: OUP.

Sodhi, M. S. and Tang, C. S. 2012. Managing Supply Chain Risk. Vol. 172. Boston, MA: Springer US.

Soni, U., Jain, V. and Kumar, S. 2014. Measuring supply chain resilience using a deterministic modeling approach. Comput. Ind. Eng. 74: 11–25.

Stapelberg, R. F. 2009. Handbook of Reliability, Availability, Maintainability and Safety in Engineering Design. London: Springer.

Tang, O. and Nurmaya Musa, S. 2011. Identifying risk issues and research advancements in supply chain risk management. International Journal of Production Economics 133(1): 25–34.

Taylor, K. 2016. Buffalo Wild Wings just unleashed a plan to crush Chipotle and Panera Bread 2016 [cited June 13 2017]. Available from http://www.businessinsider.com/buffalo-wild-wings-15-minute-lunch-guarantee-2016-7.

Taylor, L. 2014. Practical enterprise risk management: How to optimize business strategies through managed risk taking. London, UK.: Kogan Page Publishers.

Vecchi, A. and Vallisi, V. 2015. Supply chain resilience. *In*: Christiansen, B. (ed.). Handbook of Research on Global Supply Chain Management. Hershey, PA.: Business Science Reference.

Vlajic, J. V., Vorst, V. D., J., J. G. A. and Haijema, R. 2012. A framework for designing robust food supply chains. International Journal of Production Economics 137(1): 176–189.

Wang, J., Liu, C., Ton, D., Zhou, Y., Kim, J. and Vyas, A. 2011. Impact of plug-in hybrid electric vehicles on power systems with demand response and wind power. Energy Policy 39(7): 4016–4021.

Wieland, A. and Wallenburg, C. M. 2012. Dealing with supply chain risks: linking risk management practices and strategies to performance. International Journal of Physical Distribution & Logistics Management 42(10): 887–905.

Wood, D. J., Fisher, S. G. and Grimm, N. B. 1992. Pools in desert streams: Limnology and response to disturbance. Journal of the Arizona-Nevada Academy of Science 26(2): 171–179.

Wu, T. 2009. Managing Supply Chain Risk and Vulnerability : Tools and Methods for Supply Chain Decision Makers. J. Blackhurst (ed.). London, GB: Springer.

Variation Management in a Single Forward Supply Chain

A fail-safe SN can appropriately handle both (1) variations modifying its planned flow, and (2) disruptions distorting its network structure. In Chapter 2, we deal with variation management of planned flow in a single forward supply chain (see Chapter 1, Figure 1-9). First, we describe different types of variations existing in supply chains. Then, we elaborate how these variations affect supply chains' efficiency. Finally, we develop a model to select the variation management decisions for supply chains. A numerical analysis of the results provides some useful insights about variation management in supply chains.

2.1 Importance of Variation Management in Supply Chains

Today, companies are improving their competitiveness by reducing production costs, by higher productivity, by improving quality by concentrating on their core competencies and by improving their flexibility to respond to rapidly changing customer expectations. All these requirements disperse previously centralized production systems into a network of core-competency-centered companies called "Supply Chains" (SC) or, more accurately, "Supply Networks" (SN). Along with all the advantages of SCs/SNs, decentralization makes them more vulnerable to risks. This highlights the importance of risk management in SC/SN to predict, control and mitigate the effects of risk on SN performance. Risk management capability of a SC/SN is reflected mainly in one of its performance metrics, the service level. Recently, service level has become an important competition factor and many companies attempt to improve their market share by providing better service levels. For example, two well-known book retailers, Amazon and Barnes & Noble, who share more than 85 percent of online sales, initiated competition by promising the same business day delivery in different parts of the country. The same is happening in the fast food industry. Domino's, for example, provided a "30-minutes or it's free" guarantee on its deliveries. Black Angus restaurants advertise free lunch if the customer's order is not serviced in 10 minutes. Retailers such as Lucky emphasize their short checkout times. Well Fargo Bank guarantees less than five minutes wait for its customers or gives them a $5 reward. Airline companies, advertisements are based on their percentage of on-time arrival. Several independent Internet sites provide information about the company performance such as their service level warranties, back-up chargeback agreements, etc. Moreover, specifying a delivery window is common in business-to-business settings. Thus, service level is becoming one of the most important competition factors. Service level is the capability of a company to balance demand and supply quantities in their daily operations. This balancing is not easy in practice because both demand and supply processes are stochastic and have variations. By assuming perfect production systems, supply side variation is usually ignored in the extensive service level literature. However, in reality there is no perfect production system. Increasing the rate of production increases the likelihood of machinery and labor failures leading to a higher rate of non-conforming items produced (Sana 2010). Decentralized and multi-echelon production systems of SCs/SNs amplify the probability of non-conformation. These trends demand more accurate approaches towards determining appropriate service levels in the SCs'/SNs' daily operations. In this chapter by considering supply-side variations and their propagated effects on the final supply quantities of SCs, we respond to this new need of the business environment which, as will be shown later, is mainly ignored in the service level literature.

In the context of an architecture for fail-safe networks, as introduced in Section 1.3, we explain the use of reliability for risk management in SCs (see Figure 1-4). The connector is a three-tiered SC. We express the form of our architecture as an optimization model that determines the best local reliabilities (properties) in a way to maximize the total profit of the chain (relationship). This model helps us to understand the relationship between the chain's performance (service level) and the local reliabilities of its facilities (component of risk management). Summary interpretation for the problem investigated in Chapter 2 is as follows:

Table 2-1. Summary interpretation for the problem investigated in Chapter 2.

Elements	What?
Components	Reliability
Connectors	Forward supply chain
Form	**How?**
Component importance	Reliability: 1
Properties	Local reliabilities
Relationship	Supply chain profit optimization
Rationale	**Why?**
Motivation	Variation management
Assumptions	No disruption There is enough information to quantify variations
Constraints	Order amplification in echelons due to variations
Interpretation	Understanding the relationship between the chain's service level and the local reliabilities of its facilities

2.2 Literature of Variation Management in Supply Chains

In this chapter, we concentrate on the demand and supply quantity variations which are common in the SC/SN context. There has been a lot of work in the literature on variations in the SCs/SNs. Many researchers only consider demand-side variation (Sabri and Beamon 2000; Miranda and Garrido 2004; Shen and Daskin 2005; Daniel and Rajendran 2006; Romeijn et al. 2007; Ko and Evans 2007; Shen and Qi 2007; You and Grossmann 2008; Schütz et al. 2009; Pan and Nagi 2010; Park et al. 2010; Cardona-Valdés et al. 2011; Hsu and Li 2011). In our problem, in addition to demand-side variation, different supply-side variations are also considered. Variations in supply in one entity can disrupt production schedules in all subsequent entities of the SC/SN, leading to a delay in responding to customers' demands. Poor service levels lead to lost sales and long-term demand attenuation. Hence, strategies mitigating the negative effects of supply-side variations, especially in SCs/SNs with multiple supply echelons, are imperative. The problem presented here not only improves the service level estimation in SCs/SNs significantly, but also improves system reliability in preserving that service level and improving competitive capabilities. We assume that production systems in the SC's/SN's echelons are accompanied by stochastic percentages of wastage and nonconforming output making their supply quantities uncertain.

Supply-side disruption management in SC/SN has a richer literature than supply-side variation management (Santoso et al. 2005; Azaron et al. 2008; Yu et al. 2009; Chen et al. 2011; Li and Chen 2010; Li et al. 2010; Xanthopoulos et al. 2012; Baghalian et al. 2013; Listes and Dekker 2005). There are few works in the field of operational supply-side variation in the SC/SN. Chopra et al. (2007) consider product flow planning in a SN consisting of a buyer and two suppliers. The first supplier is cheaper, but prone to unreliability and the second supplier is completely reliable but more expensive. Demand in the markets is assumed to be deterministic. In this paper, only supply-side uncertainties are considered. Disruptions (strategic risks) are modeled by scenarios and operational supply variations are considered as a random variable with a given distribution function. Schmitt et al. (2010) consider optimal ordering and the required amount of the reserve product of a two-echelon SN of a firm and its suppliers. One supplier is unreliable whereas the second is completely reliable and available but more expensive. They compare single-period and multi-periods and discuss the advantages of considering multi-periods. Dada et al. (2007) consider a company with several potential suppliers both reliable and unreliable and decisions about supplier selection and order splitting are made in a way to maximize the company's expected profit. Ross et al. (2008) consider the ordering policy of a firm with a Poisson arrival demand and a single supplier with a random supply process. Supply and demand processes have time-dependent probabilities. They set a time varying ordering policy to decrease the total cost of the system. Li and Chen (2010) develop a model for inventory management of a SN with an unreliable supplier and a retailer. They investigate the impact of supply-side variation and customer differentiation on minimizing average annual cost.

In existing research, SC's/SN's supply process is restricted to one echelon and variation in the facility performance of that echelon. However, in reality, most SCs/SNs have long production chains/networks involving several echelons of suppliers of suppliers, suppliers, component manufacturers, assemblers and so on. To fill the gap, we consider a SC with a multi-echelon supply process, producing and supplying a product to a market with uncertain demand and an uncertain SC's multi-echelon supply process includes production facilities with uncertain production systems. In such a complex system, variations in the production facilities are accumulated by moving the material/product flow from the SC's upstream movement to its downstream movement leading to a larger and larger bias. As shown in a sample SC in Figure 2-1, due to the variation in the production system of the supplier, determining the conforming output of the supplier for a given input level is not possible and can change in a given range. This uncertain output of the supplier is input

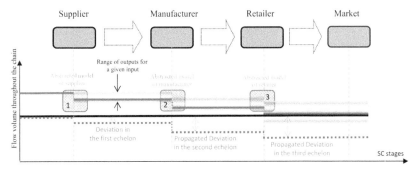

Figure 2-1. Variation propagation in a sample SC.

Black line: Product flow planned by the deterministic model;
Dashed line: Product flow that is happening in reality;
Grey line: Solution of reliable model expected to be obtained in this chapter.

to the manufacturer who also has an uncertain manufacturing system. Thus, variation of the manufacturer's system is compounded by its uncertain input level which leads to a greater variation in its qualified output. The same story repeats itself in the SC's downstream echelons. We call this phenomenon *"variation propagation"* in the SC. In such a SC, not only the local effects of these variations on the performance of their corresponding entities should be investigated, but also their global effects on the performance of the whole SC should be identified. Then it is shown that how reliable production planning can be done in this SC against all these demand and supply side variations and their propagated effect.

At first glance, the consequences of supply-side variation propagation which is introduced in this chapter and Bullwhip Effect which was already introduced in 1960s, look very similar to each other. However, the reasons behind the two, and what is amplified in these two phenomena, are completely different. Details are as follows:

Bullwhip Effect: two factors lead to Bullwhip Effect in a supply chain: (i) variation in the market (only demand side variation is considered in this phenomenon) and (ii) existence of time lag in the information transaction among the supply chain's echelons which means that all the facilities in the supply chain do not recognize demand variations simultaneously. Due to this reason, the inventory volume in the supply chain's facilities propagates by moving from downstream to upstream. Uncertain production system of facilities, or in other words, supply-side variation does not have any role in this phenomenon.

Supply-side variation propagation: this phenomenon happens due to variations in the performances of production facilities and their qualified output volumes in a supply chain with a multi-echelon production process. This variation in the qualified and acceptable flow volume propagates by the moving of material and product from upstream to downstream. The speed of information transaction among the supply chain's facilities does not have any role in this phenomenon.

2.3 Our Contribution to the Supply Chain Literature

This work contributes in the following ways to the SC literature. First, the supply-side variation in a SC with a multi-echelon supply process is considered. In the literature, all supply-side variation management work in the context of the SC is restricted to a single echelon supply process. Then, in a SC, the phenomenon of variation propagation is introduced and its importance for global performance of the SC is demonstrated.

Next, a method is proposed for reliable production planning in these chains which are formulated with mixed integer nonlinear mathematical models and an approach to solving them is developed.

This chapter is organized as follows: in Section 2.4, detailed descriptions of the operations and variation sources in a SC are provided. In Section 2.5, a mathematical model is developed for reliable production planning in the SC against all variations and their propagated effects. A solution approach is developed in Section 2.6 and the model is tested on an example in Section 2.7. Closing comments are offered in Section 2.8.

2.4 Operations and Variation in a Supply Chain

Here, we consider a SC with a multi-echelon supply process including a sequence of facilities, suppliers and manufacturer with imperfect production systems (supply-side variation). Components are procured from the supplier and, after being manufactured as the final product by the manufacturer, they are supplied to a market with a stochastic demand by a retailer (demand-side variation). The stochastic demand is an increasing function of service level and decreasing function of price. The production system of the SC's manufacturer has a stochastic percentage of defective output. After setting up machinery, each supplier's production system deteriorates after a stochastic time and shifts from in-control to out-of-control leading to a stochastic percentage of nonconforming components. In this problem, service level is defined as a percentage of the market's demand which is fulfilled immediately by the retailer's on-hand inventory and is a function of the reliability levels of the SC's facilities. Higher reliability levels in each facility improve the SC's global performance (service level) through imposing costs on the system. The goal is to determine: (i) the service level providing the highest SC profit by considering local and propagated variations; (ii) the combination of reliability levels in the SC's echelons to ensure economic service levels; and (iii) economic production planning to preserve reliability and service levels. Products for each production planning period are produced, transported and stored in the SC's retailer before the start of that period. In the rest of this section, we elaborate our general strategy to deal with variation management in multi-echelon SCs.

Optimizing service level is much more difficult in these SCs due to variation propagation. Each facility in the SC has an appropriate reliability level representing the probability that it can fulfill the order of its downstream facility completely. rl_1, rl_2 and rl_3 are the reliability levels of the SC's retailer, manufacturer and supplier respectively. The retailer selects the product stock quantity to ensure, with rl_1 probability, that this stock level fulfills the market demand and the manufacturer selects its component procurement and final product manufacturing quantities to guarantee that the qualified output is equal to the retailer's requirements with rl_2 probability. rl_3, the supplier's reliability level means that its material procurement and component production quantity fills the manufacturer's order with rl_3 probability. Thus, the SC's supplier is sure with rl_3 probability that it provides the manufacturer's complete order. The manufacturer is sure with probability rl_2 that it provides the retailer's order and the retailer is sure with probability rl_1 that its product stock quantity will fulfill the market demand. The SC's service level is: $sl = rl_1 \cdot rl_2 \cdot rl_3$. In this problem not only determining the optimal sl is important, but also it is necessary to determine the optimal reliability level combination (rl_1, rl_2, rl_3), to preserve that service level. Based on the probability distribution function of the market demand and chosen reliability level rl_1, the retailer selects the best x product order quantity from the manufacturer. SC's manufacturer receives an x product order from the retailer, but due to the probability of defective production in its own manufacturing system, the manufacturer plans to manufacture extra product Δx and orders $x + \Delta x$ components from the supplier. This protects the SC against propagated variation in the demand and the manufacturer's production system. The supplier receives $x + \Delta x$ order from the manufacturer. To compensate for its imperfect production system, the supplier produces $\Delta \hat{x}$ more components. Δx and $\Delta \hat{x}$ are determined by the stochasticity in the production systems and reliability levels rl_2 and rl_3 and protect the SC against the propagated effects of the variations (Figure 2-2).

In Sections 2.4.1, 2.4.2 and 2.4.3 the SC's facilities are considered separately step by step from downstream to upstream and production planning for each facility is discussed. The results of these sections are aggregated and formulated into a comprehensive mathematical model in

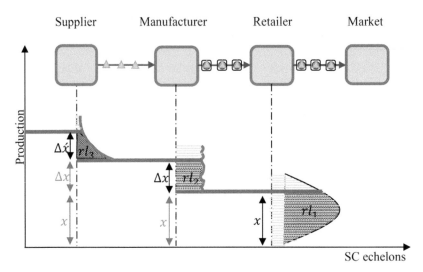

Figure 2-2. Variation propagation in the Supply Chain.

Section 2.5. The notation used in formulating this problem is summarized in Table 2-1.

2.4.1 Reliable Production Planning by the Supply Chain's Retailer

The demand of the SC is a stochastic function of its service level and retail price. The service level is a fraction of the market's realized demand that is satisfied by the retailer's on-hand inventory.

The expected market demand, $D(sl, p)$ is an increasing function of the chain's service level, sl and a decreasing function of the retail price, p. However, the actual demand, $\widehat{D}(sl, p)$, is stochastic. According to Bernstein and Federgruen (2004, 2007) demand is formulated as $\widehat{D}(sl, p) = D(sl, p) \times \varepsilon$. ε is a general continuous random variable with cumulative distribution function $G(\varepsilon)$, independent of the SC's service level and price. Without loss of generality, $E(\varepsilon)$ is normalized to $E(\varepsilon) = 1$ which implies $E(\widehat{D}(sl, p)) = D(sl, p)$. The price of the product is fixed in the market and the SC is charged a unit cost, w, for producing and supplying the product. The retailer's order is released and fulfilled by the manufacturer before the beginning of the planning period. After realizing the period's real demand, unit holding cost, h^+, and unit shortage cost, h^-, are paid by the retailer for each end-of-period inventory or backlogged demand. Then, the total cost (summation of inventory holding and shortage costs) of the retailer, Π, is:

$$MIN \quad \Pi = h^+ . E[x - \widehat{D}(sl, p)]^+ + h^- . E[\widehat{D}(sl, p) - x]^+ \tag{2-1}$$

$$S.T. \quad Pr[\widehat{D}(sl, p) \le x] \ge rl_1 \tag{2-2}$$

Table 2-2. Notation for the SC problem.

$\widehat{D}(sl, p)$	Demand of the SC's market as a function of its service level and price
$D(sl, p)$	Expected demand of the SC's market
ε	Continuous random variable representing the uncertain part of the demand function
$G(\varepsilon)$	Cumulative distribution function of ε
p	Price of the product in the market
h^+	Unit holding cost in the SC's retailer
h^-	Unit shortage cost in the SC's retailer
Π	Expected total cost of the retailer
β	Maximum wastage ratio in the production system of the SC's manufacturer
$\acute{G}(.)$	Cumulative distribution function of wastage in the production system of the SC's manufacturer
μ	Rate of shifting to an out-of-control state in the SC's supplier
γ	Percentage of defective production in the out-of-control state of the supplier
N	Available production schemes of the supplier, $N = \{n_i, i = 1,2, \ldots, \mid N\mid\}$
a_1	Unit procurement cost of the SC's supplier
a_2	Unit production cost of the SC's supplier
a_3	Set up cost of the SC's supplier
h_1	Unit inventory cost for a time unit of the SC's supplier
b_1	Unit transportation cost from the supplier to the manufacturer
b_2	Unit manufacturing cost of the SC's manufacturer
h_2	Unit inventory cost for a time unit of the SC's manufacturer
c_1	Unit transportation cost from the manufacturer to the retailer
c_2	Unit handling cost of the SC's retailer
PR_1	Production rate of the SC's supplier
PR_2	Production rate of the SC's manufacturer
SL	Set of scenarios defined for the service level of the SC, $SL = \{sl^1, sl^2, \ldots, sl^{\mid SL\mid}\}$
RL^{si}	Set of scenarios defined for service level sl^i distribution among the SC's echelons as their reliability levels, $RL_{\cdot}^{sl^i} = \{RL_1^{sl^i} = (rl_{11}^{sl^i}, rl_{12}^{sl^i}, rl_{13}^{sl^i}), RL_2^{sl^i} = (rl_{21}^{sl^i}, rl_{22}^{sl^i}, rl_{23}^{sl^i}), \ldots, RL_{\mid RL\mid^{sl^i}}^{sl^i} = (rl_{\mid RL\mid^{sl^i}1}^{sl^i}, rl_{\mid RL\mid^{sl^i}2}^{sl^i}, rl_{\mid RL\mid^{sl^i}3}^{sl^i})\}$
Variables	
rl_1	Reliability level of the SC's retailer
rl_2	Reliability level of the SC's manufacturer
rl_3	Reliability level of the SC's supplier
sl	SC's Service level in the market
x	Ordering volume of the retailer from the manufacturer

Table 2-2 contd. ...

...Table 2-2 contd.

Δx	Extra production of the manufacturer to compensate for the wastage in its production system
$\Delta \dot{x}$	Extra production units in the supplier to compensate for the wastage in its production system
y_i	1 if production scheme n_i is selected by the supplier; otherwise 0
z_{sl^i}	1 if scenario sl^i ($\forall sl^i \in SL$) is selected as the service level of the SC, otherwise 0
$w_{RL_j^{sl^i}}$	1 if scenario $RL_j^{sl^i} = (rl_{j1}^{sl^i}, rl_{j2}^{sl^i}, rl_{j3}^{sl^i})$ ($\forall RL_j^{sl^i} \in RL^{sl^i}$) is selected to distribute service level sl^i among the SC's echelons as their reliability levels, 0 otherwise

In this model x represents the ordering quantity of the retailer from the manufacturer. The ordering volume $x = D(sl, p).G^{-1}\left(\dfrac{h^-}{h^- + h^+}\right)$ minimizes the retailer's expected cost. To conserve the reliability level of the retailer we should have $x \geq D(sl, p).G^{-1}(rl_1)$, so the best order is:

$$x = D(sl, p).G^{-1}\left(Max\left\{rl_1, \frac{h^-}{h^- + h^+}\right\}\right) \qquad (2\text{-}3)$$

By substituting Eq. (2-3) for (2-1), the cost of the retailer is rewritten as follows:

$$\Pi = \left(h^+ . E\left[G^{-1}\left(Max\left\{rl_1, \frac{h^-}{h^- + h^+}\right\}\right) - \varepsilon\right]^+ \right.$$
$$\left. + h^- . E\left[\varepsilon - G^{-1}\left(Max\left\{rl_1, \frac{h^-}{h^- + h^+}\right\}\right)\right]^+\right) . D(sl, p) \qquad (2\text{-}4)$$

Thus, the SC's retailer, by ordering $x = D(sl,p).G^{-1}\left(Max\left\{rl_1, \dfrac{h^-}{h^- + h^+}\right\}\right)$ products from the manufacturer, will be sure with rl_1 probability that its product stock will fulfill all the realized demand. In Figure 2-3, a sample probability distribution function is assumed for the market's demand. As

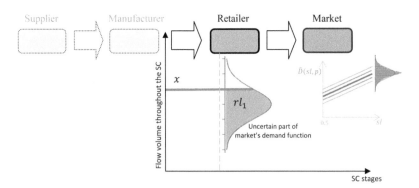

Figure 2-3. Order volume of the retailer based on its reliability level.

shown in this figure, ordering quantity x should be selected in a way that the probability of the market's demand is equal to or less than x is rl_1.

2.4.2 Reliable Production Planning for the Supply Chain's Manufacturer

The SC's manufacturer receives an order of x products from the retailer. Without loss of generality, it is assumed that a single unit of component is required per product. The production system of the manufacturer has always some wastage which is determined by the general state of its machinery and varies in range $[0, \beta\%]$ with a cumulative distribution function $G'(.)$. A manufacturer should compensate for the wastage by manufacturing more products and consequently ordering more components from the supplier. Thus, component ordering and production volumes of the manufacturer include a surplus, Δx. If the manufacturer produces x units, this batch may contain $\Delta x \in [0, x.\beta\%]$ flawed units. To compensate for this wastage, the manufacturer orders $\Delta x + x$ units from the SC's supplier. Increasing Δx improves the probability of the manufacturer to fulfill all x products ordered by the retailer; this is its reliability level, rl_2. If the rl_2 reliability level is assigned to the manufacturer, the manufacturer should order $x.G'^{-1}(rl_2) + x$ units from the supplier, Figure 2-4. Thus $x.G'^{-1}(rl_2)$ surplus order and production quantity of the manufacturer preserves rl_2 reliability level for the manufacturer against the variation in its production system.

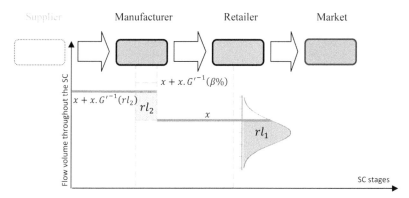

Figure 2-4. Order volume from the supplier against the retailer and manufacturer's propagated variations.

2.4.3 Reliable Production Planning for the Supply Chain's Supplier

It is assumed that the SC's supplier can use $|N|$ possible schemes to produce the order for the manufacturer, $N = \{1,2,...,|N|\}$. The binary variable y_i is defined as the production scheme selection which is equal to 1 if production scheme $i \in \{1,2,\ldots,|N|\}$ is selected by the supplier; otherwise 0. $y_i = 1$ means that the manufacturer's order is divided into i equal parts and these parts are produced in i runs after setting up the machinery. Therefore $\Sigma_{i=1}^{|N|} y_i = 1$. Using the assumptions of Rosenblatt and Lee (1986) and Lee and Rosenblatt (1987) about the production process of the supplier, after setting up the machinery, production runs start in the in-control state. However, the machinery starts to deteriorate and become out-of-control after a stochastic while with an exponential distribution with a mean $1/\mu$. All the product units produced in the in-control state are satisfactory but γ percent of those produced in the out-of-control state are defective. Once the process shifts to the out-of-control state, it stays in this state until the batch is completed because interrupting the run is either impossible or expensive. Hence, the first production scheme, $y_1 = 1$, which produces the whole order at once, has lower set up costs but leads to greater numbers of flawed units in the output and the other schemes (producing the order in $i > 1$ runs) which reduces the flawed product units at the price of a higher set-up cost.

Therefore, in each run of the supplier's production system, the number of flawless components to be produced is $\dfrac{\Delta x + x}{\Sigma_{i=1}^{|N|} y_i \cdot i}$. However, to compensate for flawed components, the supplier produces more components $\dfrac{\Delta \acute{x} + \Delta x + x}{\Sigma_{i=1}^{|N|} y_i \cdot i}$. An extra volume $\Delta \acute{x}$ is added to the production system of the supplier to replace the defective component units. If it is assumed that the production rate of the supplier is PR_1, it will take $\dfrac{\Delta \acute{x} + \Delta x + x}{(\Sigma_{i=1}^{|N|} y_i \cdot i).PR_1}$ time units to produce this volume. $\Delta \acute{x}$ preserves the reliability level rl_3 of the supplier:

$$rl_3 = \text{Pr}(\text{flawless product unit in } \frac{\Delta \acute{x} + \Delta x + x}{(\Sigma_{i=1}^{|N|} y_i \cdot i).PR_1} \text{ time unit} \geq \frac{\Delta x + x}{\Sigma_{i=1}^{|N|} y_i \cdot i})$$

$$= \text{Pr}\left[PR_1.t + (1-\gamma).PR_1.\left(\frac{\Delta \acute{x} + \Delta x + x}{\left(\Sigma_{i=1}^{|N|} y_i.i\right).PR_1} - t \right) \geq \frac{\Delta x + x}{\Sigma_{i=1}^{|N|} y_i.i} \right]$$

$$= \text{Pr}\left[t \geq \left(\frac{\Delta x + x}{\Sigma_{i=1}^{|N|} y_i.i} \right).\frac{1}{PR_1} - \left(\frac{1-\gamma}{\gamma.PR_1} \right).\left(\frac{\Delta \acute{x}}{\Sigma_{i=1}^{|N|} y_i.i} \right) \right]$$

$$= EXP\left[-\mu.\left(\left(\frac{\Delta x + x}{\Sigma_{i=1}^{|N|} y_i.i} \right).\frac{1}{PR_1} - \left(\frac{1-\gamma}{\gamma.PR_1} \right).\left(\frac{\Delta \acute{x}}{\Sigma_{i=1}^{|N|} y_i.i} \right) \right) \right] \qquad (2\text{-}5)$$

Based on Eq. (2-5), $\Delta \dot{x} = \dfrac{\gamma}{1-\gamma}\left[\dfrac{PR_1.(\Sigma_{i=1}^{|N|} y_i.\ i)}{\mu}\ \ln(rl_3) + (\Delta x + x)\right]$

units extra production in the supplier with $\Sigma_{i=1}^{|N|} y_i$. i production scheme ensures rl_3 reliability. By producing $\Delta \dot{x}$, the supplier can fulfill the entire manufacturer's order with rl_3 probability. In Figure 2-5 the probability function of qualified components in the production system of the SC's supplier is shown. The extra production $\Delta \dot{x}$ should be selected in a way that the probability of having $\Delta x + x$ qualified output equals rl_3. By producing $\Delta \dot{x}$ extra components the supplier will be able to fulfill the whole order of the manufacturer with probability rl_3, with an Δx extra product production the manufacturer will be able to fulfill the whole order of the retailer with probability rl_2 and this amount of product stock in the retailer will allow him to respond to the market demand with rl_1 probability. $\Delta \dot{x} + \Delta x + x$ production volume in the supplier leads to a volume of product in the retailer that responds to the market demand with rl_1. rl_2. rl_3 probability and preserves service level $sl = rl_1$. rl_2. rl_3 for the whole SC. This attracts $D(rl_1$. rl_2. rl_3, $p)$ demand for the SC. This leads to the following equations for x, Δx and $\Delta \dot{x}$:

$$x = D(rl_1.\ rl_2.\ rl_3,\ p).\ G^{-1}\left(Max\left\{rl_1,\ \dfrac{h^-}{h^- + h^+}\right\}\right) \tag{2-6}$$

$$\Delta x = G'^{-1}(rl_2).\ D(rl_1.\ rl_2.\ rl_3,\ p).\ G^{-1}\left(Max\left\{rl_1,\ \dfrac{h^-}{h^- + h^+}\right\}\right) \tag{2-7}$$

$$\Delta \dot{x} = \dfrac{\gamma}{1-\gamma}\left[\dfrac{PR_1.(\Sigma_{i=1}^{|N|} y_i.\ i)}{\mu}\ \ln(rl_3) + (G'^{-1}(rl_2) + 1).\ D(rl_1.\ rl_2.\ rl_3,\ p).\right.$$
$$\left. G^{-1}\left(Max\left\{rl_1,\ \dfrac{h^-}{h^- + h^+}\right\}\right)\right] \tag{2-8}$$

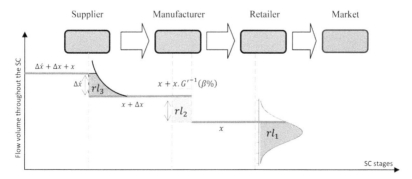

Figure 2-5. Production volume of the supplier based on the whole SC's propagated variations.

2.5 Mathematical Model of Reliable Production Planning throughout the Supply Chain

In Sections 2.4.1, 2.4.2 and 2.4.3 we found the relationship between the reliability levels of the SC's entities and their production levels. The appropriate selection of reliability levels is important because it determines service level and its captured demand and income, and affects the SC's production levels and manufacturing cost (the second term in Eq. 2-4). A mathematical model of reliable production planning determines the SC's best reliability levels by considering the tradeoff between capturable income and manufacturing cost. The mathematical model of this problem is formulated:

$$Max\ Z = \left(p - h^+ \cdot E\left[G^{-1}\left(Max\left\{rl_1 \cdot rl_2 \cdot rl_3, \frac{h^-}{h^- + h^+}\right\}\right) - \varepsilon\right]^+\right.$$

$$- h^- \cdot E\left[\varepsilon - G^{-1}\left(Max\left\{rl_1 \cdot rl_2 \cdot rl_3, \frac{h^-}{h^- + h^+}\right\}\right)\right]^+\right) \cdot D(rl_1 \cdot rl_2 \cdot rl_3, p)$$

$$- \left[a_1 \cdot (x + \Delta x + \Delta \acute{x}) - a_2 \cdot (x + \Delta x + \Delta \acute{x}) - a_3 \cdot \left(\Sigma_{i=1}^{|N|} y_i \cdot i\right) - \frac{h_1 \cdot (x + \Delta x)^2}{2.PR_1 \cdot (\Sigma_{i=1}^{|N|} y_i \cdot i)^2} - \right.$$

$$\left. b_1 \cdot (x + \Delta x) - b_2 \cdot (x + \Delta x) - \frac{h_2 \cdot (x)^2}{2.PR_2} - c_1 \cdot x - c_2 \cdot x\right] \tag{2-9}$$

Where

$$x = D(rl_1 \cdot rl_2 \cdot rl_3, p) \cdot G^{-1}\left(Max\left\{rl_1, \frac{h^-}{h^- + h^+}\right\}\right) \tag{2-10}$$

$$\Delta x = G'^{-1}(rl_2) \cdot D(rl_1 \cdot rl_2 \cdot rl_3, p) \cdot G^{-1}\left(Max\left\{rl_1, \frac{h^-}{h^- + h^+}\right\}\right) \tag{2-11}$$

$$\Delta \acute{x} = \frac{\gamma}{1 - \gamma}\left[\frac{PR_1 \cdot (\Sigma_{i=1}^{|N|} y_i \cdot i)}{\mu}\ \ln(rl_3) + (G'^{-1}(rl_2) + 1) \cdot D(rl_1 \cdot rl_2 \cdot rl_3, p) \cdot\right.$$

$$G^{-1}\left(Max\left\{rl_1, \frac{h^-}{h^- + h^+}\right\}\right)\right] \tag{2-12}$$

Subject to

$$\Sigma_{i=1}^{|N|} y_i = 1 \tag{2-13}$$

$$0 \le rl_1, rl_2, rl_3 \le 1 \tag{2-14}$$

$$y_i \in \{0,1\} \qquad (\forall i \in \{1, 2,\ldots, |N|\}) \tag{2-15}$$

In this objective function, the total profit of the SC is maximized. The first term addresses the profit of the chain in the market by selling the supplied products and their corresponding shortage and extra inventory costs. The first and second parts of the second term are the procurement and production costs in the SC's supplier. The third and fourth parts are the set-up cost of the supplier's machinery and their inventory holding costs. The fifth and sixth parts are the transportation costs of the supplier to the manufacturer and the manufacturing cost of the manufacturer. The seventh, eighth and ninth parts are inventory holding costs of the manufacturer, transportation cost from the manufacturer to the retailer and handling costs of the retailer. Equation (2-10)–(2-12), in the previous sections, specify the relationship between production quantities in the SC's facilities and their reliability levels. Based on constraint (2-13), only one production scheme in the chain's supplier is selected. This is a mixed integer nonlinear model with a highly nonlinear objective function. In the next section, an approach is proposed to solve this model.

Notice that there are some critical functions in this model such as $D(sl, p)$ function and cumulative distribution functions (G and G') used to quantify variation in different echelons' facilities. To implement the model of this chapter in practice these functions should be identified appropriately. Usually historical data of the same or different but similar product can be used to identify $D(sl, p)$ function. For example, by having historical triples of *demand*, *price* and *service level* we find the best fitting $D(sl, p)$ function by using different statistical approaches such as regression. By having nonconforming production rate of a facility in the previous production periods, statistical methods such as "goodness of fit" can be used to fit the best cumulative distribution function to quantify the variation of its production system.

2.6 Solution for the Supply Chain's Reliable Production Planning Model

In this section, a solution approach is proposed for the model in the previous section. Important continuous design variables in this model are rl_1, rl_2 and rl_3 which take values on the [0, 1] interval or, it would be more rational to assume, the [0.5, 1.0] interval. Having range-restricted design variables makes discretization an efficient solution approach. After discretization, nonlinear parts of the model's objective function become linear ones. Linear models are very well-formed mathematical models and are solved globally. To discretize the model, we define $SL = \{sl^1, sl^2, \ldots, sl^{|SL|}\}$, a set of scenarios for the SC's service level. For each member of SL, a set of reliability levels is defined to preserve that service level for the SC:

$$RL^{sl^i} = \left\{ RL_1^{sl^i} = (rl_{11}^{sl^i}, rl_{12}^{sl^i}, rl_{13}^{sl^i}), \; RL_2^{sl^i} = (rl_{21}^{sl^i}, rl_{22}^{sl^i}, rl_{23}^{sl^i}), \; \ldots, \; RL_{|RL^{sl^i}|}^{sl^i} = \right.$$

$$\left. (rl_{|RL^{sl^i}|1}^{sl^i}, rl_{|RL^{sl^i}|2}^{sl^i}, rl_{|RL^{sl^i}|3}^{sl^i}) \right\}.$$

z_{sl^i} $(\forall sl^i \in SL)$ and $w_{RL_j^{sl^i}}(\forall RL_j^{sl^i} \in RL^{sl^i})$ are new binary design variables to select service level, sl^i, and reliability level distribution, $RL_j^{sl^i}$. By defining the above new design variables, the following terms in the mathematical model of the problem are revised as:

$$x = \sum_{SL}\sum_{RL^{sl^i}} z_{sl^i} \cdot w_{RL_j^{sl^i}} \cdot \left[D(rl_{j1}^{sl^i} \cdot rl_{j2}^{sl^i} \cdot rl_{j3}^{sl^i}, p) \cdot G^{-1}\left(Max\left\{ rl_{j1}^{sl^i}, \frac{h^-}{h^- + h^+} \right\}\right) \right] \quad (2\text{-}16)$$

$$x^2 = \sum_{SL}\sum_{RL^{sl^i}} z_{sl^i} \cdot w_{RL_j^{sl^i}} \cdot \left[D(rl_{j1}^{sl^i} \cdot rl_{j2}^{sl^i} \cdot rl_{j3}^{sl^i}, p) \cdot G^{-1}\left(Max\left\{ rl_{j1}^{sl^i}, \frac{h^-}{h^- + h^+} \right\}\right) \right]^2 \quad (2\text{-}17)$$

$$\Delta x = \sum_{SL}\sum_{RL^{sl^i}} z_{sl^i} \cdot w_{RL_j^{sl^i}} \cdot \left[(G'^{-1}(rl_{j2}^{sl^i}) \cdot D(rl_{j1}^{sl^i} \cdot rl_{j2}^{sl^i} \cdot rl_{j3}^{sl^i}, p) \cdot G^{-1}\left(Max\left\{ rl_{j1}^{sl^i}, \frac{h^-}{h^- + h^+} \right\}\right) \right]$$

$$(2\text{-}18)$$

$$\Delta x + x = \sum_{SL}\sum_{RL^{sl^i}} z_{sl^i} \cdot w_{RL_j^{sl^i}} \cdot \left[(G'^{-1}(rl_{j2}^{sl^i}) + \right.$$

$$\left. 1). D(rl_{j1}^{sl^i} \cdot rl_{j2}^{sl^i} \cdot rl_{j3}^{sl^i}, p) \cdot G^{-1}\left(Max\left\{ rl_{j1}^{sl^i}, \frac{h^-}{h^- + h^+} \right\}\right) \right] \quad (2\text{-}19)$$

$$(\Delta x + x)^2 = \sum_{SL}\sum_{RL^{sl^i}} z_{sl^i} \cdot w_{RL_j^{sl^i}} \cdot \left[(G'^{-1}(rl_{j2}^{sl^i}) + \right.$$

$$\left. 1). D(rl_{j1}^{sl^i} \cdot rl_{j2}^{sl^i} \cdot rl_{j3}^{sl^i}, p) \cdot G^{-1}\left(Max\left\{ rl_{j1}^{sl^i}, \frac{h^-}{h^- + h^+} \right\}\right) \right]^2 \quad (2\text{-}20)$$

$$\Delta \dot{x} + \Delta x + x = \sum_{N}\sum_{SL}\sum_{RL^{sl^i}} y_k \cdot z_{sl^i} \cdot w_{RL_j^{sl^i}} \cdot \frac{\gamma}{1-\gamma}\left[\frac{PR_1.k}{\mu} \ln(rl_{j3}^{sl^i}) + \left(G'^{-1}(rl_{j2}^{sl^i}) + \right. \right.$$

$$\left. 1). D(rl_{j1}^{sl^i} \cdot rl_{j2}^{sl^i} \cdot rl_{j3}^{sl^i}, p) \cdot G^{-1}\left(Max\left\{ rl_{j1}^{sl^i}, \frac{h^-}{h^- + h^+} \right\}\right) \right] \quad (2\text{-}21)$$

The first five of these equations are linear functions of z_{sli}. $w_{RL_j^{sli}}$ and the last term is a linear function of y_k. z_{sli}. $w_{RL_j^{sli}}(\forall sl^i \in SL, \forall RL_j^{sli} \in RL^{sli}, \forall k \in N)$. By defining $zw_{sl^i,RL_j^{sli}} = z_{sl^i}$. $w_{RL_j^{sli}}$ and $yzw_{k,sl^i,RL_j^{sli}} = y_k$. z_{sl^i}. $w_{RL_j^{sli}}$ Eq. (2-16)–(2-21) become completely linear. However, the following constraints must be added:

$$(z_{sl^i} + w_{RL_j^{sli}} - 1) \leq zw_{sl^i,RL_j^{sli}} \leq \frac{z_{sl^i} + w_{RL_j^{sli}}}{2} \tag{2-22}$$

$$zw_{sl^i,RL_j^{sli}} \leq M. \, z_{sl^i} \tag{2-23}$$

$$zw_{sl^i,RL_j^{sli}} \leq M. \, w_{RL_j^{sli}} \tag{2-24}$$

$$zw_{sl^i,RL_j^{sli}} \in \{0,1\} \tag{2-25}$$

$$\left(y_k + z_{sl^i} + w_{RL_j^{sli}} - 2\right) \leq yzw_{k,sl^i,RL_j^{sli}} \leq \frac{y_k + z_{sl^i} + w_{RL_j^{sli}}}{3} \tag{2-26}$$

$$yzw_{k,sl^i,RL_j^{sli}} \leq M. \, z_{sl^i} \tag{2-27}$$

$$yzw_{k,sl^i,RL_j^{sli}} \leq M. \, w_{RL_j^{sli}} \tag{2-28}$$

$$yzw_{k,sl^i,RL_j^{sli}} \leq M. \, y_k \tag{2-29}$$

$$yzw_{k,sl^i,RL_j^{sli}} \in \{0,1\} \tag{2-30}$$

By substituting these equations into the mathematical model (9-15), the model becomes:

$$\textbf{Max } Z = \sum_{SL} \sum_{RL^{sli}} [zw_{sl^i,RL_j^{sli}} \times \left(D\left(rl_{j1}^{sli}. \, rl_{j2}^{sli}. \, rl_{j3}^{sli}, p\right)\right) \times$$

$$\left(p - h^+. \, E\left[G^{-1}\left(Max \left\{rl_{j1}^{sli}. \, rl_{j2}^{sli}. \, rl_{j3}^{sli}, \frac{h^-}{h^- + h^+}\right\}\right) - \varepsilon\right]^+ - h^-. \, E\left[\varepsilon - \right.\right.$$

$$G^{-1}\left(Max \left\{rl_{j1}^{sli}. \, rl_{j2}^{sli}. \, rl_{j3}^{sli}, \frac{h^-}{h^- + h^+}\right\}\right)\right]^+\right)]$$

$$- a_1. \, (x + \Delta x + \Delta \acute{x}) - a_2. \, (x + \Delta x + \Delta \acute{x}) - a_3. \left(\Sigma_{i=1}^{|N|} y_i. \, i\right)$$

$$- \frac{h_1(x + \Delta x)^2}{2.PR_1.(\Sigma_{i=1}^{|N|} y_i.i)^2} - b_1. \, (x + \Delta x) - b_2. \, (x + \Delta x) - \frac{h_2(x)^2}{2.PR_2} - c_1. \, x - c_2. \, x \tag{2-31}$$

Where

$$x = \sum_{SL}\sum_{RL^{sli}} zw_{sli,RL_j^{sli}} \cdot \left[D\left(rl_{j1}^{sli}. \, rl_{j2}^{sli}. \, rl_{j3}^{sli}, p\right) \times G^{-1}\left(Max\left\{rl_{j1}^{sli}, \frac{h^-}{h^- + h^+}\right\}\right)\right] \qquad (2\text{-}32)$$

$$x^2 = \sum_{SL}\sum_{RL^{sli}} zw_{sli,RL_j^{sli}} \cdot \left[D\left(rl_{j1}^{sli}. \, rl_{j2}^{sli}. \, rl_{j3}^{sli}, p\right) \times G^{-1}\left(Max\left\{rl_{j1}^{sli}, \frac{h^-}{h^- + h^+}\right\}\right)\right]^2 \qquad (2\text{-}33)$$

$$\Delta x + x = \sum_{SL}\sum_{RL^{sli}} zw_{sli,RL_j^{sli}} \cdot \left[\left(G'^{-1}\left(rl_{j2}^{sli}\right) + 1\right) \times D\left(rl_{j1}^{sli}. \, rl_{j2}^{sli}. \, rl_{j3}^{sli}, p\right) \times\right.$$
$$\left. G^{-1}\left(Max\left\{rl_{j1}^{sli}, \frac{h^-}{h^- + h^+}\right\}\right)\right] \qquad (2\text{-}34)$$

$$(\Delta x + x)^2 = \sum_{SL}\sum_{RL^{sli}} zw_{sli,RL_j^{sli}} \cdot \left[\left(G'^{-1}\left(rl_{j2}^{sli}\right) + 1\right) \times D(rl_{j1}^{sli}. \, rl_{j2}^{sli}. \, rl_{j3}^{sli}, p) \times\right.$$
$$\left. G^{-1}\left(Max\left\{rl_{j1}^{sli}, \frac{h^-}{h^- + h^+}\right\}\right)\right]^2 \qquad (2\text{-}35)$$

$$\Delta\dot{x} + \Delta x + x = \sum_{N}\sum_{SL}\sum_{RL^{sli}} yzw_{k,sli,RL_j^{sli}} \cdot \frac{\gamma}{1-\gamma}\left[\frac{PR_1.n_k}{\mu} \ln(rl_{j3}^{sli}) + \left(G'^{-1}\left(rl_{j2}^{sli}\right) + 1\right) \times\right.$$
$$\left. D(rl_{j1}^{sli}. \, rl_{j2}^{sli}. \, rl_{j3}^{sli}, p) \times G^{-1}\left(Max\left\{rl_{j1}^{sli}, \frac{h^-}{h^- + h^+}\right\}\right)\right] \qquad (2\text{-}36)$$

Subject to:

$$\sum_{i=1}^{|N|} y_i = 1 \qquad (2\text{-}37)$$

$$\sum_{SL} z_{sli} = 1 \qquad (2\text{-}38)$$

$$\sum_{RL^{sli}} w_{RL_j^{sli}} = z_{sli} \qquad (\forall RL_j^{sli} \in RL^{sli}, \forall sl^i \in SL) \qquad (2\text{-}39)$$

$$\left(z_{sli} + w_{RL_j^{sli}} - 1\right) \le zw_{sli,RL_j^{sli}} \le \frac{z_{sli} + w_{RL_j^{sli}}}{2} \qquad (\forall RL_j^{sli} \in RL^{sli}, \forall sl^i \in SL) \qquad (2\text{-}40)$$

$$zw_{sli,RL_j^{sli}} \le M. \, z_{sli} \qquad (\forall RL_j^{sli} \in RL^{sli}, \forall sl^i \in SL) \qquad (2\text{-}41)$$

$$zw_{sli,RL_j^{sli}} \le M. \, w_{RL_j^{sli}} \qquad (\forall RL_j^{sli} \in RL^{sli}, \forall sl^i \in SL) \qquad (2\text{-}42)$$

$$\left(y_k + z_{sl^i} + w_{RL_j^{sl^i}} - 2 \right) \leq yzw_{k,sl^i,RL_j^{sl^i}} \leq \frac{y_k + z_{sl^i} + w_{RL_j^{sl^i}}}{3}$$

$$(\forall sl^i \in SL, \forall RL_j^{sl^i} \in RL^{sl^i}, \forall k \in N) \quad (2\text{-}43)$$

$$yzw_{k,sl^i,RL_j^{sl^i}} \leq M. z_{sl^i} \qquad (\forall sl^i \in SL, \forall RL_j^{sl^i} \in RL^{sl^i}, \forall k \in N) \quad (2\text{-}44)$$

$$yzw_{k,sl^i,RL_j^{sl^i}} \leq M. w_{RL_j^{sl^i}} \qquad (\forall sl^i \in SL, \forall RL_j^{sl^i} \in RL^{sl^i}, \forall k \in N) \quad (2\text{-}45)$$

$$yzw_{k,sl^i,RL_j^{sl^i}} \leq M. y_k \qquad (\forall sl^i \in SL, \forall RL_j^{sl^i} \in RL^{sl^i}, \forall k \in N) \quad (2\text{-}46)$$

$$z_{sl^i}, w_{RL_j^{sl^i}}, y_{j'}, zw_{sl^i,RL_j^{sl^i}}, yzw_{k,sl^i,RL_j^{sl^i}} \in \{0,1\} \ (\forall sl^i \in SL, \forall RL_j^{sl^i} \in RL^{sl^i}, \forall k \in N)$$

$$(2\text{-}47)$$

The only nonlinear term in this model is $\dfrac{h_1(x + \Delta x)^2}{2.PR_1.(\Sigma_{i=1}^{|N|} y_i.i)^2}$ in the objective function. By the above substitutions its numerator is linearized and by using the same approach elaborated above for linearizing the $z_{sl^i}. w_{RL_j^{sl^i}}$ multiplication, the denominator can be linearized too. Thus, this term transforms into a linear fractional term. Several approaches have been proposed in the literature to linearize fractional linear terms. We utilized the approach proposed by Chang (2001). Based on constraint (2-38), only one service level scenario is selected by the SC. According to constraint (2-39), only one reliability level distribution scenario for the desired service level is selected. Thus, the model becomes linear with binary design variables.

2.7 Computational Results

In this section, a sample SC is considered. The price of its product is $12.00, holding cost of inventory at the end of the planning period is $0.30 and the cost of unmet demand is $0.70. The SC's supplier procures the required material with a cost of $a_1 = \$2.50$ and manufactures the component with $a_2 = \$1.50$ cost. The production rate is $PR_1 = 9000$ (components per time unit). The supplier's machinery has a setup cost $a_3 = \$100$, and starts in an in-control state. After an exponential time with $\mu = 2$ (average number of shifts in time unit), the machinery shifts to an out-of-control state with $\gamma = 2\%$ of non-conforming production. Qualified components are transported to the manufacturer with unit cost $b_1 = \$0.50$. The manufacturer produces the final product at a rate of $PR_2 = 8000$ (products per time unit), a unit manufacturing cost $b_2 = \$2.00$, and conveys them to the retailer with unit transportation cost $c_1 = \$1.00$. The manufacturer's production system has a wastage percentage uniformly distributed on the $[0, \beta = 10\%]$ level. The retailer's unit handling costs are $c_2 = \$1.50$. Only one production scheme is possible for the supplier and all planned material is produced at once, $|N| = 1$. Unit inventory holding costs of the supplier and manufacturer per unit time are $h_1 = \$0.40$ and $h_2 = \$0.40$ respectively. The stochastic part of the demand in the market, ε, follows a uniform distribution on the $[0.7, 1.3]$ interval. As seen in Table 2-2, in this problem, $SL = \{sl^1 = 0.82, sl^2 = 0.83, \dots, sl^{|SL|} = 0.93\}$. Reliability level sets for some of service level values are listed below:

✓ Reliability levels of facilities preserving $sl^1 = 0.82$ is $RL^{0.82} = \{RL_1^{0.82} = (rl_{11}^{0.82} = 0.91, rl_{12}^{0.82} = 0.91, rl_{13}^{0.82} = 0.99), RL_2^{0.82} = (rl_{21}^{0.82} = 0.91, rl_{22}^{0.82} = 0.99, rl_{23}^{0.82} = 0.91), RL_3^{0.82} = (rl_{31}^{0.82} = 0.99, rl_{32}^{0.82} = 0.91, rl_{33}^{0.82} = 0.91)\}$.

✓ Reliability levels of facilities preserving $sl^1 = 0.91$ is $RL^{0.91} = \{RL_1^{0.91} = (rl_{11}^{0.91} = 0.91, rl_{12}^{0.91} = 1.0, rl_{13}^{0.91} = 1.0), RL_2^{0.91} = (rl_{21}^{0.91} = 1.0, rl_{22}^{0.91} = 0.91, rl_{23}^{0.91} = 1.0), RL_3^{0.91} = (rl_{31}^{0.91} = 1.0, rl_{32}^{0.91} = 1.0, rl_{33}^{0.91} = 0.91)\}$.

The mathematical model of this problem is formulated and solved on an Intel(R)Core(TM)4 Duo CPU, 3.6 GHz, with 12276 MB RAM using the default settings. CPLEX is used to solve the linearized mathematical model of the problem and it takes less than 1 minute to solve it. The solution obtained is, $rl_1 = 1.0$, $rl_2 = 1.0$ and $rl_3 = 0.90$.

The SC's profit with respect to its service level is shown in Figure 2-6; it is equal to $rl_1 \cdot rl_2 \cdot rl_3$. When the service level is less than 0.90, incrementing the service level leads to higher profit. When the service level is 0.90, the SC has the greatest profit. Beyond 0.90, incrementing the service level leads to lower profit which means that the negative effect of service level augmentation on the system's cost is more than its positive effect on the system's income. Thus 0.90 is the best choice for this SC (Table 2). However, finding the best service level is not enough. There are many rl_1, rl_2 and rl_3 combinations with $rl_1 \cdot rl_2 \cdot rl_3 = 0.90$ (see the white arrow in Figure 2-6) but the profit of the SC is different for each combination, Table 2-3. Formulating and solving the mathematical model of this problem helps

Table 2-3. Best capturable profit of the Supply Chain with respect to its service level.

Service level	0.82	0.83	0.84	0.85	0.86	0.87	0.88	0.89	0.90	0.91	0.92	0.93
Profit	$ 6056.7	$ 6079.9	$ 6105.6	$ 6125.3	$ 6146.6	$ 6165.5	$ 6179.3	$ 6193.5	$ 6199.6	$ 6158.9	$ 6118.6	$ 6078.5

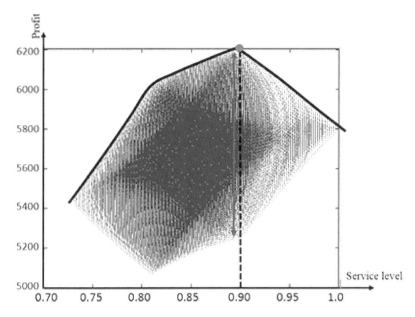

Figure 2-6. Profit of the supply chain with respect to its service level.

Table 2-4. Profit of the Supply Chain with respect to different reliability level combinations in service level 0.90.

Row	rl_1	rl_2	rl_3	Profit	Row	rl_1	rl_2	rl_3	Profit
1	0.970	0.940	0.985	$5637	2	0.970	0.945	0.980	$5662
3	0.970	0.955	0.970	$5712	4	0.970	0.960	0.970	$5720
5	0.970	0.975	0.950	$5812	6	0.980	0.915	1.000	$5600
7	0.980	0.920	0.995	$5626	8	0.980	0.940	0.975	$5729
9	0.985	0.910	1.000	$5619	10	0.985	0.930	0.980	$5723
11	0.990	0.905	1.000	$5638	12	0.990	0.910	0.995	$5665
13	0.990	0.920	0.990	$5701	14	0.990	0.930	0.975	$5769
15	0.995	0.900	1.000	$5657	16	0.995	0.915	0.985	$5736
17	0.995	0.925	0.975	$5789	18	0.995	0.945	0.955	$5892
19	1.000	0.900	0.995	$5702	20	1.000	0.900	1.000	$5687
21	1.000	0.910	0.985	$5755	22	1	1	0.900	$6199

us find the best combination of reliability levels in the different echelons of the SC (black dot in Figure 2-6). $rl_1 = 1.0$, $rl_2 = 1.0$ and $rl_3 = 0.90$ are the best reliability levels for service level 0.90 in this SC (row 22 in Table 2-3).

2.8 Closing Remarks

Controlling material/product flow in SCs is difficult because of their decentralized production systems. It is much more complicated when there are also variations in the performance of the entities inside the chain/network and variations in environmental factors. Here a SC is considered with a multi-echelon supply process involving unreliable production facilities supplying products to markets with uncertain demands. It is shown that: (i) calculation and determination of service level is critical but not easy; (ii) investigating the local effects of these variations in the performance of the corresponding facilities may not be enough; it is necessary to consider their cumulative effects on the SC performance; (iii) variation propagation in SCs is introduced and quantified; (iv) models and solution methods are proposed to provide reliable production plans for a SC protected against demand and supply side variations and propagated effects.

This problem is an example in the business environment, but it can easily be applied to problems in other fields in which variation has a significant role and where a high service level is critical. For example, it can be applied to humanitarian relief planning where a high service level is critical. Also, this model can be applied by transportation companies dealing only with product distribution. These companies do not have production facilities but variation also exists in the performance of transportation and warehousing facilities in the distribution process. Transportation and inventory holding processes always include stochastic percentage of broken, lost, spoiled and even expired items which makes their qualified output uncertain. Using the approach developed in this chapter, we will not only improve service level estimation for these SCs but also offer the foundations for service level improvement. In this problem, we assumed that production adjustment in the SC's facilities is the only option to deal with demand and supply side variations. However, keeping an inventory is the other option that can be used to deal with this problem. So, including inventory decisions in this problem can be a useful future research for this problem.

In the context of an architecture for fail-safe networks, the focus of this chapter is on variation management in forward SCs. The mathematical model of this chapter is extended in Chapter 3 to two correlated SCs servicing pre- and after-sales markets, respectively.

Acknowledgement

Figures and tables in Chapter 2 are reprinted from Transportation Research, Part E: Logistics and Transportation Review, volume 73 (January), by

Shabnam Rezapour, Janet K. Allen and Farrokh Mistree, "Uncertainty Propagation in a Supply Chain or Supply Network." pp. 185–206, 2015, with permission from Elsevier.

References

Azaron, A., Brown, K., Tarim, S. and Modarres, M. 2008. A multi-objective stochastic programming approach for supply chain design considering risk. International Journal of Production Economics 116(1): 129–138.

Baghalian, A., Rezapour, S. and Farahani, R. Z. 2013. Robust supply chain network design with service level against disruptions and demand uncertainties: A real-life case. European Journal of Operational Research 227(1): 199–215.

Bernstein, F. and Federgruen, A. 2004. A general equilibrium model for industries with price and service competition. Operations Research 52(6): 868–886.

Bernstein, F. and Federgruen, A. 2007. Coordination mechanisms for supply chains under price and service competition. Manufacturing & Service Operations Management 9(3): 242–262.

Cardona-Valdés, Y., Álvarez, A. and Ozdemir, D. 2011. A bi-objective supply chain design problem with uncertainty. Transportation Research Part C: Emerging Technologies 19(5): 821–832.

Chang, C.-T. 2001. On the polynomial mixed 0–1 fractional programming problems. European Journal of Operational Research 131(1): 224–227.

Chen, Q., Li, X. and Ouyang, Y. 2011. Joint inventory-location problem under the risk of probabilistic facility disruptions. Transportation Research Part B: Methodological 45(7): 991–1003.

Chopra, S., Reinhardt, G. and Mohan, U. 2007. The importance of decoupling recurrent and disruption risks in a supply chain. Naval Research Logistics (NRL) 54(5): 544–555.

Dada, M., Petruzzi, N. C. and Schwarz, L. B. 2007. A newsvendor's procurement problem when suppliers are unreliable. Manufacturing & Service Operations Management 9(1): 9–32.

Daniel, J. S. R. and Rajendran, C. 2006. Heuristic approaches to determine base-stock levels in a serial supply chain with a single objective and with multiple objectives. European Journal of Operational Research 175(1): 566–592.

Hsu, C.-I. and Li, H.-C. 2011. Reliability evaluation and adjustment of supply chain network design with demand fluctuations. International Journal of Production Economics 132(1): 131–145.

Ko, H. J. and Evans, G. W. 2007. A genetic algorithm-based heuristic for the dynamic integrated forward/reverse logistics network for 3PLs. Computers & Operations Research 34(2): 346–366.

Lee, H. L. and Rosenblatt, M. J. 1987. Simultaneous determination of production cycle and inspection schedules in a production system. Management Science 33(9): 1125–1136.

Li, J., Wang, S. and Cheng, T. E. 2010. Competition and cooperation in a single-retailer two-supplier supply chain with supply disruption. International Journal of Production Economics 124(1): 137–150.

Li, X. and Chen, Y. 2010. Impacts of supply disruptions and customer differentiation on a partial-backordering inventory system. Simulation Modelling Practice and Theory 18(5): 547–557.

Listes, O. and Dekker, R. 2005 A stochastic approach to a case study for product recovery network design. Europian Journal of Operational Research 160: 268–287.

Miranda, P. A. and Garrido, R. A. 2004. Incorporating inventory control decisions into a strategic distribution network design model with stochastic demand. Transportation Research Part E: Logistics and Transportation Review 40(3): 183–207.

Pan, F. and Nagi, R. 2010. Robust supply chain design under uncertain demand in agile manufacturing. Computers & Operations Research 37(4): 668–683.

Park, S., Lee, T.-E. and Sung, C. S. 2010. A three-level supply chain network design model with risk-pooling and lead times. Transportation Research Part E: Logistics and Transportation Review 46(5): 563–581.

Romeijn, H. E., Shu, J. and Teo, C.-P. 2007. Designing two-echelon supply networks. European Journal of Operational Research 178(2): 449–462.

Rosenblatt, M. J. and Lee, H. L. 1986. Economic production cycles with imperfect production processes. IIE transactions 18(1): 48–55.

Ross, A. M., Rong, Y. and Snyder, L. V. 2008. Supply disruptions with time-dependent parameters. Computers & Operations Research 35(11): 3504–3529.

Sabri, E. H. and Beamon, B. M. 2000. A multi-objective approach to simultaneous strategic and operational planning in supply chain design. Omega 28(5): 581–598.

Sana, S. S. 2010. An economic production lot size model in an imperfect production system. European Journal of Operational Research 201(1): 158–170.

Santoso, T., Ahmed, S., Goetschalckx, M. and Shapiro, A. 2005. A stochastic programming approach for supply chain network design under uncertainty. European Journal of Operational Research 167(1): 96–115.

Schmitt, A. J., Snyder, L. V. and Shen, Z.-J. M. 2010. Inventory systems with stochastic demand and supply: Properties and approximations. European Journal of Operational Research 206(2): 313–328.

Schütz, P., Tomasgard, A. and Ahmed, S. 2009. Supply chain design under uncertainty using sample average approximation and dual decomposition. European Journal of Operational Research 199(2): 409–419.

Shen, Z.-J. M. and Daskin, M. S. 2005. Trade-offs between customer service and cost in integrated supply chain design. Manufacturing & Service Operations Management 7(3): 188–207.

Shen, Z.-J. M. and Qi, L. 2007. Incorporating inventory and routing costs in strategic location models. European Journal of Operational Research 179(2): 372–389.

Xanthopoulos, A., Vlachos, D. and Iakovou, E. 2012. Optimal newsvendor policies for dual-sourcing supply chains: A disruption risk management framework. Computers & Operations Research 39(2): 350–357.

You, F. and Grossmann, I. E. 2008. Design of responsive supply chains under demand uncertainty. Computers & Chemical Engineering 32(12): 3090–3111.

Yu, H., Zeng, A. Z. and Zhao, L. 2009. Single or dual sourcing: decision-making in the presence of supply chain disruption risks. Omega 37(4): 788–800.

CHAPTER 3

Variation Management in Pre- and After-Sales Supply Chains of Non-Repairable Products

In Chapter 3, we describe how the approach developed in Chapter 2 can be extended and used for complicated chains of companies providing both pre- and after-sales services for customers for their products which cannot be repaired (see Chapter 1, Figure 1-9). First, we show that there are two highly convoluted forward and after-sales supply chains in those companies. Then, we explain what interactions exist between these two chains that justify the requirement for their concurrent flow planning. Finally, we develop a model to select variation management decisions concurrently for forward and after-sales SCs. The numerical analysis of results concludes with some useful insight about variation management in forward and after-sales SCs.

3.1 Importance of the After-sales Supply Chains for Products with Non-Repairable Components

After-sales service is a marketing strategy used by manufacturers to assure customers of product quality. Hyundai Motor Company changed customer perception about its products by providing an extensive warranty, thus signaling to customers that the quality of its cars had improved (Business Week 2004). Khajavi et al. (2014) and Baines et al. (2007) believe that in today's markets, the focus of competition has shifted from quality and price to the delivery of value. They believe that customers now value an assurance that the product will work. Recently, companies have become more aware of the profitability of after-sales service and have started to invest in it further. In high-tech product markets, Lenovo provides after-sales maintenance services for its PC customers (Li et al. 2014). Dell sells its laptops under a default hardware warranty that states "1 Yr Ltd Warranty, 1 Yr Mail-In Service, and 1 Yr Technical Support." However, customers are offered a 3-year warranty plan for an additional price (Dell.com 2010).

According to Gallagher et al. (2005), providing after-sales service by supplying spare parts for household appliances, automobiles, copy machines, heating and air conditioning is a business worth more than $200 billion. In 2009, the US military spent $194 billion on their spare parts supply chain (SC) and logistics based on data from the United States Logistics and Material Readiness Office, with $104, $70, and $20 billion related to supply, repair, and transportation, respectively. At the end of that year, the value of the spare parts inventory was $94 billion. In the automobile industry, retailers of General Motor, Volkswagen and Toyota provide 4S (sale, spare parts, service and survey) services for their customers (Li et al. 2014). Fiat uses TNT Post to handle its distribution of spare parts in Europe and South America. TNT has 2,000 employees and 3 million square feet of warehouse space, handles 120,000 tons of shipments and processes 34.6 million order lines a year on Fiat's behalf. These numbers illustrate that even a small improvement in the product and its spare parts SCs can lead to a significant gain in profitability.

The after-sales business is an important part of the economy and is nearly twice as profitable as the original product business (Kim et al. 2007). Based on the work of Dennis and Kambil (2003), GM's after-sales revenue of $9 billion generated a profit of $2 billion. This profit is considerably greater than GM's profit from the $150 billion in revenue from its car sales. On average, after-sales services contribute 25 percent of the total revenue but generate more than 40–50 percent of the total profit.

For these reasons, providing after-sales service is an important part of daily operations in successful companies. These companies have a forward SC and an after-sales SC. Whereas the forward SC involves producing and supplying the original products to the target pre-market, the after-sales SC provides the required spare parts to fulfill the after-sales commitments. Production planning in companies with both forward and after-sales SCs is extremely complex. In addition to having to address two SCs, these chains are not independent. The events occurring in one SC affect the performance of the other chain. Appropriate concurrent flow planning throughout the forward and after-sales SCs is critical to providing good service in the pre- and after-sales markets. Although a company's pre-market service level is typically defined as the product's demand fulfillment rate to avoid lost sales, the after-sales service is a function of: (i) warranty length and (ii) just-in-time fulfillment of the required spare parts inside the warranty period. In the remainder of this chapter, the spare parts' demand fulfillment rate is called the after-sales service level. Improving the after-sales service imposes more costs on the after-sales SC but also improves the attractiveness of the product for the customers in the pre-market and stimulates product demand. This is an important interaction between the two SCs. Higher product sales volumes in the pre-market, augment the spare part or repair requests in the after-sales market. This means that the after-sales demand is a function of the total sales realized in the forward SC. This is another important interaction between the two SCs. These interactions justify the rationality of their concurrent flow planning.

Boone et al. (2008) conducted a Delphi study in 18 industries in which senior service part managers were asked about the challenges in their industries. The main challenge mentioned was "lack of holistic perspective and system integration among SC partners." This result illustrates the strong need to improve integration in after-sales operations. In the academic literature, there is a lack of research with an integrated perspective in the after-sales domain (Bacchetti and Saccani 2012). According to Boone et al. (2008), Cohen et al. (2006), Wagner and Lindemann (2008) and McAvoy (2008), the main challenges in the after-sales domain are the lack of (i) systematic approaches for spare parts management, (ii) consideration of SC relationships, (iii) accurate models for predicting the demand for spare parts, and (iv) practical models for determining appropriate inventory levels. In this chapter, we fill the first and second voids by integrating all after-sales operations as an after-sales SC to consider their relationships. A consideration of the interactions between the forward and after-sales SCs improves the after-sales demand prediction, significantly the third deficiency. We also determine the inventory levels of the product and its spare parts to preserve the best pre- and after-sales service levels for the SCs, i.e., the fourth deficiency.

In the context of an architecture for fail-safe networks, as introduced in Section 1.3, we explain the use of reliability for risk management in two correlated SCs (see Figure 1-4). The connector is forward and after-sales SCs. We express the form of our architecture as an optimization model that determines the best local reliabilities (properties) for the chains' facilities in a way to maximize the total profit in pre- and after-sales markets (relationship). This model helps us to understand the relationship between the chains' performances (pre- and after-sales service levels) and the local reliability of the facilities (component of risk management). Summary interpretation for the problem investigated in Chapter 3 is as follows:

Table 3-1. Summary interpretation for the problem investigated in Chapter 3.

Elements	What?
Components	Reliability
Connectors	Forward and after-sales supply chains
Form	**How?**
Component importance	Reliability: 1
Properties	Local reliabilities
Relationship	Profit optimization in pre- and after-sales markets
Rationale	**Why?**
Motivation	Variation management
Assumptions	No disruption There is enough information to quantify variations
Constraints	Order amplification in echelons due to variations Market demand depends on service levels, pre-sales market price and after-sales market warranty
Interpretation	Relationship between the chain's service levels in pre- and after-sales markets and the local reliability of its facilities Relationship between pre- and after-sales marketing factors

3.2 Literature of the After-sales Operations for Products with Non-Repairable Components

In this section, we review some of the work performed in the after-sales literature to highlight the gaps. Detailed information is provided in Table 3-1.

For capital goods (Column 2 in Table 3-1), such as computer networks, and complex technical systems, such as medical or defense systems, the most frequent after-sales services offered by manufacturers are: (i) material contracts; (ii) performance-based warranties; and (iii) end-of-life (EOL) warranties. In these systems, operational interruptions can lead to considerable losses and the loss becomes greater as the duration of the disruption increases. In material contracts, customers pay the manufacturer for parts, other resources, and labor (Kim et al. 2007). In performance-based warranties (Column 11 in Table 3-1), there is an agreement with respect to the availability of the system in the field (Chakravarthy and Gómez-Corral 2009; Chen and Chien 2007; Chien 2005; de Smidt-Destombes et al. 2006, 2007, 2009; Finkelstein 2009; Jhang 2005; Jung and Park 2003; Kuo and Wan 2007; Li and Li 2012; Lieckens et al. 2013; Marseguerra et al. 2005; Nourelfath and Ait-Kadi 2007; Öner et al. 2010; Sahba and Balcıog 2011; Wang et al. 2009; Yeh et al. 2005). EOL warranties (Column 10 in Table 3-1) ensure after-sales service without a time limit. The company provides the required service if the products are in use, even if their production has been discontinued (Kim and Park 2008).

For durable consumer goods (Column 3 in Table 3-1), which are considered in this chapter, rebate warranties and failure-free warranties are the most common after-sales policies. Rebate warranties (Column 8 in Table 3-1) are typically used for non-repairable goods and manufacturers commit to refund customers some portion of the sale price if the product fails during the warranty period. Goods such as automobile batteries and tyres are typically sold with this type of warranty. Failure-free warranties (Column 9 in Table 3-1) are commonly used for household appliances and electronic devices and with these warranties, manufacturers commit to repair products free of charge during the warranty period. As highlighted by Cohen et al. (2006), Niemi et al. (2009), Wagner and Lindemann (2008), little work has been completed on warranty service and spare parts management for failure-free warranties. See Bacchetti and Saccani (2012) for a review of the literature of spare parts classifications and demand prediction for stock control. According to Kleber et al. (2011), the focus of authors in most of the work performed in spare parts management has been only on inventory management (Columns 18–27 and 30 in Table 3-1). For example, Chien and Chen (2008) have developed a model for optimal spare parts ordering for a non-repairable product under a rebate warranty. They assume that the lead times to fulfill the orders are stochastic and follow a given probability distribution. They determine the ordering policy to maximize profit, which is expressed as the difference between rebate gains and the total cost, including ordering, storage and holding expenses. These papers overlook the manufacturing systems supporting the inventory systems and the flow transactions that exist between these two portions.

A great deal of the after-sales work focuses on the marketing aspect of after-sales services, such as investigating the trade-off between the repair/replacement cost and the income without incorporating the SC supporting its operations (Chu and Chintagunta 2009; Kurata and Nam 2010, 2013; Majid et al. 2012; Su and Shen 2012; Zhou et al. 2009; Chen et al. 2012; Esmaeili et al. 2014; Jung et al. 2014; Wei et al. 2014; Li et al. 2014; Li et al. 2012). For example, Zhou et al. (2009) have developed a model to determine the best price and warranty for a product dynamically in its lifecycle by considering the purchase pattern of customers. Chen et al. (2012) investigate pricing strategies for a company with two competing retailers servicing markets with warranty-dependent demands. Kurata and Nam (2013, 2010) explore the interaction of basic and optional after-sales services for durable consumer products. Esmaeili et al. (2014) have determined the optimal sale price, warranty period and warranty price for a manufacturer under three-level service contacts (Columns 13–16 and 28 in Table 3-1 correspond to these decisions). These papers only concentrate on the downstream marketing effects of after-sales services. They overlook the upstream manufacturing operations in the SCs that support these marketing strategies. In this chapter, upstream manufacturing operations are included in our problem by considering the forward and after-sales SCs that back up the marketing strategies in the pre- and after-sales markets.

Recently, various researchers have considered the engineering aspects of after-sales services in addition to their marketing aspects, e.g., making decisions about the reliability of the product (Huang et al. 2007; Hussain and Murthy 2003; Kamrad et al. 2005; Öner et al. 2010; Sheu and Chien 2005; Wu et al. 2006; Chen and Chu 2001; Lin and Shue 2005). Columns 17 and 29 in Table 3-1 correspond to these decisions. For example, Huang et al. (2007) have proposed a model for simultaneously determining product reliability, retail price and warranty for a repairable product sold with a free replacement-repair warranty to maximize the total achievable profit. They assume that the product sales rate is an increasing function of warranty length and a decreasing function of retail price. Öner et al. (2010) have developed a model to support a manufacturer that designs and supplies a system to its customers through a service contract. This model selects the best reliability level for a critical component of the system. These papers only concentrate on the design and marketing aspects of the supplied products and ignore their manufacturing processes. We incorporate the manufacturing process into our problem by considering the SCs of the product and its spare parts.

This review illustrates that the literature has largely ignored the manufacturing facilities supporting after-sales services and the integration between these facilities. This has led to a lack of holistic integration and a lack of comprehensive planning in the facilities supporting these services. In this chapter, we fill this gap by considering the after-sales SC including all facilities supporting the after-sales services. We consider not only the interactions of facilities inside the after-sales SC but also the interactions of this chain with the forward SC. To the best of our knowledge, these interactions are ignored in the literature (Columns 6 and 7 in Table 3-1). To fill these gaps, we answer the following question in this chapter:

What is the most profitable integrated production plan for companies having both forward and after-sales SCs to service pre- and after-sales markets?

In this chapter, we consider a company that produces and supplies a durable consumer product to a target market through its forward SC. These products are sold warranting that all the failures of the product's components will be repaired free of charge. The spare parts required to repair the returned products are produced and supplied through the after-sales SC. We develop a mathematical model to concurrently determine the most profitable production plan in the forward and after-sales SCs. Flow transactions between facilities involving marketing and production operations and interactions between the forward and after-sales SCs are considered in this model. In the next section, we explain the variations considered in this integrated production plan model.

3.3 Literature of Variation in the After-sales Operations of Products with Non-Repairable Components

We consider two groups of variations in the flow planning of the SCs: (i) demand-side variations, including the variation in the product and after-sales service demand and (ii) supply-side variations related to the imperfect production systems of the SCs' production facilities.

Although there is a large body of work that considers variation in the product demand of the pre-markets (Baghalian et al. 2013; Cardona-Valdés et al. 2011; Daniel and Rajendran 2006; Hsu and Li 2011; Ko and Evans 2007; Pan and Nagi 2010; Park et al. 2010; Romeijn et al. 2007; Schütz et al. 2009; Shen and Qi 2007; You and Grossmann 2008; Mohammaddust et al. 2015; Rezapour et al. 2013; Rezapour and Zanjirani Farahani 2014; Rezapour et al. 2014a; Rezapour et al. 2014b; Rezapour et al. 2015a; Rezapour et al. 2015b) and the repair demand of the after-sales markets (Kurata and Nam 2010; Rappold and Van Roo 2009; Van Ommeren et al. 2006; Wang et al. 2009; Wang 2012; Wu et al. 2009; Faridimehr and Niaki 2012; Lin and Shue 2005), variation in the performance of the production systems in the SCs' facilities is often ignored (Column 33 in Table 3-1).

In the literature, it is mainly assumed that SCs' production facilities are perfect and only have a conforming output (Rezapour et al. 2015a; Rezapour et al. 2015b). However, there is no perfect production system. Due to machinery and labor failures, production systems always have some stochastic proportion of nonconforming output (Sana 2010). We fill this gap of the literature by determining the best pre- and after-sales service levels in the presence of both demand- and supply-side variations. To fill this gap, we answer the following question in this chapter:

What are the best service levels in the pre- and after-sales markets in the presence of demand- and supply-side variations?

A consideration of supply-side variations is critical for a service-level estimation in SCs. The service level indicates the capability of a SC to balance supply and demand. Therefore, a consideration of possible variations in a SC's qualified supply quantity improves the accuracy of its service level estimation significantly. In this chapter, we aim to determine the best service level for the forward and after-sales SCs in the presence of demand- and supply-side variations. We demonstrate that in SCs with several stochastic production facilities, the qualified flow depreciates when moving from upstream to downstream, which affects its service level adversely. To neutralize the negative effects of flow depreciation, we develop an approach that amplifies the orders among the SCs' facilities from downstream to upstream. Therefore, the development of a reliable flow in the forward and after-sales SCs against flow depreciation to preserve the pre- and after-sales service levels is the other contribution of this problem.

Detailed information of various relevant works is summarized in Table 3-1. The "Product" column of the table indicates the type of the investigated good: capital or consuming. The "Operation" column indicates whether the pre- or after-sales market operations (or both) are considered. The "Warranty" column indicates the good's warranty type: rebate, failure-free, EOL, or performance-based. The "Output" column indicates the decisions determined by the models of the papers. The objective functions and constraints of the models are listed in the "Objective" and "Constraint" columns, respectively. The stochastic parts of the models are summarized in the "Variation" column of the table.

3.4 Our Contributions to the After-sales Operations of Products with Non-Repairable Components

In this chapter, we propose an integrated mathematical model for coordinating all the facilities involved in the complex production system of manufacturing companies that provide a product/after-sales service package for their customers. The contributions of this work are as follows:

✓ **After-sales servitization:** In addition to downstream marketing effects of the after-sales services, we also incorporate their supporting upstream manufacturing operations in our model. Integration of after-sales providers and merchandiser facilities fills the *"lack of system integration"* gap noted in the literature review (the flow transactions between these facilities are explained in Section 3.5 and quantified in Section 3.6.2);

✓ **Integration of forward and after-sales SCs:** The operations of the forward and after-sales SCs are typically planned separately in the literature (see Columns 6–7 in Table 3-1). In this chapter, we determine the important interactions that exist between these two SCs and justify the necessity of their concurrent flow planning. Incorporating these interactions not only improves the demand and required inventory predictions in pre- and after-sales markets but also strengthens the holistic perspective and system integration in product/after-sales

Table 3-2. Literature review of after-sales service.

Paper	Belongs to capital goods	Belongs to durable consumer goods	Pre-market operations	After-sales market operations	Rebate Warranty	Failure-free warranty	EOL warranty	Performance-based logistics	Topology of after-sales network	Price of the spare part/product	Warranty length	Warranty parameters	Warranty reserve funding/Warranty cost per product	Reliability allocation	Location of Inventory	Volume of Inventory	Location of capacity	Volume of capacity	Maintenance schedule	Availability/service level	Demand prediction	Spare parts ordering time (from the customer point of view)	Spare parts ordering time (from the manufacturer point of view)	Safety stock of spare parts	Buyback price of returned products	Redundancy allocation	Replacement time (based on the deterioration degree and residual warranty period)	Objective	Constraint	Variations
Barabadi et al. (2014)	*			*																	*							Min Spare part number and cost	-	Failure time
Chien and Chen (2008)		*		*	*																	*						Min per unit time cost & Max cost effectiveness	-	Lifetime of a product & lead time for delivering a spare

Table 3-2 contd. ...

Paper	Belongs to capital goods	Belongs to durable consumer goods	Pre-market operations	After-sales market operations	Rebate Warranty	Failure-free warranty	EOL warranty	Performance-based logistics	Topology of after-sales network	Price of the spare part/product	Warranty length	Warranty parameters	Warranty reserve funding/Warranty cost per product	Reliability allocation	Location of Inventory	Volume of Inventory	Location of capacity	Volume of capacity	Maintenance schedule	Availability/service level	Demand prediction	Spare parts ordering time (from the customer point of view)	Spare parts ordering time (from the manufacturer point of view)	Safety stock of spare parts	Buyback price of returned products	Redundancy allocation	Replacement time (based on the deterioration degree and residual warranty period)	Objective	Constraint	Variations
Glickman and Berger (1976)		*		*		*				*	*																	Max Profit	-	Number of repairs under warranty
Huang et al. (2007)		*		*		*				*	*			*														Max Profit	-	Failure time
Kim and Park (2008)	*			*			*			*	*												*					Max Profit	-	-
Kim et al. (2007)	*			*				*				*				*												Max Utility	Service Level	

Reference	Max Profit / Min cost	Flow and price selection constraints	Failure type
Kleber et al. (2011)	Max Profit	-	-
Menke (1969)	-	-	Failure time of product
Murthy (1990)	Max Profit	-	Failure time of product
Nguyen and Murthy (1984)		-	Failure time of product
Nguyen and Murthy (1988)	Min manufacturing + servicing costs	-	Failure time of product
Oner et al. (2010)	Min cost	Reliability boundary	Failure and repair time
Sahba and Balcioglu (2011)	Min cost	-	Failure and repair time
Wang (2012)	Min inventory + shut down costs	-	Plant failure
Wang et al. (2009)	Min cost	-	Uncertain deterioration of each unit
Anderson (1977)	Max Profit	Price is more than manufacturing cost	Failure time
Díaz and Fu (1997)	-	Service level	Failure rate & repair time
Graves (1985)	-	Service level	Failure rate & repair time
Sherbrooke (1968)	-	Service level	Failure rate & repair time

Table 3-2 contd. ....

...Table 3-2 contd.

Paper	Belongs to capital goods	Belongs to durable consumer goods	Pre-market operations	After-sales market operations	Rebate Warranty	Failure-free warranty	EOL warranty	Performance-based logistics	Topology of after-sales network	Price of the spare part/product	Warranty length	Warranty parameters	Warranty reserve funding/Warranty cost per product	Reliability allocation	Location of Inventory	Volume of Inventory	Location of capacity	Volume of capacity	Maintenance schedule	Availability/service level	Demand prediction	Spare parts ordering time (from the customer point of view)	Spare parts ordering time (from the manufacturer point of view)	Safety stock of spare parts	Buyback price of returned products	Redundancy allocation	Replacement time (based on the deterioration degree and residual warranty period)	Objective	Constraint	Variations
Perlman et al. (2001)	*			*																				*				Min sum of backorders	-	Failure rate & repair time
Sleptchenko et al. (2002)	*			*											*	*												Max Availability	-	Failure rate & repair time
Hussain and Murthy (2003)		*		*		*								*														Min manufacturing + warranty cost	-	Failure rate & reliability improvement of parts

Reference	Objective function	Constraint	Uncertainty
Hussain and Murthy (2000)	Min manufacturing + warranty cost	-	Failure rate & reliability of parts
Zuo et al. (2000)	Min warranty cost	-	Failure & deterioration rate of parts
Lieckens et al. (2013)	Max Profit	Service level	Failure rate & processing time
Lin and Shue (2005)	Max Profit	-	Failure rate
Van Ommeren et al. (2006)	Min total expected cost	Service level	Demands and repair times
Rappold and Roo (2009)	Min total expected cost	-	Demands and repair times
Gross and Pinkus (1979)	Min total expected cost	Service level	Failure rates and repair times
Wu et al. (2009)	Min Cost	-	Failure rate
Chen et al. (2012)	Max Profit	-	-
Faridimehr and Niaki (2012)	Min Cost	-	Failure rate
Kurata and Nam (2010)	Max profit	-	Customer needs

[1] Wholesale price of the manufacturer.
[2] Warranty length of the retailer.

service provider companies (the interactions between the SCs are explained in Section 3.5, quantified in Sections 3.6.1 and 3.6.2, and incorporated in the integrated mathematical model developed in Section 3.6.3);

✓ **Managing supply-side variations in SCs:** In the literature, the performances of production facilities in SCs are assumed to be perfect (see Column 33 in Table 3-1). In this chapter, we relax this assumption by considering that inherent variations exist in the imperfect production systems of the practical world. We demonstrate that in SCs with imperfect facilities, qualified and presentable flow depreciates when moving from upstream to downstream. Flow depreciation affects service levels in markets adversely. We suggest that amplifying orders from the downstream to the upstream of the SCs neutralizes flow depreciation and helps to preserve the desired service levels in pre- and after-sales markets (neutralizing flow depreciation in the forward and after-sales SCs is explained in Sections 3.6.1 and 3.6.2, respectively).

The remainder of this chapter is organized as follows. The problem definition is presented in Section 3.5. The problem is modeled in Section 3.6. After a discussion of the model's specific characteristics, a solution method is proposed in Section 3.7. The model and its solution approach are used to solve a sample problem in Section 3.8. The computational results reveal correlations among the company's marketing strategies. Closing remarks are given in Section 3.9.

3.5 Problem Description

This problem considers a company producing and supplying a durable product to a target market. The production and distribution processes of this product are implemented in the facilities of the forward SC. This product includes r critical components manufactured by suppliers of the first echelon. The components are transported to a manufacturer in the second echelon and after assembly, the final product is supplied to the final customers through a retailer (Figure 3-1). The products of each sale period are produced, transported and stored in the SC's retailer before the beginning of that period.

The product demand is stochastic and depends on the product's price, its availability in the pre-market (called the pre-market service level), the spare parts' availability after-sales (called the after-sales service level), and the warranty length. Whenever a product is sold, a failure-free warranty

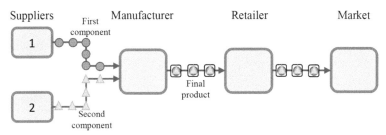

Figure 3-1. Network structure and flow dynamics through the forward SC.

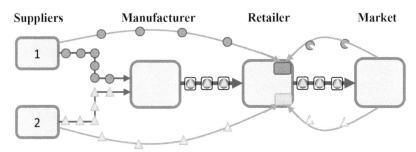

Figure 3-2. Network structure and flow dynamics through the after-sales SC.

is provided, which is implementable from the time of sale. Any failure in the product, which is mainly caused by the failure of its key components, is repaired without charge within this warranty period. Without loss of generality, it is assumed that typically, the first n_i $(i = 1, 2,..., r)$ failures of these components are repaired but that failed components are substituted with new components stored by the retailer.

The components required to provide after-sales services for customers are produced and supplied by the company's after-sales SC. The components required to fulfill the after-sales commitments of each sales period are produced by the suppliers (there is only one supplier for each component) and directly transported to the retailer and stored there before the beginning of that period (Figure 3-2). Accurate prediction of the required components is an important element of this problem and plays a key role in preserving the recommended after-sales service level.

Two important interactions between these two SCs are: (1) the dependence of the demand of the forward SC in the pre-market on the service level provided by the after-sales SC and (2) the dependence of the after-sales demand of the components on the total products supplied by the forward SC to the market and the quality of the product's components. These interactions are incorporated in the concurrent flow planning of these two SCs.

We consider several different sources of variation in this problem. (1) *Demand-side variation*: there are several sources of demand-side variation in this problem. The first variation is related to the product's demand in the pre-market. The pre-market's demand is assumed to be a stochastic function of price, warranty length and service levels in the pre- and after-sales markets. The after-sales demands for spare parts are functions of the quantity of product sales in the pre-market and the quality of the product's components. Both factors are nondeterministic. We assume that the failure times of the product's components are stochastic and follow given density functions depending on their reliability parameters. (2) *Supply-side variation*: to make the problem more compatible with actual conditions, it is assumed that the production systems of the SCs' facilities are not perfect and that their output always has a stochastic percentage of nonconforming production. In our problem, the performance of the suppliers and the manufacturer includes a stochastic percentage of nonconforming output.

In a company with these specifications, it is important to make the following decisions to maximize the total profit: (1) the best marketing strategy for this company (price, warranty length and service levels); and (2) the best reliable flow dynamics throughout the SCs, preserving the service levels in the pre- and after-sales markets.

3.6 Mathematical Model

The problem here includes two distinct but highly interconnected parts: the forward SC and the after-sales SC. There are several interactions between the forward and after-sales SCs. For example, the total product sales in the forward SC determine the potential demand for the spare parts in the after-sales market. Additionally, the after-sales services provided by the after-sales SC, such as warranty and spare parts availability, play an important role in the forward SC's captured demand in the pre-market. Therefore, there is synergy in the simultaneous flow planning of the forward and after-sales SCs.

In the remainder of this section, we first address planning flow dynamics through the forward SC with stochastic facilities and then shift to the after-sales SC. Thereafter, a comprehensive mathematical model that yields the most profitable marketing strategies (price, warranty and service levels) and preserves the flow plan for the company under consideration, is proposed by considering the interactions between these two SCs. The solution of this model includes the synergy of concurrent coordination compared to a hierarchical decision-making process that is easier but leads to sub-optimal solutions for this problem.

The notations used in this chapter are summarized in Table 3-3.

Table 3-3. Notations.

Variables	
rl_1	Local reliability of the retailer
rl_2	Local reliability of the manufacturer
rl_3	Local reliability of the suppliers
sl_p	Service level in the pre-market
sl_a	Service level in the after-sales market
w	Warranty time
x	Product order quantity by the retailer
Δx	Additional production volume for the manufacturer
$\Delta \acute{x}_i$	Additional production volume for Supplier i for the forward SC ($i = 1, 2, 3, ..., r$)
x_i	Order quantity of Component i by the retailer ($i = 1, 2, 3, ..., r$)
$\Delta x_i''$	Additional production volume for Supplier i for the after-sales SC ($i = 1, 2, 3, ..., r$)
yrl_{1^i}	Binary variable equal to 1 if the local reliability $rl1^i$ is selected from set $RL1$ for the retailer and equal to 0 otherwise ($\forall rl1^i \in RL1$)
yrl_{2^i}	Binary variable equal to 1 if the local reliability $rl2^i$ is selected from set $RL2$ for the manufacturer and equal to 0 otherwise ($\forall rl2^i \in RL2$)
yrl_{3^i}	Binary variable equal to 1 if the local reliability $rl3^i$ is selected from set $RL3$ for the suppliers and equal to 0 otherwise ($\forall rl3^i \in RL3$)
z_{wi}	Binary variables equal to 1 if the warranty length w^i is selected from set W ($\forall w^i \in W$)
Parameters	
Π	Profit of the company
C	Total cost of the retailer
T	Length of the sale period
p	Price of the product in the pre-market
$\widehat{D}(p, sl_p, sl_a, w)$	Stochastic product demand function in the pre-market
$D(p, sl_p, sl_a, w)$	Expected product demand in the pre-market
ε	Random part of the pre-market demand
$G(.)$	Cumulative distribution function of ε
h^+	Unit holding cost of additional product inventory at the end of the sale period for the retailer
h^-	Unit shortage cost of lost product sales at the end of the sale period for the retailer
r	Number of critical components in the product

Table 3-3 contd. ...

...Table 3-3 contd.

Parameters	
$\acute{G}(.)$	Cumulative distribution function of the wastage ratio for the manufacturer
β	Maximum wastage ratio for the manufacturer of the sample problem
μ_i	Average number of failures in the time unit for Supplier i ($i = 1, 2, 3, ..., r$)
γ_i	Defective component ratio in the out-of-control state of Supplier i ($i = 1, 2, 3, ..., r$)
a_{1i}	Unit procurement cost of material for Supplier i ($i = 1, 2, ..., r$)
a_{2i}	Unit production cost of Component i for Supplier i ($i = 1, 2, ..., r$)
h_{1i}	Unit inventory holding cost for a time unit for Supplier i ($i = 1, 2, ..., r$)
b_{1i}	Unit transportation cost of product from Supplier i to the manufacturer ($i = 1, 2, ..., r$)
b_2	Unit product manufacturing cost for the manufacturer
h_2	Unit inventory holding cost for a time unit for the manufacturer
c_1	Unit transportation cost of product from the manufacturer to the retailer
c_2	Unit handling cost of product in the retailer
c_{3i}	Unit transportation cost of Component i from Supplier i to the retailer ($i = 1, 2, ..., r$)
PR_{1i}	Production rate of Supplier i ($i = 1, 2, ..., r$)
PR_2	Production rate of the manufacturer
λ_i	Reliability parameter of Component i ($i = 1, 2, 3, ..., r$)
$f_i(.)$	Density function of failure time of Component i ($i = 1, 2, 3, ..., r$)
$F_i(.)$	Cumulative distribution function of failure time of Component i ($i = 1, 2, 3, ..., r$)
$F_i^{(m)}(.)$	Cumulative distribution function of total time to the mth failure of Component i ($i = 1, 2, 3, ..., r$)
n_i	Number of first failures of Component i that are repairable ($i = 1, 2, 3, ..., r$)
cn_i	Unit repair cost of Component i ($i = 1, 2, 3, ..., r$)
cr	Average repair cost of the product unit;
Num_i	Random number of Component i substitutions for a product unit in the warranty period ($i = 1, 2, 3, ..., r$)
E_i	Average number of Component i substitutions for a product unit in the warranty period ($i = 1, 2, 3, ..., r$)
σ_i^2	Variance of number of Component i substitutions for a product unit in the warranty period ($i = 1, 2, 3, ..., r$)

Table 3-3 contd. ...

...Table 3-3 contd.

Parameters	
D_i	Average number of Component i substitutions in the warranty period in the after-sales market ($i = 1, 2, 3, ..., r$)
k_1	Number of sale periods inside the warranty period
T'	Longest time period inside the sales period in which it is logical to assume that the product demand occurs at the beginning of the period
k_2	Number of T's inside the sale period
D_{ij}	Required quantity of Component i to repair product lot x/k_2 in the jth period T of its selling time
RL1	Set of scenarios for the local reliability of the retailer $RL1 = \{rl1^1, rl1^2, ..., rl1^{|RL1|}\}$
RL2	Set of scenarios for the local reliability of the manufacturer $RL2 = \{rl2^1, rl2^2, ..., rl2^{|RL2|}\}$
RL3	Set of scenarios for the local reliability of the suppliers $RL3 = \{rl3^1, rl3^2, ..., rl3^{|RL3|}\}$
W	Set of warranty length $W = \{w^1, w^2, ..., w^{|w|}\}$

3.6.1 *Mathematical Formulation for Flow Planning in the Forward Supply Chain*

In this section, only the decisions related to the flow dynamics in the forward SC will be considered. As noted above, there are several sources of variation in the forward SC: (i) variation in the product demand in the pre-market and (ii) variation in the performance of the manufacturer and suppliers' production systems. In the remainder of this section, all the forward SC's facilities are sequentially investigated from downstream to upstream and a procedure for reliable flow planning is implemented in each facility against its corresponding variation. In addition to investigating the local effects of these variations, we also investigate their global effects on the performance of the entire forward SC.

As shown in Figure 3-3, the forward SC considered here has three echelons and the facilities in each are faced with various variations. The retailer of the first echelon faces uncertain market demand, which has a given distribution function. The production system of the manufacturer in the second echelon is always accompanied with some stochastic waste. After setup, the production processes of the suppliers in the third echelon start their machinery in a state of control. However, the state of the machinery deteriorates and shifts to an out-of-control state after a stochastic amount of time, which leads to a stochastic percentage of nonconforming output. Due to the imperfect production systems of the suppliers, the precise volume of their qualified component output for a given material input quantity cannot be determined. Thus, the qualified

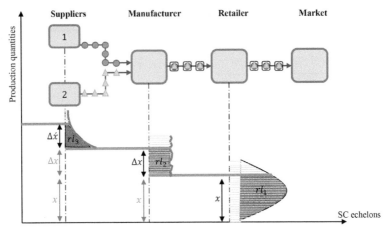

Figure 3-3. Qualified flow depreciation in the forward SC.

output volumes can change and are stochastic. The output components of the suppliers are the input for the manufacturer. Variation in the input volume of the manufacturer is amplified because of the stochastic wastage ratio for the manufacturer's production system, which leads to a higher variation in the qualified product output of the manufacturer. This process continues by moving material, components, and product from upstream to downstream in multi-echelon SCs with imperfect facilities. We call this phenomenon "variation propagation", which leads to the qualified flow depreciation throughout the SCs' networks (see Figure 3-3).

Determining the optimal service level is more difficult in such a SC due to the flow depreciation that occurs by moving the flow from upstream to downstream. In such a network with multiple stochastic facilities, a local reliability is assigned to each facility to manage the variation of its own system. It is assumed that rl_1, rl_2, and rl_3 represent the local reliability in the retailer, manufacturer and suppliers of the SC, respectively (without loss of generality, we consider similar reliabilities for the suppliers; the same logic can be applied for different reliabilities).

In this problem, we exploit the newsboy problem style to manage the inventory system of the retailer. Based on this system, products should be procured and stocked by the retailer before the beginning of each sales period and by realizing its actual demand because transferring additional products between the manufacturer and retailer is not possible during the period. Thus, rl_1, the local reliability of the retailer, suggests that before the beginning of the next sale period, the retailer must select its product stock quantity to ensure with rl_1 probability that this stock level can respond to the market demand. The retailer orders the required products from the manufacturer. Furthermore, the local reliability of the manufacturer, rl_2, means that the manufacturer must manufacture an appropriate product quantity to guarantee that the qualified output is equal to the order of the retailer with a probability of rl_2. The local reliability of each supplier, rl_3, means that the material procurement and component production quantity should preserve the order of the manufacturer with a probability of rl_3. We assume that each facility either completely fulfills the order of its downstream facility and sends a complete package equal to its order, or misses the order and sends nothing. Flow transactions less than orders is not possible among facilities. In this case, the suppliers will be confident with a probability of $rl_3{}^r$ that they can fulfill the manufacturer's component orders. The manufacturer will be confident with a probability of rl_2 that it can provide the complete order of the retailer and the retailer will be confident with a probability of rl_1 that its product stock quantity can fulfill the demand of the market. Therefore, the final service level of the forward SC in the pre-market is $sl_p = rl_1.rl_2.(rl_3)^r$. In this problem, in addition to determining the optimal sl_p, it is also essential to determine the optimal local reliability combination (rl_1, rl_2, rl_3) that preserves that service level.

3.6.1.1 Retailer in the forward supply chain

The company positions itself in the market by choosing its service levels in the pre- and after-sales markets, its warranty time and its retail price. The expected product demand in the pre-market $D(p, sl_p, sl_a, w)$ in the sales period T is an increasing function of the chains' service levels and warranty time and a decreasing function of the product's price. However, the actual demand is a stochastic function and deviates from its mean value. It is assumed that the stochastic demand function of the pre-market has a multiplicative form: $\widehat{D}(p, sl_p, sl_a, w) = D(p, sl_p, sl_a, w) \times \varepsilon$ (Bernstein and Federgruen 2004, 2007), where ε is a general continuous random variable with a stationary distribution function and a cumulative distribution function, $G(\varepsilon)$, which are independent of the service levels, warranty time and price. Without loss of generality, $E(\varepsilon) = 1$ is normalized, which implies that $E[\widehat{D}(p, sl_p, sl_a, w)] = D(p, sl_p, sl_a, w)$.

Companies typically provide the price (p) and warranty (w) information of products to customers directly. However, there are several channels through which customers can acquire information about pre- and after-sales services provided by companies indirectly. There are thousands of independent websites that review products and provide useful information about the pre- and after-sales performance of companies, such as their service level warranties, spare parts availability and back-up chargeback agreements (e.g., ConsumerReports.org, Epinions.

com). This information helps customers make informed decisions and affect the average demand. Recently, most companies have started to advertise their service levels. For example, Sunning and Gome, the largest and second-largest suppliers of home electronic appliances in China respectively, recently started to advertise their after-sales service level commitments to compete for customers. Both are selling similar models of air conditioners at the same price. To stimulate demand, both offer to clean sold air conditioners at least once a year. However, to dominate their rival, Gome has started to commit to a response time of no more than 72 hours for a customer's request for an air conditioner cleaning (Li et al. 2014). As another example, most automobile manufacturers, such as BMW, Volkswagen, and Ford, prominently state the average waiting time for car maintenance per customer in their 4S retailers. They also employ third-party agencies to monitor the service level provided by their retailers (Li et al. 2014). These examples illustrate that not only providing better after-sales services, such as longer warranty length, but also the quality of the service provided inside the commitment period, such as a higher service level and shorter waiting time, are important for customers in competitive markets. Therefore, we assume that (1) the warranty length, w, and after-sales service level, sl_a, are two mutually independent factors with different importance affecting customer purchasing decisions and the captured demand of the company and (2) customers are informed of the after-sales service level commitment when they make a purchasing decision (Li et al. 2014; Allon and Federgruen 2009).

The effect of the second assumption can be mitigated by substituting the $\theta \times sl_a$ term instead of sl_a in the $D(p, sl_p, sl_a, w)$ function ($0 \leq \theta \leq 1$). θ represents the level of information availability about the after-sales service level commitment ($\theta = 0$ means that no information is available and $\theta = 1$ means that complete information is available to customers).

In this section, we only focus on the operation of the forward SC. Therefore, the pre-market's service level is the focus here. The pre-market's service level is defined as the fraction of the pre-market's realized product demand that can be satisfied from the on-hand product inventory available in the retailer (Rezapour 2011). The retailer must order the product stock, x, from the manufacturer before the beginning of the sale period. By realizing the period's real product demand, the unit holding cost, h^+ and unit shortage cost, h^-, are paid by the retailer for each end-of-period additional inventory and lost sale, respectively. The expected value of the retailer's cost, C, is computed with Eq. (3-1). Constraint (3-2) preserves the retailer's local reliability, which guarantees that the retailer's product stock can fulfill the pre-market's product demand for rl_1 percent of cases.

Thus, the product order quantity of the retailer from the manufacturer can be computed as

$$MIN \quad C = h^+ . E[x - \widehat{D}(p, sl_p, sl_a, w)]^+ + h^- . E[\widehat{D}(p, sl_p, sl_a, w) - x]^+ \qquad (3\text{-}1)$$

$$S.T. \quad Pr\,[\widehat{D}(p, sl_p, sl_a, w) \le x] \ge rl_1 \qquad (3\text{-}2)$$

Based on the objective function, $x = D(p, sl_p, sl_a, w).\ G^{-1}(\dfrac{h^-}{h^- + h^+})$ minimizes the expected cost of the retailer, and to preserve the constraint, $x \ge D(p, sl_p, sl_a, w).\ G^{-1}(rl_1)$. Accordingly, the best product ordering amount of the retailer from the manufacturer is

$$x = D(p, sl_p, sl_a, w).\ G^{-1}\!\left(Max\left\{rl_1, \dfrac{h^-}{h^- + h^+}\right\}\right) \qquad (3\text{-}3)$$

By substituting Eq. (3-3) into (3-1), the lowest total cost of the retailer can be calculated as

$$C = \left(h^+ . E\left[G^{-1}\!\left(Max\left\{rl_1, \dfrac{h^-}{h^- + h^+}\right\}\right) - \varepsilon\right]^+ + h^- . E\left[\varepsilon - G^{-1}\!\left(Max\left\{rl_1, \dfrac{h^-}{h^- + h^+}\right\}\right)\right]^+\right).$$
$$D(p, sl_p, sl_a, w) \qquad (3\text{-}4)$$

When the retailer orders x product units from the manufacturer, this protects the pre-market's product demand such that it can be fulfilled from the retailer's on-hand product inventory with a probability of rl_1 (see the retailer in Figure 3-3). Section 3.6.1.2 illustrates how this product's flow quantity must be amplified by moving backward to the manufacturer in the forward SC.

3.6.1.2 Manufacturer in the forward supply chain

The forward SC's manufacturer receives an order of x product units from the retailer and then orders the required components from the suppliers. Without loss of generality, it is assumed that one unit of each component is required to produce one unit of product. However, the production system of the manufacturer is always accompanied by some wastage. The ratio of wastage to qualified product depends on the general state of its machinery, which varies from time to time. It is assumed that the wastage ratio of the manufacturer's output changes over the range $[0, \beta]$ with a cumulative distribution function $G'(.)$. The manufacturer attempts to compensate for this wastage in its production system by manufacturing additional product and consequently orders additional components from the suppliers.

If the manufacturer produces x product units, this production lot contains less than $\Delta x = \alpha \cdot x$ ($\alpha \in [0, \beta]$) flawed product units with $G'(\alpha)$ probability. Therefore, the manufacturer plans to produce $\Delta x + x$ product units to be confident with a probability of $G'(\alpha)$ that the entire order of the retailer is fulfilled. Because the local reliability of the manufacturer is assumed to be rl_2 ($= G'(\alpha)$), the additional production quantity of the manufacturer is $\Delta x = G^{-1}(rl_2) \cdot x$. Thus, the manufacturer should order $\Delta x + x$ component units from each supplier in the forward SC. As noted above, the manufacturer only fulfills the x product order of the retailer before the beginning of the next period, and additional product acquisition during the next sales period is impossible.

Producing $\Delta x + x$ product units by the manufacturer ensures that it can fulfill the x product order of the retailer with a probability of rl_2 (see the manufacturer in Figure 3-3). Section 3.6.1.3 provides a discussion of how these component flow quantities are amplified by moving backward to the suppliers of the forward SC.

3.6.1.3 Suppliers in the forward supply chain

Each supplier receives an order of $\Delta x + x$ component units from the manufacturer. After setting up the system, the production run starts in an in-control state of Supplier i's machinery ($i = 1, 2, \ldots, r$). However, the machinery state deteriorates and shifts to an out-of-control state after a period of time. The time for deterioration is stochastic and has an approximately exponential distribution with mean $1/\mu_i$ (Lee and Rosenblatt 1987; Rosenblatt and Lee 1986). All the component units produced in the in-control state are qualified, but from the units produced in the out-of-control state, γ_i percent are defective. Once the process shifts to the out-of-control state, it stays in this state until the entire production batch is finished because interrupting the machinery is either impossible or too expensive.

Each supplier should produce $\Delta x + x$ flawless component units. To compensate for the flawed component production in its production system, the supplier should plan to produce more components, $\Delta \acute{x}_i + \Delta x + x$. The additional quantity of units, $\Delta \acute{x}_i$ is added to the production system of Supplier i to replace the defective component units. If it is assumed that the production rate of Supplier i is PR_{1i}, it takes $\dfrac{\Delta \acute{x}_i + \Delta x + x}{PR_{1i}}$ time units to produce this component volume. The additional volume $\Delta \acute{x}_i$ should be determined in such a manner to preserve the local reliability of the supplier, rl_3:

$$rl_3 = \text{Pr}(\textit{flawless component units produced in } \frac{\Delta \dot{x}_i + \Delta x + x}{PR_{1i}} \textit{ time units} \geq \Delta x + x)$$

$$= \text{Pr} \left[PR_{1i}. \, t + (1 - \gamma_i). \, PR_{1i}. \left(\frac{\Delta \dot{x}_i + \Delta x + x}{PR_{1i}} - t \right) \geq \Delta x + x \right]$$

$$= \text{Pr} \left[t \geq \left(\frac{\Delta x + x}{PR_{1i}} \right) - \left(\frac{1 - \gamma_i}{\gamma_i \cdot PR_{1i}} \right). (\Delta \dot{x}_i) \right]$$

$$= EXP \left[-\mu_i. \left(\left(\frac{\Delta x + x}{PR_{1i}} \right) - \left(\frac{1 - \gamma_i}{\gamma_i \cdot PR_{1i}} \right). (\Delta \dot{x}_i) \right) \right] \qquad (3\text{-}5)$$

Based on the equation above, $\Delta \dot{x}_i = \frac{\gamma_i}{1 - \gamma_i} \left[\frac{PR_{1i}}{\mu_i} \ln(rl_3) + (\Delta x + x) \right]$
units of additional component production for Supplier i ensures the local reliability for that supplier with a probability of rl_3. This means that with this amount, $\Delta \dot{x}_i$, the supplier can fulfill the order of the manufacturer rl_3 percent of the time and preserve the local reliability rl_3 for itself (see the suppliers in Figure 3-3). Therefore, with these values of $\Delta \dot{x}_i$ (i = 1, 2, ..., r), the suppliers can fulfill the orders of the manufacturer with a probability of rl_3^r. With the amount of Δx determined in Section 3.6.1.2, the manufacturer can fulfill the product order of the retailer with a probability of rl_2. With a product volume of x, the retailer can respond to the realized product demand of the pre-market with a probability of rl_1. Thus, supplier production volumes of $\Delta \dot{x}_i + \Delta x + x$ (i = 1, 2, ..., r) are able to fulfill the product demand in the pre-market with a probability of $rl_1.rl_2.rl_3^r$ and preserve the service level $sl_p = rl_1.rl_2.rl_3^r$ for the entire forward chain against variation propagation in its entities (Figure 3-3).

3.6.2 *Mathematical Formulation for Flow Planning in the After-sales Supply Chain*

This section considers the flow planning decisions in the after-sales SC. The after-sales SC has several variations: (i) variation in the demand for spare parts in the retailer to repair or substitute failed components of returned products and (ii) variation in the performance of the production systems in the suppliers. In the remainder of this section, the performance of the after-sales SC's facilities is formulated sequentially from the retailer in the downstream to the suppliers in the upstream. Here, flow planning in the after-sales SC is determined, which will not only assure appropriate reliabilities for the chain's facilities against their variations locally but also yield an acceptable performance for the entire after-sales SC.

3.6.2.1 *Retailer in the after-sales supply chain*

Based on Section 3.6.1, if it is assumed that rl_1 and rl_3 represent the local reliabilities in the retailer and suppliers, respectively, then the service levels provided by the forward and after-sales SCs are $sl_p = rl_1.rl_2.rl_3$, and $sl_a = (rl_1.rl_3)^r$, respectively. Like the forward SC, in the after-sales SC, the first after-sales operation starts in the retailer. Variation in the after-sales SC's retailer is related to the demand for spare parts. The demand for spare parts in the retailer is caused by the failed components in returned products that require part substitution. Thus, the demand for spare parts in the after-sales market is a function of the total product sales in the pre-market and the reliability of the product's key components. Then, for a given product sales in the pre-market, x and a given component reliability, λ_i $(i = 1, 2, ..., r)$, it is necessary to find an appropriate density function for the demand of the component.

The performances of the components in the product are assumed to be independent. The failure time of Component i has a density function f_i and cumulative density function F_i, including the reliability parameter λ_i $(i = 1, 2, ..., r)$. Lower values of the parameter λ_i imply a higher reliability and lower failure of Component i. It is typically assumed that for each product, the retailer must repair the first n_i failures of Component i with repair cost cn_i, but after that, the failed component is replaced with a new one. $n_i = 0$ implies a non-repairable component in the product. We also assume that the breakdown probability of a failed component does not change after repair and that the time required for the repair or substitution of components is negligible compared to the warranty time, w (Nguyen and Murthy 1984).

If $F_i^{(m)}$ is defined as the cumulative density function of the total time to the mth failure and $Num_i(w)$ represents the random number of failures in $[0, w]$, then we have (Nguyen and Murthy 1984)

$$\Pr\{Num_i(w) = m\} = F_i^{(m)}(w, \lambda_i) - F_i^{(m+1)}(w, \lambda_i) \qquad (\forall i = 1, 2, ..., r) \qquad (3\text{-}6)$$

The following can be stated based on Eq. (3-6):

Lemma 3-1: The average number of Component i substitutions, $E_i(w, n_i)$, for a product unit is calculated as follows (see the proof in Appendix 3.A):

$$E_i(w, n_i) = (n_i)F_i^{(n_i+1)}(w, \lambda_i) + \sum_{j=n_i+1}^{+\infty} F_i^{(j)}(w, \lambda_i) \qquad (\forall i = 1, 2, ..., r) \qquad (3\text{-}7)$$

Lemma 3-2: The variance in the number of Component i substitutions, $\sigma_i^2(w, n_i)$, for a product unit is calculated as follows (see the proof in Appendix 3.A):

$$\sigma_i^2(w, n_i) = (n_i + 1)^2 F_i^{(n_i+1)}(w, \lambda_i) + \sum_{j=n_i+2}^{+\infty}[2j-1]. F_i^{(j)}(w, \lambda_i) - [(n_i)F_i^{(n_i+1)}(w, \lambda_i) +$$

$$\sum_{j=n_i+1}^{+\infty} F_i^{(j)}(w, \lambda_i)]^2 \qquad\qquad (\forall i = 1, 2, ..., r) \qquad (3\text{-}8)$$

Now, the total number of required Component i substitutions for a lot size of x product units can be estimated to represent the demand for Component i in the after-sales market, D_i. D_i is the sum of required Component i substitutions for x individual units. Since x is large, the following can be stated based on the central limit theorem:

Lemma 3-3: The demand of Component i in the after-sales market, D_i, can be approximated as being normally distributed with a mean of $x. E_i(w, n_i)$ and variance of $x. \sigma_i^2(w, n_i)$:

$$D_i \sim Normal \left(\mu_{D_i} = x. E_i(w, n_i), \sigma_{D_i}^2 = x. \sigma_i^2(w, n_i)\right) \qquad (\forall i = 1, 2, ..., r) \qquad (3\text{-}9)$$

Thus, the after-sales SC is faced with a normally distributed random demand for components. Because a local reliability of rl_1 is assumed for the retailer, the stock quantity of Component i that preserves this local reliability in the retailer is

$$x_i = x. E_i(w, n_i) + \left(z_{rl_1}. \sqrt{x. \sigma_i^2(w, n_i)}\right) \qquad (\forall i = 1, 2, ..., r) \qquad (3\text{-}10)$$

We assume that the retailer provides the same reliability for both forward and after-sales SCs. The problem would be simplified by assigning different reliabilities for the retailer because in that case, the service levels of the forward and after-sales SCs are independent.

Assuming that the first n_i failures of Component i in each product are repaired by the retailer with a repair cost cn_i, the average repair cost of the product at the retailer is

$$cr = \sum_{i=1}^{r}\sum_{j=1}^{n_i} j. cr_i. \text{PR}\{Num_i(w) = j\} = \sum_{i=1}^{r}\sum_{j=1}^{n_i} j. cr_i.[F_i^{(j)}(w, \lambda_i) - F_i^{(j+1)}(w, \lambda_i)]$$
$$(3\text{-}11)$$

In Eq. (3-10), the prediction of the demand for spare parts in the sales period, T, is based on w, which is typically longer than the sales period: $w = k_1.T$. For a detailed explanation regarding this topic, refer to Appendix 3.B.

3.6.2.2 Suppliers in the after-sales supply chain

In the previous section, it is shown that the following stock quantity of Component i is required for a local reliability of rl_1 in the after-sales SC's retailer:

$$x_i = x. E_i(w, n_i) + \left(z_{rl_1}. \sqrt{x. \sigma_i^2(w, n_i)}\right) \qquad (\forall i = 1, 2, ..., r)$$

These quantities of components are ordered directly by the retailer from their corresponding suppliers. Hence, the supplier of Component i should not only produce and supply $\Delta x + x$ units of Component i to the manufacturer to assemble and produce the final product but also produce and supply x_i units of Component i to the chain's retailer to substitute the failed Components i of the returned products that have already been repaired n_i times. Thus, the total component order received by Supplier i is $x_i + \Delta x + x$ units. However, to compensate for the nonconforming output of its production system, it should plan to produce some additional components, represented by $\Delta \acute{x}_i$. In Section 3.6.1.3, the quantity of $\Delta \acute{x}_i$ is determined by assuming that $\Delta x + x$ component units are ordered from this supplier. However, as explained here, in addition to this order for the forward SC, another order with x_i quantity is received from the after-sales SC. In this section, we revise the quantity of $\Delta \acute{x}_i$ to consider the requirements of the after-sales SC. By following the approach described in Section 3.6.1.3 and the local reliability of the suppliers, rl_3, the additional production quantity of the suppliers should be modified as follows:

$$\Delta \acute{x}_i = \frac{\gamma_i}{1-\gamma_i} \left[\frac{PR_{1i}}{\mu_i} \ln(rl_3) + x_i + \Delta x + x \right] \qquad (\forall i = 1, 2, ..., r) \qquad (3\text{-}12)$$

We assume that the shortage in fulfilling the component order is divided proportionally between the order of the manufacturer and the order of the retailer. In this case, we are confident with a probability of rl_3 that the conforming output of Supplier i can fulfill the order of the retailer. With a stock of x_i of Component i, the retailer is confident with a probability of rl_1 that it can respond to all Component i substitutions needed to repair the returned products. Therefore, the after-sales SC is confident with a probability of rl_1. rl_3 that it will be able to respond to all Component i substitutions needed for the returned products inside the sale period. By considering all key components of the product, the after-sales SC's service level is $sl_a = (rl_1.rl_3)^r$.

3.6.3 Mathematical Model for Concurrent Flow Planning in the Supply Chains

The appropriate selection of local reliabilities in different echelons of the SCs and the warranty time is critical for our problem. As described in the previous sections, the chains' service levels in the pre- and after-sales markets are functions of these reliabilities. Higher local reliabilities increase the company's service levels and thus the quantum of sales in the pre-market. Alternately, higher reliabilities lead to higher production volumes in the facilities, which incur more costs to the system. The same issue is true for the warranty time. Longer warranty times make the product more attractive to customers and increase the pre-market's demand quantity.

However, longer warranty times also impose more after-sales costs on the system. By considering these tradeoffs and interactions among the forward and after-sales SCs, we develop a comprehensive mathematical model to determine the best service levels and warranty times for the company in its pre- and after-sales markets and they preserve the best local reliabilities and flow plan to maximize the company's total profit. This mathematical model is formulated as follows:

Max Π =

$$
\left(p - h^+ . E\left[G^{-1}\left(Max\left\{ rl_1 . rl_2 . rl_3^r , \frac{h^-}{h^- + h^+} \right\} \right) - \varepsilon \right]^+ \right.
$$

$$
- h^- . E\left[\varepsilon - G^{-1}\left(Max\left\{ rl_1 . rl_2 . rl_3^r , \frac{h^-}{h^- + h^+} \right\} \right) \right]^+
$$

$$
\left. - cr \right) . D(p, (rl_1 . rl_2 . rl_3^r , (rl_1 . rl_3)^r , w)
$$

$$
- \left[\sum_{i=1}^r (a_{1i} + a_{2i}) . (x + \Delta x + x_i + \Delta \acute{x}_i) + \sum_{i=1}^r \frac{h_{1i} . (x + \Delta x + x_i)^2}{2 . PR_{1i}} \right.
$$

$$
+ \sum_{i=1}^r b_{1i} . (x + \Delta x) + b_2 . (x + \Delta x) + \frac{h_2 . (x)^2}{2 . PR_2} + (c_1 + c_2) . x + \sum_{i=1}^r c_{3i} . x_i \right]
$$

$$
\tag{3-13}
$$

Subject to

$$
x = D(p, rl_1 . rl_2 . rl_3^r , (rl_1 . rl_3)^r , w) . G^{-1}\left(Max\left\{ rl_1 , \frac{h^-}{h^- + h^+} \right\} \right)
\tag{3-14}
$$

$$
\Delta x = G'^{-1}(rl_2) . x
\tag{3-15}
$$

$$
x_i = x . E_i(w, n_i) + \left(z_{rl_1} . \sqrt{x . \sigma_i^2(w, n_i)} \right) \qquad (\forall i = 1, 2, ..., r) \tag{3-16}
$$

$$
\Delta \acute{x}_i = \frac{\gamma_i}{1 - \gamma_i}\left[\frac{PR_{1i}}{\mu_i} \ln(rl_3) + x + \Delta x + x_i \right] \qquad (\forall i = 1, 2, ..., r) \tag{3-17}
$$

$$
0 \le rl_1, rl_2, rl_3 \le 1
\tag{3-18}
$$

$$
w \ge 0
\tag{3-19}
$$

The first term of the objective function is used to compute the profit captured by the retailer of the company in the pre-market. In this term, the average additional inventory, average shortage and average repair costs are removed from the captured income (see Eqs. 3-4 and 3-11). The second term is the sum of procurement, production, inventory holding and transportation costs throughout the forward and after-sales SCs. The first item of the second term is the sum of procurement and production costs in the suppliers. The second and fifth items are the inventory holding costs in the suppliers and manufacturer, respectively. The third and seventh items are the product transportation costs from the suppliers to the manufacturer and the spare parts transportation costs from the suppliers to the retailer, respectively. The fourth term is the manufacturing cost of the manufacturer. The sixth term is the sum of the transportation costs from the manufacturer to the retailer and the handling cost of the retailer. Equations (3-14) to (3-17) represent the relationships between the local reliability of the facilities and their production volumes.

This model is a nonlinear formulation with highly nonlinear terms in the objective function and constraints. The forms of some of these terms are not fixed and depend on the density functions of the variations (Eqs. 3-14 and 3-15). Solving this type of model is not straightforward. However, our model has some unique characteristics that differentiate it from other models. In the next section, we propose a solution approach to solve the model.

3.7 Solution Approach

Not only is the model proposed in Section 3.6 for concurrent flow planning in the forward and after-sales SCs highly nonlinear, but the mathematical forms of some of its nonlinear terms, such as Eqs. (3-14) and (3-15), also depend on the density functions considered for modeling variation. This means that changing the type of density function causes the mathematical form of these terms to change. This makes solving the model even more challenging. Alternately, important design variables, such as rl_1, rl_2, and rl_3, take values on a highly restricted interval, [0, 1]; it is also reasonable to assume that this interval is [0.5, 1.0] (if we ignore density functions and only consider their medians in the problem, we can easily preserve a 0.5 reliability for facilities; therefore, the main challenge occurs when we look for higher reliabilities for facilities). In addition, warranty lengths of 6 months, 1 year, 18 months and 2 years are common. These properties of this model make discretization an appropriate method for solving it.

To discretize the model, it is necessary to define some new notations. $RL3 = \{rl3^1, rl3^2, ..., rl3^{|RL3|}\}$, $RL2 = \{rl2^1, rl2^2, ..., rl2^{|RL2|}\}$, and $RL1 = \{rl1^1, rl1^2, ..., rl1^{|RL1|}\}$ are defined as sets of scenarios for the local reliability of the suppliers, manufacturer and retailer, respectively. For scenario selections from these sets, we must define some new binary variables. The binary variables y_{rl1^i} ($\forall rl1^i \in RL1$), y_{rl2^i} ($\forall rl2^i \in RL2$) and y_{rl3^i} ($\forall rl3^i \in RL3$) are equal to 1 if the local reliabilities $rl1^i$, $rl2^i$ and $rl3^i$ are selected from the sets $RL1$, $RL2$ and $RL3$ for the retailer, manufacturer and suppliers, respectively; otherwise, they are equal to 0. In the same manner, we define a set of warranty lengths $W = \{w^1, w^2, \ldots, w^{|w|}\}$ and binary design variables z_{w^i} ($\forall w^i \in W$) for warranty selection from this set. Only one local reliability and warranty length can be selected from these sets:

$$\sum_{i=1}^{|RL1|} y_{rl1^i} = 1 \tag{3-20}$$

$$\sum_{i=1}^{|RL2|} y_{rl2^i} = 1 \tag{3-21}$$

$$\sum_{i=1}^{|RL3|} y_{rl3^i} = 1 \tag{3-22}$$

$$\sum_{i=1}^{|W|} z_{w^i} = 1 \tag{3-23}$$

By defining these new sets and variables, we revise Eqs. (2-14) to (3-18) to represent the relationships between the production volume and local reliability of the SCs' facilities:

$$x = \sum_{i=1}^{|RL1|} \sum_{j=1}^{|RL2|} \sum_{k=1}^{|RL3|} \sum_{t=1}^{|W|} y_{rl1^i} \cdot y_{rl2^j} \cdot y_{rl3^k} \cdot z_{w^t} \cdot D(p, rl1^i, rl2^j, (rl3^k), (rl1^i, rl3^k)^r, w^t).$$
$$G^{-1}\left(Max \left\{rl1^i, \frac{h^-}{h^- + h^+}\right\}\right) \tag{3-24}$$

$$\Delta x = \sum_{i=1}^{|RL1|} \sum_{j=1}^{|RL2|} \sum_{k=1}^{|RL3|} \sum_{t=1}^{|W|} y_{rl1^i} \cdot y_{rl2^j} \cdot y_{rl3^k} \cdot z_{w^t} \cdot G'^{-1}(rl2^j) \cdot D(p, rl1^i, rl2^j, (rl3^k)^r, (rl1^i, rl3^k)^r, w^t).$$
$$G^{-1}\left(Max \left\{rl1^i, \frac{h^-}{h^- + h^+}\right\}\right) \tag{3-25}$$

$$x_i = \sum_{i=1}^{|RL1|} \sum_{j=1}^{|RL2|} \sum_{k=1}^{|RL3|} \sum_{t=1}^{|W|} y_{rl1^i} \cdot y_{rl2^j} \cdot y_{rl3^k} \cdot z_{w^t}.$$
$$\left[D(p, rl1^i, rl2^j, (rl3^k)^r, (rl1^i, rl3^k)^r, w^t) \cdot G^{-1}\left(Max \left\{rl1^i, \frac{h^-}{h^- + h^+}\right\}\right) \cdot E_i(w^t, n_i) + \right.$$
$$\left. \left(z_{rl1^i} \cdot \sqrt{D(p, rl1^i, rl2^j, (rl3^k)^r, (rl1^i, rl3^k)^r, w^t) \cdot G^{-1}\left(Max \left\{rl1^i, \frac{h^-}{h^- + h^+}\right\}\right) \cdot \sigma_i^2(w^t, n_i)} \right) \right]$$
$$(\forall i = 1, 2, \ldots, r) \tag{3-26}$$

$$\Delta \dot{x}_i = \sum_{i=1}^{|RL1|} \sum_{j=1}^{|RL2|} \sum_{k=1}^{|RL3|} \sum_{t=1}^{|W|} y_{rl1i} \cdot y_{rl2j} \cdot y_{rl3k} \cdot z_{w^t} \cdot \left(\frac{\gamma_i}{1-\gamma_i} \cdot \left[-\frac{PR_{1i}}{\mu_i} \ln(rl3^k) \right] \right.$$

$$+ (G'^{-1}(rl2^j) + 1) \cdot D(p, rl1^i \cdot rl2^j \cdot (rl3^k)^r, (rl1^i \cdot rl3^k)^r, w^t) \cdot G^{-1}\!\left(Max\left\{rl1^i, \frac{h^-}{h^- + h^+}\right\}\right)$$

$$+ D(p, rl1^i \cdot rl2^j \cdot (rl3^k)^r, (rl1^i \cdot rl3^k)^r, w^t) \cdot G^{-1}\!\left(Max\left\{rl1^i, \frac{h^-}{h^- + h^+}\right\}\right) \cdot E_i(w^t, n_i)$$

$$+ z_{rl1i} \cdot \sqrt{D(p, rl1^i \cdot rl2^j \cdot (rl3^k)^r, (rl1^i \cdot rl3^k)^r, w^t) \cdot G^{-1}\!\left(Max\left\{rl1^i, \frac{h^-}{h^- + h^+}\right\}\right) \cdot \sigma_i^2(w^t, n_i)} \right)$$

$$(\forall i = 1, 2, \ldots, r) \qquad (3\text{-}27)$$

After substituting these equations into the objective function (Eq. 3-13) and linearizing the multiplication of binary variables, the mathematical model of the problem is transformed into a mixed integer linear model with binary variables, which can be solved globally, using software like CPLEX, GAMS, GROOBI or LINGO. We used CPLEX to solve this model (for the entire linearized mathematical model, refer to Appendix 3.C).

3.8 Results and Discussions

This section considers a company that produces and supplies a durable consumer product to a target market with a stochastic and elastic demand function for the retail price p = $10.00. This product includes two critical components, Components 1 and 2. Components 1 and 2 are manufactured by Suppliers 1 and 2 respectively with procurement and production costs of $a_{11} + a_{21}$ = $3.00 and $a_{12} + a_{22}$ = $2.50, respectively. Then, these components are transported to the manufacturer and assembled into the final product with a cost of $b_2 + b_{11}$ = $b_2 + b_{12}$ = $1.00. After that, the final products are transported and handled by the retailer with a cost of $c_1 + c_2$ = $0.5. Based on historical sales, the average product demand in the pre-market is treated as a linear function of the retail price, warranty time and service levels: $D(p, sl_p, sl_a, w)$ = 500 + 200 × w − 250 × (p − 10) − 500 × (1 − sl_a) − 900 × (1 − sl_p).

The products of this company are offered with a warranty. The company has four options for the warranty length: 6, 12, 18, or 24 months. A dead inventory and lost sales at the end of the sales period impose unit costs of h^- = $0.10 and h^+ = $0.15 on the company, respectively. Components 1 and 2 of this product have reliability parameters λ_1 = 0.1 and λ_2 = 0.4. Component 1 is not repairable. Thus, if the failure of a returned product inside the warranty time is due to Component 1, that part is replaced with a new one by the retailer. However, the circumstances are different for Component 2. It is more economical to repair Component 2 the first time it fails, but after the first failure, it is substituted with a new component. Similar to the final product, the required components for repairing returned products should be produced and stored with the retailer before the beginning of the sale period. The components are produced by the first and second suppliers with production rates (number per time unit) of $PR_1 = 8000$ and $PR_2 = 9000$, respectively. The average deterioration times in the first and second suppliers are similar and equal to $1/\mu_{1 \text{ and } 2} = 0.5$. After deterioration, 10 and 20 percent of Component 1 and Component 2 production in the first and second suppliers is non-conforming ($\gamma_1 = 0.10$ and $\gamma_2 = 0.20$). The uncertain part of the pre-market's demand function, ε, is normally distributed with a mean of 0.0 and variance of 1.0. In addition, the flawed production rate for the manufacturer is uniformly distributed over the range $[0, \beta = 0.15]$. Components 1 and 2 produced by Suppliers 1 and 2 for after-sales market operations are transported directly to the retailer with transportation costs $c_{31} = c_{32} = \$1.00$. Solving the mathematical model of this problem leads to the following results: the local reliabilities in the retailer, manufacturer and suppliers are $rl_1 = 0.99$, $rl_2 = 0.99$ and $rl_3 = 0.88$, respectively. The best warranty option is 6 months. To preserve these local reliabilities, $x = 552.7$ product units are ordered by the retailer from the manufacturer. To fulfill this order of the retailer, the manufacturer plans to manufacture $\Delta x = 82.07$ additional product units to compensate for the malfunction of its system. To produce this product volume, the required components are ordered from the corresponding suppliers. In addition to this component order from the manufacturer, the suppliers receive another order from the retailer, x_i ($i = 1$ and 2), to provide the required components for repairing returned products. Similarly, the first and second suppliers plan to procure and produce $\Delta x'_1 = 18.14$ and $\Delta x'_2 = 19.46$ additional units of Component 1 and Component 2, respectively, to compensate for defective production in their production systems. This flow planning leads to a profit of $\Pi = \$715.3$ for the company, which is the highest in retail price $p = \$10.00$.

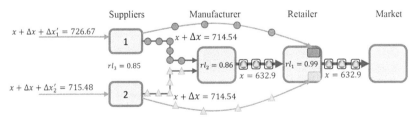

Figure 3-4. Flow dynamics in the SC.

As explained before, the local reliability of imperfect facilities has a critical role in the service levels provided by the SCs in the pre- and after-sales markets. Increasing local reliabilities causes an increase in service levels, which leads to higher product demand and a higher income. Alternately, a higher local reliability in a facility means higher production in that facility, which imposes a higher cost. Therefore, the reliabilities of facilities should be determined in such a way as to facilitate an appropriate tradeoff between their cost and income. Figures 3-5 and 3-6 present the profit of the company, Π, with respect to its service level in the pre-market, $sl_p = rl_1 . rl_2 . rl_3^2$ and the after-sales market, $sl_a = (rl_1 . rl_3)^2$, respectively. Because the service levels are functions of local reliabilities, there are several local

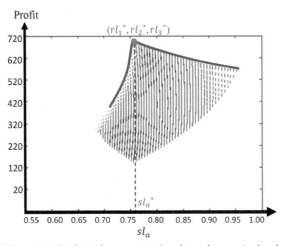

Figure 3-5. Profit with respect to the after-sales service level.

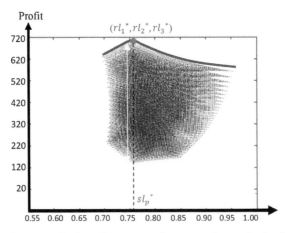

Figure 3-6. Profit with respect to the pre-market service level.

reliability triples, (rl_1, rl_2, rl_3), that may lead to a single service level, which is why there is more than one profit value in Figures 3-5 and 3-6 for each service level. Each value corresponds to one (rl_1, rl_2, rl_3) triple, which leads to the following observation:

Observation 1: *In SCs with imperfect facilities, it is not sufficient to find the best service level; it is also necessary to find the least costly local reliability triples, $(rl_1{}^*, rl_2{}^*, rl_3{}^*)$, corresponding to that service level.*

For example, in Figure 3-5, all the points along the yellow arrow correspond to (rl_1, rl_2, rl_3) triples, leading to $sl_p{}^* = 0.76$. As seen, the profits of the companies corresponding to these triples differ significantly. Solving the proposed mathematical model helps us to find the least costly triple that is equal to $(rl_1{}^* = 0.99, rl_2{}^* = 0.99, rl_3{}^* = 0.88)$.

In the model proposed in this chapter and the sample problem solved in this section, the retail price of the product is assumed to be a fixed exogenous factor. However, the retail price has always been one of the most important competitive factors for rivals in the markets. Determining the appropriate retail price is not straightforward because of its conflicting effects on the company's sales volume and unit marginal profit. The price increment augments the unit marginal profit of each sale but reduces the attractiveness of the product for customers and leads to lower sales volume. In the remainder of this section, we analyze the correlation between the retail price and after-sales service of the company via sensitivity analysis. It is assumed that the retail price of the product can be selected on the [$9.0, $13.5] interval. This interval is determined by different factors, such as the retail price of similar rival or substitutable products and governmental regulations to support domestic production or customers. The mathematical model of the problem is solved for different values of the price on the [$9.0, $13.5] interval and different variants of the warranty time. The results are shown in Figure 3-7.

As seen in Figure 3-7, the price increment has similar effects on the company's profit for different warranty length options. Initially, the price increment leads to a higher profit for the company because the positive effect of unit marginal profit increment on the profit of the company dominates the negative effect on the sales reduction. Thus, the company's profit gradually starts to increase. For the 6-month warranty length, the highest profit is achieved for $p^* = \$10.75$, which is equal to $\varPi = \$782.20$. At this price, the difference between the positive and negative effects of the price increment becomes zero and beyond that, its negative effect dominates the positive effect. Thus, the company's profit starts to decrease. Therefore, the retail price increments have heterogeneous effects on the company's profit for all warranty options. As shown in Figure 3-7, by increasing the warranty length, the profit function shifts to the right. This

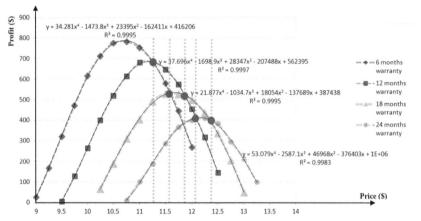

Figure 3-7. Profit of the company with respect to the retail price for different warranty lengths.

means that a higher retail price is needed to preserve the same profit value for a longer warranty length. Therefore, there is a positive correlation between price and warranty length. These results are summarized in the following observations:

Observation 2: *Increases/decreases in the price have a heterogeneous effect on the company's profit for all warranty options, meaning that the $\dfrac{\Delta \varPi}{\Delta p}$ ratio is not constant for different p values. For each warranty option, w, this effect is positive for all price values less than the optimal price of that warranty option, p_w^*. For price values, greater than p_w^*, this effect is negative. Therefore, managers should be careful, as any price increment beyond p_w^* is not advisable for each warranty option.*

Observation 3: *A longer warranty length imposes a higher cost on a company, which is compensated for by a higher price value. Therefore, changing the warranty strategy for a product requires a positively correlated change in the retail price of that product.*

Now, we seek to determine the best priority for the warranty options for different price values. The priority of a warranty option is determined by its profitability. This means that a warranty option with the highest priority is the most profitable (optimal) one. However, by determining the priority of all warranty options, we provide more information for decision makers regarding the profitability of the other warranty options. For this purpose, we solve the mathematical model of the test problem for different values of the retail price and different warranty options. Then, a function representing the profit function of the company for each warranty length with respect to the retail price values is fitted. These functions are shown in Figure 3-7. These profit functions have several intersections, indicated by red dots in this figure. These dots represent critical retail price values at which the priority and profitability of the warranty options change. In the test problem, these critical price values are $p_1 = 11.25$, $p_2 = 11.57$, $p_3 = 11.82$, $p_4 = 12.07$, and $p_5 = 12.37$. As shown in Figure 3-7, in the first price interval,[3] [$9.00, $11.25], the profit function corresponding to $w = 6$ (*months*) is the highest function, which means that it is the most profitable one. Therefore, $w^* = 6$ (*months*) is the optimal warranty option and has the highest priority. After $w = 6$ (*months*), the second highest function corresponds to $w = 12$ (*months*). This means that the $w = 12$ (*months*) warranty option is the second most profitable warranty option and that its priority order is 2. In the same manner, the $w = 18$ (*months*) and $w = 25$ (*months*) warranty options have the third and fourth priorities, respectively. Thus, the priority order of the warranty options in the first price interval is 6, 12, 18, and 24 (*months*). In the second price interval,[4] [$11.25, $11.57], the priority order of the profit functions changes to 12, 6, 18, and 24 (*months*). This means that the optimal warranty option is $w^* = 12$ (*months*). The priority order of the warranty options in different price intervals is as follows:

- If $p < p_1 = \$11.25$ *then the priority of the warranty options is: 6, 12, 18 and 24 months.*

- If $p_1 < p \le p_2 = \$11.57$ *then the priority of the warranty options is: 12, 6, 18 and 24 months.*

- If $p_2 < p \le p_3 = \$11.82$ *then the priority of the warranty options is: 12, 18, 6 and 24 months.*

- If $p_3 < p \le p_4 = \$12.07$ *then the priority of the warranty options is: 18, 12, 24 and 6 months.*

- If $p_4 < p \le p_5 = \$12.37$ *then the priority of the warranty options is: 18, 24, 12 and 6 months.*

- If $p_5 = 12.37 < p$ *then the priority of the warranty options is: 24, 18, 12 and 6 months.*

Based on these results, the best warranty strategy in different price intervals is summarized in Table 3-3.

These results are summarized in the following observation:

---

[3] The lower bound of this interval is the lower bound of the feasible price interval, [$9.0, $13.5] and the upper bound is the first critical price value.
[4] The lower and upper bounds of this interval are equal to the first and second critical price values, respectively.

Table 3-4. Best warranty strategy in different price intervals.

Price interval	$p < \$11.25$	$\$11.25 < p \le \$11.82$	$\$11.82 < p \le \$12.37$	$\$12.37 < p$
Best warranty	$w^* = 6$ (*mo.*)	$w^* = 12$ (*mo.*)	$w^* = 18$ (*mo.*)	$w^* = 24$ (*mo.*)

Observation 4: *The priority order of the warranty options changes with the critical price values, but it remains stable in the price intervals between two sequential critical price values.*

Next, we analyze how this behavior changes in price- and warranty-sensitive markets. We first start with price-sensitive markets. For this purpose, the price sensitivity parameter of the pre-market is doubled (an increase from 250 to 500) and all the models are re-computed with this new parameter. The results are summarized in Figure 3-8. In the price-sensitive market, the priority order of the warranty options is as follows:

- If $p < p_1 = \$10.90$ *then the priority of the warranty options is: 6, 12, 18 and 24 months.*

- If $p_1 < p \le p_2 = \$11.05$ *then the priority of the warranty options is: 12, 6, 18 and 24 months.*

- If $p_2 < p \le p_3 = \$11.20$ *then the priority of the warranty options is: 12, 18, 6 and 24 months.*

- If $p_3 < p \le p_4 = \$11.38$ *then the priority of the warranty options is: 18, 12, 24 and 6 months.*

- If $p_4 < p \le p_4 = \$11.55$ *then the priority of the warranty options is: 18, 24, 12 and 6 months.*

- If $p_4 < p$ *then the priority of the warranty options is: 24, 18, 12 and 6 months.*

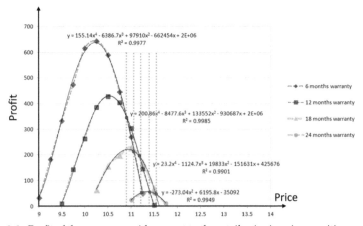

Figure 3-8. Profit of the company with respect to the retail price in price-sensitive markets.

Table 3-5. Best warranty strategy in the price-sensitive market.

Price interval	$p < \$10.90$	$\$10.90 < p \le \$11.20$	$\$11.20 < p \le \$11.55$	$\$11.55 < p$
Best warranty	$w^* = 6$ (*mo.*)	$w^* = 12$ (*mo.*)	$w^* = 18$ (*mo.*)	$w^* = 24$ (*mo.*)

In Table 3-4, we summarize the best warranty strategy in different price intervals based on these results.

As seen in Figure 3-8, the optimal price for all the warranty functions shifts to the left. This means that in price-sensitive markets, the highest profit of the company occurs at lower retail prices regardless of the warranty length. Alternately, the differences between the profit functions of the warranty options become more significant. This means that an inappropriate selection of the warranty length leads to a higher profit loss in this market compared with less price-sensitive markets. In addition, the price intervals between the critical retail price values in which the priority of the warranty options changes become smaller. In this type of market, the priority of the warranty options is more fragile and changes more rapidly with retail price variations. These outcomes lead to Observation 5.

Observation 5: *An inappropriate warranty length for products leads to higher profit loss in markets with higher price sensitivity. In addition, the priority order of the warranty options is more fragile in these markets and remains stable within smaller price intervals. Even a small change in the price may change the most profitable warranty option. This means that managers of companies working in price-sensitive markets should be more careful with respect to price changes. It is more likely that a small change in the retail price requires a new warranty strategy.*

Next, we analyze how this behavior changes in warranty-sensitive markets. For this purpose, the warranty sensitivity parameter of the market in the problem is doubled (an increase from 200 to 400), and all the models are re-computed with this new parameter. The results are summarized in Figure 3-9.

In the warranty-sensitive market, the priority order of the warranty options is as follows:

- If $p < p_1 = \$11.17$ *then the priority of the warranty options is: 6, 12, 18 and 24 months.*
- If $p_1 < p \le p_2 = \$11.57$ *then the priority of the warranty options is: 12, 6, 18 and 24 months.*
- If $p_2 < p \le p_3 = \$11.95$ *then the priority of the warranty options is: 12, 18, 6 and 24 months.*
- If $p_3 < p \le p_4 = \$12.40$ *then the priority of the warranty options is: 18, 12, 24 and 6 months.*

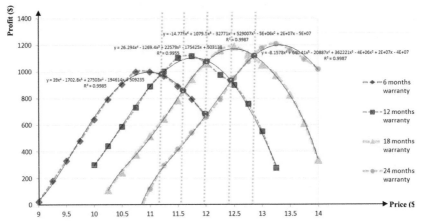

Figure 3-9. Profit of the company with respect to the retail price in warranty-sensitive markets.

Table 3-6. Best warranty strategy in the warranty-sensitive market.

Price interval	$p < \$11.17$	$\$11.17 < p \le \$11.95$	$\$11.95 < p \le \$12.75$	$\$12.75 < p$
Best warranty	$w^* = 6$ (*mo.*)	$w^* = 12$ (*mo.*)	$w^* = 18$ (*mo.*)	$w^* = 24$ (*mo.*)

- If $p_4 < p \le p_4 = \$12.75$ *then the priority of the warranty options is: 18, 24, 12 and 6 months.*

- If $p_4 < p$ *then the priority of the warranty options is: 24, 18, 12 and 6 months.*

In Table 3-5, we present the best warranty strategy in different price intervals based on these results.

As seen in Figure 3-9, in this case, the warranty options with higher lengths are more attractive and the highest profit is achieved with the $w^* = 24$ (*months*) warranty option. Furthermore, a longer warranty length justifies the optimality of a higher retail price in this market, as the positive effect of the warranty increment dominates the negative effects of price augmentation on the market's demand volume. The optimal retail price is $p^* = \$13.30$ in this case. In warranty-sensitive markets, the critical priority changing causes the price points to get farther away from each other. This means that the optimal warranty strategy is more stable in this market and that the priority of the warranty options is more stationary with respect to variations in the retail price. These results are summarized in Observation 6.

Observation 6: *In warranty-sensitive markets, the optimal retail prices are higher and the price intervals between sequential critical price values are larger. This means that the optimal warranty strategy of companies and the priority order of their warranty options are stationary in a larger price interval. In other* *words, managers of companies working in warranty-sensitive markets do not need to be particularly concerned with small price variations that occur far from the critical price values.*

3.9 Closing Remarks

In this chapter, we develop a mathematical model that determines the most profitable integrated production plan for companies servicing both pre- and after-sales markets. Variation in the performance of production facilities, called supply-side variations and demands of markets, called demand-side variations, are considered in this model. Having an integrated production plan is critical for the companies because in addition to having to address two SCs (i.e., forward and after-sales SCs), these chains are not independent. The events occurring in one SC affect the performance of the other chain. In this chapter, we identified two interactions between the chains that justify the necessity of their integrated and concurrent flow planning. This model fills the "lack of holistic perspective and system integration among SC partners" gap raised by both industrial managers and academic researchers. The contributions of this work to the literature are as follows:

- **Integration in after-sales activities**: In addition to the downstream marketing effects of the after-sales services, we also incorporate their support of upstream manufacturing operations in our model. This integration strengthens the holistic perspective and system integration among facilities involved in after-sales activities.

- **Integration of forward and after-sales SCs**: The interactions between the operations of the forward and after-sales SCs are typically ignored in the literature and they are planned separately. These interactions are quantified and incorporated in our integrated model. Incorporating these interactions not only improves demand and required inventory predictions in pre- and after-sales markets but also strengthens the holistic perspective and system integration in product/after-sales service provider companies.

- **Managing supply-side variations in SCs**: The performances of production facilities are typically assumed to be perfect in the SC literature. In this chapter, we consider the inherent variations existing in imperfect production systems of the practical world. To improve the service level in pre- and after-sales markets and mitigate qualified flow depreciation in SCs with imperfect facilities, we suggest that orders should be amplified from the downstream to the upstream of the SCs.

Analyzing the computational results of the model reveals some interesting insights:

- *In SCs with imperfect facilities, it is not sufficient to determine the best service level; it is also necessary to find the least costly local reliability triples corresponding to that service level.*

- *Increases/decreases in price have a heterogeneous effect on the company's profit for all warranty options. However, changing the warranty strategy for a product requires a positively correlated change in the retail price of that product.*

- *The priority order of the warranty options changes for the critical price values, but it remains stable in the price intervals between two sequential critical price values. These orders are more fragile in price-sensitive markets and more stable in warranty-stable markets.*

The model presented in this chapter is applicable to companies supplying durable consumer products with failure-free warranties for customers. Customers are informed by the companies' retailers about the after-sales service level commitment, or this information is available for customers through their own evaluation or viewing of independent Internet product-service evaluation websites.

Although this work focuses on durable consumer products for which repairing the returned products is the main responsibility of the after-sales SCs and a failure-free warranty strategy is considered, this formulation can be modified for other product types with different warranty strategies, e.g., non-repairable products with rebate warranties. In addition, the concepts developed here can be modified to make them applicable for capital goods, such as computer networks, medical and defence systems, and infrastructure, for which performance-based contracts are common. In these industries, the development, installation, or construction of systems is completed by forward SCs and the maintenance of such systems to keep them performing at an acceptable level of availability, is the responsibility of after-sales SCs.

In the context of an architecture for fail-safe networks, the focus of this chapter is on variation management in two correlated forward and after-sales SCs supplying an original product and its spare parts, respectively. The defective parts of the products are not repairable and should be replaced with new parts. The mathematical model of this chapter will be extended in Chapter 4 to the correlated chains of repairable products.

Acknowledgement

Figures and tables in Chapter 3 are reprinted from Transportation Research, Part E: Logistics and Transportation Review, volume 93 (September), by

Shabnam Rezapour, Janet K. Allen and Farrokh Mistree, "Reliable Flow in Forward and After-sales Supply Chains Considering Propagated Uncertainty." pp. 409–436, 2016, with permission from Elsevier.

References

Allon, G. and Federgruen, A. 2009. Competition in service industries with segmented markets. Management Science 55(4): 619–634.

Anderson, E. E. 1977. Product price and warranty terms: an optimization model. J. Oper. Res. Soc. 28(3): 739–741. http://dx.doi.org/10.1057/jors.1977.150.

Bacchetti, A. and Saccani, N. 2012. Spare parts classification and demand forecasting for stock control: Investigating the gap between research and practice. Omega 40(6): 722–737.

Baghalian, A., Rezapour, S. and Farahani, R. Z. 2013. Robust supply chain network design with service level against disruptions and demand uncertainties: A real-life case. European Journal of Operational Research 227(1): 199–215.

Baines, T., Lightfoot, H., Evans, S., Neely, A., Greenough, R., Peppard, J., Roy, R., Shehab, E., Braganza, A., Tiwari, A., Alcock, J., Angus, J., Bastl, M., Cousens, A., Irving, P., Johnson, M., Kingston, J., Lockett, H., Martinez, V. and Michele, P. 2007. State-of-the-art in product-service systems. Proceedings of the Institution of Mechanical Engineering–Part B: Journal of Engineering. Manufacturing 221(10): 1543–1552.

Barabadi, A., Barabady, J. and Markeset, T. 2014. Application of reliability models with covariates in spare part prediction and optimization—a case study. Reliab. Eng. Syst. Saf. 123: 1–7. http://dx.doi.org/10.1016/j.ress.2013.09.012.

Bernstein, F. and Federgruen, A. 2004. A general equilibrium model for industries with price and service competition. Operations Research 52(6): 868–886.

Bernstein, F. and Federgruen, A. 2007. Coordination mechanisms for supply chains under price and service competition. Manufacturing & Service Operations Management 9(3): 242–262.

Boone, C. A., Craighead, C. W. and Hanna, J. B. 2008. Critical challenges of inventory management in service parts supply: A Delphi study. Operations Management Research 1(1): 31–39.

Business Week. 2004. Hyundai: Kissing Clunkers Goodbye—A Five-year Focus on Quality has sent Customer Satisfaction Soaring. Business Week (16 May).

Cardona-Valdés, Y., Álvarez, A. and Ozdemir, D. 2011. A bi-objective supply chain design problem with uncertainty. Transportation Research Part C: Emerging Technologies 19(5): 821–832.

Chakravarthy, S. R. and Gómez-Corral, A. 2009. The influence of delivery times on repairable k-out-of-N systems with spares. Applied Mathematical Modelling 33(5): 2368–2387.

Chen, J. A. and Chien, Y. H. 2007. Renewing warranty and preventive maintenance for products with failure penalty post-warranty. Quality and Reliability Engineering International 23(1): 107–121.

Chen, M.-S. and Chu, M.-C. 2001. The analysis of optimal price control model in matching problem between production and sales. Asia-Pacific Journal of Operational Research 18(2): 131.

Chen, X., Li, L. and Zhou, M. 2012. Manufacturer's pricing strategy for supply chain with warranty period-dependent demand. Omega 40(6): 807–816.

Chien, Y.-H. 2005. Determining optimal warranty periods from the seller's perspective and optimal out-of-warranty replacement age from the buyer's perspective. International Journal of Systems Science 36(10): 631–637.

Chien, Y.-H. and Chen, J.-A. 2008. Optimal spare ordering policy under a rebate warranty. European Journal of Operational Research 186(2): 708–719.

Chu, J. and Chintagunta, P. K. 2009. Quantifying the economic value of warranties in the US server market. Marketing Science 28(1): 99–121.

Cohen, M. A., Agrawal, N. and Agrawal, V. 2006. Winning in the aftermarket. Harvard Business Review 84(5): 129.

Daniel, J. S. R. and Rajendran, C. 2006. Heuristic approaches to determine base-stock levels in a serial supply chain with a single objective and with multiple objectives. European Journal of Operational Research 175(1): 566–592.

De Smidt-Destombes, K. S., Van Der Heijden, M. C. and Van Harten, A. 2006. On the interaction between maintenance, spare part inventories and repair capacity for a k-out-of-N system with wear-out. European Journal of Operational Research 174(1): 182–200.

De Smidt-Destombes, K. S., Van Der Heijden, M. C. and Van Harten, A. 2007. Availability of k-out-of-N systems under block replacement sharing limited spares and repair capacity. International Journal of Production Economics 107(2): 404–421.

De Smidt-Destombes, K. S., Van Der Heijden, M. C. and Van Harten, A. 2009. Joint optimisation of spare part inventory, maintenance frequency and repair capacity for k-out-of-N systems. International Journal of Production Economics 118(1): 260–268.

Dell.Com. 2010. web site 2010 [cited April 28 2010]. Available from http://www.dell.com/home/.

Dennis, M. J. and Kambil, A. 2003. Service management: building profits after the sale. Supply Chain Management Review 7(3): 42–48.

Díaz, A. and Fu, M. C. 1997. Models for multi-echelon repairable item inventory systems with limited repair capacity. Eur. J. Oper. Res. 97(3): 480–492. http://dx.doi.org/10.1016/S0377-2217(96)00279-2.

Esmaeili, M., Shamsi, N. and Asgharizadeh, E. 2014. Three-Level Warranty Service Contract among Manufacturer, Agent and Customer: A Game-Theoretical Approach. Vol. 239.

Faridimehr, S. and Niaki, S. T. A. 2012. A note on optimal price, warranty length and production rate for free replacement policy in static demand markets. Omega 40(6): 805–806.

Finkelstein, M. 2009. On systems with shared resources and optimal switching strategies. Reliability Engineering & System Safety 94(8): 1358–1362.

Gallagher, T., Mitchke, M. D. and Rogers, M. C. 2005. Profiting from spare parts. The McKinsey Quarterly 2: 1–4.

Glickman, T. S. and Berger, P. D. 1976. Optimal price and protection period decisions for a product under warranty. Manage. Sci. 22(12): 1381–1390. http://dx. doi.org/10.1287/mnsc.22.12.1381.

Graves, S. C. 1985. A multi-echelon inventory model for a repairable item with one-for-one replenishment. Manage. Sci. 31(10): 1247–1256. http://dx.doi.org/10.1287/mnsc.31.10.1247.

Gross, D. and Pinkus, C.E. 1979. Designing a support system for repairable items. Comput. Oper. Res. 6 (2): 59–68. http://dx.doi.org/10.1016/0305-0548(79)90017-0.

Hsu, C.-I. and Li, H.-C. 2011. Reliability evaluation and adjustment of supply chain network design with demand fluctuations. International Journal of Production Economics 132(1): 131–145.

Huang, H.-Z., Liu, Z.-J. and Murthy, D. 2007. Optimal reliability, warranty and price for new products. Lie Transactions 39(8): 819–827.

Hussain, A. Z. M. O. and Murthy, D. N. P. 2000. Warranty and optimal redundancy with uncertain quality. Math. Comput. Model. 31(10–12): 175–182. http://dx.doi.org/10.1016/S0895-7177(00)00085-6.

Hussain, A. and Murthy, D. 2003. Warranty and optimal reliability improvement through product development. Mathematical and Computer Modelling 38(11-13): 1211–1217.

Jhang, J.-P. 2005. The optimal used period of repairable product with leadtime after the warranty expiry. International Journal of Systems Science 36(7): 423–431.

Jung, G. M. and Park, D. H. 2003. Optimal maintenance policies during the post-warranty period. Reliability Engineering & System Safety 82(2): 173–185.

Jung, K., Park, M. and Ho Park, D. 2014. Cost Optimization Model Following Extended Renewing Two-phase Warranty. Vol. 79.

Kamrad, B., Lele, S. S., Siddique, A. and Thomas, R. J. 2005. Innovation diffusion uncertainty, advertising and pricing policies. European Journal of Operational Research 164(3): 829–850.

Khajavi, S. H., Partanen, J. and Holmström, J. 2014. Additive manufacturing in the spare parts supply chain. Computers in Industry 65(1): 50–63.

Kim, B. and Park, S. 2008. Optimal pricing, EOL (end of life) warranty, and spare parts manufacturing strategy amid product transition. European Journal of Operational Research 188(3): 723–745.

Kim, S.-H., Cohen, M. A. and Netessine, S. 2007. Performance contracting in after-sales service supply chains. Management Science 53(12): 1843–1858.

Kleber, R., Zanoni, S. and Zavanella, L. 2011. On how buyback and remanufacturing strategies affect the profitability of spare parts supply chains. International Journal of Production Economics 133(1): 135–142.

Ko, H. J. and Evans, G. W. 2007. A genetic algorithm-based heuristic for the dynamic integrated forward/reverse logistics network for 3PLs. Computers & Operations Research 34(2): 346–366.

Kuo, W. and Wan, R. 2007. Recent advances in optimal reliability allocation. IEEE Transactions on Systems, Man, and Cybernetics-Part A: Systems and Humans 37(2): 143–156.

Kurata, H. and Nam, S.-H. 2010. After-sales service competition in a supply chain: Optimization of customer satisfaction level or profit or both? International Journal of Production Economics 127(1): 136–146.

Kurata, H. and Nam, S.-H. 2013. After-sales service competition in a supply chain: Does uncertainty affect the conflict between profit maximization and customer satisfaction? International Journal of Production Economics 144(1): 268–280.

Lee, H. L. and Rosenblatt, M. J. 1987. Simultaneous determination of production cycle and inspection schedules in a production system. Management Science 33(9): 1125–1136.

Li, G., Huang, F. F., Cheng, T. C. E., Zheng, Q. and Ji, P. 2014. Make-or-buy service capacity decision in a supply chain providing after-sales service. European Journal of Operational Research 239(2): 377–388.

Li, K., Mallik, S. and Chhajed, D. 2012. Design of extended warranties in supply chains under additive demand. Production and Operations Management 21(4): 730–746.

Li, S. and Li, Z. 2012. Spare parts allocation by improved genetic algorithm and Monte Carlo simulation. International Journal of Systems Science 43(6): 997–1006.

Lieckens, K. T., Colen, P. J. and Lambrecht, M. R. 2013. Optimization of a stochastic remanufacturing network with an exchange option. Decision Support Systems 54(4): 1548–1557.

Lin, P.-C. and Shue, L.-Y. 2005. Application of optimal control theory to product pricing and warranty with free replacement under the influence of basic lifetime distributions. Computers & Industrial Engineering 48(1): 69–82.

Majid, H. A., Wulandhari, L. A., Samah, A. A. and Chin, A. J. 2012. A framework in determining extended warranty by using two dimensional delay time model. Paper read at Advanced Materials Research.

Marseguerra, M., Zio, E. and Podofillini, L. 2005. Multiobjective spare part allocation by means of genetic algorithms and Monte Carlo simulation. Reliability Engineering & System Safety 87(3): 325–335.

McAvoy, J. 2008. Integrating Spare Parts Planning with Logistics. Report, Aberdeen Group.

Menke, W. W. 1969. Determination of warranty reserves. Manage. Sci. 15(10): B542–B549. http://dx.doi.org/10.1287/mnsc.15.10.B542.

Mohammaddust, F., Rezapour, S., Zanjirani Farahani, R., Mofidfar, M. and Hill, A. 2015. Developing Lean and Responsive Supply Chains: A Robust Model for Alternative Risk Mitigation Strategies in Supply Chain Designs. Vol. 183.

Murthy, D. N. P. 1990. Optimal reliability choice in product design. Eng. Optim. 15(4): 281–294. http://dx.doi.org/10.1080/03052159008941158.

Nguyen, D. and Murthy, D. 1984. A general model for estimating warranty costs for repairable products. IIE Transactions 16(4): 379–386.

Nguyen, D. G. and Murthy, D. N. P. 1988. Optimal reliability allocation for products sold under warranty. Eng. Optim. 13(1): 35–45. http://dx.doi.org/10.1080/03052158808940945.

Niemi, P., Huiskonen, J. and Kärkkäinen, H. 2009. Understanding the knowledge accumulation process—Implications for the adoption of inventory management techniques. International Journal of Production Economics 118(1): 160–167.

Nourelfath, M. and Ait-Kadi, D. 2007. Optimization of series–parallel multi-state systems under maintenance policies. Reliability Engineering & System Safety 92(12): 1620–1626.

Öner, K. B., Kiesmüller, G. P. and Van Houtum, G.-J. 2010. Optimization of component reliability in the design phase of capital goods. European Journal of Operational Research 205(3): 615–624.

Pan, F. and Nagi, R. 2010. Robust supply chain design under uncertain demand in agile manufacturing. Computers & Operations Research 37(4): 668–683.

Park, S., Lee, T.-E. and Sung, C. S. 2010. A three-level supply chain network design model with risk-pooling and lead times. Transportation Research Part E: Logistics and Transportation Review 46(5): 563–581.

Perlman, Y., Mehrez, A. and Kaspi, M. 2001. Setting expediting repair policy in a multi-echelon repairable-item inventory system with limited repair capacity. J. Oper. Res. Soc. 52(2): 198–209. http://dx.doi.org/10.1057/palgrave.jors.2601079.

Rappold, J. A. and Van Roo, B. D. 2009. Designing multi-echelon service parts networks with finite repair capacity. European Journal of Operational Research 199(3): 781–792.

Rezapour, S. 2011. Competition in supply chain. pp. 215–232. In: Farahani, R. Z., Rezapour, S. and Kardar, L. (eds.). Supply Chain Sustainability and Raw Material Management: Concepts and Processes. IGI Global, Hershey, USA.

Rezapour, S., Allen, J. K., Trafalis, T. B. and Mistree, F. 2013. Robust Supply Chain Network Design by Considering Demand-Side Uncertainty and Supply-Side Disruption. (55881):V03AT03A030.

Rezapour, S. and Zanjirani Farahani, R. 2014. Supply Chain Network Design under Oligopolistic Price and Service Level Competition with Foresight. Vol. 72.

Rezapour, S., Allen, J. and Mistree, F. 2014a. Uncertainty Propagation in a Supply Chain or Supply Network. Vol. 73.

Rezapour, S., Allen, J. K. and Mistree, F. 2014b. Uncertainty Propagation in a Supply Chain / Network With Uncertain Facility Performance. (46407):V007T07A021.

Rezapour, S., Allen, J. K. and Mistree, F. 2015a. Uncertainty propagation in a supply chain or supply network. Transportation Research Part E: Logistics and Transportation Review 73: 185–206.

Rezapour, S., Singh, R., Allen, J. K. and Mistree, F. 2015b. Stochastic Supply Networks Servicing Pre- and After-Sales Markets. (57175):V007T06A021.

Rezapour, S., Allen, J. K. and Mistree, F. 2016. Reliable Flow in Forward and After-sales Supply Chains Considering Propagated Uncertainty. Transportation Research Part E 93: 409–436.

Romeijn, H. E., Shu, J. and Teo, C.-P. 2007. Designing two-echelon supply networks. European Journal of Operational Research 178(2): 449–462.

Rosenblatt, M. J. and Lee, H. L. 1986. Economic production cycles with imperfect production processes. IIE Transactions 18(1): 48–55.

Sahba, P. and Balcıog, B. 2011. The impact of transportation delays on repairshop capacity pooling and spare part inventories. European Journal of Operational Research 214(3): 674–682.

Sana, S. S. 2010. An economic production lot size model in an imperfect production system. European Journal of Operational Research 201(1): 158–170.

Schütz, P., Tomasgard, A. and Ahmed, S. 2009. Supply chain design under uncertainty using sample average approximation and dual decomposition. European Journal of Operational Research 199(2): 409–419.

Shen, Z.-J. M. and Qi, L. 2007. Incorporating inventory and routing costs in strategic location models. European Journal of Operational Research 179(2): 372–389.

Sherbrooke, C. C. 1968. Metric: a multi-echelon technique for recoverable item control. Oper. Res. 16(1): 122–141. http://dx.doi.org/10.1287/opre.16.1.122.

Sheu, S.-H. and Chien, Y.-H. 2005. Optimal burn-in time to minimize the cost for general repairable products sold under warranty. European Journal of Operational Research 163(2): 445–461.

Sleptchenko, A., van der Heijden, M. C. and van Harten, A. 2002. Effects of finite repair capacity in multi-echelon, multi-indenture service part supply systems. Int. J. Prod. Econ. 79(3): 209–230. http://dx.doi.org/10.1016/S0925-5273(02)00155-X.

Su, C. and Shen, J. 2012. Analysis of extended warranty policies with different repair options. Engineering Failure Analysis 25: 49–62.

Van Ommeren, J., Bumb, A. F. and Sleptchenko, A. 2006. Locating repair shops in a stochastic environment. Computers & Operations Research 33(6): 1575–1594.

Wagner, S. and Lindemann, E. 2008. A case study-based analysis of spare parts management in the engineering industry. Production Planning & Control 19(4): 397–407.

Wang, L., Chu, J. and Mao, W. 2009. A condition-based replacement and spare provisioning policy for deteriorating systems with uncertain deterioration to failure. European Journal of Operational Research 194(1): 184–205.

Wang, W. 2012. A stochastic model for joint spare parts inventory and planned maintenance optimisation. European Journal of Operational Research 216(1): 127–139.

Wei, J., Zhao, J. and Li, Y. 2014. Price and Warranty Period Decisions for Complementary Products with Horizontal Firms' Cooperation/Noncooperation Strategies. Vol. 105.

Wu, C.-C., Chou, C.-Y. and Huang, C. 2009. Optimal price, warranty length and production rate for free replacement policy in the static demand market. Omega 37(1): 29–39.

Wu, C.-C., Lin, P.-C. and Chou, C.-Y. 2006. Determination of price and warranty length for a normal lifetime distributed product. International Journal of Production Economics 102(1): 95–107.

Yeh, R. H., Chen, G.-C. and Chen, M.-Y. 2005. Optimal age-replacement policy for nonrepairable products under renewing free-replacement warranty. IEEE Transactions on Reliability 54(1): 92–97.

You, F. and Grossmann, I. E. 2008. Design of responsive supply chains under demand uncertainty. Computers & Chemical Engineering 32(12): 3090–3111.

Zuo, M. J., Liu, B. and Murthy, D. N. P. 2000. Replacement–repair policy for multi-state deteriorating products under warranty. Eur. J. Oper. Res. 123(3): 519–530. http://dx.doi.org/10.1016/S0377-2217(99)00107-1.

Zhou, Z., Li, Y. and Tang, K. 2009. Dynamic pricing and warranty policies for products with fixed lifetime. European Journal of Operational Research 196(3): 940–948.

Appendices

Appendix 3.A: Proofs of Lemmas

Proof of Lemma 3-1
As explained before, the probability of the jth failure in the $[0, w]$ interval is equal to:

$$\Pr\{Num_i(w) = j\} = F_i^{(j)}(w, \lambda_i) - F_i^{(j+1)}(w, \lambda_i) \qquad (\forall i = 1, 2, \ldots, r) \qquad (3\text{-}28)$$

Therefore, the average number of failures, $E_i(w, n_i)$, is computed as

$$E_i(w, n_i) = \sum\nolimits_{j=n_i+1}^{\infty} j \times \Pr\{Num_i(w) = j\} = \sum\nolimits_{j=n_i+1}^{\infty} j \times \left[F_i^{(j)}(w, \lambda_i) - F_i^{(j+1)}(w, \lambda_i) \right]$$

$$= (n_i + 1) \times \left[F_i^{(n_i+1)}(w, \lambda_i) - F_i^{(n_i+2)}(w, \lambda_i) \right] +$$

$$(n_i + 2) \times \left[F_i^{(n_i+2)}(w, \lambda_i) - F_i^{(n_i+3)}(w, \lambda_i) \right] +$$

$$(n_i + 3) \times \left[F_i^{(n_i+2)}(w, \lambda_i) - F_i^{(n_i+3)}(w, \lambda_i) \right] + \ldots$$

$$= (n_i + 1) \times F_i^{(n_i+1)}(w, \lambda_i) + F_i^{(n_i+2)}(w, \lambda_i) + F_i^{(n_i+3)}(w, \lambda_i) + \ldots$$

$$= n_i \times F_i^{(n_i+1)}(w, \lambda_i) + \sum\nolimits_{j=n_i+1}^{\infty} F_i^{(j)}(w, \lambda_i) \qquad (3\text{-}29)$$

Proof of Lemma 3-2
The variance of the number of failures, $\sigma_i^2(w, n_i)$, is computed as

$$\sigma_i^2(w, n_i) = \sum\nolimits_{j=n_i+1}^{\infty} j^2 \times \Pr\{Num_i(w) = j\} - \left[\sum\nolimits_{j=n_i+1}^{\infty} j \times \Pr\{Num_i(w) = j\} \right]^2 \quad (3\text{-}30)$$

The second term of (31) is already computed in Lemma 1. Therefore, we first compute the first term of (31):

$$\sum\nolimits_{j=n_i+1}^{\infty} j^2 \times \Pr\{Num_i(w) = j\} = (n_i + 1)^2 \times \left[F_i^{(n_i+1)}(w, \lambda_i) - F_i^{(n_i+2)}(w, \lambda_i) \right] +$$

$$(n_i + 2)^2 \times \left[F_i^{(n_i+2)}(w, \lambda_i) - F_i^{(n_i+3)}(w, \lambda_i) \right] +$$

$$(n_i + 3)^2 \times \left[F_i^{(n_i+3)}(w, \lambda_i) - F_i^{(n_i+4)}(w, \lambda_i) \right] + \ldots$$

$$= (n_i + 1)^2 \times F_i^{(n_i+1)}(w, \lambda_i) + (3 + 2n_i). F_i^{(n_i+2)}(w, \lambda_i) + (5 + 2n_i). F_i^{(n_i+3)}(w, \lambda_i) + \ldots$$

$$= (n_i + 1)^2 \times F_i^{(n_i+1)}(w, \lambda_i) + \sum\nolimits_{j=n_i+2}^{\infty} (2j - 1). F_i^{(j)}(w, \lambda_i) \qquad (3\text{-}31)$$

By substituting Eqs. (3-31) and (3-29) into Eq. (3-30), $\sigma_i^2(w, n_i)$ is simplified as

$$\sigma_i^2(w, n_i) = (n_i + 1)^2 \times F_i^{(n_i+1)} (w, \lambda_i) + \sum_{j=n_i+2}^{\infty} (2j-1). F_i^{(j)} (w, \lambda_i) - [n_i \times F_i^{(n_i+1)} (w, \lambda_i) +$$

$$\sum_{j=n_i+1}^{\infty} F_i^{(j)} (w, \lambda_i)]^2 \tag{3-32}$$

Appendix 3.B: After-sales Demand Prediction

In this appendix, we elaborate on why w is considered in the after-sales demand prediction; see Section 3.6.2.1. We assume that the warranty length is an integer multiple of the sales period: $w = k_1. T$. In the sales period, T, we define $\acute{T}$ as the longest time period in which it is logical to assume that the product demand occurs at the beginning of the period. Again, the sales period is an integer multiple of $\acute{T}$: $T = k_2.\acute{T}$. If we assume that the rate of the product demand is nearly constant, then the product sales quantity in each period $\acute{T}$ is x/k_2. We define Dr_{ij} ($\forall i = 1, 2, ..., r$ and $\forall j = 1, 2, ..., k_1. k_2$) as the required quantity of Component i to repair the returned products in batch x/k_2 sold in the jth period of $\acute{T}$. Consider an example production system in which $w = 3T$ and $T = 4\acute{T}$. In Figure 3-10, we show the required amount of Component i in the interval $[0, \acute{T}]$ for the x/k_2 product batch sold in that interval and all the product batches already sold and their warranty times if they have not yet been completed. As seen in Figure 3-10, this total quantity is equal to $\sum_{j=1}^{k_1 k_2} Dr_{ij}$, which is equal to the required quantity of Component i for a x/k_2 product batch inside the warranty time, $w = k_1.k_2.\acute{T}$. The same quantity of Component i is required for intervals $[\acute{T}, 2\acute{T}]$, $[2\acute{T}, 3\acute{T}], ... [(k_2 - 1)\acute{T}, k_2\acute{T}]$ inside the sale period. Therefore, a quantity of $k_2. \sum_{j=1}^{k_1 k_2} Dr_{ij}$ of Component i is required inside the sale period, which is equal to the required quantity of Component i for ($x/k_2.k_2 = x$) product units inside the warranty time, w.

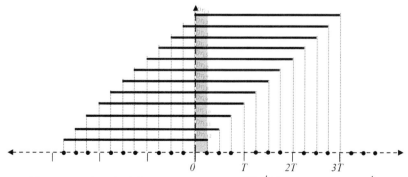

Figure 3-10. Required Component i in interval $[0, \acute{T}]$ for w = 3T and T = 4$\acute{T}$.

(Bold lines represent the interval between the sale time and the end of the warranty time for product batches of x/k_2).

Appendix 3.C: Linearization of Model

The linearized mathematical model is

Max

$$\Pi = \sum_{i=1}^{|RL1|} \sum_{j=1}^{|RL2|} \sum_{k=1}^{|RL3|} \sum_{t=1}^{|W|} v_{rl1^i, rl2^j, rl3^k, w^t} \times \left[\left[\left(p - h^+ \cdot E\left[G^{-1}\left(Max\left\{rl1^i \cdot rl2^j \cdot (rl3^k)^r,\right.\right.\right.\right.\right.$$

$$\left.\left.\left.\left.\frac{h^-}{h^- + h^+}\right\}\right)\right] - \varepsilon\right]^+ - h^- \cdot E\left[\varepsilon - G^{-1}\left(Max\left\{rl1^i \cdot rl2^j \cdot (rl3^k)^r, \frac{h^-}{h^- + h^+}\right\}\right)\right]^+ -$$

$$cr\right) \cdot D(p, rl1^i \cdot rl2^j \cdot (rl3^k)^r, (rl1^i \cdot rl3^k)^r, w^t)\right] - \left[\sum_{i=1}^{r}(a_{1i} + a_{2i}) \cdot (x + \Delta x + x_i + \Delta \acute{x}_i) +\right.$$

$$\sum_{i=1}^{r} \frac{h_{1i} \cdot (x + \Delta x + x_i)^2}{2 . PR_{1i}} + \sum_{i=1}^{r} b_{1i} \cdot (x + \Delta x) + b_2 \cdot (x + \Delta x) + \frac{h_2 . (x)^2}{2 . PR_2} + (c_1 + c_2).$$

$$x + \sum_{i=1}^{r} c_{3i} . x_i\right]$$

$$(3\text{-}33)$$

Subject to

$$x = \sum_{i=1}^{|RL1|} \sum_{j=1}^{|RL2|} \sum_{k=1}^{|RL3|} \sum_{t=1}^{|W|} v_{rl1^i, rl2^j, rl3^k, w^t} \times$$

$$\left[D(p, rl1^i \cdot rl2^j \cdot (rl3^k)^r, (rl1^i \cdot rl3^k)^r, w^t) . G^{-1}\left(Max\left\{rl1^i, \frac{h^-}{h^- + h^+}\right\}\right)\right] \qquad (3\text{-}34)$$

$$\Delta x = \sum_{i=1}^{|RL1|} \sum_{j=1}^{|RL2|} \sum_{k=1}^{|RL3|} \sum_{t=1}^{|W|} v_{rl1^i, rl2^j, rl3^k, w^t} \times$$

$$\left[D(p, rl1^i \cdot rl2^j \cdot (rl3^k)^r, (rl1^i \cdot rl3^k)^r, w^t) . G^{-1}\left(Max\left\{rl1^i, \frac{h^-}{h^- + h^+}\right\}\right) . G'^{-1}(rl2^j)\right] \quad (3\text{-}35)$$

$$x_i = \sum_{i=1}^{|RL1|} \sum_{j=1}^{|RL2|} \sum_{k=1}^{|RL3|} \sum_{t=1}^{|W|} v_{rl1^i, rl2^j, rl3^k, w^t} \times$$

$$\left[\left(D(p, rl1^i \cdot rl2^j \cdot (rl3^k)^r, (rl1^i \cdot rl3^k)^r, w^t) . G^{-1}\left(Max\left\{rl1^i, \frac{h^-}{h^- + h^+}\right\}\right) . E_i(w^t, n_i)\right) +\right.$$

$$\left(z_{rl_1^i} . \sqrt{D(p, rl1^i \cdot rl2^j \cdot (rl3^k)^r, (rl1^i \cdot rl3^k)^r, w^t) . G^{-1}\left(Max\left\{rl1^i, \frac{h^-}{h^- + h^+}\right\}\right) . \sigma_i^2(w^t, n_i)}\right)\right]$$

$$(\forall i = 1, 2, \ldots, r) \qquad (3\text{-}36)$$

$$\Delta \acute{x}_i = \sum_{i=1}^{|RL1|} \sum_{j=1}^{|RL2|} \sum_{k=1}^{|RL3|} \sum_{t=1}^{|W|} v_{rl1^i, rl2^j, rl3^k, w^t} \times \frac{\gamma_i}{1 - \gamma_i} \left[\frac{PR_{1i}}{\mu_i} \ln(rl3^k) +\right.$$

$$D(p, rl1^i \cdot rl2^j \cdot (rl3^k)^r, (rl1^i \cdot rl3^k)^r, w^t) . G^{-1}\left(Max\left\{rl1^i, \frac{h^-}{h^- + h^+}\right\}\right) . (1 + G'^{-1}(rl2^j) +$$

$$E_i(w^t, n_i)\right) +$$

$$z_{rl_1^i} \cdot \sqrt{D(p, rl1^i. rl2^j. (rl3^k)^r, (rl1^i. rl3^k)^r, w^t). G^{-1}\left(Max\left\{rl1^i, \frac{h^-}{h^- + h^+}\right\}\right). \sigma_i^2(w^t, n_i)}\,\Bigg]$$

$$(\forall i = 1, 2, \ldots, r) \qquad (3\text{-}37)$$

$$\sum_{i=1}^{|RL1|} y_{rl1^i} = 1 \qquad\qquad (\forall rl1^i \in RL1) \qquad (3\text{-}38)$$

$$\sum_{i=1}^{|RL2|} y_{rl2^i} = 1 \qquad\qquad (\forall rl2^i \in RL2) \qquad (3\text{-}39)$$

$$\sum_{i=1}^{|RL3|} y_{rl3^i} = 1 \qquad\qquad (\forall rl3^i \in RL3) \qquad (3\text{-}40)$$

$$\sum_{i=1}^{|W|} z_{w^i} = 1 \qquad\qquad (\forall w^t \in W) \qquad (3\text{-}41)$$

$$\frac{y_{rl1^i} + y_{rl2^j} + y_{rl3^k} + z_{w^t}}{4} \geq v_{rl1^i, rl2^j, rl3^k, w^t}$$

$$(\forall w^t \in W, \forall rl1^i \in RL1, \forall rl2^i \in RL2, and\ \forall rl3^i \in RL3) \qquad (3\text{-}42)$$

$$v_{rl1^i, rl2^j, rl3^k, w^t} \geq (y_{rl1^i} + y_{rl2^j} + y_{rl3^k} + z_{w^t} - 3)$$

$$(\forall w^t \in W, \forall rl1^i \in RL1, \forall rl2^i \in RL2, and\ \forall rl3^i \in RL3) \qquad (3\text{-}43)$$

$$v_{rl1^i, rl2^j, rl3^k, w^t} \leq M.\ y_{rl1^i}$$

$$(\forall w^t \in W, \forall rl1^i \in RL1, \forall rl2^i \in RL2, and\ \forall rl3^i \in RL3) \qquad (3\text{-}44)$$

$$v_{rl1^i, rl2^j, rl3^k, w^t} \leq M.\ y_{rl2^j}$$

$$(\forall w^t \in W, \forall rl1^i \in RL1, \forall rl2^i \in RL2, and\ \forall rl3^i \in RL3) \qquad (3\text{-}45)$$

$$v_{rl1^i, rl2^j, rl3^k, w^t} \leq M.\ y_{rl3^k}$$

$$(\forall w^t \in W, \forall rl1^i \in RL1, \forall rl2^i \in RL2, and\ \forall rl3^i \in RL3) \qquad (3\text{-}46)$$

$$v_{rl1^i, rl2^j, rl3^k, w^t} \leq M.\ z_{W^t}$$

$$(\forall w^t \in W, \forall rl1^i \in RL1, \forall rl2^i \in RL2, and\ \forall rl3^i \in RL3) \qquad (3\text{-}47)$$

$$rl1^i,\ rl2^j,\ rl3^k,\ w^t,\ and,\ v_{rl1^i, rl2^j, rl3^k, w^t} \in \{0, 1\}$$

$$(\forall w^t \in W, \forall rl1^i \in RL1, \forall rl2^i \in RL2, and\ \forall rl3^i \in RL3) \qquad (3\text{-}48)$$

Variation Management in the Product-Service Supply Chains of Repairable Products

In Chapter 4, we explain how the approach developed in Chapter 3 can be extended and used for the complicated supply chain of companies providing both pre- and after-sales services for customers of their repairable products (see Chapter 1, Figure 1-9). First, we explain what interactions exist between forward chains, after-sales chains and repair sections. These interactions justify the necessity of their concurrent flow planning. Finally, we develop a model to concurrently make variation management decisions for chains and repair sections. Numerical analysis of results concludes with insight about variation management in these companies.

4.1 Importance of After-sales Supply Chains for Repairable Products

In highly competitive markets, products manufactured by rivals become almost homogeneous from quality and price perspectives. In such markets, increasing number of companies try to provide better pre- and after-sales services for their customers to differentiate from rivals and to leverage competition capabilities. This marketing strategy is called "servitization" in the literature (Vandermerwe and Rada 1988). Product-service system (PSS) is introduced by Baines et al. (2007) as a special case of servitization. Servitization works as a motivational lever and signals the high quality of a product and attracts customers. Warranty and other after-sales services as types of servitization protect customers against defects in materials or workmanship, unexpected failures and unsatisfactory performance. Also, a warranty provides an opportunity for companies to build and maintain a longer relationship with the customers. For example, Hyundai changed customers' perception about the quality of its products by providing an extensive warranty. This long warranty signals the customer that the quality of its cars has improved to match the best in the market (Business Week 2004). In the same industry, Nissan has been offering 10 years/ unlimited mileage warranties for its cars.

Servitization not only improves a company's competitive capability in pre-markets, but also opens a new and profitable income resource in the after-sales markets. Based on the estimate of Gaiardelli et al. (2007), after-sales services in the consumer electronic devices, power tools, vacuum cleaners and personal computer industries, generate around $6 to 8 billion income yearly in the United States. In European car markets, 40 to 50 percent of the total revenue is related to after-sales services provided by the companies. The gross profit of this income is much greater than that resulting from new cars' sales (Bohmann et al. 2003). According to Bundschuh and Dezvane (2003), the profitability of the after-sales markets is four or five times larger than the pre-markets profitability. The importance of the after-sales services is much greater in capital intensive industries such as aerospace, defense and industrial equipment. For example, in the defense industry only 28 percent of the system's total cost is related to its development and procurement and the rest (more than 72 percent) is due to its operation and maintenance. The United States Department of Defense has a budget of about $70B (in 2007) to operate and maintain its systems. Thus, there is a severe competition among supporting industries to offer better after-sales services.

In addition, there are governmental regulations that require companies to provide warranties for their customers. The United States Congress passed the Magnusson Moss Act and the European Union passed legislation requiring two-year warranties for all products.

These economic and non-economic reasons make it necessary to consider and service after-sales markets. However, considering after-sales markets made supply networks of companies much more complicated. These companies not only include a forward supply chain (SC) producing and transshipping products to pre-markets, but also include an after-sales SC dealing with replacing and repairing defective products which have been returned within the warranty period. The considerable interactions between these SCs highlight the importance of concurrent design and flow planning. For example, the total product supplied by a forward SC to a pre-market constitutes the potential demand for the after-sales SC that can be realized as repair requests. Also, providing a high service level in the after-sales SC improves the product's attractiveness in the pre-market and increases the forward SC's sales. Due to these interactions, a huge synergy can be achieved by concurrent flow planning through these SCs. In this chapter, we deal with concurrent flow planning in the forward and after-sales SCs of a company servicing both pre- and after-sales markets. This company supplies a durable product to the pre-market with a failure free warranty. While the product is produced and transported by the forward SC, the after-sales SC is responsible for repairing defective products returned inside the warranty period.

In the context of an architecture for fail-safe networks, as introduced in Section 1.3, we explain the use of reliability for risk management in two correlated SCs and repair sections (see Figure 1-4). The connector is forward and after-sales SCs. We express the form of our architecture as an optimization model that determines the best local reliabilities (properties) and warranty strategy in a way to maximize the total profit in pre- and after-sales markets (relationship). This model helps us to understand the relationship between the chains' performances (pre- and after-sales service levels) and the local reliabilities of the facilities (component of risk management) and the relationships among the optimal service levels, price and warranty. Summary interpretation for the problem investigated in Chapter 4 is as follows:

Table 4-1. Summary interpretation for the problem investigated in Chapter 4.

Elements	What?
Components	Reliability
Connectors	Forward and after-sales supply chains and repair sections
Form	**How?**
Component importance	Reliability: 1
Properties	Local reliabilities
Relationship	Profit optimization in pre- and after-sales markets and repair sections
Rationale	**Why?**
Motivation	Variation management
Assumptions	No disruption There is enough information to quantify variations There is enough information to quantify failure time of products
Constraints	Order amplification in echelons due to variations Market demand depends on service levels, pre-sales market price, and after-sales market warranty
Interpretation	Relationship between the chains' service levels in pre- and after-sales markets and the local reliabilities of its facilities Relationship between optimal service levels, price and warranty

4.2 Literature of After-sales Operations

After-sales and warranty services have an extensive literature. Reviews by Murthy and Djamaludin (2002) and Wang et al. (2015) provide more details. Some of the main streams of research in this field are:

I) Marketing aspect of the warranty: In these papers, warranty is treated as a competitive factor and the authors offer methods for selecting the best warranty strategies by analyzing the tradeoff among the cost and income along with other marketing factors such as price, service level, etc. (Zhou et al. 2009; Chu and Chintagunta 2009; Majid et al. 2012; Su and Shen 2012; Jiang and Zhang 2011; Esmaeili et al. 2014; Aggrawal et al. 2014; Wei et al. 2015; Huang et al. 2015; Li et al. 2012). For example, Zhou et al. (2009) propose a mathematical model to determine price and warranty policy dynamically for a repairable product with a fixed life cycle. First, they study the purchase pattern of customers with a fixed warranty length and a linearly decreasing price function. Then, they use this pattern to determine optimal price and warranty strategies. Wei et al. (2015) develop five models to formulate competition between two manufacturers producing complementary products and a common retailer selling their products to end customers. These models determine the optimal strategies for price and warranty period for the products in different cooperation/noncooperation strategies and bargain powers. Esmaeili et al. (2014) present a three-level warranty among a manufacturer, an agent and a customer by using a game theory approach. The customer faces several warranty options with the sales volume being sensitive to the price of each option. Their model determines optimal sales price, warranty price, warranty period for the manufacturer and the best repair cost for the agent. Aggrawal et al. (2014) use two-dimensional innovation diffusion models to demonstrate product sales cycles and develop an approach to determine optimal price and warranty length for a product. Huang et al. (2015) perform cost analysis to determine an appropriate two-dimensional warranty policy, considering both time and usage, for a repairable product. They consider two customer groups: (1) a customer group whose warranty ends because the warranty time has reached its limit and (2) a customer group whose warranty ends because the warranty usage has reached its limit.

The papers in this research stream treat warranty as a marketing variable in their models which should be optimized by analyzing cost and income tradeoffs in retail outlets in monopoly cases or be equalized in the competition of sellers and buyers in duopoly cases. The focus of these papers is only on downstream marketing activities in after-sales SCs and ignores upstream manufacturing activities required to fulfill customers' claims inside the warranty period. In this chapter, we develop an integrated model considering both upstream manufacturing operations and downstream marketing operations in after-sales SCs.

II) Marketing and engineering aspects of the warranty: By considering that engineering factors such as product reliability and quality have an important role in the warranty service cost, the authors of these papers simultaneously analyze the marketing and engineering aspects of the warranty (Murthy 1990; Balachandran and Radhakrishnan 2005; Kamrad et al. 2005; Öner et al. 2010; Lin and Shue 2005; Huang et al. 2007). For examples, Murthy (1990) proposes a model to determine price, warranty length, and reliability jointly for a new product to maximize the total profit. Öner et al. (2010) consider a company producing and selling a system to its customers with a service contract. To fulfill the after-sales commitment of the company, they develop a model that determines spare parts inventory levels and best reliabilities for the system's critical components. Huang et al. (2007) determine product reliability, retail price, and warranty concurrently for a repairable product. They assume that the product demand is a positively correlated function of its warranty length and a negatively correlated function of the retail price. They consider free replacement and repair warranty for the product.

The papers of this group focus on the product design decisions and analyze their impacts on the after-sales costs in companies. They ignore the fact that to realize these design and marketing decisions, two highly convoluted forward and after-sales SCs are working in the companies. To provide an integrated framework, integrating manufacturing operations in SCs with design and marketing operations is necessary. In this chapter, we fill this gap by incorporating forward and after-sales SCs.

III) Warranty cost: In these papers, authors focus on minimizing the warranty cost by scheduling appropriate maintenance (replace and repair) activities (Chen and Chien 2007; Chukova et al. 2007; Williams 2007; Wu and Li 2007; Rao 2011; Vahdani et al. 2011; Su and Shen 2012; Wang 2008; Wang 2012; Tsoukalas and Agrafiotis 2013; Vahdani et al. 2013; Shahanaghi et al. 2013; Park et al. 2013; Anastasiadis et al. 2013; Liu et al. 2013). Rao (2011), for example, proposes a decision support model for repair and replacement decisions for a repairable product sold under a failure free warranty so that total warranty cost is minimized. He assumes that the product lifecycle follows a phase type distribution in which phases represent the product condition. In the automobile industry, Anastasiadis et al. (2013) test whether there is a relationship between the variability of the driving pattern of a vehicle and the frequency and size of warranty claims made for it. Their results show that there is a positive relationship between the variability of the driving pattern and the expected warranty cost per vehicle. Liu et al. (2013) use a Markov model with continuous time to measure vulnerability of multiple components in a product. Then they calculate the warranty claim probability for the product and use it to estimate warranty costs in varied warranty periods. Su and Shen (2012) compare two extended warranty policies from the manufacturer's perspective: (1) one-dimensional extended warranty and (2) two-dimensional non-renewing extended warranty. To calculate the warranty cost for these strategies, three repair options are considered: (1) minimal repair, (2) imperfect repair combined with minimal repair and (3) complete repair combined with minimal repair. The criterion used to select optional warranty policy and repair option is expected profit. Examples from the automobile industry are used as case problems. Wang (2012) develops a stochastic optimization model that simultaneously determines spare parts ordering intervals, spare parts ordering quantities and the preventive maintenance inspection interval to minimize the total cost. He employs an enumeration algorithm to find the joint optimal solutions. Vahdani et al. (2013) determine the optimal replacement-repair policy for a special group of discretely degrading products by renewing free warranties. The policy is determined to minimize the manufacturer's expected warranty servicing cost per item sold.

The papers of this group consider after-sales services such as warranty as a sort of cost imposing commitments. Therefore, they focus only on minimizing their costs by selecting appropriate replacement-repair policies. They ignore positive effects of after-sales services on the profitability of forward SCs in pre-markets. This problem is there in all papers investigating forward and after-sales SCs separately. In this chapter, we fill this gap of the literature by concurrently considering forward and after-sales SCs. Therefore, both positive impacts of after-sales services on profitability of companies through their forward SCs and their imposing costs through after-sales SCs are considered in our problem.

IV) Repair process as a part of the after-sales services: The emphasis of this group of papers is on the repair process of a system's key parts to improve its availability (Sleptchenko et al. 2002, 2003; Sahba and Balcıog 2011; Barabadi et al. 2014; Avsar and Zijm 2000). As examples, Sleptchenko et al. (2003) investigate a multi-echelon and multi-indenture part supply process for repairable items. In this process, failed parts are received by a repair shop (in the first echelon). These parts are immediately sent to a central repair facility (in the second echelon) for maintenance and are replaced by repaired ones from the shop's stock if they are available; otherwise, the desired part is backordered. The order is filled whenever an item is repaired and sent back to the shop from the central repair facility. This problem is formulated as a multi-class and multi-server queuing system. The goal is to maximize the system's availability by considering the trade-off between the repair capacity and inventories of spare parts. Barabadi et al. (2014) develop a model to determine the number of spare parts in the repair process of an item, drill bits in the Jajarm Bauxite Mine, by considering the influence of different factors such as operational environment, maintenance policy and operator skill. Sahba and Balcıog (2011) consider a system of fleets of machines at different locations. The machines are subject to failure due to a critical repairable component. They study whether these fleets should be served by smaller onsite repair shops dedicated to them or by a centralized repair shop serving all fleets. They show that when transportation costs are reasonable, repair shop pooling is a better alternative.

The papers of this group consider the repair process of failed components as a separate system. They overlook how providing an appropriate after-sales service level by this system affects the attractiveness of the original products/systems in pre-markets and stimulates demand for forward SCs. To consider and analyze interactions between pre- and after-sales markets' operations, we need to have an integrated model including both (i) forward SC dealing with pre-markets' operations and (ii) after-sales SC dealing with producing new spare parts and repairing returned parts to fulfill after-sales commitments. In this chapter, we provide such an integrated model considering interactions between highly convoluted forward and after-sales SCs. In Table 4-1, we show a list of carefully selected papers strongly related to the scope of this article. In this table, we clearly present what new features are considered in this chapter in comparison with the related papers.

As seen from the preceding literature review, the lack of a holistic and SC view in the after-sales research streams is clear. This has already been discovered by many academic and industrial researchers. For example, the Aberdeen Research Group highlights that the key challenges faced by managers in the product-service providing companies are: (i) lack of systematic flow management approaches, and (ii) ignoring the SC relationships among the different sections of the companies leading to inaccurate demand predictions and inefficient production, storage and transportation plans (Boone et al. 2008; McAvoy 2008; Cohen et al. 2006; Wang 2008). Also, a survey has been done by the senior service parts managers of 18 industries and the results show that the top challenge in systems is a *"lack of holistic perspective and system integration among SC partners"* (Boone et al. 2008; Bacchetti and Saccani 2012). This gap in the literature and the needs of manufacturers are filled in this chapter

Table 4-2. New features of the model presented in the chapter.

Papers	Marketing Decisions		Engineering Decisions (Product or System reliability)	After-sales SC Operations					Variation	
				Maintenance process		Repair Process of failed parts		Interaction with forward SC operations		
	Price	Warranty		Repair or replace	Spare parts inventory decisions	Repair or capacity	Spare parts inventory decisions		Demand	Supply
Aggrawal et al. (2014)	✓	✓							✓	
Esmaeili et al. (2014)	✓	✓							✓	
Huang et al. (2015)		✓							✓	
Jung et al. (2015)				✓					✓	
Su and Shen (2012)		✓		✓					✓	
Wei et al. (2015)	✓	✓							✓	
Oner et al. (2010)			✓		✓				✓	
Wang (2012)				✓	✓				✓	
Huang et al. (2007)	✓	✓	✓						✓	

Table 4-2 contd. ...

...Table 4-2 contd.

Papers	Marketing Decisions		Engineering Decisions (Product or System reliability)	After-sales SC Operations					Variation	
				Maintenance process		Repair Process of failed parts		Interaction with forward SC operations		
	Price	Warranty		Repair or replace	Spare parts inventory decisions	Repair or capacity	Spare parts inventory decisions		Demand	Supply
Vahdani et al. (2013)										
Barabadi et al. (2014)					✓				✓	
Sahba and Balcioglu (2011)						✓	✓		✓	
Sleptchenko et al. (2003)						✓	✓		✓	
Chien and Chen (2008)					✓				✓	
Huang and Yen (2009)		✓							✓	
Rao (2011)				✓					✓	
This chapter	✓	✓		✓	✓	✓	✓	✓	✓	✓

by concurrently planning flow in the forward and after-sales SCs while considering their critical interactions. This concurrent consideration improves the accuracy of demand predictions in the pre- and after-sales markets and the efficiency of the production, storage and transportation plans in the presence of different sources of variation.

In this chapter, we consider a company including both forward and after-sales SCs which respectively services pre- and after-sales markets. The product is produced in facilities in the different echelons of the forward SC and supplied to the pre-market under a retail price and a failure free warranty. Defective products returned inside the warranty period, are fixed by the company free of (Rao 2011) charge. The spare parts required are provided by the after-sales SC. Several sources of variation are considered:

i) Demand-side variations include variations in the prediction of product demand in the pre-market and the prediction of demand for spare parts in the after-sales market and

ii) Supply-side variations include variations in the qualified output of imperfect production facilities.

Demand-side variations have been extensively investigated in the literature (You and Grossmann 2008; Schütz et al. 2009; Pan and Nagi 2010; Park et al. 2010; Cardona-Valdés et al. 2011; Hsu and Li 2011; Rao 2011; Wang 2012; Su and Shen 2012; Lieckens et al. 2013; Vahdani et al. 2013; Park et al. 2013; Baghalian et al. 2013; Barabadi et al. 2014; Rezapour et al. 2015; Mohammaddust et al. 2015; Fattahi et al. 2015; Keyvanshokooh et al. 2016). These papers focus only on downstream variations in the product demand in pre-markets and spare parts demands in after-sales markets (see "*Variation*" column in Table 4-1). They assume that performance of facilities in SCs is perfect and all production units in their production batches are sound and usable. This assumption is not consistent with reality. Real production systems always have a stochastic number of nonconforming and defective units in their production batches. The papers of this group ignore variations in qualified product quantity of SCs' facilities, called supply-side variations. The supply-side variations are often ignored in the literature (Rezapour et al. 2015). Further, when the rate of production increases, the rate of non-conforming output in the production facilities also increases (Sana 2010; Sarkar and Saren 2016). Higher production rates mean higher machinery and labor failure possibilities. By considering both demand- and supply-side variations, we not only fill this gap in the literature but also improve the accuracy of the service level estimates in the pre- and after-sales markets.

4.3 Our Contribution to the Literature of After-Sales Supply Chains for Repairable Products

In this chapter, we propose an integrated mathematical framework for coordinating all facilities involved in the complicated production systems of manufacturing companies producing repairable products and providing product—warranty packages for their customers. The contribution of this work lies in three domains:

- *Considering SC integration between facilities involved in after-sales operations:* In this work, we consider marketing impacts of after-sales services, such as warranty, in the capturable demand of retailers and we also incorporate the manufacturing operations in production facilities, such as suppliers and their repair sections, to produce new spare parts and repair returned parts, to fulfill the after-sales commitment. In this chapter, we consider all the involved facilities as an after-sales SC.

- *Concurrent flow planning in forward and after-sales SCs of repairable products:* Pre- and after-sales markets' operations are usually investigated separately in the literature. In this chapter, we show that there are several important interactions between forward and after-sales SCs of repairable products. Considering these interactions through concurrent flow planning, not only improves demand predictions in pre- and after-sales markets but also induces more efficient production and transportation planning in both SCs.

- *Considering both demand- and supply-side variations:* To be more consistent with reality, we assume that performance of production systems in the manufacturing facilities of the SCs is imperfect. Considering that imperfect facilities always have a stochastic number of nonconforming and defective units in their production batches, we show that the quantity of qualified flow depreciates when moving from upstream to downstream in SCs with imperfect facilities. To preserve an appropriate service level in markets, we suggest that qualified flow depreciation should be neutralized by amplifying orders while moving from downstream to upstream.

The rest of the chapter is organized as follows: a detailed problem description is presented in Section 4.4. Flow planning in the facilities of the forward and after-sales SCs in the presence of demand- and supply-side variations is modeled in Sections 4.5.1 and 4.5.2 respectively. Finally, these flow planning equations are used to develop a mathematical model to determine the best price, warranty, and pre- and after-sales service levels.

In Section 4.6 we present a solution approach for solving the mathematical model developed in the previous section. Computational results for an example from the automotive industry are presented and analyzed in Section 4.7. The chapter is concluded in Section 4.8.

4.4 Problem Description: Operations and Variations in the Forward and After-sales Supply Chains of Repairable Products

In this problem, we consider a company producing and supplying a product to a target market through its forward SC. This product is sold to the customer under a retail price and a warranty period. This product includes several key components which are produced by suppliers in the first echelon. These components are transported to a manufacturer in the second echelon. After assembly, final products are supplied to the market through a retailer. The flow of components and final products through the forward SC are displayed in Figure 4-1 for a sample product with two key components.

The products of this company are sold under a warranty and all the defective products returned within the warranty period must be fixed free of charge. The flow of returned defective products is represented by orange lines in Figure 4-2. Spare parts required to fix these returned products are provided through the after-sales SC. The after-sales SC has repair sections inside the suppliers to repair failed components of the returned products. As seen in Figure 4-2, defective components are sent by the retailer to the repair sections for repair. Then, the repaired components are returned and stored by the retailer for use in repairing the next defective product.

If there is no repaired component with the retailer, new components provided and stored by the suppliers with the retailer are used for the repairs. The storage of new components by the retailer preserves an appropriate service level for the after-sales SC. The flow of the repaired and new components through the after-sales SC are displayed in Figure 4-2 by gray and orange lines respectively.

The required products and new components needed to fulfill the product demand and inside-warranty repair requests for each sales period are produced by the forward and after-sales SCs respectively and stored with the retailer before its beginning. Before the beginning of each sales period, the retailer orders the required products and components from the manufacturer and suppliers respectively. Based on the retailer's order and the performance of its production system, the manufacturer orders the required components from the suppliers. This means that suppliers receive two orders: one order from the manufacturer and another order

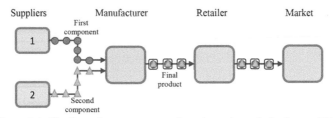

Figure 4-1. The flow of components and products through the forward SC. (for a product with two key components)

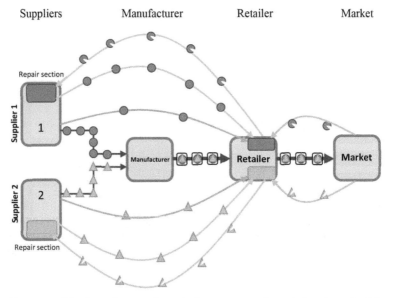

Figure 4-2. The flow of new and repaired components through the after-sales SC. (for a product with two key components)

from the retailer. Then, based on the capabilities of their production systems, the suppliers estimate and order the required material.

As discussed in Section 4.1, we consider two types of variation in this problem: (i) demand-side variations, and (ii) supply-side variations. The demand-side represents the variation in the prediction of product demand in the pre-market and the prediction of demand for spare parts in the after-sales. Supply-side variations are related to imperfect production systems in the SCs' production facilities (e.g., the suppliers and the manufacturer). Production in the production facilities is always accompanied by a stochastic percentage of non-conforming output which depends on the state of the machinery and labor and varies from time to time. The variations in the qualified output of the facilities accumulate and become larger and larger by moving the flow from the upstream to

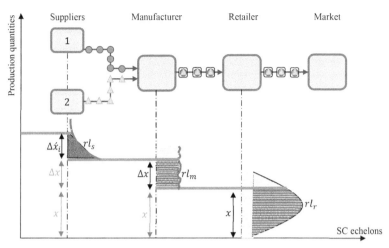

Figure 4-3. Flow depreciation in the forward SC.

the downstream of the chains. In this chapter, we term this "variation propagation". Due to variation propagation, the quantity of the qualified flow depreciates by moving from the upstream to the downstream which leads to a stochastic qualified supply quantity in the last echelon (see Figure 4-3). The capability of the forward and after-sales SCs in balancing the stochastic supply and demand quantities in the pre- and after-sales markets is the pre- and after-sales service levels respectively. These service levels represent the capability of the chains to fulfill demand. The product demand in the pre-market is an increasing function of the warranty length and service levels and a decreasing function of the retail price.

In this complex production system, which includes two interactive SCs with multiple stochastic facilities and services pre- and after-sales markets with stochastic demand, we want to determine the best marketing strategies (price, warranty and service levels) for the company and the best reliable flow dynamics through its SCs preserving the marketing strategies in the most profitable way. The assumptions in the problem are summarized in Appendix 4.A.

4.5 Mathematical Model for Concurrent Flow Planning in the Forward and After-sales Supply Chains of Repairable Products

The production system in the problem has two SCs with different missions: (i) the forward SC servicing the pre-market and (ii) the after-sales SC fulfilling the after-sales commitments. Operations in the forward and after-sales SCs are analyzed separately in Section 4.5.1 and 4.5.2 respectively.

Finally, with the help of the equations derived in these two sections, we develop a mathematical model in Section 4.5.3 for concurrent reliable flow planning through the networks of these SCs. The nomenclature of the terms used in this chapter is in Appendix 4.B.

4.5.1 Mathematical Model for Flow Planning in the Forward Supply Chain

In this section, the focus is on producing and supplying products through the forward SC. The forward SC, as shown in Figure 4-1, includes a retailer, a manufacturer and suppliers. Each of these facilities faces variation. The retailer faces variation in product demand in the pre-market. The manufacturer always has a stochastic percentage of defective assemblies in its production system. In the suppliers, after setting up the equipment, the production process starts in an in-control state. But after a stochastic time, the production process shifts to an out-of-control state in which a given percent of output is non-conforming. Due to the imperfect performance of the facilities along the SC, the quantity of the qualified output (variation in the qualified output) decreases (accumulates and increases) by moving the flow from the upstream to the downstream. In this section, we propose a method to neutralize the negative effects of this flow depreciation (variation propagation) though the chain. Based on this method, the order quantities are amplified by moving from the downstream to the upstream of the chain (Figure 4-3).

To model the flow depreciation, we assume rl_r, rl_m, and rl_s represent the local reliabilities of the retailer, manufacturer and suppliers respectively. The market's actual demand in each sales period is stochastic with a given density function. Before the beginning of each period, the retailer orders the required products, x, from the manufacturer based on its local reliability, rl_r. This amount of product stock ensures that the entire product demand will be fulfilled by the retailer with rl_r probability. Therefore, the manufacturer receives an order of x products from the retailer. To compensate for the defective assemblies in its production system, the manufacturer must plan to manufacture extra products, Δx. The size of Δx depends on the local reliability of the manufacturer, rl_m (see Figure 4-3). By manufacturing $x + \Delta x$ products, the manufacturer must be sure with rl_m probability that it can fulfill the whole order of the retailer. Thus, the manufacturer orders $x + \Delta x$ components from each supplier. Supplier i ($i = 1,2,\ldots, N$) receives an order of $x + \Delta x$ Component i units from the manufacturer. To compensate for the non-conforming output of its production system, Supplier i plans to produce extra components, $\Delta \dot{x}_i$. The local reliability of the supplier, rl_s, governs the amount of $\Delta \dot{x}_i$ (see Figure 4-3). By $\Delta \dot{x}_i$ extra production, Supplier i will be sure with rl_s probability that it can fulfill the entire order of the manufacturer. As seen above, we neutralize the negative effect of the flow depreciation by amplifying the orders transferred between the facilities form the downstream to the upstream.

This is a complicated problem. To reduce its complexity and make it manageable, we use some simplifying assumptions. We assume that each facility either completely fulfills the order of its downstream facility and sends a complete package equal to its order, or misses the order and sends nothing. Flow transactions less than orders is not possible among facilities. This assumption is widely used in the yield-uncertainty literature and is called the Bernoulli supply process (Parlar et al. 1995; Tomlin and Wang 2005; Dada et al. 2003; Swaminathan and Shanthikumar 1999). In the Bernoulli supply processes, the order fulfillment rate of a resource is 1 with probability of θ and is 0 with probability of $1 - \theta$. θ is referred as the reliability of the resource. If flow transactions less than orders are permitted among facilities, service levels in the markets become higher than what is computed in the chapter. This means we consider the worst-case service levels in the chapter.

In this case, the manufacturer will be sure that with rl_s^N probability, it will receive all the ordered components. With Δx extra production, the manufacturer will be sure with rl_m probability that it can fulfill the whole order of the retailer. Product stock x ensures that the retailer will be able to fulfill the entire product demand with rl_r probability. Therefore, the forward SC will be able to fulfill the pre-market's demand with $sl_p = rl_s^N \cdot rl_m \cdot rl_r$ probability, which is its service level, sl_p. The forward SC's service level, sl_p, determines the percent of the pre-market's demand that is fulfilled immediately by the retailer's on-hand inventory. The forward SC's service level depends on the reliability of its included facilities.

We analyze the relationship between rl_r, rl_m, and rl_s (local reliabilities) and x, Δx, and $\Delta \dot{x}_i$ (order and production quantities) in the retailer, manufacturer, and suppliers in the following sections.

The relationship between the order quantity of the retailer and its local reliability

In this section, we analyze the retailer's performance in the forward SC. In each sales period, the product demand in the pre-market is $\hat{D}(p, sl_p, sl_a, w) = D(p, sl_p, sl_a, w) \times \varepsilon$. $D(p, sl_p, sl_a, w)$ is a deterministic decreasing function of the price (p) and an increasing function of the pre-market service level (sl_p), the after-sales service level (sl_a) and the warranty length (w). ε is a random variable with a given cumulative distribution function, $G(\varepsilon)$, which is independent of p, sl_p, sl_a, and w. Without loss of generality, we assume that $E(\varepsilon) = 1$ which implies $E[\hat{D}(p, sl_p, sl_a, w)] = D(p, sl_p, sl_a, w)$. After the start of each sales period and based on its local reliability, the retailer selects its product stock quantity represented by x. Higher x means higher reliability in the retailer to fulfill the entire demand and increases the probability of having extra inventory at the end of the period. Unit holding cost h^+ is incurred by the retailer for each extra inventory unit. Lower values for x increase the probability of lost sales at the end of the period. The unit shortage cost h^- is incurred by the retailer for each lost sales unit. To make an appropriate tradeoff between these two cost components, the retailer determines the stock quantity by solving the following:

$$MIN \ TC_r = h^+ . E \ [x - \widehat{D}(p, sl_{p'}, sl_{a'}, w)]^+ + h^- . E \ [\widehat{D}(p, sl_{p'}, sl_{a'}, w) - x]^+ \quad (4\text{-}1)$$

$$S.T. \ \ Pr[\widehat{D}(p, sl_{p'}, sl_{a'}, w) \le x] \ge rl_r \quad (4\text{-}2)$$

Objective function (1) is the sum of expected extra inventory cost and expected lost sales cost which should be minimized. Constraint (4-2) preserves the retailer's local reliability.

The product order quantity $x = D(p, sl_{p'}, sl_{a'}, w). \ G^{-1}(\dfrac{h^-}{h^- + h^+})$ minimizes the expected total cost of the retailer. To conserve the retailer's local reliability, we should have $x \ge D(p, sl_{p'}, sl_{a'}, w). \ G^{-1}(rl_r)$. Accordingly, the best product order quantity of the retailer from the manufacturer is:

$$x = D(p, sl_{p'}, sl_{a'}, w). \ G^{-1}\left(Max\left\{rl_{r'}, \dfrac{h^-}{h^- + h^+}\right\}\right) \quad (4\text{-}3)$$

Substituting Eq. (4-3) into (4-1) leads to the following least cost to the retailer:

$$TC_r = \left(h^+ . \ E\left[G^{-1}\left(Max\left\{rl_{r'}, \dfrac{h^-}{h^- + h^+}\right\}\right) - \varepsilon\right]^+ + h^- . \right.$$

$$\left. E\left[\varepsilon - G^{-1}\left(Max\left\{rl_{r'}, \dfrac{h^-}{h^- + h^+}\right\}\right)\right]^+\right). \ D(p, sl_{p'}, sl_{a'}, w) \quad (4\text{-}4)$$

In the above equation, the first term, $h^+ . \ E\left[G^{-1}\left(Max\left\{rl_{r'}, \dfrac{h^-}{h^- + h^+}\right\}\right) - \varepsilon\right]^+ + h^- . \ E\left[\varepsilon - G^{-1}\left(Max\left\{rl_{r'}, \dfrac{h^-}{h^- + h^+}\right\}\right)\right]^+$, is the average unit handling cost of the product in the retailer. Equation (4-3) represents the relationship between the retailer's local reliability, rl_r, and its product order quantity, x. By ordering x product units from the manufacturer, the retailer is able to fulfill the realized product demand with rl_r probability (see the retailer in Figure 4-3). In the next section, we describe how the order of the retailer is amplified in the manufacturer.

The relationship between the production quantity of the manufacturer and its local reliability

The manufacturer receives an order of x product units from the retailer. But the manufacturer knows that its production system is always accompanied with a stochastic percentage of defective assembly. To compensate for the defective assemblies, the manufacturer must plan to produce some extra products, Δx, and consequently order some extra components from the suppliers. We assume the rate of defective assembly in the manufacturer is in the range $[0,\beta]$ with a given cumulative distribution function, $G'(.)$. Also without loss of generality, we assume that to produce a product unit, a unit of each component is required.

Producing x product units by the manufacturer leads to, at the most $a.x$ ($a \in [0,\beta]$) defective assemblies with $G'(a)$ probability. Therefore, $\Delta x = \acute{G}^{-1}(rl_m)$. x extra production enables the manufacturer to fulfill the whole order of the retailer with rl_m probability. Assembling $\acute{G}^{-1}(rl_m)$. $x + x$ product units preserves rl_m local reliability for the manufacture (see the manufacturer in Figure 4-3).

Equation (4-5) represents the relationship between the local reliability of the manufacturer and its production quantity.

$$\Delta x + x = [\acute{G}^{-1}(rl_m) + 1].\, x \tag{4-5}$$

For producing $\Delta x + x$ product units, the manufacturer orders $\Delta x + x$ component units from each supplier. In the next section, we describe how the orders of the manufacturer are amplified in the suppliers.

The relationship between the production quantity of the suppliers and their local reliabilities

Each supplier receives an order of $\Delta x + x$ component units from the manufacturer. But the production system of the suppliers is not perfect. According to Rosenblatt and Lee (1986) and Lee and Rosenblatt (1987), we assume the production run of each supplier starts in an in-control state after setting up its equipment. However, they deteriorate and shift to an out-of-control state after a stochastic time following exponential distribution with $1/\mu_i$ ($i = 1, 2, ..., N$) mean. However, in-control production systems only produce conforming components, γ_i ($i = 1, 2, ..., N$) percentage of the components produced in the out-of-control state is nonconforming. Once the production system shifts to an out-of-control state, it stays in that state until the end of the production period, because Interruption of machines to return them into in-control state is prohibitively expensive.

Supplier i ($i = 1, 2, ..., N$) receives an order of $\Delta x + x$ component units from the manufacturer. To compensate for the nonconforming components of its production system, Supplier i plans to produce $\Delta \acute{x}_i + \Delta x + x$

units of Component i. $\Delta \dot{x}_i + \Delta x + x$ production units in Supplier i should preserve with rl_s probability that this supplier will have $\Delta x + x$ sound output to fulfill the order of the manufacturer. Thus, we have

$$rl_s = \text{Pr} \left[sound\ component\ units\ produced\ in\ \frac{\Delta \dot{x}_i + \Delta x + x}{PR_{1i}}\ time\ unit \geq \Delta x + x \right]$$

$$= \text{Pr} \left[PR_{1i} \cdot t + (1 - \gamma_i) \cdot PR_{1i} \cdot \left(\frac{\Delta \dot{x}_i + \Delta x + x}{PR_{1i}} - t \right) \geq \Delta x + x \right]$$

$$= \text{Pr} \left[t \geq \left(\frac{\Delta x + x}{PR_{1i}} \right) - \left(\frac{1 - \gamma_i}{\gamma_i \cdot PR_{1i}} \right) \cdot (\Delta \dot{x}_i) \right]$$

$$= EXP \left[-\mu_i \cdot \left(\left(\frac{\Delta x + x}{PR_{1i}} \right) - \left(\frac{1 - \gamma_i}{\gamma_i \cdot PR_{1i}} \right) \cdot (\Delta \dot{x}_i) \right) \right] \tag{4-6}$$

where PR_{1i} is the production rate in Supplier i ($i = 1, 2, \ldots, N$). Based on Eq. (4-6), to preserve rl_s local reliability, Supplier i should plan to produce

$$\Delta \dot{x}_i = \frac{\gamma_i}{1 - \gamma_i} \left[\frac{PR_{1i}}{\mu_i}\ \ln(rl_s) + (\Delta x + x) \right] \tag{4-7}$$

extra components in its production system (see the suppliers in Figure 4-3). We assume that extra product and component units produced in each period in the manufacturer and the suppliers cannot be kept to be used in the next period. The assumption of keeping no stock at facilities holds at times when there is no storage capability in facilities because of economic or physical reasons (Perlman et al. 2001).

$\Delta \dot{x}_i$ ($i = 1, 2, \ldots, N$) extra production ensures that Supplier i will be able to fulfill the order of the manufacturer with rl_s probability. In this case, the manufacturer will be sure with rl_s^N probability that it will receive all the component orders issued to the suppliers. With Δx extra product assembly, the manufacturer will be sure with rl_m probability that it can fulfill the whole order of the retailer. By ordering x product units, the retailer will be able to fulfill the whole product demand of the pre-market with rl_r probability. Therefore, (rl_r, rl_m, rl_s) the local reliability combination in the retailer, manufacturer and suppliers provides $sl_p = rl_r \cdot rl_m \cdot rl_s^N$ service level for the forward SC in the pre-market. The equation, $sl_p = rl_r \cdot rl_m \cdot rl_s^N$, is used to determine the relationship between the service level of the forward SC and the local reliabilities of its stochastic facilities. Equations (4-3), (4-5), and (4-7) indicate the way orders should be amplified from the downstream to the upstream of the forward SC to neutralize the negative effect of flow depreciation throughout its network. Similar equations are developed for the after-sales SC in Section 4.5.2.

4.5.2 *Mathematical Model for Flow Planning in the After-Sales Supply Chain*

Since failure free warranty is provided, the company must also provide the required spare parts to repair defective products returned within the warranty period. These parts are produced and provided through the after-sales SC. The prerequisite for production planning in the after-sales SC is estimating the after-sales demands of the spare parts. First, we describe the failure processes to estimate after-sales demand for the product and its components. Second, we model the performance of the repair sections in the suppliers to compute the percentage of the after-sales demands that can be fulfilled by repaired components. Then we determine how many new components should be ordered by the retailer from the suppliers to preserve a given after-sales service level. Finally, we show how the orders of the retailer should be amplified in the suppliers.

After-sales demand estimation

Demand of each component in the after-sales depends on: (i) the total number of products supplied through the forward SC to the pre-market (this constitutes the potential demand for each component in the after-sales market) and (ii) the reliability index of that component, τ_i ($i = 1, 2, ..., N$).

We assume that the performance of the components is independent and the failure time of each Component i ($i = 1, 2, ..., N$) is a random variable with an F_i cumulative distribution function. F_i is a function of the component's reliability index, τ_i. Lower τ_i value implies higher reliability and vice versa. When a product with a defective Component i is returned within the warranty period, its defective part is removed and immediately substituted with another repaired or new component if the inventory level of Component i in the retailer is positive. Otherwise, the customer must wait until a repaired component is sent to the retailer from the repair section. The removed defective Component i is sent to the repair section of Supplier i for repair. Also, it is assumed the probability of failure of the component does not change after repair.

We define $F_i^{(m)}$ as the cumulative distribution function of total time up to the mth failure in Component i. $Num_i(w)$ is a random variable representing the number of failures inside the warranty interval, $[0,w]$. Based on Nguyen and Murthy (1984), we have:

$$\Pr\{Num_i(w) = m\} = F_i^{(m)}(w, \tau_i) - F_i^{(m+1)}(w, \tau_i) \qquad (\forall i = 1, 2,..., N) \qquad (4\text{-}8)$$

As seen in Eq. (4-8), the average number of failures, $E_i(w)$, for a unit of Component i within the warranty time is:

$$E_i(w) = \sum_{j=1}^{+\infty} F_i^{(j)}(w, \tau_i) \qquad (\forall i = 1, 2,..., N) \qquad (4\text{-}9)$$

In each sales period, on an average, $x. sl_p$ product units are available with the retailer to supply to the market through the forward SC. Thus, the highest expected number of products which can be sold to customers and may be returned as defective is equal to $x. sl_p$. Therefore, the highest expected number of Component i failures for each sales period within the warranty period, λ_i, is (for more details refer to Appendix 4.C):

$$\lambda_i = x. sl_p. E_i(w) \qquad\qquad (\forall i = 1, 2,..., N) \qquad (4\text{-}10)$$

We use this highest number of failures to compute service level in the after-sales SC, sl_a. In this case, the after-sales SC will be able to preserve sl_a service level in the worst case with the highest failure rate. In the other periods with lower sales quantity, $D < x$, after-sales service level will be higher than sl_a. Therefore, we are very conservative by assuring that the after-sales service level felt by customers is never less than sl_a. Assuming the total cost for repairing a unit of Component i (this is the sum of the unit transportation cost from the retailer to Supplier i (cr_i^{rs}), the unit service cost in Supplier i (cr_i^s) and the unit transportation cost from Supplier i to the retailer (cr_i^{sr})) is $cr_i (\forall i = 1, 2,..., N)$, the average repair cost for a unit of product, cr, is:

$$cr = \sum_{i=1}^{N} \sum_{n=1}^{\infty} n. cr_i. \Pr\{Num_i(w) = n\} = \sum_{i=1}^{N} \sum_{n=1}^{\infty} n. cr_i. [F_i^{(n)}(w, \tau_i) - F_i^{(n+1)}(w, \tau_i)]$$
$$(4\text{-}11)$$

The repair process of the defective components

Defective components of the returned products are sent to the repair sections of their corresponding suppliers for repair. The repair process of each component is treated as a two-echelon system with one server center (the repair section) and one user (the retailer). When a defective product is returned to the retailer, fault diagnosis is preformed first to discover the source of the problem. Assume that the problem is related to Component i ($i = 1, 2,..., N$). Then the retailer sends the defective component to the repair section of Supplier i. When the failed component enters the repair section, if there is no queue, it immediately receives the repair service. Otherwise, it waits in a queue. The repair time, t_i, is stochastic with a given distribution function.

When the repair process is completed, the repaired component is sent back to the retailer. There is storage capacity only with the retailer. Also, the retailer has a safety stock, s_i ($i = 1, 2,..., N$), this includes new components manufactured and stocked by the supplier before the beginning of each sales period. This safety stock preserves local reliability rl_r for the retailer in the after-sales services. In Figure 4-4, we represent the queuing system in the repair section of Component i ($i = 1, 2,..., N$).

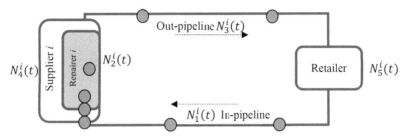

Figure 4-4. Queuing system in the repair section of Component i.

The inventory policy of the components in the retailer is $(S, S-1)$. This means whenever a failed component is found in a returned product, the retailer sends it to the supplier's repair section and supplies a repaired one from the repair section. $N_k^i(t)$ is a random variable that represents the number of components in state k ($k = 1, 2, 3, 4,$ and 5) at time t. These states are shown in Figure 4-4. $N_1^i(t)$, $N_2^i(t)$, and $N_3^i(t)$ represent respectively the number of components in the in-pipeline transferring the defective components from the retailer to the repair section, the number of waiting components or components being serviced in the repair section and the number of repaired components in the out-pipeline being transferred from the repair section to the retailer. $N_4^i(t)$ and $N_5^i(t)$ are the inventory levels at the repair and retail section respectively.

Demands are fulfilled when the inventory levels are positive. Otherwise, they become outstanding orders. $B_0^i(t)$ and $B_1^i(t)$ represent the backorder levels in the repair and retail section respectively. Therefore, we have:

$$B_0^i(t) = Max\{-N_4^i(t), 0\} = Max\{N_1^i(t) + N_2^i(t), 0\} \qquad (4\text{-}12)$$

$$B_1^i(t) = Max\{-N_5^i(t), 0\} = Max\{N_3^i(t) + B_0^i(t) - s_i, 0\} \qquad (4\text{-}13)$$

In Eq. (4-12), term $N_1^i(t) + N_2^i(t)$ represents the total number of the components in the server and in-pipeline. For each of these components, the repair section has received an order from the retailer which has not been fulfilled yet. In Eq. (4-13), terms $N_3^i(t)$ and $B_0^i(t)$ represent the released but not fulfilled orders of the retailer which shows Component i's demand in the retail section and s_i represents the stock quantity in the retail section. Therefore, the retailer's backorder is the difference between these two terms. To show that we are dealing only with steady-state quantities of the above system, we remove the t argument henceforth. In this problem, the probability of having no backorders in the retail section, $Pr(N_3^i(t) + B_0^i(t) \leq s_i)$, is important because it represents the retailer's local reliability, rl_i, in the after-sales. To compute this probability, it is critical to find the distribution function of $N_3^i(t) + B_0^i(t)$. If we assume a mutual independence between the pipelines and the repair section's server, the above problem reduces to two convolutions: (i) obtaining the distribution of $B_0^i(t)$ at the repair section from the distribution of the components in the in-pipeline ($N_1^i(t)$) and the distribution of the components being repaired ($N_2^i(t)$) in the server and (ii) obtaining the distribution of inventory at the retailer ($N_5^i(t)$) from the repair section's backorder distribution ($B_0^i(t)$) which is derived from the first convolution and the distribution of the components in the out-pipeline ($N_3^i(t)$).

Diaz and Fu (1997) show that a negative binomial distribution approximates both convolutions with great accuracy. We use this approximation to simplify the calculations. Then the mean and variance of the outstanding orders in Repair Section i must be calculated to determine the parameters a_0^i and b_0^i of the negative binomial approximating the distribution function of B_0^i.

$$E[B_0^i] = \sum_{x=0}^{\infty} (x) . \frac{\Gamma(x + a_0^i)}{x!\,\Gamma(a_0^i)}\, b_0^{i\,a_0^i}(1 - b_0^i)^x \qquad (4\text{-}14)$$

where $a_0^i = \mu_0^i \Big/ \left[\left(\sigma^{2^i}_0 \Big/ \mu_0^i\right) - 1\right]$, $b_0^i = \mu_0^i \Big/ \sigma^{2^i}_0$, $\mu_0^i = E[N_1^i(t)] + E[N_2^i(t)]$, and $\sigma^{2^i}_0 =$

$Var[N_1^i(t)] + Var[N_2^i(t)]$.

In the same way, parameters a_1^i and b_1^i are computed to generate the negative binomial distribution function of B_1^i in the retailer. Then, the expected backorder and backorder probability in the retailer is:

$$E[B_1^i] = \sum_{x=s_i}^{\infty} (x - s_i) . \frac{\Gamma(x + a_1^i)}{x!\,\Gamma(a_1^i)}\, b_1^{i\,a_1^i}(1 - b_1^i)^x \qquad (4\text{-}15)$$

$$\Pr(N_3^i(t) + B_0^i(t) \geq s_i) = \sum_{x=s_i}^{\infty} \frac{\Gamma(x + a_1^i)}{x!\,\Gamma(a_1^i)}\, b_1^{i\,a_1^i}(1 - b_1^i)^x \qquad (4\text{-}16)$$

where $a_0^i = \mu_1^i \Big/ \left[\left(\sigma^{2^i}_1 \Big/ \mu_1^i\right) - 1\right]$, $b_1^i = \mu_1^i \Big/ \sigma^{2^i}_1$, $\mu_1^i = E[N_3^i(t)] + E[B_0^i(t)]$, and $\sigma^{2^i}_1 =$

$Var[N_3^i(t)] + Var[B_0^i(t)]$.

If we assume the $M/G/1$ queuing system for the repair process in the repair section in which $E[t_i^s]$ represents the sth moment of the service time, then we have:

$$E[N_2^i] = \rho_i + \frac{(\lambda_i)^2 . E[t_i^2]}{2.(1 - \rho_i)} \qquad\qquad \rho_i = \lambda_i . E[t_i] \qquad (4\text{-}17)$$

$$Var[N_2^i] = \frac{(\lambda_i)^3 \cdot E[t_i^3]}{3.(1-\rho_i)} + \frac{(\lambda_i)^4 \cdot (E[t_i^2])^2}{2.(1-\rho_i)^2} + \frac{(\lambda_i)^3 \cdot E[t_i^2] \cdot E[t]}{(1-\rho_i)} + \frac{(\lambda_i)^2 \cdot E[t_i^2] \cdot (3-2\rho_i)}{(1-\rho_i)} +$$

$$\rho_i - (E[N_2^i])^2 \tag{4-18}$$

Considering $M/G/1$ queuing system for the repair process requires the assumption that the failure time of Component i follows an exponential distribution. This means the failure mode of this component is Poisson. We also model the in-pipeline and the out-pipeline as $M/G/\infty$ queuing systems which is consistent with the assumption of independence of the numbers of components in the server and in the pipelines. Therefore, we have $E[N_1^i(t)] = Var[N_1^i(t)] = \lambda_i . O_i$ and $E[N_3^i(t)] = Var[N_3^i(t)] = \lambda_i . O_i$ (Mirasol 1963). In these equations, O_i represents the shipment time between the retailer and the repair section of Supplier i ($i = 1, 2, \ldots, N$). The main objective of the above calculations is to determine the distribution function of $N_3^i(t) + B_0^i(t)$. This negative binomial distribution is used to determine the relationship between the retailer's local reliability and its safety stocks. If we assume G_{NB}^i represents the negative binomial cumulative distribution function approximating the density of $N_3^i(t) + B_0^i(t)$, then we have:

$$Pr(N_3^i(t) + B_0^i(t) \leq s_i) = rl_r \tag{4-19}$$

$$s_i = G_{NB}^{i^{-1}}(rl_r) \tag{4-20}$$

This means that, in order to preserve the rl_r local reliability for the retailer in the after-sales SC in each sales period, the retailer should order s_i ($i = 1, 2, \ldots, N$) new Component i's from Supplier i before the beginning of that period. In the next section, we explain how this order of the retailer will be amplified in the suppliers.

Safety stock production in the suppliers

Each supplier not only receives the order of $\Delta x + x$ component units from the manufacturer to produce new products, but also the order of s_i component units from the retailer to fulfill a part of the after-sales demand that cannot be fulfilled by the repaired components. Therefore, each supplier should produce $s_i + \Delta x + x$ component units for the forward and after-sales SCs. Based on this, a new order, s_i, is issued by the retailer from the suppliers and we modify the extra production quantity of the suppliers (Eq. 4-7) proposed in Section 4.5.1 as follows:

$$\Delta \dot{x}_i = \frac{\gamma_i}{1-\gamma_i} \left[\frac{PR_{1i}}{\mu_i} \ln(rl_s) + (s_i + \Delta x + x) \right] \quad (i = 1, 2, 3, \ldots, N) \tag{4-21}$$

If a supplier does not fulfill the whole $s_i + \Delta x + x$ order, the unfulfilled part of this order is divided proportionally between the forward

$(\dfrac{\Delta x + x}{s_i + \Delta x + x})$ and after-sales SCs $(\dfrac{\Delta s_i}{s_i + \Delta x + x})$. Therefore, each supplier is able to fulfill the component order of the retailer with rl_s probability. The retailer by ordering s_i component units from the supplier is sure with rl_r probability that the order can fulfill the whole after-sales demand of Component i. In this case, the fulfillment rate of Component i's demand is rl_r, rl_s. Since the product includes N critical components, the after-sales SC's service level in fulfilling the after-sales demand of all components is $sl_a = (rl_r \cdot rl_s)^N$.

4.5.3 Mathematical Model for Concurrent Flow Planning

Theoretically, decisions in SCs are made in a centralized or decentralized way. In centralized SCs, all decisions are made at the corporate level by a responsible central authority. In decentralized SCs, the entities make their own decisions individually at a business unit level. In practice, SCs are not completely centralized or decentralized. Most commonly, the strategic decisions are made centrally while operational decisions are decentralized (Chang and Harrington 2000; Saharidis et al. 2009).

In our problem, the production system includes several facilities such as the suppliers, manufacturer, and retailer. They are separate entities working together through long term contracts. Therefore, each facility as a separate entity makes local decisions about its own production system, such as extra production, by considering only the local variation of its own system and their corresponding costs. However, a leadership team monitors the performance of the whole system and its performance in the market. This team dictates local reliabilities for the facilities to maximize the expected profit of the whole system. Therefore, decisions of the SCs are made as follows:

- Operational decisions in SCs are short term decisions that are usually made in a weekly or monthly basis such as production decisions in manufacturing facilities and ordering decisions in outlets. These decisions are made individually by facilities by considering their corresponding local variations and costs but they should satisfy the whole SCs' strategic goals (as shown in Sections 4.5.1 and 4.5.2, production decisions in the manufacturer and the suppliers and ordering decision in the retailer are made individually). However, these decisions are made in a way so as to satisfy the service level and its corresponding local reliabilities that are dictated by a leader team;
- Strategic decisions in SCs have a longer time horizon and determine their competitive advantages or goals in markets in the next couple of

years. These decisions are usually made corporately such as product quality, customer service level, warranty, etc. (as shown in this section, the SCs' service levels and their corresponding local reliabilities and the product's warranty strategy are made corporately by the leadership team).

In this section, we develop a mathematical model from the leadership team perspective to optimize local reliabilities. We use the equations derived in Sections 4.5.1 and 4.5.2 (Equations (4-3), (4-4), (4-5), (4-11), (4-20) and (4-21)), to concurrently determine the best flow through the network of forward and after-sales SCs in a way so as to maximize the total profit of the whole company. The model is as follows:

Max Π =

$$
\left[\left(p - h^+ \cdot E\left[G^{-1}\left(Max\left\{rl_s^N \cdot rl_m \cdot rl_r, \frac{h^-}{h^- + h^+}\right\}\right) - \varepsilon\right]^+\right.\right.
$$

$$
- h^- \cdot E\left[\varepsilon - G^{-1}\left(Max\left\{rl_s^N \cdot rl_m \cdot rl_r, \frac{h^-}{h^- + h^+}\right\}\right)\right]^+ - cr\right)
$$

$$
\times D(p, (rl_s^N \cdot rl_m \cdot rl_r), (rl_r \cdot rl_s)^N, w)\bigg]
$$

$$
- \left\{\left[\sum_{i=1}^{N}(ca_{1i} + ca_{2i}) \cdot (x + \Delta x + s_i + \Delta \acute{x}_i)\right] + \left[\sum_{i=1}^{N}\frac{ch_{1i} \cdot (x + \Delta x + s_i)^2}{2.PR_{1i}}\right]\right.
$$

$$
+ \left[\sum_{i=1}^{N}cb_{1i} \cdot (x + \Delta x)\right] + [cb_2 \cdot (x + \Delta x)] + \left[\frac{ch_m \cdot (x)^2}{2.PR_m}\right] + [cc_1 \cdot x]
$$

$$
+ \left[\sum_{i=1}^{N}cc_{3i} \cdot s_i\right]\right\}
\tag{4-22}
$$

Where

$$
x = D(p, (rl_s^N \cdot rl_m \cdot rl_r), (rl_r \cdot rl_s)^N, w). G^{-1}\left(Max\left\{rl_r, \frac{h^-}{h^- + h^+}\right\}\right)
\tag{4-23}
$$

$$
\Delta x = G'^{-1}(rl_m). D(p, (rl_s^N \cdot rl_m \cdot rl_r), (rl_r \cdot rl_s)^N, w). G^{-1}\left(Max\left\{rl_r, \frac{h^-}{h^- + h^+}\right\}\right)
\tag{4-24}
$$

$$
s_i = G_{NB}^{i\,-1}(rl_r) \qquad\qquad (\forall i = 1, 2,\ldots, N)
\tag{4-25}
$$

$$\Delta \dot{x}_i = \frac{\gamma_i}{1-\gamma_i} \left[\frac{PR_{1i}}{\mu_i} \ln(rl_s) + G_{NB}^{i^{-1}}(rl_r) \right.$$

$$+ (G'^{-1}(rl_m)$$

$$\left. + 1). D(p, (rl_s^N \cdot rl_m \cdot rl_r), (rl_r \cdot rl_s)^N, w). G^{-1}\left(Max\left\{rl_r, \frac{h^-}{h^- + h^+}\right\}\right)\right]$$

$$(\forall i = 1, 2, ..., N) \qquad (4\text{-}26)$$

Subject to

$$0.5 \le rl_r, rl_m, rl_s \le 1 \qquad\qquad\qquad\qquad (4\text{-}27)$$

$$p, w \ge 0 \qquad\qquad\qquad\qquad\qquad (4\text{-}28)$$

The first term in the objective function (4-22) represents the average profit made by the retailer through selling the products in the pre-market. This term is equal to the retailer's income, $p. D(p, sl_p, sl_a, w)$, minus the average handling cost, Eq. (4-4), and average repair cost, Eq. (4-11), of the products in the retailer. The second term of (22) represents the cost of producing and supplying the products and components in the SCs' first and second echelons. The first item in the second term is the cost of procuring material and producing the components in the suppliers. The second item in the second term is the average holding cost of the qualified components produced and stocked in the suppliers. The third item is the transportation cost of the qualified components from the suppliers to the manufacturer. The fourth item is the cost of assembling the products in the manufacturer. The fifth term is the average holding cost of the qualified products in the manufacturer. The sixth and seventh terms respectively represent the transportation cost of the products and components from the manufacturer and suppliers to the retailer. The relationships between the local reliabilities of the echelons and their production quantities are shown by Equations (4-23), (4-24), (4-25), and (4-26) explained in Sections 4.5.1. and 4.5.2.

Using this mathematical model, we determine the best local reliabilities for the SCs' facilities (and consequently the best pre- and after-sales service levels), price and warranty length for the company to maximize the total profit. This formulation of the problem is a mathematical model with a strictly nonlinear objective function and continuous variables. In Section 4.6, a method is proposed to solve this model.

4.6 Solution Approach

The mathematical model formulated for the problem in Section 4.5 includes a strictly nonlinear objective function. Finding the best solution is not straightforward for nonlinear models. Analyzing the model shows the most important variables which mainly appear in the nonlinear terms of the model are rl_r, rl_m and rl_s. These variables take values from a very restricted range, [0.5, 1]. Having a very restricted feasible range justifies discretizing these variables. By discretizing on the [0.5, 1] range, substituting this interval with a set of discrete values, and assuming that rl_r, rl_m, and rl_s variables take values only from this set, we transform the problem's nonlinear model to a linear one which is much easier to solve globally.

The other variable in the model is warranty length, w. This variable does not have a restricted feasible range but, in reality, a few warranty options are available in markets and usually offered by companies for customers such as 6, 12, 18 and 24 months. But the price variable, p, does not have either a restricted feasible range or a few options. Therefore, in this section, we assume that the product price is given exogenously. By introducing price as a parameter in the model, discretizing reliability and warranty variables looks an appropriate technique to linearize and solve this model globally. In Section 4.7, we determine the best price for the company by a sensitivity analysis of the results.

We discretize the feasibly continuous range of rl_r by defining a set of discrete values $RL1 = \{rl1^1, rl1^2, ..., rl1^{|RL1|}\}$. To use this set, we define new binary variables y_{rl1^r} ($\forall rl1^r \in RL1$) for selecting scenarios from this set. Variable y_{rl1^r} is equal to 1 if the reliability scenario $rl1^i$ is selected from this set and 0 otherwise. In the same way, sets $RL2 = \{rl2^1, rl2^2, ..., rl2^{|RL2|}\}$ and $RL3 = \{rl3^1, rl3^2, ..., rl3^{|RL3|}\}$ and their corresponding binary variables y_{rl2^m} ($\forall rl2^m \in RL2$) and y_{rl3^s} ($\forall rl3^s \in RL3$) are defined to discretize the continuous ranges of rl_m and rl_s. Set $W = \{w^1, w^2, ..., w^{|w|}\}$ represents the available warranty length options and binary variables z_{w^t} ($\forall w^t \in W$) are defined for warranty strategy selection from this set. By defining these new sets and variables, the important nonlinear terms of Model (22-28) can be linearized. The linearized form of Eq. (4-23) is shown in Eq. (4-30). Linearized forms of Eq. (4-24), (4-25), (4-26) and the objective function (4-22) are shown in Appendix 4.D.

$$x = \sum_{r=1}^{|RL1|} \sum_{m=1}^{|RL2|} \sum_{s=1}^{|RL3|} \sum_{t=1}^{|W|} y_{rl1^r} \cdot y_{rl2^m} \cdot y_{rl3^s} \cdot z_{w^t} \cdot \left[\begin{array}{c} D(p, (rl1^r \cdot rl2^m \cdot rl3^{sN}), (rl1^r \cdot rl3^s)^N, w^t). \\[1em] G^{-1}\left(Max\left\{rl1^r, \dfrac{h^-}{h^- + h^+}\right\}\right) \end{array} \right]$$

$$(4\text{-}29)$$

Also, notice that only one reliability and one warranty option can be selected from the sets. Therefore, the following constraints are added:

$$\sum_{r=1}^{|RL1|} y_{rl1r} = 1 \tag{4-30}$$

$$\sum_{m=1}^{|RL2|} y_{rl2m} = 1 \tag{4-31}$$

$$\sum_{s=1}^{|RL3|} y_{rl3s} = 1 \tag{4-32}$$

$$\sum_{t=1}^{|W|} z_{wt} = 1 \tag{4-33}$$

By treating the price as an exogenously given factor and discretizing the feasible range of the warranty and reliability variables, the mathematical model of the problem is transformed to a mixed integer linear model with binary variables which can be solved globally by the available software such as CPLEX, GAMS, GROOBI and LINGO. We used CPLEX to solve it.

The solution time of the linearized model depends mainly on the number of binary variables, $|W|.|RL1|.|RL2|.|RL3|$. The number of the binary variables depends on the discretizing step of the local reliability variables. To reduce complexity, we start with a large step to find a rough approximation of the best solution. Then we make the steps finer around the rough approximation to improve the solution's accuracy. Solution times for all the examples solved in Section 4.7, Computational Results, are less than a minute. In the next section, by analyzing the sensitivity of the company's profit with respect to the price, we determine the optimal value for the product's price.

4.7 Computational Results

4.7.1 A Test Problem from the Automotive Industry

The test problem in this chapter is based on the need of a company, SMAC (due to confidentiality issues, we do not disclose the names of companies), located in the Middle East and supplying products to the regional automotive manufacturers of that area such as IKC. SMAC is a well-known Reverse Idler Gear Shaft (RIGS) supplier in the automotive industry in that region. However, recently the entrance of some new external suppliers with comparable prices and warranties has made the markets more competitive. In such competitive markets, determining the best price and warranty length as well as providing appropriate pre- and after-sales service levels is mandatory to keep customers. Due to low efficiency and the high rate of defective production, variations in the qualified output of the production facilities is significant. Therefore, considering supply-side variations in balancing demand and supply and estimating service levels is necessary.

The main components of RIGS are CK45 steel and barbed pins procured from companies YIIC and AKC respectively. There are long term contracts between SMAC and its suppliers, YIIC and AKC. A fixed part of production capacity in YIIC and AKC is dedicated to SMAC. Strategic decisions about these dedicated capacities are made by a leadership team in SMAC. After shipping the conforming CK45 steel order from YIIC to SMAC, several processes are performed on the steel such as stretching it to the required diagonal, cutting stretched steel to suitable lengths and rough grinding. Then the first puncturing, bathing, milling, second puncturing and tapping are done on the work pieces. After plating and smoothing, the work piece is assembled with barbed pin procured from AKC. Then the final product is cleaned and inspected. In the inspection process, defective products are removed from the batch and returned to the manufacturing process. Qualified products are sent to the retailer to supply to the market. The network structure of the RIGS SC is shown in Figure 4-5. This SC includes CK45 and barbed pin suppliers in the third echelon (YIIC and AKC), one RIGS manufacturer in the second echelon (SMAC) and a retailer in the first echelon supplying the SC's product to the market.

This company provides a failure free warranty for its customers. The products returned inside the warranty period are checked by the retailer to determine whether the problem is related to the work piece made from

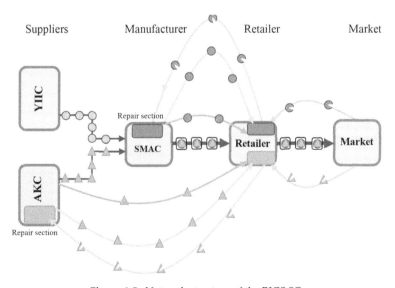

Figure 4-5. Network structure of the RIGS SC.

CK45 steel or the barbed pin. If it is related to the steel work piece, the defective work piece is sent to SMAC's repair section and a repaired piece is ordered from this section. If the problem is related to the barbed pin, the defective pin is sent to AKC's repair section and a repaired pin is ordered from it (Figure 4-5).

This product includes two critical components: Component 1 (CK45) and Component 2 (barbed pin). Components 1 and 2 are manufactured with the procurement and production costs of $ca_{11} + ca_{21} = \$3.5$ and $ca_{12} + ca_{22} = \$2.5$ respectively. The sound components are shipped to the manufacturer and assembled into the final products with cost a of $cb_{11} = cb_{12} = \$0.2$ and $cb_2 = \$0.8$. After inspection, the qualified final products are shipped to the retailer with transportation cost $cc_1 = \$0.5$. Analyzing the company's historical sales data shows the pre-market demand can be approximated as a linear function of price, warranty length, and service levels: $D(p, sl_p, sl_a, w) = 500 + 200 \times w - 250 \times (p - 10) - 500 \times (1 - sl_a) - 900 \times (1 - sl_p)$. The company has four options for warranty length - 6, 12, 18, and 24 months. Cost components $h^- = \$0.10$ and $h^+ = \$0.15$ are considered for unit extra inventory and unit lost sales at the end of each sales period.

The CK45 work piece and the barbed pin respectively have reliability indices $\tau_1 = 0.1$ and $\tau_2 = 0.3$. The repair cost of components and the moments of their service time in the repair sections are: $cr_1 = \$1.5$, $cr_2 = \$1.0$, $E[t_1^2] = 0.0044$, $E[t_1^3] = 0.0003$, $E[t_2^2] = 0.0027$, and $E[t_2^3] = 0.0046$. The transportation times of the defective components from the retailer to the repair sections of SMAC and AKC are $O_1 = 0.05$ (*month*) and $O_2 = 0.05$ (*month*) respectively. The CK45 work pieces and the barbed pins are produced in the suppliers with $PR_1 = 8000$ (number in time unit) and $PR_2 = 9000$ (number in time unit) production rates. The average deterioration time in the production system of the suppliers is equal to $1/\mu_{1 \, and \, 2} = 0.5$. In the out-of-control state, the rates of nonconforming production for CK45 and barbed pin are $\gamma_1 = 0.10$ and $\gamma_2 = 0.20$ respectively. The stochastic part of the pre-market demand, ε, follows a normal distribution with mean 0.0 and variance 1.0. SMAC's defective assembly rate has uniform density in the range $[0, \beta = 0.15]$. The transportation cost of the repaired components from SMAC and AKC to the retailer is $cc_{31} = cc_{32} = \$1$.

In this problem, the flow of defective CK45 components is somewhat different. Instead of the supplier, they are returned to the manufacturer, SMAC. Thus, we modify Equations (4-24) and (4-26) as follows:

$$\Delta x = G'^{-1}(rl_m). \left[D(p, (rl_r \cdot rl_m \cdot rl_s^N), (rl_r \cdot rl_s)^N, w). \ G^{-1}\left(Max\left\{rl_r, \frac{h^-}{h^- + h^+}\right\}\right) + G_{NB}^{1\,-1}(rl_r) \right]$$

$$(4\text{-}34)$$

$$\Delta \acute{x}_1 = \frac{\gamma_1}{1-\gamma_1} \left[\frac{PR_{11}}{\mu_1} \ln(rl_s) + (G'^{-1}(rl_m) + \right.$$

$$1). \left[D(p, (rl_r \cdot rl_m \cdot rl_s^N), (rl_r \cdot rl_s)^N, w). G^{-1} \left(Max \left\{ rl_r, \frac{h^-}{h^- + h^+} \right\} \right) + G_{NB}^{1-1}(rl_r) \right] \quad (4\text{-}35)$$

$$\Delta \acute{x}_2 = \frac{\gamma_2}{1-\gamma_2} \left[\frac{PR_{12}}{\mu_2} \ln(rl_s) + G_{NB}^{2-1}(rl_r) + (G'^{-1}(rl_m) + \right.$$

$$1). \left[D(p, (rl_r \cdot rl_m \cdot rl_s^N), (rl_r \cdot rl_s)^N, w). G^{-1} \left(Max \left\{ rl_r, \frac{h^-}{h^- + h^+} \right\} \right) \right] \quad (4\text{-}36)$$

Solving the mathematical model of this example leads to the following results: local reliabilities in the SCs' echelons are $rl_r = 0.95$, $rl_m = 0.95$ and $rl_s = 0.94$ respectively.

For retail price $p = \$16.0$, the optimal warranty strategy is 6 months. Based on local reliabilities, $x = 263$ RIGS units are ordered by the retailer at the beginning of each sales period. To fulfill this order and the required CK45 work pieces as the retailer's safety stock ($s_1 = 3$), SMAC plans for $\Delta x = 41$ extra production. The required CK45 and barbed pins are ordered from YIIC and AKC respectively. In addition to SMAC's order, AKC receives another barbed pin order from the retailer, $s_2 = 6$, to preserve the retailer's local reliability in the after-sales market. In the same way, YIIC and AKC plan to procure and produce $\Delta \acute{x}_1 = 6$ and $\Delta \acute{x}_2 = 7$ extra units of CK45 and barbed pin to compensate for their non-conforming production. The results are summarized in Figure 4-6. This flow planning leads to $\Pi = \$1841.4$ profit for the company which is the highest for the retail price $p = \$16.0$.

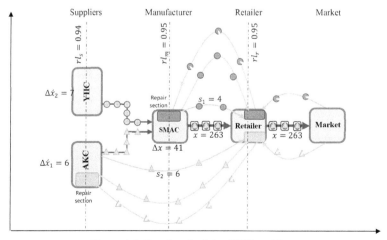

Figure 4-6. Results of solving RIGS problem.

4.7.2 Sensitivity Analysis

In Sections 4.5 and 4.6, it is assumed the price is given exogenously. However, price has always been one of the strongest competitive advantages for companies in the markets. In reality, the appropriate selection of the retail price is critical. Therefore, in this section, we consider the price as a variable to be optimized by the company. We assume the price is selected in the range [p_{min} = \$15, p_{max} = \$17.65]. Several factors should be considered to determine this feasible range for price, for example, the product's manufacturing cost, the prices of rival products in the market, and the governmental regulations supporting consumers' rights. In the rest of this section, first we analyze the sensitivity of the company's profit with respect to price and warranty length to determine the correlation between these two marketing strategies. For different values of price in the feasible range and warranty options, we solve the model. The results are summarized in Figure 4-7, 4-8, and 4-9. In Figure 4-7 the profit of the company with respect to the price for different warranty options is shown.

As seen in Figure 4-7, for a 6 month warranty the best price that leads to the highest profit (\$1934) is \$16.32. However, solving the model for different combinations of price and warranty leads to better results. As seen in Figure 4-7, the best price and warranty combination is p = \$17.12 and w = 18 months which yields the highest profit Π^* = \$2017 for the company. In different warranty options, the behavior of the profit function with respect to the price is similar but shifts to the right by the warranty length increment. This means that changing the warranty does not change the effect of the price on the company's profitability. By increasing the

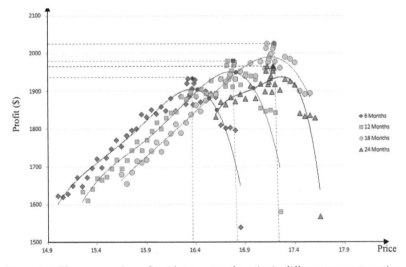

Figure 4-7. The company's profit with respect to the price in different warranty options.

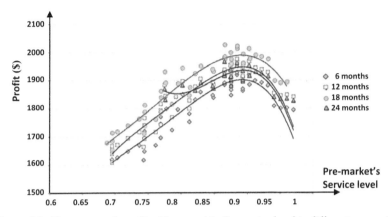

Figure 4-8. The company's profit with respect to the service level in different warranty options.

price, first the company's profit starts to increase because the positive effect of the price increment on the marginal profit is more than its negative effect on the demand. The difference of these effects becomes zero at the best price for that warranty option. After the best price, the negative effect of the price increment dominates its positive effect. Therefore, the profit starts to decrease. As expected, a longer warranty length leads to a higher best price.

The red dots in Figure 4-7 represent the intersections of the profit functions for different warranty options. These dots show the critical price values at which the priority (or, in the other words, the profitability) of the warranty options changes. Based on these price values, the priority of the warranty options in different price intervals is as follows:

- If $p < p_1 = \$16.41$ *then the priority of the warranty options is: 6, 12, 18 and 24 (months).*

- If $p_1 < p \leq p_2 = \$16.54$ *then the priority of the warranty options is: 12, 6, 18 and 24 (months).*

- If $p_2 < p \leq p_3 = \$16.63$ *then the priority of the warranty options is: 12, 18, 6 and 24 (months).*

- If $p_3 < p \leq p_4 = \$16.82$ *then the priority of the warranty options is: 12, 18, 24 and 6 (months).*

- If $p_4 < p \leq p_5 = \$16.95$ *then the priority of the warranty options is: 18, 12, 24 and 6 (months).*

- If $p_5 < p \leq p_6 = \$17.65$ *then the priority of the warranty options is: 18, 24, 12 and 6 (months).*

- If $p_6 < p$ *then the priority of the warranty options is: 24, 18, 12 and 6 (months).*

	$16.82 < p \le $16.95	$16.95 < p \le $17.65	$17.65 < p$
$sl_p \le 0.785$	-	-	24, 18, 12 and 6
$0.78 < sl_p \le 0.817$	-	18, 24, 12 and 6	
$0.81 < sl_p$	18, 12, 24 and 6	-	-

Figure 4-9. Combinations of the best price, service level, and priority of warranty options.

The profit of the company with respect to the pre-market's service level, $sl_p = rl_r \cdot rl_m \cdot rl_s^2$, for different warranty options is shown in Figure 4-8. As seen in this figure, the behavior of the profit function with respect to the service level is similar for all the warranty options without any significant shift to the left or right. This means these profit functions have almost similar optimal service levels. Therefore, finding the best service level for one warranty option gives us a good approximation of the best service level for the other options. Therefore, it is seen that there is a very weak correlation between the warranty length and service level and they can be selected separately. Based on Figure 4-8, the highest profit corresponds to an 18-month warranty and occurs at $sl_p^* = 0.865$. However, the functions cross each other a few times, the red dots represent the pre-market's service level values at which the priority (or, in the other words, the profitability) of the warranty options changes

Based on these results, we have:

- If $sl_p < sl_p^1 = 0.785$ *then the priority of the warranty options is: 24, 18, 12, and 6 (months).*
- If $sl_p^1 < sl_p \le sl_p^1 = 0.817$ *then the priority of the warranty options is: 18, 24, 12, and 6 (months).*
- If $sl_p^1 < sl_p$ *then the priority of the warranty options is: 18, 12, 24, and 6 (months).*

Summarizing the results in Figure 4-9 and 4-10 leads to the following best combinations of the price, service level and priority of the warranty options (Figure 4-9):

In Figure 4-10 the positive correlation between the price and service level for different warranty options is shown. As seen in the figure, the trend of this correlation is similar for different warranty options. Increasing the warranty length only shifts the price and service level function to the right. This means that regardless of the warranty length, a

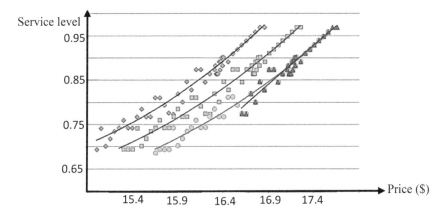

Figure 4-10. The price and service level correlation in different warranty options.

given increment in the service level leads to almost the same increment in the price. However, the ratio of the best price increment to the best service level increment decreases at higher prices.

As expected, for a given warranty length, increasing the product's price is always accompanied with a service level increment because the positive effect of the service level increment compensates for the negative effect of the price increment on the market's demand. Also for a given retail price, the service level improvement leads to reduction in the warranty length. For a given service level, the price increment leads to selecting a longer warranty.

4.8 Closing Remarks

In this chapter, we consider a manufacturing company producing a repairable product and providing a product-service package for its customers in a pre-market with a stochastic demand function. This company includes two SCs: forward and after-sales SCs servicing pre- and after-sales markets respectively. In our model, we consider two important interactions between these two SCs which justifies the necessity of concurrent flow planning: (i) the after-sales service level provided by the after-sales SC directly affects the product demand in the forward SC and (ii) the total products supplied by the forward SC to the pre-market constitutes the after-sales SC's potential demand for the after-sales services. In this chapter, a mathematical model is developed to determine the best marketing strategies, the best (price, warranty and service levels) triple, for the company and the best flow plan in its SCs to support marketing strategies against different variations.

In this problem, we consider different variations: (i) supply-side variations related to the imperfect performance of the production systems in the SCs' production facilities and (ii) demand-side variations related to the stochastic demand for the product in the pre-market and for the spare parts in the after-sales market. We show that supply-side variations propagate by moving the flow from the SC's upstream to its downstream which yields qualified flow depreciation throughout the networks. We suggest the method of order amplification between the SCs' facilities from the downstream to the upstream to neutralize the negative effects of the flow depreciation. We show that the SCs' service levels in the pre- and after-sales markets are functions of local facilities in the stochastic facilities. This method is used in the mathematical model to plan reliable flow throughout the SCs' networks. The results of solving this model for an example in the automobile industry reveal the following insights:

- ✓ **The critical price and service level values:** There are critical price and service level values in which the priority of the warranty options changes. By combining these critical values, we determine the most profitable price and service level intervals for each priority of the warranty options.

- ✓ **The effect of warranty length on the trend of profit changes with respect to the price:** In different warranty options, the behavior of the profit function with respect to the price is almost similar but only shifts to right (increases) by the increment of warranty length. This means that changing the warranty length does not change the price effects on the company's profitability.

- ✓ **The effect of warranty length on the trend of the change of profit with respect to the service level:** The behavior of the profit function with respect to the service level is similar for all the warranty options without any significant shift to the left (decrease) or right (increase). This means that these profit functions have almost the same optimal service level. Therefore, finding the best service level for one warranty option gives us a good approximation of the best service level for other options. This shows that there is a very weak correlation between the warranty length and service level and they can be selected separately.

- ✓ **The effect of warranty length on the correlation between the price and service level:** The trend of the price and service level correlation is similar for different warranty options. Increasing the warranty length only shifts the price and service level function to the right (increase). This means that regardless of the warranty length, a given increment in the service level and price leads to almost the same increment in the price and service level respectively. However, the ratio of the best price increment to the best service level increment decreases in higher prices.

A failure free warranty is the after-sales service considered in this chapter. However, the procedures in this chapter can be extended to cover other kinds of after-sales services such as rebate warranties, end-of-life (EOL) warranties and performance-based logistics. Considering supply-side variations and their propagated effects significantly improves the accuracy of the service level estimation. Therefore, the methods presented in this chapter for reliable flow planning can be extended to non-profit domains in which providing a high service level is critical such as in humanitarian logistics. In the problem presented here, we only consider the supply-side variations in the performance of production facilities. There are similar variations in the connecting links between the SCs' facilities. Considering the variations in the connecting links of the chains improves the flow planning reliability.

In the context of an architecture for fail-safe networks, the focus of this chapter is on variation management in two correlated forward and after-sales SCs supplying an original product and its spare parts, respectively. The defective parts of the returned products are repaired and supplied along with new spare parts through the after-sales SC. The mathematical model of this chapter will be extended in Chapter 5 to supply networks with more than one facility in each echelon.

Acknowledgement

Figures and tables in Chapter 4 are reprinted from Transportation Research, Part E: Logistics and Transportation Review, volume 95 (November), by Shabnam Rezapour, Janet K. Allen and Farrokh Mistree, "Reliable Product-service Supply Chains for Repairable Products." pp. 299–321, 2016, with permission from Elsevier.

References

Aggrawal, D., Anand, A., Singh, O. and Singh, J. 2014. Profit maximization by virtue of price & warranty length optimization. High Technol. Manage. Res. 25(1): 1–8.

Anastasiadis, S., Anderson, B. and Chukova, S. 2013. Auto warranty and driving patterns. Reliability Engineering & System Safety 116: 126–134.

Avsar, Z. M. and Zijm, W. H. 2000. Resource-Constrained Two-Echelon Inventory Models for Repairable Item Systems. In Memorandum. Enschede.

Bacchetti, A. and Saccani, N. 2012. Spare parts classification and demand forecasting for stock control: Investigating the gap between research and practice. Omega 40(6): 722–737.

Baghalian, A., Rezapour, S. and Farahani, R. Z. 2013. Robust supply chain network design with service level against disruptions and demand uncertainties: A real-life case. European Journal of Operational Research 227(1): 199–215.

Baines, T., Lightfoot, H., Evans, S., Neely, A., Greenough, R., Peppard, J., Roy, R., Shehab, E., Braganza, A., Tiwari, A., Alcock, J., Angus, J., Bastl, M., Cousens, A., Irving, P., Johnson, M., Kingston, J., Lockett, H., Martinez, V. and Michele, P. 2007. State-of-the-art in product-service systems. Proceedings of the Institution of Mechanical Engineering–Part B: Journal of Engineering. Manufacturing 221(10): 1543–1552.

Balachandran, K. R. and Radhakrishnan, S. 2005. Quality implications of warranties in a supply chain. Management Science 51(8): 1266–1277.

Barabadi, A., Barabady, J. and Markeset, T. 2014. Application of reliability models with covariates in spare part prediction and optimization–a case study. Reliability Engineering & System Safety 123: 1–7.

Bohmann, E., Rosenberg, J. and Stenbrink, P. 2003. Overhauling European auto distribution. McKinsey Quarterly 1: 134–142.

Boone, C. A., Craighead, C. W. and Hanna, J. B. 2008. Critical challenges of inventory management in service parts supply: A Delphi study. Operations Management Research 1(1): 31–39.

Bundschuh, R. G. and Dezvane, T. M. 2003. How to make after-sales services pay off. McKinsey Quarterly (4): 116–127.

Business Week. 2004. Hyundai: kissing clunkers goodbye—A five-year focus on quality has sent customer satisfaction soaring. Business Week, 16 May.

Cardona-Valdés, Y., Álvarez, A. and Ozdemir, D. 2011. A bi-objective supply chain design problem with uncertainty. Transportation Research Part C: Emerging Technologies 19(5): 821–832.

Chang, M.-H. and Harrington, J. E. 2000. Centralization vs. Decentralization in a multi-unit organization: A computational model of a retail chain as a multi-agent adaptive system. Management Science 46(11): 1427–-1440.

Chien, Y. H. and Chen, J. A. 2008. Optimal spare ordering policy under a rebate warranty. Eur. J. Oper. Res. 186: 708–719.

Chen, J. A. and Chien, Y. H. 2007. Renewing warranty and preventive maintenance for products with failure penalty post-warranty. Quality and Reliability Engineering International 23(1): 107–121.

Chu, J. and Chintagunta, P. K. 2009. Quantifying the economic value of warranties in the US server market. Marketing Science 28(1): 99–121.

Chukova, S., Hayakawa, Y. and Johnston, M. 2007. Optimal two-dimensional warranty repair strategy. Proceedings of the Institution of Mechanical Engineers, Part O: Journal of Risk and Reliability 221(4): 265–273.

Cohen, M. A., Agrawal, N. and Agrawal, V. 2006. Winning in the aftermarket. Harvard Business Review 84(5): 129.

Dada, M., Petruzzi, N. C. and Schwarz, L. B. 2003. A Newsvendor Model with Unreliable Suppliers. University of Illinois at Urbana-Champaign, College of Business.

Diaz, A. and Fu, M. C. 1997. Models for multi-echelon repairable item inventory systems with limited repair capacity. European Journal of Operational Research 97(3): 480–492.

Esmaeili, M., Shamsi, N. and Asgharizadeh, E. 2014. Three-level warranty service contract among manufacturer, agent and customer: A game-theoretical approach. Vol. 239.

Fattahi, M., Mahootchi, M., Moattar Husseini, S. M., Keyvanshokooh, E. and Alborzi, F. 2015. Investigating replenishment policies for centralised and decentralised supply chains using stochastic programming approach. International Journal of Production Research 53(1): 41–69.

Gaiardelli, P., Saccani, N. and Songini, L. 2007. Performance measurement of the after-sales service network—Evidence from the automotive industry. Computers in Industry 58(7): 698–708.

Hsu, C.-I. and Li, H.-C. 2011. Reliability evaluation and adjustment of supply chain network design with demand fluctuations. International Journal of Production Economics 132(1): 131–145.

Huang, H.-Z., Liu, Z.-J. and Murthy, D. 2007. Optimal reliability, warranty and price for new products. Lie Transactions 39(8): 819–827.

Huang, Y. S. and Yen, C. 2009. A study of two-dimensional warranty policies with preventive maintenance. IIE Trans. 41: 299–308.

Huang, Y.-S., Gau, W.-Y. and Ho, J.-W. 2015. Cost analysis of two-dimensional warranty for products with periodic preventive maintenance. Reliability Engineering & System Safety 134: 51–58.

Jiang, B. and Zhang, X. 2011. How does a retailer's service plan affect a manufacturer's warranty? Management Science 57(4): 727–740.

Kamrad, B., Lele, S. S., Siddique, A. and Thomas, R. J. 2005. Innovation diffusion uncertainty, advertising and pricing policies. European Journal of Operational Research 164(3): 829–850.

Keyvanshokooh, E., Ryan, S. M., and Kabir, E. 2016. Hybrid robust and stochastic optimization for closed-loop supply chain network design using accelerated Benders decomposition. European Journal of Operational Research 249(1): 76–92.

Lee, H. L. and Rosenblatt, M. J. 1987. Simultaneous determination of production cycle and inspection schedules in a production system. Management Science 33(9): 1125–1136.

Li, K., Mallik, S. and Chhajed, D. 2012. Design of extended warranties in supply chains under additive demand. Production and Operations Management 21(4): 730–746.

Lieckens, K. T., Colen, P. J. and Lambrecht, M. R. 2013. Optimization of a stochastic remanufacturing network with an exchange option. Decision Support Systems 54(4): 1548–1557.

Lin, P.-C. and Shue, L.-Y. 2005. Application of optimal control theory to product pricing and warranty with free replacement under the influence of basic lifetime distributions. Computers & Industrial Engineering 48(1): 69–82.

Liu, Y., Liu, Z. and Wang, Y. 2013. Customized warranty offering for configurable products. Reliability Engineering & System Safety 118: 1–7.

Majid, H. A., Wulandhari, L. A., Samah, A. A. and Chin, A. J. 2012. A framework in determining extended warranty by using two dimensional delay time model. Paper read at Advanced Materials Research.

McAvoy, J. 2008. Integrating Spare Parts Planning with Logistics. Report, Aberdeen Group.

Mirasol, N. M. 1963. A queueing approach to logistics systems. Oper. Res. 12: 707–724.

Mohammaddust, F., Rezapour, S., Zanjirani Farahani, R., Mofidfar, M. and Hill, A. 2015. Developing Lean and Responsive Supply Chains: A Robust Model for Alternative Risk Mitigation Strategies in Supply Chain Designs. Vol. 183.

Murthy, D. 1990. Optimal reliability choice in product design. Engineering Optimization+ A35 15(4): 281–294.

Murthy, D. and Djamaludin, I. 2002. New product warranty: A literature review. International Journal of Production Economics 79(3): 231–260.

Nguyen, D. and Murthy, D. 1984. A general model for estimating warranty costs for repairable products. IIE Transactions 16(4): 379–386.

Öner, K. B., Kiesmüller, G. P. and Van Houtum, G.-J. 2010. Optimization of component reliability in the design phase of capital goods. European Journal of Operational Research 205(3): 615–624.

Pan, F. and Nagi, R. 2010. Robust supply chain design under uncertain demand in agile manufacturing. Computers & Operations Research 37(4): 668–683.

Park, M., Jung, K. M. and Park, D. H. 2013. Optimal post-warranty maintenance policy with repair time threshold for minimal repair. Reliability Engineering & System Safety 111: 147–153.

Park, S., Lee, T.-E. and Sung, C. S. 2010. A three-level supply chain network design model with risk-pooling and lead times. Transportation Research Part E: Logistics and Transportation Review 46(5): 563–581.

Parlar, M., Wang, Y. and Gerchak, Y. 1995. A periodic review inventory model with Markovian supply availability. International Journal of Production Economics 42(2): 131–136.

Perlman, Y., Mehrez, A. and Kaspi, M. 2001. Setting expediting repair policy in a multi-echelon repairable-item inventory system with limited repair capacity. Journal of the Operational Research Society 52(2): 198–209.

Rao, B. M. 2011. A decision support model for warranty servicing of repairable items. Computers & Operations Research 38(1): 112–130.

Rezapour, S., Allen, J. K. and Mistree, F. 2015. Stochastic supply networks servicing pre- and after-sales markets. ASME International Design Engineering Technical Conferences, Boston, USA.

Rezapour, S., Allen, J. K. and Mistree, F. 2016. Reliable product-service supply chains for repairable products. Transportation Research Part E; 95: 299–321.

Rosenblatt, M. J. and Lee, H. L. 1986. Economic production cycles with imperfect production processes. IIE Transactions 18(1): 48–55.

Saharidis, G. K. D., Kouikoglou, V. S. and Dallery, Y. 2009. Centralized and decentralized control polices for a two-stage stochastic supply chain with subcontracting. International Journal of Production Economics 117(1): 117–126.

Sahba, P. and Balcıog, B. 2011. The impact of transportation delays on repairshop capacity pooling and spare part inventories. European Journal of Operational Research 214(3): 674–682.

Sana, S. S. 2010. An economic production lot size model in an imperfect production system. European Journal of Operational Research 201(1): 158–170.

Sarkar, B. and Saren, S. 2016. Product inspection policy for an imperfect production system with inspection errors and warranty cost. European Journal of Operational Research 248(1): 263–271.

Schütz, P., Tomasgard, A. and Ahmed, S. 2009. Supply chain design under uncertainty using sample average approximation and dual decomposition. European Journal of Operational Research 199(2): 409–419.

Shahanaghi, K., Noorossana, R., Jalali-Naini, S. G. and Heydari, M. 2013. Failure modeling and optimizing preventive maintenance strategy during two-dimensional extended warranty contracts. Engineering Failure Analysis 28: 90–102.

Sleptchenko, A., Van Der Heijden, M. and Van Harten, A. 2002. Effects of finite repair capacity in multi-echelon, multi-indenture service part supply systems. International Journal of Production Economics 79(3): 209–230.

Sleptchenko, A., Van Der Heijden, M. and Van Harten, A. 2003. Trade-off between inventory and repair capacity in spare part networks. Journal of the Operational Research Society 54(3): 263–272.

Su, C. and Shen, J. 2012. Analysis of extended warranty policies with different repair options. Engineering Failure Analysis 25: 49–62.

Swaminathan, J. M. and Shanthikumar, J. G. 1999. Supplier diversification: effect of discrete demand. Operations Research Letters 24(5): 213–221.

Tomlin, B. and Wang, Y. 2005. On the value of mix flexibility and dual sourcing in unreliable newsvendor networks. Manufacturing & Service Operations Management 7(1): 37–57.

Tsoukalas, M. Z. and Agrafiotis, G. 2013. A new replacement warranty policy indexed by the product's correlated failure and usage time. Computers & Industrial Engineering 66(2): 203–211.

Vahdani, H., Chukova, S. and Mahlooji, H. 2011. On optimal replacement-repair policy for multi-state deteriorating products under renewing free replacement warranty. Computers & Mathematics with Applications 61(4): 840–850.

Vahdani, H., Mahlooji, H. and Jahromi, A. E. 2013. Warranty servicing for discretely degrading items with non-zero repair time under renewing warranty. Computers & Industrial Engineering 65(1): 176–185.

Vandermerwe, S. and Rada, J. 1988. Servitization of business: Adding value by adding services. European Management Journal 6(4): 314–324.

Wang, W. 2012. A stochastic model for joint spare parts inventory and planned maintenance optimisation. European Journal of Operational Research 216(1): 127–139.

Wang, Y.-W. 2008. Locating battery exchange stations to serve tourism transport: A note. Transportation Research Part D: Transport and Environment 13(3): 193–197.

Wang, Y., Wallace, S. W., Shen, B. and Choi, T.-M. 2015. Service supply chain management: A review of operational models. European Journal of Operational Research 247(3): 685–698.

Wei, J., Zhao, J. and Li, Y. 2015. Price and warranty period decisions for complementary products with horizontal firms' cooperation/noncooperation strategies. Journal of Cleaner Production 105: 86–102.

Williams, D. P. 2007. Study of the warranty cost model for software reliability with an imperfect debugging phenomenon. Turkish Journal of Electrical Engineering & Computer Sciences 15(3): 369–381.

Wu, S. and Li, H. 2007. Warranty cost analysis for products with a dormant state. European Journal of Operational Research 182(3): 1285–1293.

You, F. and Grossmann, I. E. 2008. Design of responsive supply chains under demand uncertainty. Computers & Chemical Engineering 32(12): 3090–3111.

Zhou, Z., Li, Y. and Tang, K. 2009. Dynamic pricing and warranty policies for products with fixed lifetime. European Journal of Operational Research 196(3): 940–948.

Appendices

Appendix 4.A: Assumptions of the Problem

Assumptions of the problem are as follows:

- In the production system of the company, there are several separate facilities (suppliers, manufacture and retailer) working together through long term contracts. Each facility makes local decisions about its production system, such as extra production, by only considering the local variation of its own system. However, a leader team monitors the performance of the whole system and its performance in the market. This team dictates local reliabilities for the facilities to maximize the profit of the whole system.

- We assume that in the SCs each facility either completely fulfills the order of its downstream facility and sends a complete package equal to its order, or misses the order and sends nothing.

- In each sales period, the product demand in the pre-market is a deterministic decreasing function of the price (p) and an increasing function of the pre-market service level (sl_p), the after-sales service level (sl_a) and the warranty length (w).

- The defective rate of assembly in the manufacturer is in the range $[0, \beta]$ with a given cumulative distribution function, $G'(.)$.

- The production run of each supplier starts in an in-control state after setting up its equipment. However, they deteriorate and shift to an out-of-control state after a stochastic time following exponential distribution with $1/\mu_i$ ($i = 1, 2, ..., N$) mean. However, in-control production systems only produce conforming components, γ_i ($i = 1, 2, ..., N$) is the percentage of the components produced in the out-of-control state which are nonconforming. Once the production system shifts to an out-of-control state, it stays in that state until the end of the production period, because interrupting production is prohibitively expensive.

- We assume that the performance of the product components is independent and the failure time of each Component i ($i = 1, 2, ..., N$) is a random variable with an F_i cumulative distribution function. F_i is a function of the component's reliability index, τ_i. The probability of failure of the component does not change after repair.

- We assume a mutual independence between the pipelines and the server in the repair sections. We assume a M/G/1 queuing system for the repair process in the repair section in which $E[t_i^s]$ represents the sth moment of the service time. We also model the in-pipeline and the out-pipeline as an M/G/∞ queuing systems which is consistent with the assumption of independence of the numbers of components in the server and in the pipelines.

Appendix 4.B: Notation

Nomenclature

Variables

w	Warranty length of product;
s_i	Safety stock of Component i in the retailer $(i = 1, 2, …, N)$;
rl_r	Local reliability of retailer;
rl_m	Local reliability of manufacturer;
rl_s	Local reliability of suppliers;
sl_a	After-sales SC's service level;
sl_p	Forward SC's service level;
x	Product order quantity of retailer from manufacturer;
Δx	Extra product assembly quantity in the manufacturer;
$\Delta\acute{x}_i$	Extra component production in Supplier i $(i = 1, 2, …, N)$;
p	Price of the product supplied to the market by the company;
y_{rl1^i}	1 if reliability scenario $rl1^i$ is selected from $RL1$ set and 0 otherwise;
y_{rl2^i}	1 if reliability scenario $rl2^i$ is selected from $RL2$ set and 0 otherwise;
y_{rl3^i}	1 if reliability scenario $rl3^i$ is selected from $RL3$ set and 0 otherwise;
zw^t	1 if warranty scenario w^i is selected from W set and 0 otherwise;

Parameters and Functions

N	Number of product's components $(i = 1, 2, …, N)$;
K	Number of sale periods inside the warranty;
$\acute{K}$	Number of time units inside the sale period;
T	Sale period;
$\acute{T}$	Time unit;
$\widehat{D}(p, sl_p, sl_a, w)$	Stochastic function of product demand in the pre-market. We assume that $\widehat{D}(p, sl_p, sl_a, w) = D(p, sl_p, sl_a, w) \times \varepsilon$ and $E[\widehat{D}(p, sl_p, sl_a, w)] = D(p, sl_p, sl_a, w)$;

ε	Random variable representing the stochastic part of product demand function;
$G(.)$	Cumulative density function of ε variable;
h^+	Unit holding cost of extra inventory at the end of sale period in the retailer;
h^-	Unit shortage cost of lost sale at the end of sale period in the retailer;
β	Maximum defective assembly rate in the manufacturer;
$G'(.)$	Cumulative density function of defective assembly rate in the manufacturer;
μ_i	Average rate of shifting from in-control to out-of-control for the machineries of Supplier i in producing each production batch ($i = 1, 2, ..., N$);
γ_i	Average rate of non-conforming production in the out-of-control state of supplier i's machineries ($i = 1, 2, ..., N$);
PR_{1i}	Production rate of Supplier i ($i = 1, 2, ..., N$);
PR_m	Production rate of the Manufacturer;
τ_i	Reliability index of Component i ($i = 1, 2, ..., N$);
F_i	Cumulative distribution function of Component i's failure time ($i = 1, 2, ..., N$);
$F_i^{(m)}$	Cumulative distribution function of total time up to the mth failure in Component i ($i = 1, 2, ..., N$);
$Num_i(w)$	Random variable represents the number of Component i's failures inside the warranty interval ($i = 1, 2, ..., N$);
$E_i(w)$	Average number of failures for a unit of Component i inside the warranty time ($i = 1, 2, ..., N$);
λ_i	Expected failure number of Component i during each sale period ($i = 1, 2, ..., N$);
t_i	Random variable represents the repair time of Component i in the repair section of its corresponding supplier ($i = 1, 2, ..., N$);
N_1^i	Steady state number of Component i in the in-pipeline ($i = 1, 2, ..., N$);
N_2^i	Steady state number of Component i in the repair section of Supplier i($i = 1, 2, ..., N$). These parts are either waiting in the queue or being serviced;
$N_3^i(t)$	Steady state number of Component i in the out-pipeline ($i = 1, 2, ..., N$);
N_4^i	Steady state inventory level at the repair section of Supplier i ($i = 1, 2, ..., N$);
N_5^i	Steady state inventory level of Component i in the retailer ($i = 1, 2, ..., N$);

B_0^i	Steady state backorder level in the repair section of Supplier i ($i = 1, 2, ..., N$);
B_1^i	Steady state backorder level of Component i in the retailer ($i = 1, 2, ..., N$);
$E[t_i^s]$	s^{th} moment of service time in the Repair Section i ($i = 1, 2, ..., N$);
O_i	Average shipment time between retailer and repair section of Supplier i ($i = 1, 2, ..., N$);
ρ_i	Utilization of repair section of Supplier i ($i = 1, 2, ..., N$);
a_0^i	Number of success parameter of negative binomial distribution used to approximate first convolution;
b_0^i	Success probability parameter of negative binomial distribution used to approximate first convolution;
a_1^i	Number of success parameter of negative binomial distribution used to approximate second convolution;
b_1^i	Success probability parameter of negative binomial distribution used to approximate second convolution;
μ_0^i	Expected number of Component i in the corresponding in-pipeline and repair section ($i = 1, 2, ..., N$);
$\sigma^2{}_0^i$	Variance of number of Component i in the corresponding in-pipeline and repair section ($i = 1, 2, ..., N$);
μ_1^i	Expected number of Component i backordered by the repair section or transferring to the retailer through the out-pipeline ($i = 1, 2, ..., N$);
$\sigma^2{}_1^i$	Variance of number of Component i backordered by the repair section or transferring to the retailer through the out-pipeline ($i = 1, 2, ..., N$);
G_{NB}^i	Negative binomial cumulative distribution function used to approximate density of $N_3^i(t) + B_0^i(t)$;
TC_r	Total inventory and shortage cost in the retailer;
cr_i^{rs}	Unit transportation cost of Component i from retailer to Supplier i ($i = 1, 2, ..., N$);
cr_i^s	Unit service cost in the repair section of Supplier i ($i = 1, 2, ..., N$);
cr_i^{sr}	Unit transportation cost of Component i from Supplier i to the Retailer i ($i = 1, 2, ..., N$);
cr_i	Total cost of repairing unit of Component i ($i = 1, 2, ..., N$);
cr	Average repair cost of the product unit;
Π	Total profit of the whole company;
ca_{1i}	Unit procurement cost of material in Supplier i ($i = 1, 2, ..., N$);
ca_{2i}	Unit production cost of Component i in Supplier i ($i = 1, 2, ..., N$);

ch_{1i}	Unit inventory holding cost for a time unit in Supplier i ($i = 1, 2, ..., N$);
cb_{1i}	Unit transportation cost of component from Supplier i to the manufacturer ($i = 1, 2, ..., N$);
cb_2	Unit product assembling cost in the manufacturer;
ch_m	Unit inventory holding cost for a time unit in the manufacturer;
cc_1	Unit transportation cost of product from manufacturer to the retailer;
cc_{3i}	Unit transportation cost of Component i from Supplier i to the retailer ($i = 1, 2, ..., N$);
$RL1$	Set of discretized values that can be selected as the local reliability of retailer, $RL1 = \{rl1^1, rl1^2, ..., rl1^{|RL1|}\}$;
$RL2$	Set of discretized values that can be selected as the local reliability of manufacturer; $RL2 = \{rl2^1, rl2^2, ..., rl2^{|RL2|}\}$;
$RL3$	Set of discretized values that can be selected as the local reliability of suppliers; $RL3 = \{rl3^1, rl3^2, ..., rl3^{|RL3|}\}$;
W	Set of available options for warranty, $W = \{w^1, w^2, ..., w^{|W|}\}$;

Appendix 4.C: After-sales Demand in Each Sales Period

Here, we explain why the average number of failures inside the warranty time, $E_i(w)$, is used to estimate the after-sales demand in each sales period. This is a further explanation to the matter in Section 4.5.2.

In this problem, we consider a single sales period and need to determine the number of failures in the components inside that period. For this purpose, we assume that the warranty period is an integer multiple of the sales period which is consistent with what happens in reality, $w = K. T$ (K is an integer number). In the same way, we consider the sales period as an integer multiple of time unit, $\acute{T}$, which means $T = \acute{K}.\acute{T}$ ($\acute{K}$ is an integer number). If we assume that the pre-market rate of demand is almost constant, then in each time unit $^{x.sl_p}/_K$ products are supplied to the market on an average. In Figure 4-11, we consider the beginning of a sales period as the origin of the time on the horizontal axis. We want to determine how many Component i failures will be received during this sales period. First, we do it for the first-time unit of the sales period. The procedure for the other time units is similar. As shown in Figure 4-5, the warranty period for the supply lot size $^{x.sl_p}/_K$ which was sold $\acute{K}.K$ time units before is finished. But warranty period for the other lot sizes are as follows:

- For the lot size $x.sl_p/_K$ sold $\acute{K}$. $K-1$ time units before we will receive

$$\frac{x.sl_p}{K}.\left[E_i(w)-E_i\left(\frac{\acute{K}.K-1}{\acute{K}.K}w\right)\right] \text{ failures on average;}$$

- For the lot size $x.sl_p/_K$ sold $\acute{K}$. $K-2$ time units before we will receive

$$\frac{x.sl_p}{K}.\left[E_i\left(\frac{\acute{K}.K-1}{\acute{K}.K}w\right)-E_i\left(\frac{\acute{K}.K-2}{\acute{K}.K}w\right)\right] \text{ failures on an average;}$$

- For the lot size $x.sl_p/_K$ sold $\acute{K}$. $K-3$ time units before we will receive

$$\frac{x.sl_p}{K}.\left[E_i\left(\frac{\acute{K}.K-2}{\acute{K}.K}w\right)-E_i\left(\frac{\acute{K}.K-3}{\acute{K}.K}w\right)\right] \text{ failures on an average;}$$

- ...

- For the lot size $x.sl_p/_K$ which is sold 0 time units before we will receive

$$\frac{x.sl_p}{K}.\left[E_i\left(\frac{\acute{K}.K-(\acute{K}.K-1)}{\acute{K}.K}w\right)-E_i(0)\right] \text{ failures on an average;}$$

Therefore, $\dfrac{x.sl_p}{K}.E_i(w)$ failures will be received in the first-time unit of the sales period. There are K time units inside the sales period. Thus, the retailer will receive $x. sl_p. E_i(w)$ Component i failures in each sales period ($\forall i = 1, 2,..., N$).

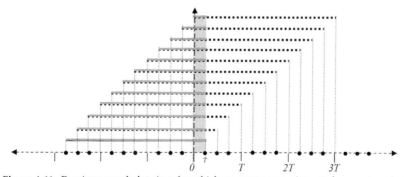

Figure 4-11. Previous supply lot sizes for which warranty commitments have not expired by the end of the $[0, T']$ time interval (in this figure it is assumed that $w = 3T$ and $T = 4T'$).

Appendix 4.D: Model Linearization

Linearized form of Equations (4-24), (4-25), (4-26), and the first term of the objective function (4-22)

$$\Delta x = \sum_{r=1}^{|RL1|} \sum_{m=1}^{|RL2||RL3|} \sum_{s=1}^{|W|} \sum_{t=1} y_{rl1^r} \cdot y_{rl2^m} \cdot y_{rl3^s} \cdot z_{w^t} \cdot \left[\begin{array}{c} G'^{-1}(rl2^m) \cdot D(p, (rl1^r \cdot rl2^m \cdot rl3^{sN}), (rl1^r \cdot rl3^s)^N, w^t). \\ G^{-1}\left(Max \left\{ rl1^r, \dfrac{h^-}{h^- + h^+} \right\} \right) \end{array} \right]$$

$$(4\text{-}37)$$

$$s_i = \sum_{r=1}^{|RL1|} \sum_{t=1}^{|W|} y_{rl1^r} \cdot \left[G_{NB}^{i \; -1}(rl^r) \right] \qquad (\forall i = 1, 2, \dots, N) \qquad (4\text{-}38)$$

$$\Delta \acute{x}_i = \sum_{r=1}^{|RL1|} \sum_{m=1}^{|RL2|} \sum_{s=1}^{|RL3|} \sum_{t=1}^{|W|} y_{rl1^r} \cdot y_{rl2^m} \cdot y_{rl3^s} \cdot z_{w^t} \cdot \left[\dfrac{\gamma_i}{1-\gamma_i} \left[\dfrac{PR_{1i}}{\mu_i} \ln(rl3^s) + (G_{NB}^{i \; -1}(rl1^r) \right. \right.$$

$$+ (G'^{-1}(rl2^m)$$

$$\left. \left. + 1). D(p, (rl1^r \cdot rl2^m \cdot rl3^{sN}), (rl1^r \cdot rl3^s)^N, w^t). G^{-1}\left(Max \left\{ rl1^r, \dfrac{h^-}{h^- + h^+} \right\} \right) \right] \right]$$

$$(\forall i = 1, 2, \dots, N) \qquad (4\text{-}39)$$

Since the product of binary variables can be linearized easily, the items appearing in the second term of the objective function will be linear. Also the first term of the objective function can be rewritten as:

$$\left[\left(p - h^+. E\left[G^{-1}\left(Max \left\{ rl_s^N \cdot rl_m \cdot rl_r, \dfrac{h^-}{h^- + h^+} \right\} \right) - \varepsilon \right]^+ \right. \right.$$

$$- h^-. E\left[\varepsilon - G^{-1}\left(Max \left\{ rl_s^N \cdot rl_m \cdot rl_r, \dfrac{h^-}{h^- + h^+} \right\} \right) \right]^+ - cr \right)$$

$$\left. \times D(p, (rl_s^N \cdot rl_m \cdot rl_r), (rl_r \cdot rl_s)^N, w) \right]$$

$$= \sum_{r=1}^{|RL1|} \sum_{m=1}^{|RL2|} \sum_{s=1}^{|RL3|} \sum_{t=1}^{|W|} y_{rl1^r} \cdot y_{rl2^m} \cdot y_{rl3^s} \cdot z_{w^t} \cdot \left[D(p, (rl1^r \cdot rl2^m \cdot rl3^{sN}), (rl1^r \cdot rl3^s)^N, w^t). \right.$$

$$\left(p - h^+. E\left[G^{-1}\left(Max \left\{ rl1^r \cdot rl2^m \cdot rl3^{sN}, \dfrac{h^-}{h^- + h^+} \right\} \right) - \varepsilon \right]^+ - h^-. E\left[\varepsilon - \right. \right.$$

$$\left. \left. G^{-1}\left(Max \left\{ rl1^r \cdot rl2^m \cdot rl3^{sN}, \dfrac{h^-}{h^- + h^+} \right\} \right) \right]^+ - cr \right) \right] \qquad (4\text{-}40)$$

In this way, the first term of the objective function will also be linear.

CHAPTER 5

Variation Management in Supply Networks

In Chapter 5, we explain how the approaches and models developed in Chapters 3 and 4 for pre- and after-sales supply chains can be extended and used for complicated supply networks with more than one facility in each echelon (see Chapter 1, Figure 1-9).

5.1 Reliable Flow Planning in Supply Networks

In this chapter, we want to show how the models proposed in Chapters 3 and 4 for concurrent flow planning in pre- and after-sales supply chains (SCs) can be extended to companies having pre- and after-sales supply networks (SNs) instead of SCs. In this chapter, we consider a company including both a pre-sales SN producing and supplying products to markets and an after-sales SN providing spare parts to fulfill the after-sales commitments. Variations in estimating product demands in the pre-markets and spare parts demands in the after-sales markets and qualified outputs of production facilities throughout these two networks are considered in this problem. We propose a mathematical model for determining the best marketing strategies for this company (price, warranty length and service levels) in the markets and preserving reliable flow dynamics throughout the networks. Finally, the model is tested on a test problem defined in the engine industry and some managerial insights are provided by analyzing the results.

In the context of an architecture for fail-safe networks, as introduced in Section 1.3, we explain the use of reliability for risk management in two correlated SNs (see Figure 1-4). The connector is forward and after-sales SNs. We express the form of our architecture as an optimization model that determines the best local reliabilities (properties) for the networks' facilities in a way as to maximize the total profit in pre- and after-sales markets (relationship). This model helps us to understand the relationship between the networks' performances (pre- and after-sales service levels) and the local reliabilities of the facilities (component of risk management). Summary interpretation for the problem investigated in Chapter 5 is as follows:

Table 5-1. Summary interpretation for the problem investigated in Chapter 5.

Elements	What?
Components	Reliability
Connectors	Forward and after-sales supply networks
Form	**How?**
Component importance	Reliability: 1
Properties	Local reliabilities
Relationship	Profit optimization in pre- and after-sales markets
Rationale	**Why?**
Motivation	Variation management
Assumptions	No disruption There is enough information to quantify variations
Constraints	Order amplification in echelons due to variations Market demands depend on service levels, pre-sales market retail prices, and after-sales market warranties
Interpretation	Relationship between the networks' service levels in pre- and after-sales markets and the local reliabilities of their facilities Relationship between pre- and after-sales marketing factors

5.2 Literature in the After-sales Operations

In today's highly competitive markets, products manufactured by rivals become almost homogeneous from quality and price perspectives. In such markets to differentiate their products from those of rivals and to leverage competition capabilities, an increasing number of companies try to provide better pre- and after-sales services for their customers (Penttinen and Palmer 2007; Johnson and Mena 2008; Bijvank et al. 2010; Rezapour and Zanjirani Farahani 2014; Rezapour et al. 2016c, 2016a; Rezapour et al. 2017; Hasani and Khosrojerdi 2016; Rezapour et al. 2016b; Mohammaddust et al. 2015). This marketing strategy has been called "servitization" in the literature (Vandermerwe and Rada 1988). Product-service system (PSS) is introduced by (Baines et al. 2007) as a special case of servitization. Servitization motivates the customers to buy and stimulates demand. In the competitive markets with homogeneous products (from quality and price facets), customers tend to buy from the rival providing better service commitment. To stimulate demand, service commitment must be guaranteed. To keep the brand reputation, actual service experienced by the customers in the pre- and after-sales markets can be higher than the commitment but should never be lower.

Servitization is an important marketing strategy for most of the pioneer manufacturers. For example, Rolls-Royce supplies its jet engines to the airlines under a service commitment to repair and maintain them for many years (Davies et al. 2006). Dell Company sells its laptops under a default hardware warranty that states "1 Yr Ltd Warranty, 1 Yr Mail-In Service and 1 Yr Technical Support". However, at the additional price of \$119, customers are offered an optional 3-year warranty plan (Dell. com 2010). After-sales services are critical in the automobile industry; the Hyundai Company offers a 5 year/60.000-mile bumper-to-bumper and 10 year/100,000-mile powertrain protection warranty for all its automobiles sold in US. Distributors for companies like General Motor, Volkswagen and Toyota provide 4S services (sale, spare parts, service and survey) for their customers (Xu et al. 2014).

In the past, after-sales services were considered as a necessary cost generator but today this role has changed and they are considered a source of competitive advantages and business opportunity (Lele 1997). After-sales service is also considered as an important income resource. After-sales markets are usually four or five times larger than their corresponding products and their profits are at lease three times larger than the profit from the products' markets (Bundschuh and Dezvane 2003).

Due to these reasons, the number of companies providing after-sales services for their customers and servicing after-sales markets are growing every day. Gaiardelli et al. (2007) highlight that SC and process-oriented literature dealing with after-sales services is very limited and overcoming obstacles of this industry, mainly related to relationships between the entities involved, is necessary. As highlighted by Boone et al. 2008; McAvoy 2008; Cohen et al. 2006; Wagner and Lindemann 2008; Bacchetti and Saccani 2012, most of the mangers lament (i) the lack of system perspective in servicing after-sales markets and (ii) weakness of considering relationships in all SC operations (procurement, production, distribution and inventory management). In this chapter, we plan to fill this gap in the literature by considering all the after-sales operations and their responsible entities in the form of an after-sales SN.

After-sales service capacity can be provided in two different ways: (i) in-house which means the company itself provides the requirements (such as spare parts availabilities and repair and service capacities) to fulfill the after-sales service request; this in-house capacity—called *"prior service capacity"*—should be ready before the after-sales service demand realization, or (ii) providing it from outsourcing the market which is usually called *"service spot market"*; in this case service provision is done after demand realization (Morley et al. 2006). Although spot market is usually introduced as a hedge against service demand variation, its cost and service capacity are inherently uncertain. That is why most of the companies with well-known brands prefer to use prior service capacity (in-house option) not only because it is more reliable but also due to intellectual property protection. These companies build suitable prior service capacity which maximizes their expected profit. However, dealing simultaneously with product and service complicates the operations of these companies significantly. These companies deal with two SNs: (i) pre-sales SN producing and supplying products to markets and (ii) after-sales SN fulfilling after-sales service requests. The operations of these two networks are highly convoluted. But for simplicity, these two chains are investigated separately in the literature. Based on Xu et al. 2014; Johnson and Mena 2008, SC literature is very sparse on product-service system. Nordin 2005 highlights that little academic research has been done about after-sales services in the manufacturing context. By considering pre- and after-sales SNs of a manufacturing company simultaneously, we fill this gap of the literature.

Research on after-sales service covers the following streams:

- ✓ Maintenance and replacement activities to prevent systems' failures (Wang 2012; Park et al. 2013; Shahanaghi et al. 2013; Vahdani et al. 2013; Rao 2011)

- ✓ Repair services in systems' failures (Öner et al. 2010; Rappold and Van Roo 2009; Sahba and Balcıog 2011; Sleptchenko et al. 2002; Van Ommeren et al. 2006)

- ✓ Spare parts management to fulfill after-sales commitments (Chien and Chen 2008; Kleber et al. 2011; Lieckens et al. 2013; Thonemann et al. 2002). As mentioned by (Boylan and Syntetos 2009), spare parts are very varied and have different costs, demand patterns and requirements. So, classification of spare parts is critical for appropriate inventory management (Zhou and Fan 2007; Ng 2007; Kalchschmidt et al. 2006).

- ✓ Appropriate warranty service selection (Chu and Chintagunta 2009; Hartman and Laksana 2009; Huang et al. 2007; Su and Shen 2012; Tsoukalas and Agrafiotis 2013; Wu et al. 2009; Zhou et al. 2009).

- ✓ Managing customer relationships (Gupta and Lehmann 2005). This research stream illustrates the value of understanding how marketing dollars affect customer profitability and why this focus may lead to very different conclusions than those obtained from traditional approaches.

✓ After-sales demand prediction (Barabadi et al. 2014; Chu and Chintagunta 2009; Dolgui and Pashkevich 2008; Gutierrez et al. 2008; Hua et al. 2007). The demand of a large portion of spare parts is lumpy and intermittent which requires a new forecasting method and on the other hand their demands depend on some explanatory variables such as product failure probability and system maintenance activities. This topic has a voluminous literature.

✓ Competition between new and remanufactured products in markets (Atasu et al. 2008; Ferrer and Swaminathan 2006; Mitra and Webster 2008; Wu 2012).

✓ After-sales service competition (Kameshwaran et al. 2009; Kurata and Nam 2010). This research stream is about modeling competition of rivals in a market by considering after-sales service as one of their marketing strategies.

✓ Configuration of after-sales networks (Amini et al. 2005; Khajavi et al. 2014; Nordin 2005; Saccani et al. 2007). This research stream refers to how SC configuration is designed with respect to the activities carried out within it.

Based on this literature review, the lack of holistic and process-oriented consideration in after-sales operations and ignoring interactions between pre- and after-sales SNs (product-service interplay) are clear. We fill this gap by concurrent planning of flow dynamics in all entities of pre- and after-sales markets' operations in the form of pre- and after-sales SNs. The other important factor that is considered in this chapter is variation management in the flow dynamics of the chains. Three variations are mainly considered in the after-sales research:

✓ Variation in the failure time/rate of product/system to determine after-sales demand (Barabadi et al. 2014; Faridimehr and Niaki 2012; Lieckens et al. 2013; Matis et al. 2008; Öner et al. 2010; Park et al. 2013; Rao 2011; Rappold and Van Roo 2009; Sahba and Balcıog 2011; Su and Shen 2012; Vahdani et al. 2013; Van Jaarsveld and Dekker 2011; Wang 2012; Wang and Lin 2009; Wu et al. 2009).

✓ Variation in the repair time of product/system (Lieckens et al. 2013; Öner et al. 2010; Rappold and Van Roo 2009; Sahba and Balcıog 2011; Van Ommeren et al. 2006).

✓ Variation in the repair cost (Zhou et al. 2009).

As seen above, most of the work in the literature does not include a holistic view and only concentrates on downstream of after-sales SNs such as repair demand prediction and repair process management and their corresponding variations. They ignore the upstream production facilities producing and providing the requirements (such as spare parts) for the after-sales services. In this chapter, we consider the upstream production facilities of the after-sales SN and their corresponding variations. Three groups of variations are considered in this problem: (1) demand-side variation; (2) supply-side variation and (3) variation in the performances of the product's components. Demand-side variation includes the variation in the prediction of pre-markets' product demands and after-sales markets' spare parts' demands. Supply-side variation includes imperfect production systems of production facilities such as suppliers and manufacturers which lead to stochastic qualified outputs and supply quantities of these facilities. Supply-side variations are mainly ignored in the literature of not only after-sales SNs but also pre-sales SNs. This variation is critical because there is not any perfect production system and non-conforming production rates in the production systems have increased recently due to a higher production rate which led to higher number of machinery and labor failures (Rezapour et al. 2015; Sana 2010). In this chapter, we fill this gap in the literature and bring supply-side variations into consideration. We notice that in SNs with multiple stochastic echelons, variations propagate and accumulate by moving flow of products and spare parts from upstream to the downstream of the networks. These variation propagations should be formulated throughout the networks to quantify stochastic qualified supply quantities of product and spare parts. Introducing and modeling variation propagation in stochastic SNs and using it to quantify qualified supply quantities in the last echelon of their networks, are the other contributions of this work.

All in all, in this chapter we consider a company including pre- and after-sales SNs with several demand and supply side variations. In such a complex production system, we want to determine the best marketing strategies (such as price, warranty length and service levels) and their preserving reliable flow dynamics in the SNs. The contributions of this research in comparison with the literature are as follows:

✓ Introducing and quantifying variation propagation throughout the stochastic pre- and after-sales SNs;

✓ Finding out the relationship between service levels of the SNs and local reliabilities of their including facilities;

✓ Finding out the relationship between local reliabilities of facilities and their flow quantities;

✓ Proposing a comprehensive mathematical model for concurrent flow planning in the pre- and after-sales SNs and optimizing the company's marketing strategies in the presence of demand and supply side variations.

This chapter is organized as follows: Section 5.3 includes detailed descriptions of operations and variation sources in the SNs, assumptions and expected outputs. The modeling method and solution approach are proposed in Sections 5.4–5.7 and 5.8 respectively and tested on a test problem from the engine industry in Section 5.9. Closing comments are offered in Section 5.10.

5.3 Operations and Variations in Supply Networks

In this problem, we consider a company producing and supplying products to pre-markets through a pre-sales SN. These products are sold to the customers under a specific retail price and warranty strategy. This product includes several key components which are produced by suppliers in the first echelon. These components are transported to manufacturers in the second echelon and after assembling, final products are supplied to pre-markets through retailers. The products are sold with a failure-free warranty and all defective products returned by customers within the warranty period should be fixed free of charge. Spare parts required to fix the returned products are provided by an after-sales SN. The after-sales SN has two echelons: (i) the suppliers in the first echelon produce the required components to fix the returned products and (ii) these parts are transported to the retailers in the second echelon for substitution and repair. The required products and spare parts to fulfill the pre-market product demands and the warranty repair requests (called the after-sales market demands) of each sales period are produced in these pre- and after-sales SNs and stored in the retailers before the beginning of that sales period.

Before the beginning of each sales period, the retailers order the required products of the pre-markets and the spare parts of the after-sales markets from the manufacturers and suppliers respectively. Based on the retailers' orders and performance of their production systems, the manufacturers' order the required components from the suppliers. The suppliers receive the orders of the manufacturers and retailers and based on the performance of their own production systems, order the required materials from outside suppliers. We consider different variations in modeling this problem: (i) variation in the pre- and after-sales market demands, (ii) variation in the qualified supply quantities of the suppliers, (iii) stochastic flow deterioration in the intermediate manufacturing nodes and (iv) variation in the performance of the components. The demand variations include variation in the product demand prediction in the pre-markets and the spare parts demands prediction in the after-sales markets. The variations of the supply and intermediate manufacturing facilities are related to imperfect production systems of these facilities including a stochastic percent of nonconforming production. Thus, qualified flow deteriorates by moving from upstream to downstream in these networks and this deterioration increases as the variation propagates. In such complex production systems, the following questions arise by considering these variations:

1. What are the best service levels for the entire pre- and after-sales SNs?
2. What are the best local reliabilities for the SNs' stochastic facilities supporting their service levels?
3. What are the best material, component, and product flow through the SNs supporting the local reliabilities of the facilities?
4. What are the best price and warranty strategies for the company?
5. What are the correlations between the best marketing strategies (service levels, price and warranty) of the company?

5.4 Path Concepts in Supply Networks

Without loss of generality and for modeling the problem, we consider a sample three-echelon pre-sales SN including suppliers, manufacturers and retailers. The modeling approach proposed here is applicable for any kind of network with any number of echelons. The notations used in this chapter are summarized in the Appendix 5.A. In Figure 5-1, a sample pre-sales SN is shown with three suppliers ($S = \{s_1, s_2, s_3\}$), one manufacturer ($M = \{m_1\}$) and two retailers ($R = \{r_1, r_2\}$). The product of this SN includes two critical components, $N = \{n_1, n_2\}$. The first component is provided by a first group of suppliers, $S^{(n_1)} = \{s_1, s_2\}$, including the first and second suppliers. The second component is provided by the third supplier which alone is considered as a second group of suppliers, $S^{(n_2)} = \{s_3\}$. Flow streams of components starting from the suppliers in the first echelon are assembled in the manufacturer and as final products transported to the retailers in the last echelon to supply to the markets. In the structure of the pre-sales SN, there are several potential paths that can be used to produce and supply products to the markets.

In the sample, SN of Figure 5-1, each path starts from a set of suppliers in the first echelon (one supplier for each component), passes through the manufacturer in the intermediate echelon, and ends at a retailer in the last echelon. The potential paths of the sample pre-sales SN are shown in Figure 5-1. Here each path corresponds to a triple, $t = (s, \acute{s}, r) \ \forall s \in S^{(n_1)}$, $\forall \acute{s} \in S^{(n_2)}$ and $\forall r \in R$. It includes the starting suppliers of the first and second components and the final retailer. As there is a single manufacturer in this example, it is not included in the path definition. However, this must be considered in a problem with several manufacturers.

Using the concept of path in modeling this problem helps us to be able to use the developed mathematical model for any kind of network after a little manipulation. In a different network, we only need to modify

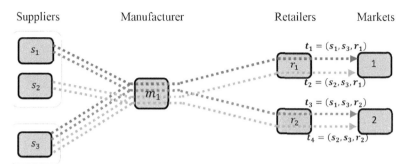

Figure 5-1. Potential paths in the structure of the sample pre-sales SN.

the definition of path and apply it in the same way in the mathematical model.

The set of potential paths for the sample SN of Figure 5-1 is $T = \{t_1 = (s_1, s_3, r_1), t_2 = (s_2, s_3, r_1), t_3 = (s_1, s_3, r_2), t_4 = (s_2, s_3, r_2)\}$. The most profitable subset of these paths must be selected to produce and supply the products to the pre-markets. The products of this chain are supplied to the market with a specific price, p and failure free warranty, w strategies. Eventually a stochastic percentage of the supplied products is returned by the customers to the retailers and their defective components should be fixed free of charge. The components required to fix these defective products must be provided by the suppliers. We assume that the required components to fix the defective items supplied by a path should be provided by the corresponding suppliers of that path. For example, if we assume that t_1 is a selected active path in the sample pre-sales SN in Figure 5-1 and its flow quantity is x_{t_1}, the required first and second components to repair the returned items of these x_{t_1} products, which are represented by $\acute{x}_{t_1}^{(n_1)}$ and $\acute{x}_{t_1}^{(n_2)}$, will be supplied directly by the associated suppliers of path t_1 (s_1 and s_3) to its ending retailer, r_1 (Figure 5-2). So, by determining the selected paths of the pre-sales SN and their assigned flow quantities, the active paths of the after-sales SN and their corresponding flow quantities are determined automatically.

In this problem, we consider demand- and supply-side variations by assuming that demand prediction in the demand nodes is stochastic and the performance of the production systems in the supply and intermediate manufacturing facilities is imperfect. Imperfect production systems in the supply and manufacturing facilities mean that their qualified output quantities are stochastic. Having several uncertain echelons in the SN leads to a problem which we call variation propagation. Considering and quantifying this propagation of variation is critical for determining service levels in the pre- and after-sales markets. The variation propagation occurs through all the active paths of the networks. We display one of the paths of the pre-sales SN as a sample in Figure 5-2. In the rest of this section, we

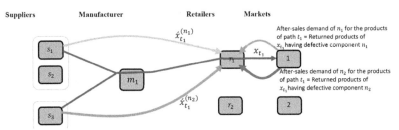

Figure 5-2. The after-sales services provided by the active Path t_1.

describe the process of quantifying variation propagation throughout this path of the pre-sales SN.

5.5 Variation Management in the Pre-sales Supply Network

The pre- and after-sales markets' service levels show the global reliabilities of the pre- and after-sales networks against all the variations and their propagated effect. The service levels which represent the capability of the networks in balancing the supply and demand quantities depend on the local reliabilities of its constituting facilities. In this problem, we introduce and use the concept of paths to produce and supply products and spare parts to the markets. Therefore, in this section (Section 5.5) and Section 5.6 respectively, we explain how to manage the flow in the paths of the pre- and after-sales SNs against variations. Then we use the findings of these sections in Section 5.7 to develop a comprehensive mathematical model to manage the performance of the entire system.

In this section, we elaborate a way to quantify variation propagation and plan a reliable flow through the paths of the pre-sales SN. The paths of the pre-sales network include a retailer, a manufacturer and suppliers (one supplier for each component). However, in each path of the after-sales SN there are a retailer and suppliers (one supplier for each component, Figure 5-2).

We assume that the local reliability of Retailer r, Manufacturer m and Supplier s are represented by rl_r, rl_m and rl_s respectively. To quantify variation propagation through each path, in Section 5.5.1, we start from the last echelon including a retailer, then variations of the manufacturer and suppliers are addressed in Sections 5.5.2 and 5.5.3.

5.5.1 Variation Management in the Pre-sales Supply Network's Retailers

The company positions itself in the markets by choosing its pre- and after-sales service levels, warranty length and retail price. The average product demand in Market r, $\bar{D}_r(sl_p, sl_a, w, p)$, in a sales period is an increasing function of the service levels, (sl_p, sl_a), and warranty length, w and a decreasing function of price, p. However, the realized actual demand is stochastic and has a deviation from its mean. Consistently with Bernstein and Federgruen 2004, 2007, we assume that the stochastic actual demand in a market is multiplicative as $D_r(sl_p, sl_a, w, p) = \varepsilon_r \times \bar{D}_r(sl_p, sl_a, w, p)$. Where ε_r is a general continuous random variable with a cumulative distribution function, $G_r(\varepsilon_r)$, which is independent of the service levels, warranty length and retail price. Without loss of generality, we assume $E(\varepsilon_r) = 1$ which means $E[D_r(sl_p, sl_a, w, p)] = \bar{D}_r(sl_p, sl_a, w, p)$.

Before the beginning of each sales period, Retailer r ($\forall r \in R$) orders the required products from the manufacturers. These products are provided by the active paths ending with this retailer, $\sum_{T(r)} x_t$, before the beginning of the period. Additional product transactions during the period and after real demand realization, are not possible. The demand of Market r is stochastic with $G_r(.)$ cumulative distribution function (demand-side variation). Extra inventory and inventory shortage at the end of each sales period impose unit cost h_r^+ and h_r^- to the retailer respectively. Thus, subject to the local reliability of Retailer r (rl_r), the product ordering quantity of the retailer, $\sum_{T(r)} x_t$, should be determined in a way as to minimize its end-of-period total cost.

Product ordering quantity of Retailer r is:

$$MIN \quad \Pi_r = h_r^+ . E[\sum_{T(r)} x_t - D_r(sl_p, sl_a, w, p)]^+ + h_r^- . E[D_r(sl_p, sl_a, w, p) - \sum_{T(r)} x_t]^+ \tag{5-1}$$

$$S.T. \quad \Pr[D_r(sl_p, sl_a, w, p) \leq \sum_{T(r)} x_t] \geq rl_r \tag{5-2}$$

The first term of the objective function (5-1) is the expected holding cost of the end-of-period extra inventory and the second term is the expected shortage cost in Retailer r. Therefore, the objective function is minimizing the total cost in the retailer. Constraint (5-2) preserves the local reliability of the retailer (Figure 5-3). Minimizing the model's objective function without considering constraint (5-2) leads to $\sum_{T(r)} x_t = \bar{D}_r(sl_p, sl_a, w, p). G_r^{-1}(\frac{h_r^-}{h_r^- + h_r^+})$.

Also, to preserve the local reliability of the retailer, we have $\sum_{T(r)} x_t \geq \bar{D}_r(sl_p, sl_a, w, p). G_r^{-1}(rl_r)$. Accordingly, the best amount of the product that should be ordered by the retailer is $\sum_{T(r)} x_t = \bar{D}_r(sl_p, sl_a, w, p). G_r^{-1}\left(Max\left\{rl_r, \frac{h_r^-}{h_r^- + h_r^+}\right\}\right)$.

This order is distributed among the active paths ending at this retailer and

Path t's share from this order is x_t (assuming that Path t ends at Retailer r). Therefore, x_t products must be provided by the manufacturer of this path. In the next section, we study the manufacturer's performance with respect to the retailers' order.

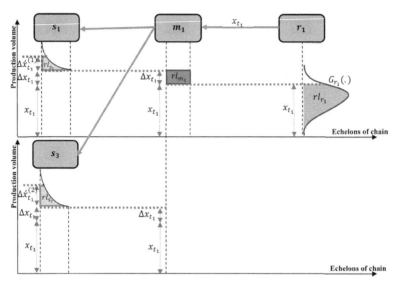

Figure 5-3. Variation propagation in Path $t_1 = (s_1, s_3, r_1)$ of the pre-sales SN.

5.5.2 *Variation Management in the Pre-sales Supply Network's Manufacturers*

The order share of each path should be produced by the manufacturer of that path. By assuming that Path t is passing through Manufacturer m, this manufacturer should produce x_t qualified products for this path. But the production system of the manufacturer is not perfect and is always accompanied by a stochastic percentage of defective items. To compensate for these defective items, the manufacturer should plan to produce some extra products represented by Δx_t. The amount of Δx_t depends on the local reliability of Manufacturer m. Δx_t should be determined in a way that the manufacturer can be sure with rl_m probability that it can fulfill the whole product order assigned to the path. The probability that the defective product quantity in the manufacturing process of Path t's ordered products, $D_{m,t}$, will be less than Δx_t should be equal to rl_m ($\acute{G}_{m,t}$ is the cumulative distribution function assumed for $D_{m,t}$):

$$\Pr(D_{m,t} \leq \Delta x_t) = rl_m \qquad \rightarrow \qquad \Delta x_t = \acute{G}_{m,t}^{-1}(rl_m) \qquad (5\text{-}3)$$

For example, if we assume that the defective production rate in Manufacturer m is a stochastic variable, α_m, uniformly distributed on $[0, \beta_m]$, then the appropriate value of Δx_t becomes:

$$\text{Pr}\left(\alpha_m . \, x_t \leq \Delta x_t\right) = \text{Pr}\left(\alpha_m \leq \frac{\Delta x_t}{x_t}\right) = rl_m \qquad \rightarrow \qquad \Delta x_t = rl_m . \, \beta_m . \, x_t \qquad (5\text{-}4)$$

To preserve its local reliability, rl_m, the manufacturer plans to produce $x_t + \Delta x_t$ products for Path t. Accordingly, it should order $x_t + \Delta x_t$ components from the suppliers of this path. In Section 5.5.3, we study the performance of Path t's suppliers with respect to the component orders received from the manufacturer.

5.5.3 *Variation Management in the Pre-sales Supply Network's Suppliers*

We assume that Supplier s is a supplier of Path t. This supplier receives an order of $x_t + \Delta x_t$ component units from the manufacturer. But we know that his production system is not perfect and has some nonconforming output. To compensate for these nonconforming items, the supplier plans to produce extra components, $\Delta \acute{x}_t^{(s)}$. The amount of $\Delta \acute{x}_t^{(s)}$ depends on the local reliability of Supplier s. $\Delta \acute{x}_t^{(s)}$ ensures the supplier with rl_s probability that it can fulfill the manufacturer's order. Therefore, the probability that the nonconforming component quantity in the production process of Path t's order, $D_{s,t}$, is less than $\Delta \acute{x}_t^{(s)}$ and is equal to rl_s ($G''_{s,t}$ is the cumulative distribution function assumed for $D_{s,t}$):

$$\text{Pr}\left(D_{s,t} \leq \Delta \acute{x}_t^{(s)}\right) = rl_s \qquad \rightarrow \qquad \Delta \acute{x}_t^{(s)} = G''^{-1}_{s,t}(rl_s) \qquad (5\text{-}5)$$

For example, we assume that in the supplier, after setting up the machines to produce the required components, the machines start to work in an in-control state in which all the produced components are qualified. Gradually their state deteriorates and after a stochastic time, they shift to an out-of-control state in which γ_s percent of components is nonconforming. According to Rosenblatt and Lee 1986; Lee and Rosenblatt 1987, we assume the deterioration time follows exponential distribution with $1/\mu_s$ mean. After shifting to the out-of-control state, they stay in that state until the whole batch is completed because interrupting the machines is prohibitively expensive. To fulfill the component order of Path t, $\Delta \acute{x}_t^{(s)} + \Delta x_t + x_t$ components should be produced by this supplier. By considering PR_s as the production rate of the supplier, it takes $\dfrac{\Delta \acute{x}_t^{(s)} + \Delta x_t + x_t}{PR_s}$ time units to produce this batch. Assuming rl_s as the supplier's local reliability, the probability that the quantity of non-conforming components produced during this time period is less than $\Delta \acute{x}_t^{(s)}$ should be equal to rl_s. Thus, the probability that the conforming component quantity is greater than or equal to $\Delta x_t + x_t$ should be equal to rl_s:

$$rl_s = \Pr(\text{conforming component units produced in } \frac{\Delta \acute{x}_t^{(s)} + \Delta x_t + x_t}{PR_s} \text{ time units} \geq \Delta x_t + x_t)$$

$$= \Pr\left[PR_s . t + (1 - \gamma_s). PR_s . \left(\frac{\Delta \acute{x}_t^{(s)} + \Delta x_t + x_t}{PR_s} - t\right) \geq \Delta x_t + x_t\right]$$

$$= \Pr\left[t \geq \left(\frac{\Delta x_t + x_t}{PR_s}\right) - \left(\frac{1 - \gamma_s}{\gamma_s . PR_s}\right). (\Delta \acute{x}_t^{(s)})\right] = EXP\left[-\mu_s . \left(\left(\frac{\Delta x_t + x_t}{PR_s}\right) - \left(\frac{1 - \gamma_s}{\gamma_s . PR_s}\right). (\Delta \acute{x}_t^{(s)})\right)\right]$$

(5-6)

$$\rightarrow \Delta \acute{x}_t^{(s)} = \frac{\gamma_s}{1 - \gamma_s}\left[\frac{PR_s}{\mu_s} \ln(rl_s) + (\Delta x_t + x_t)\right] \tag{5-7}$$

This means that with this $\Delta \acute{x}_t^{(s)}$ extra production, Supplier s will be sure with rl_s probability that it can fulfill the order of the manufacturer.

To sum up, with $\Delta \acute{x}_t^{(s)}$ ($\forall s \in t$—all the suppliers of Path t) extra production, the suppliers of Path t in the first echelon will be sure with $\prod_{(\forall s \in t)} rl_s$ probability that they can fulfill the whole component order of this path's manufacturer. Also, the manufacturer by producing Δx_t extra products, will be sure with rl_m probability that he can fulfill the product order of the path's retailer. By ordering x_t products from this path, the retailer will be sure with rl_r probability that he can fulfill a $x_t / \sum_{T^{(r)}} x_t$ portion of the corresponding pre-market's demand in the coming sales period. The global reliability provided by this path is:

Global reliability of Path t $= (\prod_{(\forall s \in t)} rl_s) \times rl_m \times rl_r$ ($\forall t \in T$)   (5-8)

The demand of each pre-market and the order of its corresponding Retailer r can be fulfilled by all the potential paths ending at that retailer, $\forall t \in T^{(r)}$. To determine the active paths of this set, we define binary variables $y_t (\forall t \in T)$. Variable y_t is 1 if potential Path t is active and used to produce and supply products and 0 otherwise.

Therefore, Retailer r will be sure with $\prod_{(\forall t \in T^{(r)})}\left[\left(\left(\prod_{(\forall s \in t)} rl_s\right) \times rl_m \times rl_r\right). y_t + (1 - y_t)\right]$ probability that he can fulfill the demand of its corresponding market in the next sales period. Thus, the service level (demand fulfillment rate) of the pre-sales SN in the pre-market of Retailer r will be:

Pre – market Service Level in Retailer r $= \prod_{(\forall t \in T^{(r)})}\left[\left(\left(\prod_{(\forall s \in t)} rl_s\right) \times rl_m \times rl_r\right). y_t + (1 - y_t)\right]$

($\forall r \in R$)   (5-9)

5.6 Variation Management in the After-sales Supply Network

We assume that the after-sales services of the products supplied by a path to a market should be provided by the facilities of that path. The first step in planning flow dynamics of the after-sales SN, described in Section 5.6.1, is to predict the after-sales requests for the products of each path. After determining the after-sales flow of each path, this flow is amplified from downstream to upstream to deal with variation propagation in that path; this step in described in Section 5.6.2.

5.6.1 Variation Management in the After-sales Supply Network's Retailers

Assume that x_t products are supplied by Path $t \in T^{(r)}$ of the pre-sales SN to the pre-market of Retailer r. The required components to repair the defective products of x_t returned by the customers within the warranty period is the after-sales demand for Path t. Here, we compute the quantity of this demand for each component. This demand depends on the product quantity supplied by Path t in the pre-sales SN, the length of the warranty and the reliability of the components represented by θ_n ($\forall n \in N$). We assume that the performance of the product's components is independent and the failure time of Component n is a random variable with $f_n(\theta_n)$ density and $F_n(\theta_n)$ cumulative density function. Lower θ_n means higher reliability for Component n and longer time between failures. We assume the first λ_n failures of Component n are repairable but after that it is more economical to replace it with a new one. The repair cost of Component n is cr_n. We assume that the behavior of the components does not change after repair; the repaired and new components have similar breakdown behavior. Assuming that $F_n^{(m)}$ and $Num_n(w)$ represents the cumulative distribution function of total time up to the mth failure and the number of failures of Component n in $[0,w]$ interval, we have Nguyen and Murthy (1984):

$$\Pr\{Num_n(w) = m\} = F_n^{(m)}(w, \theta_n) - F_n^{(m+1)}(w, \theta_n) \qquad (\forall n \in N) \qquad (5\text{-}10)$$

Then the average number of new Component n required to repair a unit of product inside the warranty period, $AD_n(w, \theta_n, \lambda_n)$, is:

$$AD_n(w, \theta_n, \lambda_n) = \sum_{m=\lambda_n+1}^{+\infty} F_n^{(m)}(w, \theta_n) \qquad (\forall n \in N) \qquad (5\text{-}11)$$

In the same way, the variance of the number of new Component n required to repair a unit of the product within the warranty period, $VD_n(w, \theta_n, \lambda_n)$, is:

$$VD_n(w, \theta_n, \lambda_n) = \sum_{m=\lambda_n+1}^{+\infty} [2.(m - \lambda_n) - 1]. F_n^{(m)}(w, \theta_n) - [\sum_{m=\lambda_n+1}^{+\infty} F_n^{(m)}(w, \theta_n)]^2$$

$$(\forall n \in N) \qquad (5\text{-}12)$$

By using the Central Limit theorem, the total Component n required in the after-sales market of Path t, $\acute{D}^n_t$, has a normal distribution with the following features:

$$\acute{D}^n_t \sim Normal\ (\mu_{\acute{D}^n_t} = x_t.\ AD_n\ (w,\ \theta_n,\ \lambda_n),\ \sigma^2_{\acute{D}^n_t} = x_t.\ VD_n\ (w,\ \theta_n,\ \lambda_n))$$
$$(\forall n \in N; \forall t \in T) \qquad (5\text{-}13)$$

If Path t ends at Retailer r ($r \in t$) and its local reliability is rl_r, the quantity of Component n ordered by Retailer r from Path t is (z'_{rl_r} is a standard normal distribution for which $P_r(Z \le z'_{rl_r}) = rl_r$:

$$x'^{(n)}_t = x_t.\ AD_n\ (w,\ \theta_n,\ \lambda_n) + (z'_{rl_r}.\ \sqrt{x_t.\ VD_n\ (w,\ \theta_n,\ \lambda_n)})\ (\forall n \in N) \qquad (5\text{-}14)$$

By ordering $x'^{(n)}_t$ units of Component n, the retailer will be sure with rl_r probability that it is able to fulfill the after-sales demand of Component n for path t's products.

5.6.2 Variation Management in the After-sales Supply Network's Suppliers

Retailer r not only orders x_t ($t \in T^{(r)}$) products from the manufacturer of Path t, but also orders $x'^{(n)}_t$ ($\forall n \in N$) units of Component n from the path's corresponding Supplier s($s \in t$ and $s \in S^{(n)}$) providing Component n for this path. Supplier s receives an order of $\Delta x_t + x_t$ component units from the manufacturer of this path (pre-sales SN) and an order of $x'^{(n)}_t$ component units from the retailer of this path (after-sales SN). Thus, the total order received by Supplier s includes $x'^{(n)}_t + \Delta x_t + x_t$ component units. To compensate for the nonconforming output of its production system, it plans to produce extra components $\Delta \acute{x}^{(s)}_t$. In Section 5.5.3, the quantity of $\Delta \acute{x}^{(s)}_t$ is determined by assuming that $\Delta x_t + x_t$ component order is received by this supplier. But in addition to this order of the pre-sales SN, another order with $\Delta \acute{x}^{(n)}_t$ quantity is received from the after-sales SN. In this section, we revise the quantity of $\Delta \acute{x}^{(s)}_t$ to consider the order of the after-sales SN:

$$rl_s = Pr(conforming\ component\ units\ produced\ in\ \frac{\Delta \acute{x}^{(s)}_t + x'^{(n)}_t + \Delta x_t + x_t}{PR_s}\ time$$
$$units \ge x'^{(n)}_t + \Delta x_t + x_t)$$

$$= Pr\left[PR_s.\ t + (1-\gamma_s).\ PR_s.\left(\frac{\Delta \acute{x}^{(s)}_t + x'^{(n)}_t + \Delta x_t + x_t}{PR_s} - t\right) \ge x'^{(n)}_t + \Delta x_t + x_t\right]$$

$$= Pr\left[t \ge \left(\frac{x'^{(n)}_t + \Delta x_t + x_t}{PR_s}\right) - \left(\frac{1-\gamma_s}{\gamma_s.PR_s}\right).(\Delta \acute{x}^{(s)}_t)\right]$$

$$= EXP\left[-\mu_s.\left(\left(\frac{x'^{(n)}_t + \Delta x_t + x_t}{PR_s}\right) - \left(\frac{1-\gamma_s}{\gamma_s.PR_s}\right).(\Delta \acute{x}^{(s)}_t)\right)\right] \qquad (5\text{-}15)$$

$$\to \Delta \dot{x}_t^{(s)} = \frac{\gamma_s}{1 - \gamma_s} \left[\frac{PR_s}{\mu_s} \ln(rl_s) + (x_t^{\prime(n)} + \Delta x_t + x_t) \right] \qquad (5\text{-}16)$$

This means that by this $\Delta \dot{x}_t^{(s)}$ extra production, Supplier s is sure with rl_s probability that it can fulfill the combined orders of the pre- and after-sales SNs.

Thus, with $\Delta \dot{x}_t^{(s)}$ ($\forall s \in t - s$ is supplying Component n) extra production, the supplier of Path t is sure with rl_s probability that it can fulfill the whole Component n order of this path's retailer. By ordering $\dot{x}_t^{(n)}$ units of Component n from the path's supplier, the retailer is sure with rl_r probability that it can fulfill the whole after-sales demand of Component n to repair the defective products of Path t. Therefore, the fulfill rate of Component n in Path t is:

fulfill rate of Component n in Path t $= rl_s \times rl_r \qquad (t \in T^{(r)}, s \in t) \qquad (5\text{-}17)$

There are n components in the product. The fulfillment rate of all components by Path t will be:

fulfill rate of all components in Path t $= \prod_{(\forall n \in N, s \in S^{(n)} \mid s \in t)} (rl_s \times rl_r) =$

$$(rl_r)^{|N|} \cdot \prod_{(\forall n \in N, s \in S^{(n)} \mid s \in t)} rl_s \qquad (t \in T^{(r)}) \qquad (5\text{-}18)$$

The after-sales demand in Retailer r is fulfilled by all the potential active paths ending at that retailer, $\forall t \in T^{(r)}$. Therefore, the service level (demand fulfillment rate) of the after-sales SN in Retailer r is:

after – sale service level in Retailer r

$$= \prod_{(\forall t \in T^{(r)})} \left[\left((rl_r)^{|N|} \cdot \prod_{(\forall n \in N, s \in S^{(n)} \mid s \in t)} rl_s \right) \cdot y_t + (1 - y_t) \right] \qquad (\forall r \in R) \qquad (5\text{-}19)$$

5.7 Concurrent Flow Planning in the Pre- and After-sales Supply Networks

With the help of the equations formulated in Sections 5.5 and 5.6, in this section we develop a comprehensive mathematical model to simultaneously determine the best marketing strategies and their preserving flow dynamics throughout the pre- and after-sales SNs. In practice, there are common options for the warranty length that are usually offered, such as 6, 12, 18, and 24 months. Therefore, in this problem, we define a new set, $W = \{W\}$, including all options available for warranty length. In the same way, we define a similar set for the service levels in the pre- and after-sales markets. Set $SL = \{sl = sl_p, sl_a)\}$ includes all possible options for the service level of the company in the pre- and after-sales markets. The options offered by the markets' rivals and government regulations are considered in determining these sets. To make decisions about warranty and service levels strategy, we define two new binary variables v_w and z_{sl}. Variable v_w is 1 if Warranty w is selected, 0 otherwise ($\forall w \in W$). Variable z_{sl} is 1 if Service level sl is selected, 0 otherwise ($\forall sl \in SL$). The mathematical model of this concurrent planning is:

$$MAX \; \sum_R \sum_W \sum_{SL} v_w \cdot z_{sl} \cdot \overline{D}_r(sl_p, sl_a, w, p) \cdot \left[p - h_r^+ \cdot E\left(G_r^{-1}\left(MAX\left\{rl_{r'} \frac{h_r^-}{h_r^+ + h_r^-}\right\}\right) - \varepsilon_r\right)^+ - \right.$$

$$\left. h_r^- \cdot E\left(\varepsilon_r - G_r^{-1}\left(MAX\left\{rl_{r'} \frac{h_r^-}{h_r^+ + h_r^-}\right\}\right)\right)^+\right]$$

$$- \sum_N \sum_{S^{(n)}} \sum_{T^{(s)}} (a_1^s + a_2^s) \cdot [x_t + \Delta x_t + x_t'^{(n)} + \Delta \acute{x}_t^{(s)}] - \sum_M \sum_{T^{(m)}} \alpha^m \cdot (x_t + \Delta x_t)$$

$$- \sum_S \sum_M \sum_{T^{(s)} \cap T^{(m)}} a_{sm}^t \cdot (x_t + \Delta x_t) - \sum_M \sum_R \sum_{T^{(m)} \cap T^{(r)}} a_{mr}^t \cdot x_t$$

$$- \sum_N \sum_{S^{(n)}} \sum_R \sum_{T^{(s)} \cap T^{(r)}} a_{sr}^t \cdot x_t'^{(n)} \tag{5-20}$$

Subject To:

$$\sum_W v_w = 1 \tag{5-21}$$

$$\sum_{SL} z_{sl} = 1 \tag{5-22}$$

$$\sum_{T^{(r)}} y_t \geq 1 \qquad\qquad (\forall r \in R) \tag{5-23}$$

$$x_t \leq BM \cdot y_t \qquad\qquad (\forall t \in T) \tag{5-24}$$

$$\sum_{T^{(r)}} x_t = [\sum_W \sum_{SL} v_w \cdot z_{sl} \cdot \overline{D}_r(sl_p, sl_a, w, p)] \cdot G_r^{-1}(Max\{rl_{r'} \frac{h_r^-}{h_r^- + h_r^+}\}) \quad (\forall r \in R) \tag{5-25}$$

$$\Delta x_t = {G'}_{m,t}^{-1}(x_t, rl_m) \cdot y_t \qquad\qquad (\forall t \in T, m \in t) \tag{5-26}$$

$$x_t'^{(n)} = x_t \cdot AD_n(w, \theta_n, \lambda_n) + z_{rlr}' \cdot \sqrt{x_t \cdot VD_n(w, \theta_n, \lambda_n)} \quad (\forall t \in T, \forall n \in N) \tag{5-27}$$

$$\Delta \acute{x}_t^{(s)} = {G''}_{s,t}^{-1}(x_t + \Delta x_t + x_t'^{(n)}, rl_s) \cdot y_t \qquad (\forall t \in T, \forall n \in N, s \in t, s \in S^{(n)}) \tag{5-28}$$

$$\sum_{SL} z_{sl} \cdot sl_p = \prod_{(\forall t \in T^{(r)})} \left[((\prod_{(\forall s \in t)} rl_s) \times rl_m \times rl_r) \cdot y_t + (1 - y_t) \right] \qquad (\forall r \in R) \tag{5-29}$$

$$\sum_{SL} z_{sl} \cdot sl_a = \prod_{(\forall t \in T^{(r)})} \left[((rl_r)^{|N|} \cdot \prod_{(\forall n \in N, \ s \in S^{(n)} \mid s \in t)} rl_s) \cdot y_t + (1 - y_t) \right] \quad (\forall r \in R) \quad (5\text{-}30)$$

$$v_w, \ z_{sl}, \ y_t \in \{0,1\} \qquad\qquad (\forall w \in W, \forall sl \in SL, \forall t \in T) \quad (5\text{-}31)$$

$$x_t, \ \Delta x_t, \ \Delta \dot{x}_t^{(s)}, \ x'^{(n)}_t \geq 0 \qquad\qquad (\forall t \in T, \forall s \in S, \forall n \in N) \quad (5\text{-}32)$$

In these equations, *BM* is a large constant. The first term of the objective function (5-20) represents the profit which is captured in the pre-markets. This term is equal to the income minus the shortage and holding cost of the inventory shortage and extra inventory at the end of the sales period. The second term is the sum of procurement and production costs in the suppliers. Manufacturing costs of the products in the manufacturers is computed in the third term. The fourth, fifth and sixth terms compute the sum of transportation costs of the pre-sales SN's components from the suppliers to the manufacturers, the pre-sales SN's products from the manufacturers to the retailers and the after-sales SN's components from the suppliers to the retailers, respectively. This objective function maximizes the net profit of the whole company.

Based on Constraints (5-21) and (5-22), only one warranty and service level strategy can be selected by the company. Constraint (5-23) ensures that at least one path is activated to fulfill the demand of each market. According to Constraint (5-24), product flow is only possible in the activated paths. Based on Constraint (5-25), the sum of the product flow through the paths ending at a retailer is equal to the pre-market demand of that retailer. In Constraint (5-26), flow amplification in the manufacturer of each path is shown. Constraint (5-27) is used to calculate the component requests of each path in the after-sales markets. Constraint (5-28) represents flow amplification in the suppliers of each path. Based on Constraint (5-29), local reliabilities assigned to the facilities must preserve the company's selected pre-market service level. In the same way, local reliabilities assigned to the facilities should preserve the company's selected after-sales service level (Constraint 5-30).

This mathematical model determines the best warranty and service level strategies in the pre- and after-sales markets and their preserving local reliabilities and flow in the system's facilities to maximize the company's total profit. The model developed for this problem is based on some assumptions. These assumptions have either been used extensively in the literature or are justifiable as stated:

- We assume that the average product demand in Market r, $\overline{D}_r(sl_p, sl_a, w, p)$, in a sales period is an increasing function of the service levels,

(sl_p, sl_a) and warranty length, w and a decreasing function of price, p. Finding this demand function for each market is straightforward. We analyze historical quadruples of price, service levels, warranty, average demand in the previous sales periods by regression methods and fit an appropriate function that is used for future sale periods as an estimation of average demand.

- We assume that the number of defective units in the production systems of facilities has a known distribution function. Finding this distribution function for a production system is straightforward. We only need to gather some historical data about the number of defective units in the production batches of that production system in the last couple of days. Then we use statistical tools such as the "goodness-of-fit" test to fit the most appropriate distribution function to represent the number of defective units.

In Sections 5.5.2, we assume that the defective production rate in Manufacturer m is a stochastic variable with a known cumulative distribution function $G'_{m,t}$ (see Eq. 5-3). Then only as an example we show how these equations can be applied for uniform distribution (see Eq. 5-4). In Sections 5.5.3, we assume that the nonconforming component quantity in Supplier s is a stochastic variable with a known cumulative distribution function $G''_{s,t}$ (see Eq. 5-5). Then, only as an example we show how these equations can be applied when deterioration time is exponential (see Eq. 5-7). This means that the method proposed in the chapter is general and does not depend on the type of distribution functions considered for the performance of facilities or demand of markets. We only apply it for a uniform and exponential cases as an example.

- We assume that the performances of the product's components are independent and the failure time of Component n is a random variable with $f_n(\theta_n)$ density and $F_n(\theta_n)$ cumulative density function. This assumption is widely used in the literature (Nguyen and Murthy 1984; Hussain and Murthy 2003; Murthy 1990; Nguyen and Murthy 1988; Jack and Murthy 2007).

This model is a mixed integer nonlinear mathematical model. Solving this kind of model is not straightforward. Especially the form of nonlinear terms in this model depends on the cumulative distribution functions defined for the stochastic parts of the problem. This means that by changing these distribution functions, the mathematical forms of these terms also change. In Section 5.8, we propose an efficient approach to solve this model and find the solution.

5.8 Solution Approach

In this section, we develop a five-step approach to solve the model proposed in the previous section (see Figure 5-15 in Appendix 5.B). First, we define Set $SL = \{sl = (sl_p, sl_a)\}$ including all feasible combinations of service levels in the pre- and after-sales markets and Set $W = \{w\}$ including all feasible warranty options for the product. Then, for each $sl = (sl_p, sl_a) \in SL$ and each $w \in W$, the following steps should be taken:

Step 1: Define a new set, $P1 = \{p1\}$, including all the path selection possibilities in the network to fulfill the demand of all markets. The largest size for this set is:

$$|P1| = \prod_{\forall r \in R} 2^{(|T^{(r)}|-1)} \tag{5-33}$$

Step 2: For each $p1 \in P1$, determine a set of facilities' local reliabilities that can provide sl_p service level in the pre-markets and sl_a service level in the after-sales markets, $P2^{(p1)} = \{p2\}$. Notice that:

$$p2 = (rl_r^{(p2)} (\forall r \in R), rl_m^{(p2)} (\forall m \in M), rl_s^{(p2)} (\forall s \in S)) \tag{5-34}$$

Determining these feasible local reliability combinations is initiated by discretizing the continuous interval of the local reliabilities. For example, by assuming that the least possible pre-market service level is 0.75 and the facilities have the same lower bounds for their local reliabilities, the lower interval bound for the local reliabilities is 0.9. After discretizing the [0.9, 1.0] interval by an acceptable step such as 0.01, these feasible local reliability combinations are determined as follows:

For $rl_r = 0.9: 0.01: 1.0 \ (\forall r \in R)$
  For $rl_m = 0.9: 0.01: 1.0 \ (\forall m \in M)$
    For $rl_s = 0.9: 0.01: 1.0 \ (\forall s \in S)$
      IF $sl_p \cong \prod_{(\forall t \in (p1 \cap T^{(r)}))} \left((\prod_{(\forall s \in t)} rl_s) \times rl_{m \mid m \in t} \times rl_{r \mid r \in t} \right)$ and
        $sl_a \cong \prod_{(\forall t \in (p1 \cap T^{(r)}))} \left((rl_r)^{|N|} \cdot \prod_{(\forall n \in N, \ s \in S^{(n)} \mid s \in t)} rl_s \right)$ $(\forall r \in R)$
        Add $(rl_r^{(p2)} = rl_r (\forall r \in R), rl_m^{(p2)} = rl_m (\forall m \in M), rl_s^{(p2)} = rl_s (\forall s \in S))$ into
set $P2$
          End;
        End;
      End;
End;   (5-35)

Having restricted feasible intervals for local reliability variables justifies the rationality of using discretizing in this step.

Step 3: For each $\forall p1 \in P1$ and $\forall p2 \in P2^{(p1)}$, solve the following linear model with continuous variables:

$$MIN \quad Cost^{(p1,P2)}(w, sl) = \bar{D}_r(sl, w, p) \cdot \left[h_r^+ \cdot E\left(G_r^{-1}\left(MAX\left\{ sl, \frac{h_r^-}{h_r^+ + h_r^-} \right\} \right) - \varepsilon_r \right)^+ + \right.$$

$$\left. h_r^- \cdot E\left(\varepsilon_r - G_r^{-1}\left(MAX\left\{ sl, \frac{h_r^-}{h_r^+ + h_r^-} \right\} \right) \right)^+ \right] + \sum_N \sum_{S(n)} \sum_{T(s)} (a_1^s + a_2^s) \cdot [x_t + \Delta x_t + x_t'^{(n)} + \Delta \acute{x}_t'^{(s)}]$$

$$+ \sum_M \sum_{T(m)} \alpha^m \cdot [x_t + \Delta x_t] + \sum_S \sum_M \sum_{T(s) \cap T(m)} a_{sm}^t \cdot [x_t + \Delta x_t]$$

$$+ \sum_M \sum_R \sum_{T(m) \cap T(r)} a_{mr}^t \cdot x_t + \sum_N \sum_{S(n)} \sum_R \sum_{T(m) \cap T(r)} a_{sr}^t \cdot x_t'^{(n)} \qquad (5\text{-}36)$$

Subject To:

$$\sum_{\forall t \in p1 \mid r \in t} x_t = \bar{D}_r(sl, w, p) \cdot G_r^{-1}\left(MAX\left\{ rl_r^{(p2)}, \frac{h_r^-}{h_r^+ + h_r^-} \right\} \right) \qquad (\forall r \in R) \quad (5\text{-}37)$$

$$\Delta x_t = G'^{-1}_{m \mid m \in t, t}(x_t, rl_m^{(p2)}) \qquad (\forall t \in p1) \quad (5\text{-}38)$$

$$x_t'^{(n)} = x_t \cdot AD_n(w, \theta_n, \lambda_n) + z'_{rl_r(p2)} \cdot \sqrt{x_t \cdot VD_n(w, \theta_n, \lambda_n)} \quad (\forall t \in T, \forall n \in N) \quad (5\text{-}39)$$

$$\Delta \acute{x}_t^{(s \mid s \in t, s \in S^{(n)})} = G''^{-1}_{s,t}(x_t + \Delta x_t + x_t'^{(n)}, rl_s^{(p2)}) \qquad (\forall t \in p1, \forall s \in t) \quad (5\text{-}40)$$

$$x_t + \Delta x_t + \Delta \acute{x}_t^{(s)}, x_t'^{(n)} \geq 0 \qquad (\forall t \in p1, \forall s \in \{s \in S \mid s \in p1\}, \forall n \in N) \quad (5\text{-}41)$$

Step 4: Compute the minimum possible cost of each $sl = (sl_p, sl_a) \in SL$ and $w \in W$ as follows:

$$MCost(w, sl) = \underset{\forall p1 \in P1}{MIN} \quad \underset{\forall p2 \in P2^{(p1)}}{MIN} \quad Cost^{(p1,p2)}(w, sl) \qquad (5\text{-}42)$$

The best path selection, flow assignment and local reliability assignment corresponding to $MCost(w, sl)$ are represented by $Y^*(w, sl)$, $X^*(w, sl)$ and $RL^*(w, sl)$ respectively.

Step 5: After computing $MCost(w, sl)$ for each $\forall sl = (sl_p, sl_a) \in SL$ and $\forall w \in W$, use the following linear binary model to find the best warranty and service level strategies (w^*, sl^*):

$$MAX \quad \sum_R \sum_W \sum_{SL} v_w \cdot z_{sl} \cdot \bar{D}_r(sl, w, p) \cdot p - \sum_W \sum_{SL} v_w \cdot z_{sl} \cdot MCost(w, sl) \quad (5\text{-}43)$$

Subject to:

$$\sum_W v_w = 1 \tag{5-44}$$

$$\sum_{SL} z_{sl} = 1 \tag{5-45}$$

$$v_w, z_{sl} \in \{0,1\} \tag{5-46}$$

By solving this model, the best service level, sl^*, and warranty, w^*, strategies are determined. Therefore, the best path selection, flow assignment, and local reliability assignment of the networks are $Y^*(w^*, sl^*)$, $X^*(w^*, sl^*)$, and $RL^*(w^*, sl^*)$. The flowchart for this algorithm is shown in appendix 5.B.

This algorithm is designed for medium-scale problems with a reasonable number of potential paths. In very large-scale problems with thousands of retailers and potential paths, a large number of model Eq. (5-35) to (5-40) should be solved. This increases the computational time significantly. For these problems, two approaches can be used:

✓ Reducing the number of retailers and corresponding paths by clustering the retailers spatially. In this case, each cluster will be assumed as a single virtual retailer, or

✓ Using meta-heuristic algorithms such as Genetic Algorithms, Simulated Annealing, or Tabu Search to find good but not the best solution for the problem.

5.9 Numerical Analysis

The problem of this chapter is defined and developed, based on the needs of a real company in engine industry. Tracking the quality of engines due to their long and complicated manufacturing process is not easy. However, this company, to preserve its reputation, tries to satisfy its customers as much as possible by providing after-sales services. Therefore, providing a suitable warranty is critical. Recently due to high rates of after-sales costs, this company decided to revise its after-sales services. By analyzing the historical data about the sales and return rates of the previous sales periods, the company wants to make scientific decisions about its marketing strategies such as retail price, warranty length, and service levels. In this section, we concentrate on one of the important engine groups of this company which has a greater share of production compared to the others.

This engine group has two critical components provided by external suppliers, *n1* and *n2* ($N = \{n_1, n_2\}$). This company has two supplier options for procuring *n1* and for providing *n2*, only one supplier exists which means $S = S^{(n1)} \cup S^{(n2)}$, $S^{(n1)} = \{s1, s3\}$ and $S^{(n2)} = \{s2\}$. Only two manufacturing centers of this company are capable of assembling this engine group, $M = \{m1, m2\}$, then they are supplied to two important markets by their corresponding retailers, $R = \{r1, r2\}$. The structure of the pre-sales SN and its potential paths, $T = \{t_{1,2,1,1}, t_{1,2,1,2}, t_{3,2,2,1}, t_{3,2,2,2}\}$, are shown in Figure 5-4. $t_{s,\acute{s},m,r}$ is the path starting from Suppliers s and s' (providing $n1$ and $n2$ respectively), passing through Manufacturer m and ending at Retailer r.

Analyzing the quadruples of *price, service levels, warranty, average demand* in the previous sales periods by regression shows that the following functions fit well with the historical demand data of this engine group. Assessing the differences between the actual realized demands and their average values by "Goodness-of-fit" tests shows that the stochastic deviations fit with normal density functions with 90 percent confidence limit.

$$D_1 (p, sl = (sl_p, sl_a), w) = (500 + 200. \; w - 250. \; (p - 10) - 500. \; (1 - sl_a) - 900. \; (1 - sl_p)). \; \varepsilon_1 \tag{5-47}$$

$$\varepsilon_1 \sim Normal(\mu_{\varepsilon_1} = 0, \sigma^2_{\varepsilon_1} = 0.1) \tag{5-48}$$

$$D_2 (p, sl = (sl_p, sl_a), w) = (400 + 200. \; w - 250. \; (p - 10) - 500. \; (1 - sl_a) - 900. \; (1 - sl_p)). \; \varepsilon_2 \tag{5-49}$$

$$\varepsilon_2 \sim Normal(\mu_{\varepsilon_2} = 0, \sigma^2_{\varepsilon_2} = 0.1) \tag{5-50}$$

The deterioration time in $S1$, $S2$, and $S3$ has exponential distribution with $\mu_1 = 2$, $\mu_2 = 2$, and $\mu_3 = 3$. The non-conforming production rate in the out-of-control state of their machines is $\gamma_1 = 10\%$, $\gamma_2 = 20\%$ and $\gamma_3 = 5\%$. Production rates of the first, second and third suppliers are 8000, 8000 and

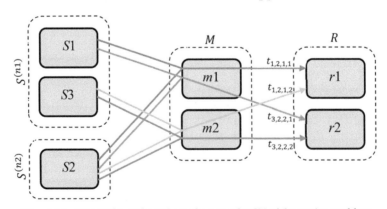

Figure 5-4. Potential supply paths in the pre-sales SN of the engine problem.

9000 component units per time unit. The cost components of this problem are summarized in Table 5-1.

The manufacturers have imperfect production systems. Defective production rate in the first and second manufacturer has a uniform distribution with $(0, \beta_{m=1} = 0.15)$ and $(0, \beta_{m=2} = 0.08)$. First, we assume the product price in the markets is fixed at its current value, $p = \$10$. In Section 5.9.1, the best price strategy is determined by analyzing the sensitivity of the results with respect to the product price. In this problem, we assume that the available warranty options are $W = \{w_1 = 0.5$ (*year*), 10 (*year*), 1.5 (*years*) 2 (*years*)$\}$. The available service level options are $SL = \{sl_1 = (sl_{1p} = 0.98, sl_{1a} = 0.96), sl_2 = (sl_{2p} = 0.90, sl_{2a} = 0.95), sl_3 = (sl_{3p} = 0.85, sl_{3a} = 0.91)\}$.

In the company, three-year records are available for the claims that have been made. To determine the failure rates of the engine, we use a statistical analysis approach proposed by Lawless 1998. Using his method, we calculate the mean and variance of the failure rate for different ages of the engine. The mean and three sigma confidence limits of the failure rates for the two critical components of this engine are shown in Figures 5-5 and 5-6.

Solving the mathematical model yields the following results: the most profitable service level and warranty strategies are $sl^* = (sl_p^* = 0.85, sl_a^* = 0.91)$ and $w^* = 1.0$ (*year*). The least costly reliabilities of the facilities preserving this service level strategy are $rl_{s=1} = 1.00$, $rl_{s=2} = 1.00$, $rl_{s=3} = 0.94$, $rl_{m=1} = 0.99$, $rl_{m=2} = 0.93$, $rl_{r=1} = 0.99$ and $rl_{r=2} = 0.99$. The best flow through the paths of the pre-sales SN are $x_1 = 49.94$, $x_2 = 40.64$, $x_3 = 949.04$, and $x_4 = 772.24$ (Figure 5-7). The best flow through the paths of the after-sales SN are $\acute{x}_1^{(1)} = 6.17$, $\acute{x}_1^{(2)} = 8.31$, $\acute{x}_2^{(1)} = 5.34$, $\acute{x}_2^{(2)} = 7.18$, $\acute{x}_3^{(1)} = 63.47$, $\acute{x}_3^{(2)} = 87.70$, $\acute{x}_4^{(1)} = 53.05$, and $\acute{x}_4^{(2)} = 73.21$ (Figure 5-8). Flow amplification in these networks' facilities are $\Delta x_1 = 7.41$, $\Delta x_2 = 6.03$, $\Delta x_3 = 70.61$, $\Delta x_4 = 57.45$, $\Delta \acute{x}_1^{(1)} = 7.06$, $\Delta \acute{x}_1^{(2)} = 16.41$, $\Delta \acute{x}_2^{(1)} = 5.78$, $\Delta \acute{x}_2^{(2)} = 13.46$, $\Delta \acute{x}_3^{(3)} = 47.23$, $\Delta \acute{x}_3^{(2)} = 276.83$, $\Delta \acute{x}_4^{(3)} = 36.69$, and $\Delta \acute{x}_4^{(2)} = 225.72$.

Table 5-2. Cost components of the engine problem.

Cost parameter	Value	Cost parameter	Value	Cost parameter	Value
$a_1^{s=1}$	$ 0.50	$a_{s=1,m=1}^t$	$ 0.05	$a_{s=1,r=1}^t$	$ 0.07
$a_2^{s=1}$	$ 0.60	$a_{s=2,m=1}^t$	$ 0.08	$a_{s=1,r=2}^t$	$ 0.07
$a_1^{s=2}$	$ 0.60	$a_{s=2,m=2}^t$	$ 0.08	$a_{s=2,r=1}^t$	$ 0.07
$a_2^{s=2}$	$ 0.70	$a_{s=1,m=2}^t$	$ 0.06	$a_{s=2,r=2}^t$	$ 0.07
$a_1^{s=3}$	$ 0.55	$a_{m=1,r=1}^t$	$ 0.05	$a_{s=3,t-1}^t$	$ 0.07
$a_2^{s=3}$	$ 0.70	$a_{m=1,r=2}^t$	$ 0.04	$a_{s=3,r=2}^t$	$ 0.07
$a^{m=1}$	$ 2.00	$a_{m=2,r=1}^t$	$ 0.05	$h_{r=1 \, and \, 2}^+$	$ 0.11
$a^{m=2}$	$ 2.15	$a_{m=2,r=2}^t$	$ 0.05	$h_{r=1 \, and \, 2}^-$	$ 0.05

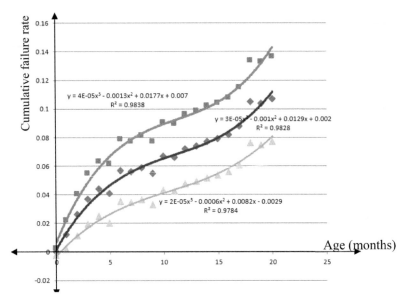

Figure 5-5. Failure rate of the first component with respect to age.

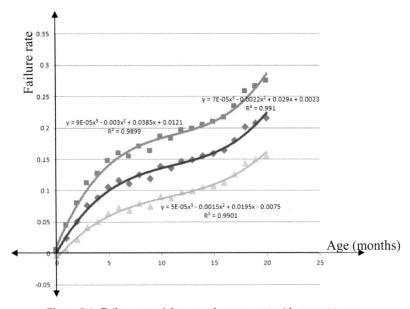

Figure 5-6. Failure rate of the second component with respect to age.

The model developed in Section 5.7 and linearized in Section 5.8 is a mixed integer linear programming (MILP) model. The solution time of MILP depends mainly on the number of binary variables that is equal to

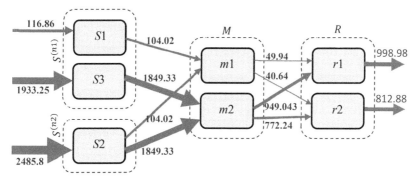

Figure 5-7. Flow through the pre-sales SN.

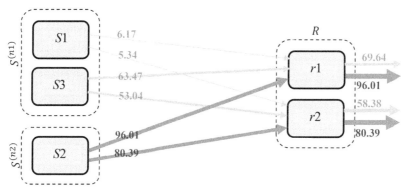

Figure 5-8. Flow through the after-sales SN.

Table 5-3. Computational capability for the developed model.

Problem	Features of SN				Computational time (hh:mm:ss)
	Number of suppliers	Number of manufacturers	Number of retailers	Number of paths	
1	3	2	2	4	< 00:00:01
2	3	2	3	6	< 00:00:01
3	3	3	5	10	00:00:48
4	3	3	7	13	00:15:08
5	3	4	8	15	02:37:10
6	3	4	10	18	17:26:55
7	3	4	12	24	> 48:00:00

$\sum_{\forall s1 \in S1} |S2^{(s1)}|$. The computational time for the case problem in this section is less than a second. Given that the case problem is simple, we check the computational capability of the model and the solution approach by solving 7 problems summarized in Table 5-2.

As seen in Table 5-2, for Problem 7 and problems larger than Problem 7 the computational time is more than 48 hours. Therefore, for this type of problem we suggest using meta-heuristic approaches to solve the model and find a good suboptimal solution in a rational computational time instead of the global optimum.

5.9.1 Optimal Price Strategy Determination

In the previous analysis, we assumed that the product price in the markets is fixed at $p = \$10$. In this section, by checking the sensitivity of the model with respect to the price, we determine the best price strategy for the company.

Based on the product's manufacturing cost and rival product prices in the markets, we assume the price should be selected from the $8–$12 range. For some sample price values from this range, we solve the mathematical model of the problem and get the results. Dark green points in Figure 5-9 represent the highest profit for these sample price values. Based on the results, a two-order polynomial function fits very well with these points. To find the best price, we find the maximum point of this fitted function which gives $p^* = \$9.77$.

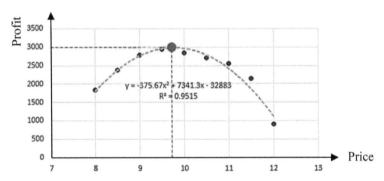

Figure 5-9. Profit with respect to price.

5.9.2 Correlation Between Price and Warranty Strategies

In this section, we analyze the correlation between the best warranty and the best price strategies in different service level options. For this purpose, for each combination of the service level and warranty options, the mathematical model is solved for some sample values in the feasible price range $8–$12. The resulting profit points and their fitted function are displayed for the third service level option ($sl_{3p} = 0.85$, $sl_{3a} = 0.91$) in Figure 5-10. The intersections of these functions correspond to the critical price values in which the priority of the warranty options changes. Based on these results, the priority of the warranty options with respect to the price values is as follows:

- If $p \leq \$8.90$ Then the priority of warranty options is 0.5, 1.0, 1.5 *and* 2.0.

- If $8.90 $< p \leq \$10.10$ Then the priority of warranty options is 1.0, 0.5, 1.5 *and* 2.0.

- If $\$10.10 < p \leq \$10.50$ Then the priority of warranty options is 1.0, 1.5, 0.5 *and* 2.0.

- If $\$10.50 < p \leq \$10.80$ Then the priority of warranty options is 1.5, 1.0, 0.5 *and* 2.0.

- If $\$10.80 < p \leq \$11.10$ Then the priority of warranty options is 1.5, 1.0, 2.0 *and* 0.5.

- If $11.10 < $p \leq \$11.45$ Then the priority of warranty options is 1.5, 2.0, 1.0 *and* 0.5.

- If $11.45 < p$ Then the priority of warranty options is 2.0, 1.5, 1.0 *and* 0.5.

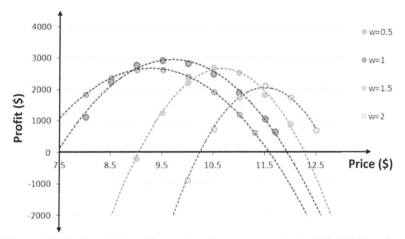

Figure 5-10. Profit variation with respect to the warranty and price in the third service level strategy.

As seen in Figure 5-10, *price increment imposes almost the same trend of changes on the profit function for the all warranty options.* Increasing price first improves the profitability of the company in each warranty option. But after the optimal price of that warranty option, the profit reduces by price increment. This means *changing the warranty length does not significantly affect the trend of changes in the profit function with respect to the price.* However, the profit function shifts to the right by increasing the warranty length. Therefore, *in the price intervals between two sequential critical price values, the effect of the price increment on the profit functions of different warranty lengths may be different.* For example, in price interval [9.00, 10.10], while the profit function of 1.5 (year) warranty option increases by the price increment, the profit function of 0.5 (year) warranty option decreases, and the profit function of 1.0 (year) warranty increases at first and decreases after a while.

Results of solving the mathematical model for different combinations of warranty and price options at the second service level option (sl_{2p} = 0.90, sl_{2a} = 0.95) and at the first service level option (sl_{1p} = 0.98, sl_{1a} = 0.96), are represented respectively in Figure 5-11 and Figure 5-12. The critical price values in the second service level option are as follows:

- If $p \leq \$10.50$ Then w = 0.5, 1.0, 1.5 *and* 2.0
- If $\$10.50 < p \leq \$11.15$ Then w = 1.0, 0.5, 1.5 *and* 2.0
- If $\$11.15 < p \leq \$11.60$ Then w = 1.0, 1.5, 0.5 *and* 2.0
- If $\$11.60 < p \leq \$11.70$ Then w = 1.5, 1.0, 0.5 *and* 2.0
- If $\$11.70 < p \leq \$12.00$ Then w = 1.5, 1.0, 2.0 *and* 0.5
- If $\$12.00 < p \leq \$12.25$ Then w = 1.5, 2.0, 1.0 *and* 0.5
- If $\$12.25 < p$ Then w = 2.0, 1.5, 1.0 *and* 0.5

The critical price values in the first service level option are as follows:

- If $p \leq \$11.83$ Then w = 0.5, 1.0, 1.5 *and* 2.0
- If $\$11.83 < p < \$12.20$ Then w = 1.0, 0.5, 1.5 *and* 2.0
- If $\$12.20 < p \leq \$12.41$ Then w = 1.0, 1.5, 0.5 *and* 2.0
- If $\$12.41 < p \leq \$12.55$ Then w = 1.5, 1.0, 0.5 *and* 2.0
- If $\$12.55 < p \leq \$12.75$ Then w = 1.5, 1.0, 2.0 *and* 0.5
- If $\$12.75 < p \leq \$12.85$ Then w = 1.5, 2.0, 1.0 *and* 0.5
- If $\$12.85 < p$ Then w = 2.0, 1.5, 1.0 *and* 0.5

A comparison of the critical price values in these three service level options reveals that by increasing the service levels, the intervals between the sequential critical price values do decrease to a large extent. This means *the correlation between the price and warranty becomes tighter by increasing the service levels. Therefore, in higher service levels, the priority of the warranty options stays stable for a smaller price interval and is more sensitive with respect to the price variations.*

A comparison of the profit functions in Figures 5-10, 5-11, and 5-12 shows that by increasing the service levels, the overlaps among the profit functions decrease and they become more separate. The profit function of each warranty option has a connected price interval inside which the profit of that warranty is positive. By increasing the service levels, these intervals of the warranty options become more distinct. This means that

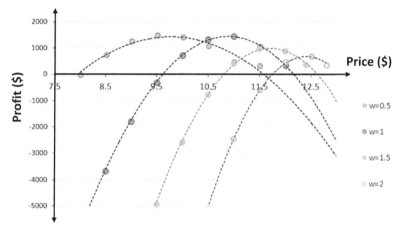

Figure 5-11. Profit variation with respect to the warranty and price in the second service level strategy.

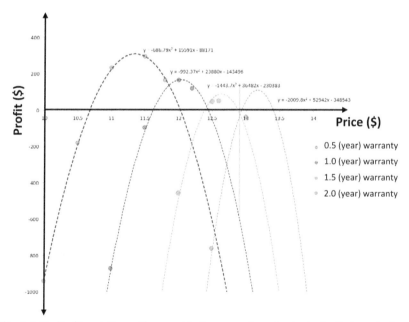

Figure 5-12. Profit variation with respect to the warranty and price in the first service level strategy.

the feasible range of price is divided to some more distinct intervals in each of which only one warranty option is profitable. Therefore, in higher service levels the positively profitable warranty options available in each price value for managers to select, is much less.

5.9.3 Correlation Between Service Level and Warranty Strategies

In this section, we analyze the relationship between the warranty length and service level in a fixed price, $p = 10$. Results of solving the mathematical model for different combinations of the warranty and service level options at $p = 10$ are represented respectively in Figure 5-13. There is no intersection among the profit functions of different service level options. This means that the priority of service level options is not changing with respect to the warranty variations. The highest profit always corresponds to the third (lowest) service level option.

Based on these results we conclude that for a given price, the priority of the service level options does not change significantly with warranty length variation and in our test problem, always the third service level option is the best. In the other words: *the priority of the service level options is very stable and is not affected easily by warranty variations. In this problem, the warranty-service level tradeoff is much more stable than the price-warranty tradeoff. However, the stability of the warranty-service level tradeoff may change by increasing the service level sensitivity parameter in the demand function.*

We summarize the outcomes of these analyses in Figure 5-14. The relationships between two marketing strategies in a given option of the third one are shown in this figure. For example, *in each warranty length option, the best price strategy is increasing with respect to the service level but the trend of this increment is different for warranty options. In shorter warranty lengths, the rate of price increment is a convex increasing function of the service levels. But this function tends to become a linear increasing and then a concave increasing by the warranty length increment.*

In the same way *for a given service levels option, the best price strategy is increasing with respect to the warranty length but the trend of this increment is different for service level options. In lower service levels, the rate of price increment*

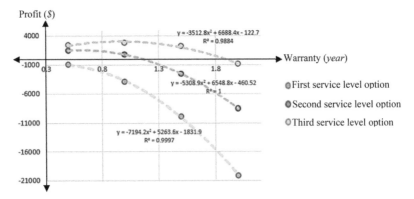

Figure 5-13. Warranty and service level correlation in p = 10 price strategy.

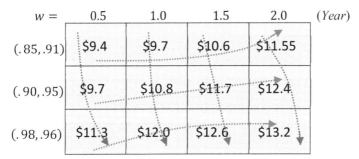

Figure 5-14. Variations of the three marketing strategies: price, service level and warranty length.

is a convex increasing function of the warranty length. But this function tends to become a linearly increasing and then a concave increasing by the increment in the service levels.

5.10 Closing Remarks

Here, we address two important issues: (i) modelling interactions in the operations of the pre- and after-sales SNs by planning the flow dynamics in their networks concurrently. There is a huge synergy in concurrent planning of these SNs which is mainly ignored in existing work; (ii) considering supply-side variations in the performance of the SNs' production facilities and their propagation throughout the networks, make our model more consistent with reality. In this chapter, we quantify the following relationships:

✓ Relationship between the local reliabilities of the facilities and the SNs' service levels,

✓ Relationship between the local reliabilities of the facilities and their flow dynamics,

✓ Relationship between the SNs' service levels and the company's other marketing strategies (price and warranty).

We use these relationships to develop a mathematical model for the problem determining the most profitable marketing strategies for the company and the least costly flow dynamics throughout its networks preserving the marketing strategies.

In this problem, we assume that the spare parts required for the after-sales operations are new and directly supplied by the suppliers. However, another option is remanufacturing the defective components which are mainly new. Including the remanufacturing option in the after-sales SN is an important future topic of research for this chapter. Also, the risk of disruptions that may distort the topology of the SN is overlooked in this chapter. Considering the risk of disruptions and variations in SNs is another future topic of research for this chapter.

In the context of an architecture for fail-safe networks, the focus of this chapter is on variation management in two correlated forward and after-sales SNs supplying an original product and its spare parts, respectively. The focus of Chapters 6, 7 and 8 is only on disruption management in SNs. The mathematical model of this chapter will be extended in Chapter 9 to SNs with both variations and disruptions.

Acknowledgement

Figures and tables in Chapter 5 are reprinted from Artificial Intelligence for Engineering Design, Analysis and Manufacturing (AIEDAM), volume 31, issue 2, by Shabnam Rezapour, Janet K. Allen and Farrokh Mistree, "Reliable Flow in Stochastic Supply Networks Servicing Pre- and After-sales Markets." pp. 120–142, 2017, with permission from Cambridge University Press.

References

Amini, M. M., Retzlaff-Roberts, D. and Bienstock, C. C. 2005. Designing a reverse logistics operation for short cycle time repair services. International Journal of Production Economics 96(3): 367–380.

Atasu, A., Sarvary, M. and Van Wassenhove, L. N. 2008. Remanufacturing as a marketing strategy. Management Science 54(10): 1731–1746.

Bacchetti, A. and Saccani, N. 2012. Spare parts classification and demand forecasting for stock control: Investigating the gap between research and practice. Omega 40(6): 722–737.

Baines, T., Lightfoot, H., Evans, S., Neely, A., Greenough, R., Peppard, J., Roy, R., Shehab, E., Braganza, A., Tiwari, A., Alcock, J., Angus, J., Bastl, M., Cousens, A., Irving, P., Johnson, M., Kingston, J., Lockett, H., Martinez, V. and Michele, P. 2007. State-of-the-art in product-service systems. Proceedings of the Institution of Mechanical Engineering–Part B: Journal of Engineering. Manufacturing 221(10): 1543–1552.

Barabadi, A., Barabady, J. and Markeset, T. 2014. Application of reliability models with covariates in spare part prediction and optimization—a case study. Reliability Engineering & System Safety 123: 1–7.

Bernstein, F. and Federgruen, A. 2004. A general equilibrium model for industries with price and service competition. Operations Research 52(6): 868–886.

Bernstein, F. and Federgruen, A. 2007. Coordination mechanisms for supply chains under price and service competition. Manufacturing & Service Operations Management 9(3): 242–262.

Bijvank, M., Koole, G. and Vis, I. F. 2010. Optimising a general repair kit problem with a service constraint. European Journal of Operational Research 204(1): 76–85.

Boone, C. A., Craighead, C. W. and Hanna, J. B. 2008. Critical challenges of inventory management in service parts supply: A Delphi study. Operations Management Research 1(1): 31–39.

Boylan, J. E. and Syntetos, A. A. 2010. Spare parts management: a review of forecasting research and extensions. IMA Journal of Management Mathematics 21(3): 227–237.

Bundschuh, R. G. and Dezvane, T. M. 2003. How to make after-sales services pay off. McKinsey Quarterly (4): 116–127.

Chien, Y.-H. and Chen, J.-A. 2008. Optimal spare ordering policy under a rebate warranty. European Journal of Operational Research 186(2): 708–719.

Chu, J. and Chintagunta, P. K. 2009. Quantifying the economic value of warranties in the US server market. Marketing Science 28(1): 99–121.

Cohen, M. A., Agrawal, N. and Agrawal, V. 2006. Winning in the aftermarket. Harvard Business Review 84(5): 129.

Davies, A., Brady, T. and Hobday, M. 2006. Charting a path toward integrated solutions. MIT Sloan Management Review 47(3): 39.

Dell.Com. 2010. web site 2010 [cited April 28 2010]. Available from http://www.dell.com/home/.

Dolgui, A. and Pashkevich, M. 2008. Demand forecasting for multiple slow-moving items with short requests history and unequal demand variance. International Journal of Production Economics 112(2): 885–894.

Faridimehr, S. and Niaki, S. T. A. 2012. A note on optimal price, warranty length and production rate for free replacement policy in static demand markets. Omega 40(6): 805–806.

Ferrer, G. and Swaminathan, J. M. 2006. Managing new and remanufactured products. Management Science 52(1): 15–26.

Gaiardelli, P., Saccani, N. and Songini, L. 2007. Performance measurement of the after-sales service network—Evidence from the automotive industry. Computers in Industry 58(7): 698–708.

Gupta, S. and Lehmann, D. R. 2005. Managing Customers as Investments: The Strategic Value of Customers in the Long Run. Upper Saddle River, NJ: Pearson Education.

Gutierrez, R. S., Solis, A. O. and Mukhopadhyay, S. 2008. Lumpy demand forecasting using neural networks. International Journal of Production Economics 111(2): 409–420.

Hartman, J. C. and Laksana, K. 2009. Designing and pricing menus of extended warranty contracts. Naval Research Logistics (NRL) 56(3): 199–214.

Hasani, A. and Khosrojerdi, A. 2016. Robust global supply chain network design under disruption and uncertainty considering resilience strategies: A parallel memetic algorithm for a real-life case study. Transportation Research Part E: Logistics and Transportation Review 87: 20–52.

Hua, Z., Zhang, B., Yang, J. and Tan, D. 2007. A new approach of forecasting intermittent demand for spare parts inventories in the process industries. Journal of the Operational Research Society 58(1): 52–61.

Huang, H.-Z., Liu, Z.-J. and Murthy, D. 2007. Optimal reliability, warranty and price for new products. Iie Transactions 39(8): 819–827.

Hussain, A. and Murthy, D. 2003. Warranty and optimal reliability improvement through product development. Mathematical and Computer Modelling 38(11-13): 1211–1217.

Jack, N. and Murthy, D. 2007. A flexible extended warranty and related optimal strategies. Journal of the Operational Research Society 58(12): 1612–1620.

Johnson, M. and Mena, C. 2008. Supply chain management for servitised products: a multi-industry case study. International Journal of Production Economics 114(1): 27–39.

Kalchschmidt, M., Verganti, R. and Zotteri, G. 2006. Forecasting demand from heterogeneous customers. International Journal of Operations & Production Management 26(6): 619–638.

Kameshwaran, S., Viswanadham, N. and Desai, V. 2009. Bundling and pricing of product with after-sale services. International Journal of Operational Research 6(1): 92–109.

Khajavi, S. H., Partanen, J. and Holmström, J. 2014. Additive manufacturing in the spare parts supply chain. Computers in Industry 65(1): 50–63.

Kleber, R., Zanoni, S. and Zavanella, L. 2011. On how buyback and remanufacturing strategies affect the profitability of spare parts supply chains. International Journal of Production Economics 133(1): 135–142.

Kurata, H. and Nam, S.-H. 2010. After-sales service competition in a supply chain: Optimization of customer satisfaction level or profit or both? International Journal of Production Economics 127(1): 136–146.

Lawless, J. F. 1998. Statistical analysis of product warranty data. International Statistical Review 66(1): 41–60.

Lee, H. L. and Rosenblatt, M. J. 1987. Simultaneous determination of production cycle and inspection schedules in a production system. Management Science 33(9): 1125–1136.

Lele, M. M. 1997. After-sales service-necessary evil or strategic opportunity? Managing Service Quality: An International Journal 7(3): 141–145.

Lieckens, K. T., Colen, P. J. and Lambrecht, M. R. 2013. Optimization of a stochastic remanufacturing network with an exchange option. Decision Support Systems 54(4): 1548–1557.

Matis, T. I., Jayaraman, R. and Rangan, A. 2008. Optimal price and pro rata decisions for combined warranty policies with different repair options. IIE Transactions 40(10): 984–991.

Mcavoy, J. 2008. Integrating spare parts planning with logistics.

Mitra, S. and Webster, S. 2008. Competition in remanufacturing and the effects of government subsidies. International Journal of Production Economics 111(2): 287–298.

Mohammaddust, F., Rezapour, S., Farahani, R. Z., Mofidfar, M. and Hill, A. 2017. Developing lean and responsive supply chains: a robust model for alternative risk mitigation strategies in supply chain designs. International Journal of Production Economics 183C: 632–653.

Morley, M., Kosnik, T., Wong-Mingji, D. J. and Hoover, K. 2006. Outsourcing vs. insourcing in the human resource supply chain: A comparison of five generic models. Personnel Review 35(6): 671–684.

Murthy, D. 1990. Optimal reliability choice in product design. Engineering Optimization+ A35 15(4): 281–294.

Ng, W. L. 2007. A simple classifier for multiple criteria ABC analysis. European Journal of Operational Research 177(1): 344–353.

Nguyen, D. and Murthy, D. 1984. A general model for estimating warranty costs for repairable products. IIE Transactions 16(4): 379–386.

Nguyen, D. and Murthy, D. 1988. Optimal reliability allocation for products sold under warranty. Engineering Optimization 13(1): 35–45.

Nordin, F. 2005. Searching for the optimum product service distribution channel: Examining the actions of five industrial firms. International Journal of Physical Distribution & Logistics Management 35(8): 576–594.

Öner, K. B., Kiesmüller, G. P. and Van Houtum, G.-J. 2010. Optimization of component reliability in the design phase of capital goods. European Journal of Operational Research 205(3): 615–624.

Park, M., Jung, K. M. and Park, D. H. 2013. Optimal post-warranty maintenance policy with repair time threshold for minimal repair. Reliability Engineering & System Safety 111: 147–153.

Penttinen, E. and Palmer, J. 2007. Improving firm positioning through enhanced offerings and buyer–seller relationships. Industrial Marketing Management 36(5): 552–564.

Rao, B. M. 2011. A decision support model for warranty servicing of repairable items. Computers & Operations Research 38(1): 112–130.

Rappold, J. A. and Van Roo, B. D. 2009. Designing multi-echelon service parts networks with finite repair capacity. European Journal of Operational Research 199(3): 781–792.

Rezapour, S. and Zanjirani Farahani, R. 2014. Supply Chain Network Design under Oligopolistic Price and Service Level Competition with Foresight. Vol. 72.

Rezapour, S., Singh, R., Allen, J. K. and Mistree, F. 2015. Stochastic Supply Networks Servicing Pre- and After-Sales Markets. (57175): V007T06A021.

Rezapour, S., Allen, J. K. and Mistree, F. 2016a. Reliable flow in forward and after-sales supply chains considering propagated uncertainty. Transportation Research Part E: Logistics and Transportation Review 93: 409–436.

Rezapour, S., Allen, J. K. and Mistree, F. 2016b. Reliable product-service supply chains for repairable products. Transportation Research Part E: Logistics and Transportation Review 95(C): 299–321.

Rezapour, S., Allen, J. K. and Mistree, F. 2016c. Reliable product-service supply chains for repairable products. Transportation Research Part E: Logistics and Transportation Review 95: 299–321.

Rezapour, S., Allen, J. K. and Mistree, F. 2017. Reliable flow in stochastic supply networks servicing pre- and after-sales markets. Artificial Intelligence for Engineering Design, Analysis and Manufacturing 31: 120–142.

Rezapour, S., Farahani, R. Z. and Pourakbar, M. 2017. Resilient supply chain network design under competition: A case study. European Journal of Operational Research 259(3): 1017–1035.

Rosenblatt, M. J. and Lee, H. L. 1986. Economic production cycles with imperfect production processes. IIE Transactions 18(1): 48–55.

Saccani, N., Johansson, P. and Perona, M. 2007. Configuring the after-sales service supply chain: A multiple case study. International Journal of Production Economics 110(1): 52–69.

Sahba, P. and Balcıog, B. 2011. The impact of transportation delays on repairshop capacity pooling and spare part inventories. European Journal of Operational Research 214(3): 674–682.

Sana, S. S. 2010. An economic production lot size model in an imperfect production system. European Journal of Operational Research 201(1): 158–170.

Shahanaghi, K., Noorossana, R., Jalali-Naini, S. G. and Heydari, M. 2013. Failure modeling and optimizing preventive maintenance strategy during two-dimensional extended warranty contracts. Engineering Failure Analysis 28: 90–102.

Sleptchenko, A., Van Der Heijden, M. and Van Harten, A. 2002. Effects of finite repair capacity in multi-echelon, multi-indenture service part supply systems. International Journal of Production Economics 79(3): 209–230.

Su, C. and Shen, J. 2012. Analysis of extended warranty policies with different repair options. Engineering Failure Analysis 25: 49–62.

Thonemann, U. W., Brown, A. O. and Hausman, W. H. 2002. Easy quantification of improved spare parts inventory policies. Management Science 48(9): 1213–1225.

Tsoukalas, M. Z. and Agrafiotis, G. 2013. A new replacement warranty policy indexed by the product's correlated failure and usage time. Computers & Industrial Engineering 66(2): 203–211.

Vahdani, H., Mahlooji, H. and Jahromi, A. E. 2013. Warranty servicing for discretely degrading items with non-zero repair time under renewing warranty. Computers & Industrial Engineering 65(1): 176–185.

Van Jaarsveld, W. and Dekker, R. 2011. Spare parts stock control for redundant systems using reliability centered maintenance data. Reliability Engineering & System Safety 96(11): 1576–1586.

Van Ommeren, J., Bumb, A. F. and Sleptchenko, A. 2006. Locating repair shops in a stochastic environment. Computers & Operations Research 33(6): 1575–1594.

Vandermerwe, S. and Rada, J. 1988. Servitization of business: Adding value by adding services. European Management Journal 6(4): 314–324.

Wagner, S. and Lindemann, E. 2008. A case study-based analysis of spare parts management in the engineering industry. Production Planning & Control 19(4): 397–407.

Wang, W. 2012. A stochastic model for joint spare parts inventory and planned maintenance optimisation. European Journal of Operational Research 216(1): 127–139.

Wang, Y.-W. and Lin, C.-C. 2009. Locating road-vehicle refueling stations. Transportation Research Part E: Logistics and Transportation Review 45(5): 821–829.

Wu, C.-C., Chou, C.-Y. and Huang, C. 2009. Optimal price, warranty length and production rate for free replacement policy in the static demand market. Omega 37(1): 29–39.

Wu, C.-H. 2012. Price and service competition between new and remanufactured products in a two-echelon supply chain. International Journal of Production Economics 140(1): 496–507.

Xu, L. D., He, W. and Li, S. 2014. Internet of things in industries: A survey. Industrial Informatics, IEEE Transactions on 10(4): 2233–2243.

Zhou, P. and Fan, L. 2007. A note on multi-criteria ABC inventory classification using weighted linear optimization. European Journal of Operational Research 182(3): 1488–1491.

Zhou, Z., Li, Y. and Tang, K. 2009. Dynamic pricing and warranty policies for products with fixed lifetime. European Journal of Operational Research 196(3): 940–948.

Appendices

Appendix 5.A: Notations Used in This Chapter

The notations used in this chapter are summarized in Table 5-4.

Table 5-4. Notations used in the chapter.

Sets:	
$S = \{s\}$	Set of suppliers in the supply network;
$M = \{m\}$	Set of manufacturers in the supply network;
$R = \{r\}$	Set of retailers in the supply network;
$N = \{n\}$	Set components in the product;
$S^{(n)} \subseteq S$	Subset of suppliers producing component n ($\forall n \in N$);
$T = \{t\}$	Set of potential paths in the supply network which can be used to fulfill markets. Each potential path starts from suppliers (one supplier per component) in the first echelon and after passing a manufacturer in the second echelon ends to a retailer in the third echelon to fulfill the demand of its corresponding retailer $t = (s_1 \in S^{(1)}, s_2 \in S^{(2)},..., s_{|N|} \in S^{(|N|)}, m \in M, r \in R)$;
$T^{(s)} \subseteq T$	Subset of potential paths starting from Supplier s ($\forall s \in S$), $T^{(s)} = \{t \mid s \in t\}$;
$T^{(m)} \subseteq T$	Subset of potential paths passing through Manufacturer m ($\forall m \in M$), $T^{(m)} = \{t \mid m \in t\}$;
$T^{(r)} \subseteq T$	Subset of potential paths ending to retailer r ($\forall r \in R$), $T^{(r)} = \{t \mid r \in t\}$;
$SL = \{sl = (sl_p, sl_a)\}$	Set of possible scenarios for the service level strategy of the company in the pre and after-sales markets;
$W = \{w\}$	Set of company's possible warranty strategies;
$S1 = \{s1\}$	Set of all the path selection possibilities in the network to fulfill the demand of all markets;
$S2^{(s1)} = \{s2\}$	Set of facilities' local reliabilities that can provide sl_p service level in the pre-markets and sl_a service level in the after-sales markets

Givens:

p	Price of product;
$D_r(sl_p, sl_a, w, p)$	Demand of retailer r's market which is considered as a product of a deterministic function, $\bar{D}_r(sl_p, sl_a, w, p)$, and a stochastic variable, ε. Without loss of generality
$\varepsilon \times \bar{D}_r(sl_p, sl_a, w, p)$	we assume $E(D_r(sl_p, sl_a, w, p)) = \bar{D}_r(sl_p, sl_a, w, p)$;
$\bar{D}_r(sl_p, sl_a, w, p)$	Average demand of retailer r's market. Retailer's average demand is an increasing function of service level and warranty length and decreasing function of price ($\forall r \in R$);
ε_r	Stochastic variable representing the uncertain part of retailer r's demand ($\forall r \in R$);
$G_r(.)$	Cumulative distribution function of ε_r variable ($\forall r \in R$);
$D_{m,t \mid m \in t}(x_t)$	Defective product quantity in manufacturer m in the manufacturing process of its passing path t ($m \in t$) order which is a stochastic increasing function of the path's flow, $x_{t \mid m \in t}$;
$G'_{m,t}(.)$	Cumulative distribution function of $D_{m,t}$ ($\forall m \in M, \forall t \in T$);
$D_{s,t \mid s \in t}(x_t)$	Nonconforming component quantity in supplier s in the production process of its ending path t ($s \in t$) order which is a stochastic increasing function of the path's flow, $x_{t \mid s \in t}$, and its reliability level, rl_s;
$G''_{s,t}(.)$	Cumulative distribution function of $D_{s,t}$ ($\forall s \in S, \forall t \in T$);
z'_α	z-score of standard normal distribution for probability of α;
a_1^s	Unit procurement cost in supplier s ($\forall s \in S$);
a_2^s	Unit production cost in supplier s ($\forall s \in S$);
a^m	Unit manufacturing cost in manufacturer m ($\forall m \in M$);
a^t_{sm}	Unit transportation cost between supplier s and manufacturer m ($\forall s \in S, \forall m \in M$);
a^t_{mr}	Unit transportation cost between manufacturer m and retailer r ($\forall m \in M, \forall r \in R$);
a^t_{sr}	Unit transportation cost between supply s and retailer r ($\forall s \in S, \forall r \in R$);
h^+_r	Unit holding cost of extra product inventory at the end of planning period in retailer r ($\forall r \in R$);
h^-_r	Unit cost of product shortage at the end of planning period in retailer r ($\forall r \in R$);
β_m	Maximum wastage ratio in manufacturer m ($\forall m \in M$);
μ_s	Average number of deterioration in the time unit in supplier s ($\forall s \in S$);

γ_s	Defective component ratio in the out-of-control state of supplier s ($\forall s \in S$);
PR_s	Production rate of supplier s ($\forall s \in S$);
θ_n	Reliability parameter of Component n ($\forall n \in N$);
$f_n(.)$	Density function of failure time of Component n ($\forall n \in N$);
$F_n(.)$	Cumulative distribution function of failure time of Component n ($\forall n \in N$);
$F_n^{(m)}(.)$	Cumulative distribution function of total time to the mth failure of Component n ($\forall n \in N$);
λ_n	Number of first failures of Component n that are repairable ($\forall n \in N$);
cr_n	Unit repair cost of Component n ($\forall n \in N$);
$Num_n(w)$	Random number of Component n failures in warranty time ($\forall n \in N$);
$AD_n(w)$	Average number of Component n substitution for a product unit in warranty time ($\forall n \in N$);
$VD_n(w)$	Variance of number of Component n substitution for a product unit in warranty time ($\forall n \in N$);
$\acute{D}_t^n$	After-market demand of component n of path t ($\forall n \in N$; $\forall t \in T$);
Π_r	Total cost of retailer r at the end of each sale period ($\forall r \in R$);

Variables:

y_t	1 if potential path t is used to supply products, 0 otherwise ($\forall t \in T$);
x_t	Product flow through path t ($\forall t \in T$);
z_{sl}	1 if service level strategy sl is selected by the company, 0 otherwise ($\forall sl \in SL$);
v_w	1 if warranty strategy w is selected by the company, 0 otherwise ($\forall w \in W$);
Δx_t	Extra production of path t in its corresponding manufacturer ($\forall w \in W, \forall t \in T$);
$\Delta \acute{x}_t^{(s)}$	Extra production of path t in supplier s of this path ($\forall s \in t$, $\forall t \in T$);
rl_s	Reliability level of supplier s ($\forall s \in S$);
rl_m	Reliability level of manufacturer m ($\forall m \in M$);
rl_r	Reliability level of retailer r ($\forall r \in R$);
$\acute{x}_t^{(n)}$	Component n flow through path t to fulfill after-sales demand ($\forall t \in T, \forall n \in N$);

Appendix 5.B: Flowchart for the Solution Algorithm Developed in Section 5.8

The flowchart for the solution algorithm developed in Section 5.8 is shown in Figure 5-15.

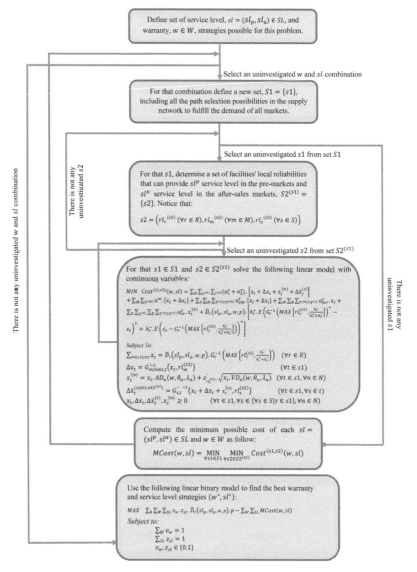

Figure 5-15. Flowchart of solution algorithm.

Disruption Management using Robust Design in Supply Networks

In Chapters 6, 7, and 8, we review the literature and explain the importance of disruption management in supply networks. We introduce robustness (Chapter 6), structural controllability (Chapter 7) and resilience (Chapter 8) as the three main elements in managing disruptions in supply networks (see Chapter 1, Figure 1-9). This follows the variation management part that is covered from Chapters 2 to 5. In this chapter, we elaborate on robustness in supply networks under disruptions while introducing a nonlinear robust design modeling approach. In addition, we examine robust design in supply networks in detail to manage disruptions and we explain the benefits of developing robust models for designing or re-designing supply networks under disruptions. In Chapter 7, we discuss structural controllability and elaborate on the relationship between structural controllability and resilience in supply networks. In Chapter 8, we discuss our three-stage model for resilience and structural controllability.

6.1 Disruptions in Supply Networks: Robustness, Structural Controllability, and Resilience in Supply Network Design

A supply network comprises of different facilities or structural components that are connected by the flow of materials, information, electricity or other resources. Disruptions can occur at any section of the network for reasons that can and do vary widely. Disruptions include company mergers, labor union strikes, regulatory changes, the destruction of production facilities, the suspension of air traffic due to bad weather or terrorism and natural disasters affecting suppliers.

Disruptions refer to rare and unexpected events with extensive effects, which mainly impact the structure of supply networks. Strategic level network design decisions determine a supply network's structure. Network design decisions deal with determining the number, location and capacity of facilities in a supply network's echelons. Furthermore, disruptions may render production facilities or transportation routes in a supply network entirely or partially inoperative.

To manage disruptions, three elements including robustness, structural controllability and resilience are essential. A robust supply network can limit the effect disruptions have on its performance, reducing its quantifiable loss of performance and maintaining its function within an acceptable range. We go on to explain robustness in greater detail in this chapter. A structurally controllable supply network has access to all its facilities through driver facilities (or controllers). In this chapter, we address robustness in supply networks to manage risk.

In the context of an architecture for fail-safe networks, as introduced in Section 1.3, we explain the use of robustness for risk management in supply networks (see Figure 1-4). The connector is the supply network, as it contains the variables used in this method. We express the form of our architecture in this chapter as an optimization model that captures component weights or importance, properties and relationships between robustness and risk management. The elements and their inter-relationships are captured using objectives like minimizing cost and maximizing service level. We use the requirements of managing the type(s) of risk to guide the selection of elements and form, along with user assumptions and system constraints, establishing the rationale of the architecture. We summarize the constituents of this architecture and our interpretation for robustness in risk management in Table 6-1.

We review the literature of disruption management in supply networks from varying perspectives in the following section.

6.2 Disruption Management in Supply Networks Literature

According to Henry and Emmanuel Ramirez-Marquez (2012), a supply network is disrupted until it initiates a recovery to reach a new, stable state with an acceptable state of performance. Disruptions are delays, natural and human-made disasters and infrastructural failures that may neutralize a portion of the elements and operations within supply networks (Gong et al. 2014). The severity of the impact of disruptions relates to the readiness of networks to manage disruptions (Craighead et al. 2007). Over

Table 6-1. Summary of architecture for robustness in risk management.

Architecture Constituents	Summary Interpretation for Fail-Safe Networks
Elements	**What?**
Components	Robustness
Connectors	Supply network
Form	**How?**
Component weights	Robustness: 1
Properties	Demand, cost, capacity, etc.
Relationship	Optimization Minimize cost and maximize service level
Rationale	**Why?**
Motivation	Disruption management
Assumptions	Linear relation between variables
Constraints	Production and transportation capacity, demand fulfilment, etc.
Interpretation	Understanding of the solution; may provide motivation for further study

a period of time, researchers have developed various strategies to manage disruptions, which we discuss in this chapter.

Tomlin (2006) investigates the neutralization of a supplier belonging to a two-echelon supply network which includes a manufacturer and two suppliers. Chopra and Sodhi (2004) analyze the appropriate selection of distortion reducing strategies in a two-echelon supply network that includes a buyer that has the option of service from two suppliers. One is reliable, and the other is unreliable but less expensive. Peng et al. (2012) develop a model that can be instrumental in designing a supply network structure that performs well under normal conditions and performs relatively well when disruptions occur at vulnerable facilities. Baghalian et al. (2013) propose a path-based approach to design a robust supply network structure with facilities and transportation routes that are vulnerable to disruptions. The papers above focus solely on employing risk mitigation strategies to protect the performance of supply networks against the effects of disruptions.

Supply network literature often addresses disruption as a sub-category within risk management. Harland et al. (2004) investigate the prevalence of sophisticated global, dynamic infrastructure networks and the increased risk of a disruption. They explain that companies collaborating globally should evaluate risk and benefits jointly to find the most appropriate strategy. Pankaj Raj et al. (2004) describe controllable and uncontrollable risks within supply networks. We can summarily define risk as a combination of the probability of a disruptive event and the impact of the occurrence (Kaplan 1997).

Disruptive event or disruption can be a supply uncertainty or the result of unreliable suppliers. Tomlin (2006) describes supply-side disruptions and proposes a model to address disruption management. Tomlin refers to destructive fires at Philips Semiconductor and Toyota production plants as examples of unavoidable disruptions in supply. The risk of disruption, or the probability of damage to a supply network, is an issue that supply networks must address (Kristianto et al. 2014). Global and highly efficient supply networks are very susceptible to disruptions. Xu et al. (2009) refer to capacity disruptions, where a company loses all or a significant portion of production capacity for a period. This loss of production capacity results in a loss of supply downstream.

A supply network must be flexible and adaptable to respond effectively to disruption (Christopher and Lee 2004). Adaptability refers to a response to a change wherein a network may return to an old state or reach a new equilibrium (Fiksel 2006) where processes and capabilities may have changed. Flexibility is a supply network's ability to respond to changes without excessive time, cost or reduction in service level (Morlok and Chang 2004). In this sense, flexibility is a system attribute, and not a response (Mohamed et al. 2006). Another word or description for flexibility is elasticity (Das and Abdel-Malek 2003). Gosling et al. (2010) summarize flexibility as either vendor or sourcing flexibility. Vendor flexibility refers to the flexibility within an individual vendor facility in operations such as production, inventory or distribution. Sourcing flexibility describes flexibility across the supply network with the selection of sourcing. A supply network with sourcing flexibility can consistently adjust to changes in the market by selecting from among a pool of suppliers (Tachizawa and Thomsen 2007; Duclos et al. 2003). Stevenson and Spring (2007) describe how flexibility empowers supply networks to adapt to disruptions while maintaining equilibrium. Retaining its fundamental characteristics and performance, as well as altering processes when faced with disruptions are critical capabilities for a successful supply network (Ivanov and Sokolov 2013). Shepherd and Günter (2006) introduce production, capacity, volume and logistics flexibility as measurable flexibility attributes. On the other hand, robustness is a critical component to manage disruptions affecting supply networks. Tang (2006) mentions the importance of designing supply chains under disruptions and proposes a set of robust managerial strategies, such as keeping additional inventory in warehouses and postponing the delivery of the end product, to manage disruptions. Park et al. (2013) present best practices and lessons learned from several catastrophic natural disasters that affected global supply chains in Japan.

Khosrojerdi et al. (2016) present a robust optimization approach for a mixed-integer nonlinear programming (MINLP) model while random failures and intentional attacks happen in a power supply network. Various mathematical models for different business environments and disruption occurrences are developed to employ robustness strategies. Aryanezhad et al. (2010) propose a stochastic integer nonlinear programming (INLP) model for the supply chain network designs that use extra inventory to decrease the impact of disruptions. Jabbarzadeh et al. (2014) propose a robust, comprehensive network design model for the blood supply during and after disasters in a real case study. Chen et al. (2011) offer an inventory-location supply chain network design (SCND) model when failures occur with predetermined probabilities. Peng et al. (2011) propose a mixed-integer linear programming (MILP) SCND model in which disruption occurrences are modeled using the robust optimization approach and p-robustness criterion.

While robustness allows a supply network to respond to disruptions, resilience gives the supply network the ability to recover efficiently. Resilience can be described as the ability to "bounce back" (Sheffi and Rice 2005), "recover quickly" (Gong et al. 2014) and return to a baseline or better operational state when faced with disruptions (Christopher and Peck 2004; Ponomarov and Holcomb 2009). The latter view accepts that flexibility and adaptability are implicit in resilience and may result in a new system configuration and performance. Francis and Bekera (2014) describe resilience as a network characteristic wherein the network can anticipate, absorb, adapt and respond to disruption. This feature is both intrinsic and strategically enhanced. Francis and Bekera (2014) also describe the widely varying definitions and strategies for resilience. Kendra and Wachtendorf (2003) find in their thorough literature review that another occasional definition for resilience is the ability to anticipate and absorb, or the ability to adapt or circumvent. Some found that resilience would require that a system must maintain its original identity (Cumming et al. 2005; Holling 1973) and others accept that a system configuration or performance may shift (Fiksel 2006). While approaches to resilience are varied, much of the supply network literature is related to recovery from disruption.

Hasani and Khosrojerdi (2016) explain the importance of considering the correlation among disruptions and its impact on disrupted global supply chains. Hassani and Khosrojerdi present a mixed-integer, nonlinear model for designing robust global supply chain networks under uncertainty. They offer six resilience strategies to mitigate the risk of correlated disruptions. Gong et al. (2014) provide a restoration model to develop resilient supply networks that can recover from disruptions while minimizing the downstream impact. They develop a mathematical representation and a restoration strategy for supply network managers.

To model the interactions and relationship among supply networks and surrounding networks, Gong and co-authors use a compact formulation of an Interdependent Layered Network (ILN). The ILN, introduced by Lee et al. (2007), represents multiple networks with layers and the logical relationships between the layers. There is no assumption of intra-network impacts on operational decisions within a supply network. However, in the event of a disruption, the impact of the disruption is propagated throughout the structure based on the relational interdependence. Using a supply network layer, power system layer, telecommunications layer and transportation layer, they employ scenarios where there is a local disruption in each of these layers. They then study the impact of possible restoration strategies on the layered network model. The solution to the multi-objective problem is found using Mixed Integer Linear Programming and a Branch and Bound algorithm using a commercial solver, CPLEX. Their work allows a supply network manager to identify priorities and to find an efficient restoration strategy.

While disruptions occur, supply network design requires not only robustness to cope with errors and uncertainties during execution, but also resilience as the ability of a network to return to its original or superior state after experiencing a disruption, which demands a combination of flexibility and adaptability. The importance of resilience manifests when maintaining, executing and recovering the baseline level or achieving a superior degree of network performance is the desired outcome. Also, as we discuss in Chapter 7, the importance of structurally controllable networks over the disruption period is extremely high. According to Liu et al. (2011), "a network is structurally controllable if, with a suitable choice of inputs, it can be driven from any initial state to any desired final state within a finite time." This definition agrees with the intuitive notion of structural controllability that is the capability to guide a network's performance toward the desired state through the appropriate manipulation of a few driver nodes. A supply network can be controlled by suitable manipulation through driver facilities wherein all other facilities in the network are accessible through these driver facilities. The accessibility facilitates transferring extra inventory to disrupted facilities and results in higher resilience. Therefore, structural controllability is another essential element, in addition to robustness and resilience, to manage disruptions in disrupted supply networks.

We discuss in this chapter the robust design of supply networks in the face of disruptions and propose a model for managing disruptions using robustness. We consider and model the power grid network as a supply network example. In the next two chapters, we introduce two other key elements in managing disruptions: structural controllability in Chapter 7 and resilience in Chapter 8. In the next section, we explain the significance of the robust supply network optimization modeling with its theoretical background.

6.3 Disruption Management using Robust Design Modeling

The contribution of this chapter to the literature of supply network risk management is in addressing the management of disruptions using robust optimization modeling. A robust design model is the representation of a sequence of solutions that are sensitive to changes in input data across scenarios to a negligible degree. The solution to a mathematical model can be robust with regard to either its optimality or its feasibility. A solution is called robust, or *solution robustness,* from the perspective of optimality if it is nearly optimal for any realization of the scenarios. The phrase *model robustness* describes a solution that is feasible in any scenario that may occur. The robust optimization Mulvey et al. (1995) address, combined an objective programming formulation with scenario-based programming that is stochastic. Their work indicates that under limited circumstances the solution may not be both optimal and feasible. A balance must be struck between solution robustness and model robustness, a trade-off, for which we will offer an explanation.

We evaluate infeasibility with a penalty function with a minimized value when the solution is nearly feasible. We measure optimality with the expected value and the variance of the objective function under all scenarios. A high variance for the objective function means that a small change in the value of uncertain parameters can cause a tremendous shift in the value of the objective function and consequently, the solution corresponds to a high-risk decision (Pan and Nagi 2010). The robust model defines two sets of variables: design and control. We determine design variable values prior to establishing the values of the uncertain parameters. Those values cannot be adjusted after the uncertain parameters have been given fixed values, although once an uncertain parameter has a fixed value, the control variables may be adjusted. There are two types of constraints: structural and control constraints with certain and uncertain input data respectively. We formulate the robust design model in this way:

$$\text{Min } c^T x + d^T y \tag{6-1}$$

s. t.

$$Ax = b \tag{6-2}$$

$$Bx + Cy = e \tag{6-3}$$

$$x, y \geq 0 \tag{6-4}$$

Here $x \in R^{n1}$ is a design variable vector and $y \in R^{n2}$ is a control variable vector. Equation (6-2) is a structural constraint in which the coefficients are fixed and certain. Equation (6-3) is a control constraint with uncertain and unstable coefficients. To consider unknown parameters, in each scenario $s \in S$ with a probability of occurrence equal to p_s the coefficients related to the control constraint are $\{d_s, B, C_s, e_s\}$, as shown in Eqs. (6-6) and (6-7). In this way, we obtain model robustness and solution robustness for any occurrence of the scenario 's'. We assess the tradeoff between solution and model robustness by using multiple-criteria decision making as in the following formula:

$$\text{Min } \sigma(x, y_1, y_2, \ldots, y_s) + \tau\varphi(\beta_1, \beta_2, \ldots, \beta_s) \tag{6-5}$$

s.t.

$$Ax = b \tag{6-6}$$

$$B_s x + C_s y_s + \beta_s = e_s \qquad\qquad s \in S \tag{6-7}$$

$$x \geq 0, y_s \geq 0 \qquad\qquad s \in S \tag{6-8}$$

Further, p_s is the probability with which the objective function takes the value of $z_s = c^T x + d_s^T y_s$.

The value of acceptable infeasibility in the control constraint under scenario 's' is measured by β_s. $\tau\varphi(\beta_1, \beta_2, \ldots, \beta_s)$ in Eq. (6-5) is the robustness value of the model; this function acts as a feasibility penalty. If any infeasibility occurs, this function penalizes any violation of the control constraint. τ represents the weight of this function. We manage the tradeoff between solution robustness and model robustness by adjusting τ. An increase in the value of τ causes model robustness to overtake solution robustness. Stated simply, we may obtain a less than optimal solution with greater feasibility.

σ is formulated by Mulvey et al. (1995) to represent the solution robustness as follows:

$$z_s = c^T x + d_s^T y_s.$$

$$\sigma = \sum_{s \in S} p_s z_s + \theta \sum_{s \in S} p_s (z_s - \sum_{s' \in S} p_{s'} z_{s'})^2 \tag{6-9}$$

In the preceding equation, θ reflects the sensitivity of the solution robustness to changes of uncertain parameters under different scenarios. The solution for the expression in Eq. (6-9), which is a nonlinear quadratic equation, requires considerable computational power. In an effort to streamline the calculation process, Yu and Li (2000) propose a model based on the absolute deviation instead of the quadratic term. In earlier work, Luckman (1972) added two non-negative deviational variables to the objective function to linearize the model. Using these improvements, the equation for solution robustness of the objective function becomes:

$$\text{Min} \sum_{s \in S} p_s z_s + \theta \sum_{s \in S} (\gamma_s^+ + \gamma_s^-) \tag{6-10}$$

s.t.

$$z_s - \sum_{s' \in S} p_{s'} z_{s'} = \gamma_s^+ - \gamma_s^- \qquad s \in S \tag{6-11}$$

$$\gamma_s^+, \gamma_s^- \geq 0 \qquad s \in S \tag{6-12}$$

In this formula γ_s^+ and γ_s^- are respectively $\{z_s - \sum_{s' \in S} p_{s'} z_{s'}\}$ if $z_s \geq \sum_{s' \in S} p_{s'} z_{s'}$ and $\{\sum_{s' \in S} p_{s'} z_{s'} - z_s\}$ if $\sum_{s' \in S} p_{s'} z_{s'} \geq z_s$. For $\theta \geq 0$ when γ_s^+ takes a non-zero value, γ_s^- will be zero and vice versa.

The objective function takes the form of Eq. (6-13) with consideration for the modifications above.

$$\text{Min} \sum_{s \in S} p_s z_s + \theta \sum_{s \in S} (\gamma_s^+ + \gamma_s^-) + \tau \sum_{s \in S} p_s \beta_s \tag{6-13}$$

In this chapter, we build on the robust design approach Mulvey et al. (1995) present and we develop it for a multi-objective, and nonlinear model and apply it to a supply network example under disruption. In the next section, we present and discuss the problem of utilizing a supply network design for modeling power grid networks.

6.4 Supply Network Modeling for Designing Power Grid Networks under Disruptions

Power systems are among the largest and most sophisticated technological infrastructure systems that human beings have developed; they are fundamental to national and international social development, economics, the quality of life and security (Zio and Aven 2011). Protecting them from intentional attacks or random failures is an area of vigorous ongoing research (Wang and Rong 2011). Accidents caused by the climate and environment, equipment malfunctions, the imbalance between supply and demand and human error can severely disrupt power grids (You et al. 2011). The European blackout of 4 November 2006 is one example of transnational infrastructure vulnerability. There is documentation of the astounding velocity and geographical reach of power failures from the European blackout in several studies (Van der Vleuten and Lagendijk 2010; ERGEG 2007; UCTE 2007). The Western North American blackouts in July and August 1996, and the major power blackout in August 2003, which lasted up to 4 days in various parts of the East Coast, impacted other critical infrastructure and caused traffic congestion (Wang and Rong 2011).

Blackouts seem to have a unique ability to remind us of the importance of the power grid and how we cannot take its availability for granted. Power network vulnerability is a key concern in modern societies which have devoted considerable effort to its analysis (Bompard et al. 2010).

The focus of research has been on the structure of power grids with a particular focus on their nodes and their connection patterns when developing models of vulnerable generation and transmission systems. Bao et al. (2009) propose a concept of power flow entropy to quantify the overall heterogeneity of load distribution. Through various simulation results of power transmission grids, they demonstrate that power flow entropy is closely related to cascading failures. Arianos et al. (2009) introduce a metric called net-ability to estimate the performance and resilience of power networks upon line removal. Albert et al. (2004) examine the power grid using a network structure point of view and measure its ability to transfer electricity from supply to demand nodes, which constitutes the transmission system, after the disruption of specific nodes. Lin et al. (2012) study the performance evaluation of a power transmission system regarding its network structure and propose a method to measure the impact of correlated failures on network reliability which they define as the probability of satisfying demand. However, they do not consider a generation system constraint (supply capacity) in their model. Sun et al. (2008) propose a new capacity allocation model to maximize the power generation profit by considering capacity allocation and network efficiency for scale-free networks and the actual network structure of the North American power grid. The model they develop considers the supply to the exclusion of demand, while also assuming that power plants are always available. Dueñas-Osorio and Vemuru (2009) study the effect of failures on the reliability and risk assessment of complex infrastructure systems. Albert et al. (2004) consider the reliability of the United States power grid. They study a network of active power plants and high voltage transmission substations. They focus on the structure of the grid and do not consider the supply, demand and power plant capacity. The majority of papers in failure analysis and modeling of power grids focus on network structure. In the literature, the purely structure-based approach of modeling generation and transmission systems does not take into account important constraints such as capacity, maintenance and the availability of power plants and electrical substation capacity and as a result, they fail to capture actual features of power systems.

A significant effort has been applied to modeling generation systems but, generally speaking, comparatively less attention has been given to the transmission system. Shahidehpour et al. (2002) address some decision-making challenges associated with modeling the production systems, including the minimization of the power generating cost while taking into account demand and power plant capacity. Xing and Wu (2002) propose a mathematical model that can be applied to power plants by considering electric demand and power capacity. The work of Billinton and Abdulwhab (2003) and Conejo et al. (2005) study power generation systems and propose deterministic models for power generation scheduling in power plants while minimizing operating cost. All these studies focus on planning for the generation system without considering the transmission system or failures in the transmission system. Power grids are integrated generation and transmission systems. Therefore each system will affect the decisions of the other.

Here we present a method of planning for the generation system taking into account its preventive maintenance while accounting for the structure of the power grid and possible disruptions. A supply chain network point of view is useful for studying the structure of the integrated power grid generation and transmission systems in which scheduling of the power plant maintenance is addressed. Considering that the power grid network is a vulnerable infrastructure and the occurrence of disruptions and maintenance is inevitable, we propose a robust design model for studying various disruption scenarios including possible disruptions of transmission lines or electrical substations. The robust design model is a multi-objective, multi-period, mixed-integer and nonlinear mathematical model, but it can be linearized. In this model, minimizing cost and maximizing the met demand are two objectives. We solve and analyze the model using a regional electric company as an example.

The objective of power grid planners is to meet the demand for electricity. There are two issues that power grid planners must consider: constraints related to the generation of electricity by power plants and possible disruptions in transmitting electricity from supply to consumer. The primary problem we address in this chapter is how power grid planners can implement a robust plan that addresses power generation and maintenance scheduling for power supply chain networks, particularly in the face of possible disruptions.

6.5 Power Grid Supply Network Modeling under Disruptions

There are different types of power plants, with different generating capacities, setup times, maintenance times and efficiencies. Hydro and wind power plants, for example, have shorter setup times and more limited capacities in comparison to combined cycle gas turbines. Furthermore, maintenance plays a critical role in decreasing the probability of sudden failures in power plants. We develop a multi-period mathematical model for supply chain power networks to determine the planning for power generation and scheduling for preventive maintenance at each period for each type of power plant. The generation system, however, is not immune to incidents within the transmission system and failures within the transmission system influence decisions regarding the generation system.

Disruptions can happen at either transmission lines or electrical substations within power grid networks. An instance of each of these disruptions decreases the supply capacity or influences the fulfillment of electricity demand. Therefore, robust design for power generation and preventive maintenance of the power grid network is required, in which various disruption scenarios may occur with the smallest possible disruption to power supply. We propose a scenario-based approach in assessing possible disruptions in the transmission system. The two objective functions of this mixed-integer nonlinear model are maximizing the met electricity demand while minimizing the setup, power generation and maintenance costs. We explain the mathematical model in detail in the next section.

We use a schematic view of its supply chain to develop a mathematical model for power generation and transmission. A four-level power supply chain network is defined by specifying interactions among the components of the production and transmission network, Figure 6-1.

Power plants are positioned on the first level. Electrical substations are positioned on the second and third levels. Two types of electrical substations are considered on each level: the first decreases the voltage, the second transmits electricity without altering the voltage. On level four, there are electrical sub-stations which correspond to the beginning of the distribution system of power grid networks. We consider the fourth level electric substations to be demand nodes.

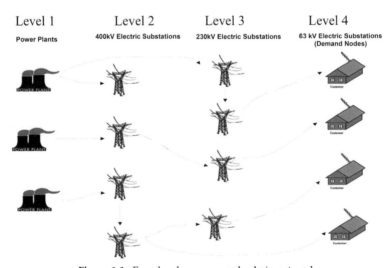

Figure 6-1. Four-level power supply chain network.

This representation, based upon three levels of electrical substations, can be expanded to fit other kinds of power grid networks. Stated simply, additional levels may be needed to represent electrical sub-stations with a range of voltages. Within this section, we demonstrate how we can model the robust design model for a power grid network as a power supply chain network.

Sets and Indices

i	:	Power plant, $i \in I$, $I = \{1,2,\ldots, |I|\}$
$j, j\grave{}$	:	High voltage electric substation, $j, j' \in J$, $J = \{1,2,\ldots, |J|\}$
$k, k\grave{}$	:	Low voltage electric substation, $k, k' \in K$, $K = \{1,2,\ldots, |K|\}$
l	:	Demand node, $l \in L$, $L = \{1,2,\ldots, |L|\}$
t	:	Time period, $t \in T$, $T = \{1,2,\ldots, |T|\}$
s	:	Scenario, $s \in S$, $S = \{1,2,\ldots, |S|\}$

Parameters

g_{imin}	:	Lower bound of power generation for power plant i
g_{imax}	:	Upper bound of power generation for power plant i
mn_i	:	Number of required preventive maintenance time periods for power plant i
u_j^s	:	Upper limit (capacity) for electric substation j under scenario s
u'^s_k	:	Upper limit (capacity) for electric substation k under scenario s
d_{il}	:	Electricity demand at electric sub-station (demand node) l in period t
cm_i	:	Maintenance cost for power plant i
cs_i	:	Setup cost for power plant i
cg_i	:	Power generation cost for power plant i
p^s	:	Probability of occurrence scenario s
w_1	:	Weight for objective function one
w_2	:	Weight for objective function two
θ	:	Sensitivity of solution robust
τ	:	Feasibility penalty of model robust

Variables

Design Variables:

g_{it}	:	Power generation at power plant i in period t
m_{it}	:	Binary variable for preventive maintenance at power plant i in period t, equal to zero for power plant i under preventive maintenance, otherwise equal to one.
o_{it}	:	Binary variable for open (active) power plant i in period t, equal to one for open (active) power plant i, otherwise equal to zero.

Control Variables:

x^s_{ijt} :   Power flow from power plant i to electric sub-station j in period t and scenario s

y^s_{ikt} :   Power flow from power plant i to electric sub-station k in period t and scenario s

z^s_{jkt} :   Power flow from electric substation j to electric sub-station k in period t and scenario s

$z'^s_{jj't}$:   Power flow from electric substation j to electric sub-station j' in period t and scenario s

w^s_{jlt} :   Power flow from electric substation j to electric sub-station l in period t and scenario s

v^s_{klt} :   Power flow from electric substation k to electric sub-station l in period t and scenario s

$v'^s_{kk't}$:   Power flow from electric substation k to electric sub-station k' in period t and scenario s

β^s_{jt} :   Infeasibility variable for the upper limit (capacity) constraint at electric sub-station j in period t and scenario s

β^s :   Summation of infeasibility variables for upper limit (capacity) constraints for scenario s ($\beta^s = \sum_j \sum_t \beta^s_{jt}$)

β'^s_{kt} :   Infeasibility variable for the upper limit (capacity) constraint at electric sub-station k in period t and scenario s

β'^s :   Summation of infeasibility variables for upper limit (capacity) constraints for scenario s ($\beta'^s = \sum_k \sum_t \beta'^s_{kt}$)

Figure 6-2 shows the schematic view of the power supply chain network for the mathematical model we propose.

Figure 6-2 shows indices and power flow variables. The figure indicates that there is a forward flow between the four levels of the network. In levels two and three, representing high and low voltage electrical sub stations respectively, there is a possibility for vertical flow between electric sub-stations at the same level.

Constraints

Equations 6-14 to 6-25 present constraints of the model. Each type of power plant has specific lower and upper limits for the capacity of electricity generation. The first two constraints, Eqs. (6-14–6-15), refer to the minimum and maximum capacity of the power generation in these power plants.

$$g_{imin} \cdot o_{it} \leq g_{it} \qquad\qquad \forall i \in I, t \in T \qquad\qquad (6\text{-}14)$$

$$g_{it} \leq g_{imax} \cdot o_{it} \qquad\qquad \forall i \in I, t \in T \qquad\qquad (6\text{-}15)$$

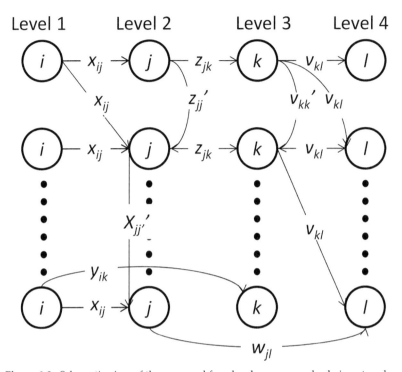

Figure 6-2. Schematic view of the proposed four-level power supply chain network.

The total power generated by all power plants in the network is transmitted to electric sub-stations in levels two and three; the storage of electricity is not possible after it is produced. The model does not consider lost energy. Equation 6-16 describes the constraint.

$$g_{it} = \sum_j x^s_{ijt} + \sum_k y^s_{ikt} \qquad \forall i \in I, t \in T, s \in S \qquad (6\text{-}16)$$

One of the constraints on the power grid transmission system is the capacity of the electric substations. The following equations are control constraints, Es. (6-17 to 6-18) and they represent the requirement that the incoming electricity flow to each electric substation cannot exceed the capacity.

$$\sum_i x^s_{ijt} + \sum_{j', j' \neq j} z'^s_{j'jt} - \beta^s_{jt} \leq u^s_j \qquad \forall j \in J, t \in T, s \in S \qquad (6\text{-}17)$$

$$\sum_i y^s_{ikt} + \sum_j z^s_{jkt} + \sum_{k', k' \neq k} v'^s_{k'kt} - \beta'^s_{kt} \leq u'^s_k \qquad \forall k \in K, t \in T, s \in S \qquad (6\text{-}18)$$

Input flow to each of the electric substations is equal to the output flow, as shown by Eqs. (6-19–6-20).

$$\sum_i x^s_{ijt} + \sum_{j',j' \neq j} z'^s_{j'jt} = \sum_k z^s_{jkt} + \sum_l w^s_{jlt} + \sum_{j',j' \neq j} z'^s_{jj't} \qquad \forall j \in J, t \in T, s \in S \quad (6\text{-}19)$$

$$\sum_i y^s_{ikt} + \sum_j z^s_{jkt} + \sum_{k',k' \neq k} v'^s_{k'kt} = \sum_l v^s_{klt} + \sum_{k',k' \neq k} v'^s_{kk't} \qquad \forall k \in K, t \in T, s \in S \quad (6\text{-}20)$$

The constraint on electrical demand at the fourth level is Eq. (6-21).

$$\sum_k v^s_{klt} + \sum_j w^s_{jlt} \leq d_{il} \qquad \forall l \in L, t \in T, s \in S \quad (6\text{-}21)$$

We present the maintenance constraints for power plants in Eq. (6-22 through 6-23). The first constraint shows the required number of periods for preventive maintenance for each power plant. A power plant cannot generate electricity within a certain period if, in that period, it is undergoing preventive maintenance as indicated in the second constraint.

$$\sum_t (1 - m_{it}) = mn_i \qquad\qquad \forall i \in I \qquad\qquad (6\text{-}22)$$

$$o_{it} \leq m_{it} \qquad\qquad \forall i \in I, t \in T \qquad\qquad (6\text{-}23)$$

The constraints Eqs. (6-24–6-25) are for binary and continuous variables.

$$g_{it}, x^s_{ijt}, y^s_{ikt}, z^s_{jkt}, z'^s_{jkt}, w^s_{jlt}, v^s_{klt}, v'^s_{klt}, \beta^s_{jt}, \beta^s, \beta'^s_{kt}, \beta'^s \geq 0$$

$$\forall i \subset I, j \in J, k \in K, l \in L, t \in T, s \in S \qquad (6\text{-}24)$$

$$m_{it}, o_{it} \in 0,1 \qquad\qquad \forall i \in I, t \in T \qquad\qquad (6\text{-}25)$$

Non-linear objective function for the robust design model

The first objective function (Z_1) refers to the minimization of cost, and the second objective function (Z_2) refers to the maximization of service level (met demand), both of which Eq. (6-26) represents. For the two objective functions, we employ a weighting method in which w_1 represents the weight of the minimization function and w_2 represents the weight of the maximization function.

$$\text{Min } z^s = w_1[\sum_i \sum_{t,t=1} cs_i \cdot o_{it} + \sum_i \sum_{t,t \neq 1} cs_i \cdot o_{it}(1 - o_{i(t-1)}) + \sum_i \sum_t cg_i \cdot g_{it} +$$

$$\sum_i \sum_t cm_i (1 - m_{it})] - w_2[\sum_l \sum_t \frac{\sum_j w^s_{jlt} + \sum_k v^s_{klt}}{d_{lt}}] \qquad (6\text{-}26)$$

$$w_1 + w_2 = 1 \qquad\qquad (6\text{-}27)$$

The first portion of Eq. (6-26) expresses the setup cost of power plant I; this makes the objective function nonlinear. The second and third portions account for the cost of power generation and the cost of maintenance, respectively. The last part denotes the percentage of the met demand. The summation of weights is equal to one as in Eq. (6-27).

We derive the scenario-based robust objective function from Eq. (6-10–6-13) and describe it in Eqs. (6-28–6-30).

$$\text{Min} \sum_s P^s \cdot Z^s + \theta \sum_s P^s (\gamma_s^+ + \gamma_s^-) + \tau \sum_s P^s (\beta^s + \beta'^s) \qquad (6\text{-}28)$$

$$Z^s - \sum_{s'} P^{s'} \cdot Z^{s'} = \gamma_s^+ - \gamma_s^- \qquad\qquad s' \in S, s' \neq s \qquad (6\text{-}29)$$

$$\gamma_s^+, \gamma_s^- \geq 0 \qquad\qquad s \in S \qquad (6\text{-}30)$$

The first portion of the objective function in Eq. (6-26) is a nonlinear equation which can be linearized with ease, as we explain in the next section.

Robust design model by linearizing the objective function

The first portion of Eq. (6-26) renders the bi-objective function a nonlinear equation, which increases the difficulty in solving the model. We use a variable change technique to linearize the equation. Using this method, we begin by defining a new variable, S_{it}, as we illustrate in Eq. (6-31).

$$S_{it} = \begin{cases} 1 & o_{it} - o_{i(t-1)} = 1 \\ 0 & o_{it} - o_{i(t-1)} \neq 1 \end{cases} \qquad (6\text{-}31)$$

This new variable replaces the non-linear portion of Eq. (6-26), with the linear objective function Eq. (6-32) and finally, we introduce an additional constraint, Eq. (6-33).

$$\text{Min } Z^s = w_1[\sum_i \sum_{t,t=1} cs_i \cdot o_{it} + \sum_i \sum_{t,t \neq 1} cs_i \cdot S_{it} + \sum_i \sum_t cg_i \cdot g_{it} +$$

$$\sum_i \sum_t cm_i (1 - m_{it})] - w_2[\sum_l \sum_t \frac{\sum_j w_{jlt}^s + \sum_k v_{klt}^s}{d_{lt}}] \qquad (6\text{-}32)$$

$$S_{it} \geq o_{it} - o_{i(t-1)} \qquad (6\text{-}33)$$

We present a mathematical model for power grid networks which applies to other types of infrastructure networks such as transportation, natural gas, and food chain networks with slight changes.

In the next section, we solve and analyze the model we propose for a regional electric company example.

6.6 Power Grid Supply Network Example: A Regional Electric Company

In this section, we consider an example of a regional electric company to apply the developed robust design model for power grid supply networks facing disruptions. We focus on generation and transmission systems that can be represented as a network. Regarding the network structure, links represent transmission lines. The power grid network example includes 400 kV and 230 kV voltage transmission lines with a length of more than 18,000 miles and 132 kV and 63 kV low voltage transmission lines (Hasani-Marzooni and Hosseini 2013). Also regarding the network structure, nodes are stand in for power plants in reference to the power generation system and stand in for electrical sub stations in reference to the transmission system.

The regional electric company example has 15 power plants of four different types (steam turbine, gas turbine, combined cycle gas turbine, and hydro technologies). The installed capacity and annual generation for these 15 power plants, based on their type, are presented in Table 6-2. The lower bound and upper bound of electricity generation, which are determined based on the minimum and the maximum number of power generation units, are shown in Figure 6-3.

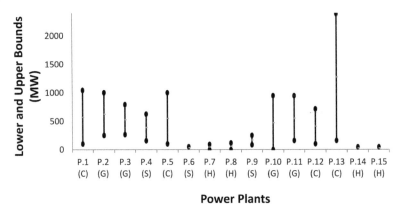

Figure 6-3. Power generation bounds (MW) – C: Combined cycle gas turbine, G: Gas turbine, S: Steam turbine, H: Hydro (TREC 2010).

Table 6-3 lists the fuel and maintenance prices for the different types of power plants. There are fourteen high voltage (400 kV) and thirty-nine low voltage (230 kV) electric sub-stations, respectively. We show the capacity of 400 kV and 230 kV electrical substations in Figures 6-4 and 6-5.

In the regional electric company for example, there are 213 of 63 kV electrical substations on the fourth level of the transmission system. The

Table 6-2. Installed capacity and average monthly generation (TREC 2010).

Generation Technology	Installed Capacities		Average Monthly Generation	
	MW	(%)	MWh	(%)
Gas turbine	2,683.0	26.7	1,169,315	21.6
Steam turbine	1,922.5	19.1	1,152,399	21.3
Cycle gas turbine	5,143.4	51.1	3,023,189	55.8
Hydro	316.0	3.1	68,262	1.3
Combined Total	10,138.3	100.0	5,413,165	100.0

Table 6-3. Fuel prices and maintenance cost.

Generation Technology	Maintenance Cost ($/MW/yr)	Fuel Types	Fuel Price
Gas turbine	2,683.0	Gas	950 ($/m³)
Steam turbine	1,922.5	Mazut and fuel oil	2000 ($/m³)
Combined cycle gas turbine	5,143.4	Diesel	3500 ($/m³)
Hydro	316.0		

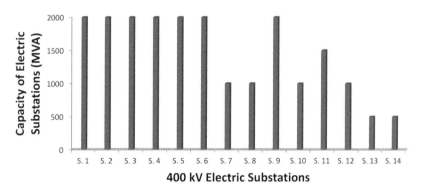

Figure 6-4. Capacity of high voltage (400 kV) electric sub-stations (kVA).

electric substations in this level of the transmission system comprise the first level of the distribution system. Level four sub-stations are demand nodes for the generation and transmission systems. The coincident power passed through all demand nodes is assumed to be the demand for the generation and transmission systems. There is a higher demand for electricity in spring and summer compared to the rest of the year. In this chapter, we consider the demand for six periods of time in spring and summer (Between April and September). We show in Figure 6-6 the peak demand for this period for each demand node.

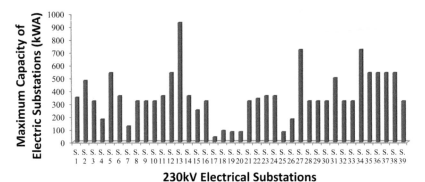

Figure 6-5. Capacity of low voltage (230 kV) electric sub-stations (kVA).

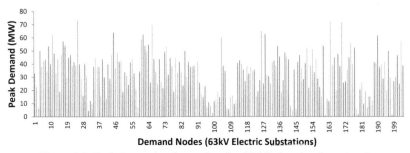

Figure 6-6. Peak demand at demand nodes (63 kV electric sub-stations).

Disruption scenarios

Power grid systems are at the core of modern infrastructure and random failures or intentional attacks can have a tremendous impact on the robustness of power generation planning or preventive maintenance scheduling. We define three different categories of disruptions. The first category is random failures at nodes. The second category is an intentional node attack, in which there will be failures on nodes with the highest degrees (highest numbers of incoming and outgoing links). The third category of disruption is random failures on links.

We define four scenarios for our proposed robust design model. In the first scenario, no failures occur. We consider this scenario to assist planners of the power grid systems to compare results of the model at times when there is no disruption to times when there is a disruption. We consider in the second scenario five random failures on electric sub-stations in levels two and three of the power supply chain network. We examine in the third scenario five failures on high degree electric sub-stations in levels two and three of the power supply chain network. We examine in the final scenario five random failures on transmission lines between level one, level two, and level three of the power supply network. We also assume that the

Table 6-4. Transmission lines and electric substations under failure scenarios.

Disruption Scenario	Scenario Description	Ps	Lines or Substations under Failure
Scenario 1	No failure	0.25	-
Scenario 2	Random node failure	0.25	j = 14, k = 16, 17, 22, 27
Scenario 3	Intentional node attack (targeted failure)	0.25	k = 4, 10, 23, 24, 33
Scenario 4	Random link failure	0.25	(j,k) = (11,10), (7,15) (j,l) = (8,86) (k,l) = (35,13) (i,l) = (6,38)

probabilities of occurrence for each of the four scenarios are equal ($Ps = 0.25$). Table 6-4 lists the details of the scenarios that address failure.

In the next section, we present and discuss the results of solving the mathematical model for the regional electric company example.

6.7 Results and Discussions: Power Grid Supply Network Modeling under Disruptions

All computations are run using the branch and bound algorithm we access via Gurobi Optimizer 5.5 on a PC Pentium V–3.16 GHz and 4 GB RAM. We coded the mathematical model utilizing the Gurobi Python 2.7 interface to use the Gurobi Optimizer 5.5. Since the value scales for objective functions are different, both objectives are normalized to a number between zero and one by using $\frac{z - z_{min}}{z_{max} - z_{min}}$. The trade-off between Objective one (minimizing cost) and Objective two (maximizing met demand) presented in Eq. (6-32) is illustrated in Figure 6-7.

The weights of objective functions (w_1 and w_2) change over the range (0, 1). Note that when (w_1, w_2) = (1, 0), the linear objective function in Eq. (6-32) is equivalent to the first objective (minimizing cost) only, and when (w_1, w_2) = (0, 1), the linear objective function in Eq. (6-32) is equivalent to only objective two (maximizing met demand). The best value of objective one (Z_1^*) is obtained for (w_1, w_2) = (1, 0), while at the same time the worst value of objective two (Z_2) is achieved. Conversely, the best value of objective two (Z_2^*) occurs when (W_1, W_2) = (0, 1), but the worst value of objective one (Z_1) is derived. Stated simply, considering only one objective sacrifices the other. We consider the trade-off between these two objective functions in the linear model in Eq. (6-32). An efficient frontier curve is shown in Figure 6-7 and allows decision makers to select suitable weights from their perspectives.

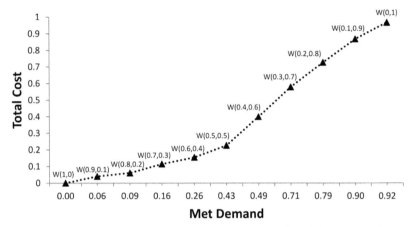

Figure 6-7. Trade-off between objective one (operating cost) and objective two (met demand).

Note that the linear model (Eq. 6-32) is to minimize operational cost (objective one) and maximize met demand (objective two) in the power supply chain network. However, after random and targeted failures, the value of these objectives can be radically different from the value in the linear model (Eq. 6-32). The model is made more robust to reduce this variation. In the robust model, the sensitivity of solution robustness (θ) and feasibility penalty of model robustness (τ) in the robust objective function are shown with two parameters (Eq. 6-28). By adjusting τ and θ, we manage the tradeoff between model robustness (feasibility) and solution robustness (optimality). By increasing the value of τ, model robustness will overtake solution robustness. In short, we may arrive at a

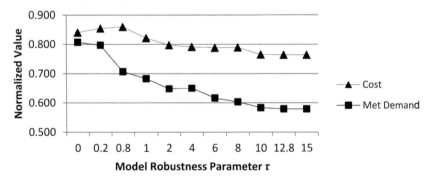

Figure 6-8. Computational results of the sensitivity analysis of the model robustness parameter (τ).

less than optimal but more feasible solution. Because of the importance of feasibility in planning for the power supply chain network, we consider the sensitivity analysis of the model robustness (feasibility) parameter in our model.

We illustrate the sensitivity analysis of the model robustness parameter in Figure 6-8, while the solution robustness (optimality) parameter is fixed ($\theta = 0.01$). The model robustness parameter increases from 0 to 15. Here we set the weights of both objective functions as 0.5 and 0.5. By increasing the model robustness parameter in the objective function, the model tends not to violate the capacity constraints at electric substations (Eqs. 6-17–6-18). In other words, by increasing the parameter, the probability of violation of the capacity constraints decreases, leading to more unmet demand as a consequence. For $\tau \geq 12.8$, the model is insensitive to the increases of the model robustness parameter.

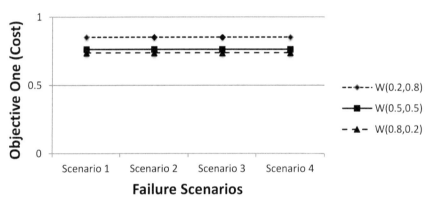

Figure 6-9. Objective one for scenario-based robust design model.

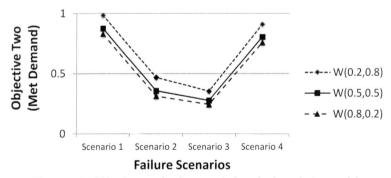

Figure 6-10. Objective two for the scenario-based robust design model.

Design variables are decided before the realization of uncertain parameters and cannot be adjusted after realization. Control variables are subject to adjustment when an occurrence of uncertain parameters is realized. In the proposed robust design model, there are only design variables in objective one (minimizing cost) and only control variables in objective two (maximizing met demand). Therefore, the values of objective one are identical for all scenarios and values for objective two can be different for each scenario. Figures 6-9 and 6-10 show the results of the robust design model for three different sets of weighting with model robustness and solution robustness set as 12.8 and 0.01, respectively.

As we illustrate in Figure 6-9 and Figure 6-10, by decreasing the weight of the second objective from 0.8 to 0.2, the percentage of the met demand decreases, while the value of the first objective function (minimizing the total cost) increases. For all weighting sets, we illustrate in Figure 6-10 that Scenario 3 has the lowest met demand (the highest unmet demand). Thus, we conclude that failures on the highly-ranked nodes (Scenario 3) in the power grid network cause more widespread blackouts (unmet demand) than random failures of other nodes or links (Scenarios 2 and 4). Therefore, the results of the proposed robust design model demonstrate that the power grid network is more vulnerable to intentional attacks (failures on high degree nodes) than the random failures of substations or transmission lines.

We then calculate the power generation planning and preventive maintenance scheduling for power plants using the proposed robust design model for six periods of time, from April to September 2010. The results, which balanced objective one and objective two in which W1 and W2 equal to 0.5 and 0.5, are presented in Table 6-5. These results are related to the planning for operational decisions of power supply chain networks. Operational decisions such as planning for electricity generation and preventive maintenance are short-term decisions (usually monthly or seasonal decisions). Therefore, based on the goals of our proposed model, solving the model for several years is unnecessary. However, for strategic decisions in a power grid network, the period analysis is for several years.

We display the results of planning for the power generation and preventive maintenance of power plants in Table 6-5. We describe here a robust solution for the power grid supply network under various failure scenarios, which causes the least disruption to power supply. As a result of including the setup cost in the first objective function, the minimum viable number of power plants are generating power in the proposed robust plan. Although combined cycle gas and gas turbines have higher setup cost, they have higher power generation capacities and fewer preventive

Table 6-5. Robust power generation and preventive maintenance of power plants for (W1, W2) = (0.5, 0.5).

Power Plants		Time Periods						Total Power Generation (MW)	Total Maintenance Periods
		t = 1	t = 2	t = 3	t = 4	t = 5	t = 6		
Power plant 1	g_{1t}	1043	890	890	890	1043	0	4756	
	$1-m_{1t}$	0	0	0	0	0	1		1
Power plant 2	g_{2t}	1000	1000	1000	1000	0	1000	5000	
	$1-m_{2t}$	0	0	0	0	1	0		1
Power plant 3	g_{3t}	0	0	0	0	792	792	1584	
	$1-m_{3t}$	0	0	0	1	0	0		1
Power plant 4	g_{4t}	0	0	0	0	0	0	0	
	$1-m_{4t}$	0	0	0	0	0	0		0
Power plant 5	g_{5t}	0	540	540	540	540	540	2700	
	$1-m_{5t}$	1	0	0	0	0	0		1
Power plant 6	g_{6t}	0	0	0	0	0	0	0	
	$1-m_{6t}$	0	0	0	0	0	0		0
Power plant 7	g_{7t}	90	90	90	0	0	0	270	
	$1-m_{7t}$	0	0	0	1	1	1		3
Power plant 8	g_{8t}	115.5	115.5	115.5	0	0	0	346.5	
	$1-m_{8t}$	0	0	0	1	1	1		3
Power plant 9	g_{9t}	247.5	247.5	247.5	247.5	247.5	0	1237.5	
	$1-m_{9t}$	0	0	0	0	0	1		1
Power plant 10	g_{10t}	0	360	360	360	360	360	1800	
	$1-m_{10t}$	1	0	0	0	0	0		1
Power plant 11	g_{11t}	0	320	320	320	320	320	1600	
	$1-m_{11t}$	1	0	0	0	0	0		1
Power plant 12	g_{12t}	0	0	0	0	0	0	0	

Table 6-5 contd. ...

...Table 6-5 contd.

Power Plants		t = 1	t = 2	t = 3	t = 4	t = 5	t = 6	Total Power Generation (MW)	Total Maintenance Periods
	$1-m_{12t}$	0	0	0	0	0	0		0
Power plant 13	g_{13t}	0	2000	2000	2000	2000	2000	10000	
	$1-m_{13t}$	1	0	0	0	0	0		1
Power plant 14	g_{14t}	0	0	0	0	0	0	0	
	$1-m_{14t}$	0	0	0	0	0	0		0
Power plant 15	g_{15t}	45	45	45	0	0	0	135	
	$1-m_{15t}$	0	0	0	1	1	1		3

*g_{it} is the power generation at power plant i in period t, $1-m_i t$ is equal to one when power plant i in period t is under maintenance)

maintenance requirements. These characteristics result in generating power mainly by combined cycle gas and gas turbines in the proposed robust plan.

6.8 Closing Remarks

In this chapter, we review the relevant literature and explain the crucial nature of disruption management in supply networks and include in the discussion three main elements in managing disruptions: robustness, structural controllability and resilience. In addition to the extensive literature review on disruption management, in this chapter, we expand on robustness in supply networks under disruptions and introduce a nonlinear robust design modeling approach for supply networks. We explain the benefits of developing robust design modeling for designing or re-designing supply networks under disruptions. Furthermore, we illustrate the role of robustness in the context of architecture for fail-safe networks as explained in Chapter 1. We summarize the constituents of this architecture and our interpretation for robustness in risk management in Table 6-1.

The example in this chapter considers a regional electric company for the application of the proposed model in this chapter. This model has its anchor in the supply network construct that aids in the design of the generation and transmission systems simultaneously with combined production and maintenance constraints of power plants, while also considering the capacity constraints and disruptions on the transmission system. Two categories of power supply disruptions, random and targeted attacks, are addressed along with disruptions due to preventive maintenance. Results of the model demonstrate that failures due to targeted attacks on nodes with higher degree cause a greater decrease in performance for these networks compared to random failures. Also, as per the results, node failures have a greater impact on network performance than link failures. This sort of contained effect is also one of the properties of scale-free networks (Barabási 2009). This observation may suggest the addition of features to power supply networks, to assist policy makers and planners in analyzing failures and designing robust networks.

In the next chapter, we explain in detail structural controllability as a key component of the resilience of supply networks enduring disruptions.

Acknowledgment

Figures and tables in Chapter 6 are reprinted from Engineering Optimization, volume 48, issue 1, by Amirhossein Khorsojerdi, Seyed Hessameddin Zegordi, Janet K. Allen and Farrokh Mistree, "A Method for Designing Power Supply Chain Networks Accounting for Failure Scenarios and Preventive Maintenance." pp. 154–172, 2016, with permission from Taylor and Francis.

References

Albert, R., Albert, I. and Nakarado, G. L. 2004. Structural vulnerability of the North American power grid. Physical Review E 69(2): 31–34.

Arianos, S., Bompard, E., Carbone, A. and Xue, F. 2009. Power grid vulnerability: A complex network approach. Chaos 19(1): 91–96.

Aryanezhad, M.-B., Jalali, S. G. and Jabbarzadeh, A. 2010. An integrated supply chain design model with random disruptions consideration. African Journal of Business Management 4(12): 2393–2401.

Baghalian, A., Rezapour, S. and Farahani, R. Z. 2013. Robust supply chain network design with service level against disruptions and demand uncertainties: A real-life case. European Journal of Operational Research 227(1): 199–215.

Bao, Z. J., Cao, Y. J., Wang, G. Z. and Ding, L. J. 2009. Analysis of cascading failure in electric grid based on power flow entropy. Physics Letters A 373(34): 3032–3040.

Barabási, A.-L. 2009. Scale-Free Networks: A Decade and Beyond. Science 325(5939): 412–413.

Billinton, R. and Abdulwhab, A. 2003. Short-term generating unit maintenance scheduling in a deregulated power system using a probabilistic approach. Generation, Transmission and Distribution, IEE Proceedings 150(4): 463–468.

Bompard, E., Napoli, R. and Xue, F. 2010. Extended topological approach for the assessment of structural vulnerability in transmission networks. Iet Generation Transmission & Distribution 4(6): 716–724.

Chen, Q., Li, X. and Ouyang, Y. 2011. Joint inventory-location problem under the risk of probabilistic facility disruptions. Transportation Research Part B: Methodological 45(7): 991–1003.

Chopra, S. and Sodhi, M. S. 2004. Managing risk to avoid supply-chain breakdown: by understanding the variety and interconnectedness of supply-chain risks, managers can tailor balanced, effective risk-reduction strategies for their companies. MIT Sloan Management Review 46(1): 53.

Christopher, M. and Lee, H. 2004. Mitigating supply chain risk through improved confidence. International Journal of Physical Distribution & Logistics Management 34(5): 388–396.

Christopher, M. and Peck, H. 2004. Biuilding the resilient supply chain. The International Journal of Logistics Management 15(2): 1–13.

Conejo, A. J., Garcia-Bertrand, R. and Diaz-Salazar, M. 2005. Generation maintenance scheduling in restructured power systems. Power Systems, IEEE Transactions on 20(2): 984–992.

Craighead, C. W., Blackhurst, J., Rungtusanatham, M. J. and Handfield, R. B. 2007. The severity of supply chain disruptions: design characteristics and mitigation capabilities. Decision Sciences 38(1): 131–156.

Cumming, G. S., Barnes, G., Perz, S., Schmink, M., Sieving, K. E., Southworth, J., Binford, M., Holt, R. D., Stickler, C. and Van Holt, T. 2005. An exploratory framework for the empirical measurement of resilience. Ecosystems 8(8): 975–987.

Das, S. K. and Abdel-Malek, L. 2003. Modeling the flexibility of order quantities and lead-times in supply chains. International Journal of Production Economics 85(2): 171–181.

Duclos, L., Vokurka, R. and Lummus, R. 2003. A conceptual model of supply chain flexibility. Industrial Management + Data Systems 103(5/6): 446.

Dueñas-Osorio, L. and Vemuru, S. M. 2009. Cascading failures in complex infrastructure systems. Structural Safety 31(2): 157–167.

Ergeg. 2007. Final report: The lessons to be learned from the large disturbance in the European power system on the 4th of November 2006. E06-BAG-01-06, Brussels.

Fiksel, J. 2006. Sustainability and resilience: toward a systems approach. Sustainability: Science Practice and Policy 2(2): 14–21.

Francis, R. and Bekera, B. 2014. A metric and frameworks for resilience analysis of engineered and infrastructure systems. Reliability Engineering & System Safety 121: 90–103.

Gong, J., Mitchell, J. E., Krishnamurthy, A. and Wallace, W. A. 2014. An interdependent layered network model for a resilient supply chain. Omega 46: 104–116.

Gosling, J., Purvis, L. and Naim, M. M. 2010. Supply chain flexibility as a determinant of supplier selection. International Journal of Production Economics 128(1): 11–21.

Harland, C., Zheng, J., Johnsen, T. and Lamming, R. 2004. A conceptual model for researching the creation and operation of supply networks. British Journal of Management 15(1): 1–21.

Hasani-Marzooni, M. and Hosseini, S. H. 2013. Dynamic analysis of various investment incentives and regional capacity assignment in Iranian electricity market. Energy Policy 56(0): 271–284.

Hasani, A. and Khosrojerdi, A. 2016. Robust global supply chain network design under disruption and uncertainty considering resilience strategies: A parallel memetic algorithm for a real-life case study. Transportation Research Part E: Logistics and Transportation Review 87: 20–52.

Henry, D. and Emmanuel Ramirez-Marquez, J. 2012. Generic metrics and quantitative approaches for system resilience as a function of time. Reliability Engineering & System Safety 99: 114–122.

Holling, C. S. 1973. Resilience and stability of ecological systems. Resilience and Stability of Ecological Systems 4: 1–23.

Ivanov, D. and Sokolov, B. 2013. Control and system-theoretic identification of the supply chain dynamics domain for planning, analysis and adaptation of performance under uncertainty. European Journal of Operational Research 224(2): 313–323.

Jabbarzadeh, A., Fahimnia, B. and Seuring, S. 2014. Dynamic supply chain network design for the supply of blood in disasters: A robust model with real world application. Transportation Research Part E: Logistics and Transportation Review 70: 225–244.

Kaplan, S. 1997. The words of risk analysis. Risk Analysis 17(4): 407–417.

Kendra, J. M. and Wachtendorf, T. 2003. Elements of resilience after the World Trade Center disaster: Reconstituting New York City's Emergency Operations Centre. Disasters 27(1): 37–53.

Khosrojerdi, A., Zegordi, S. H., Allen, J. K. and Mistree, F. 2016. A method for designing power supply chain networks accounting for failure scenarios and preventive maintenance. Engineering Optimization 48(1): 154–172.

Kristianto, Y., Gunasekaran, A., Helo, P. and Hao, Y. 2014. A model of resilient supply chain network design: A two-stage programming with fuzzy shortest path. Expert Systems with Applications 41(1): 39–49.

Lee, E. E., Mitchell, J. E. and Wallace, W. A. 2007. Restoration of services in interdependent infrastructure systems: A network flows approach. Systems, Man, and Cybernetics, Part C: Applications and Reviews, IEEE Transactions on 37(6): 1303–1317.

Lin, Y.-K., Chang, P.-C. and Fiondella, L. 2012. A study of correlated failures on the network reliability of power transmission systems. International Journal of Electrical Power & Energy Systems 43(1): 954–960.

Liu, Y.-Y., Slotine, J.-J. and Barabási, A.-L. 2011. Controllability of complex networks. Nature 473(7346): 167–73.

Luckman, J. 1972. Principles of operations research: With applications to managerial decisions. Journal of the Royal Statistical Society Series C-Applied Statistics 21(1): 94–94.

Mohamed, M. N., Andrew, T. P., Robert, J. M. and Nicola, B. 2006. The role of transport flexibility in logistics provision. The International Journal of Logistics Management 17(3): 297–311.

Morlok, E. K. and Chang, D. J. 2004. Measuring capacity flexibility of a transportation system. Transportation Research Part A 38(6): 405–420.

Mulvey, J. M., Vanderbei, R. J. and Zenios, S. A. 1995. Robust Optimization of Large-Scale Systems. Operations Research 43(2): 264–281.

Pan, F. and Nagi, R. 2010. Robust supply chain design under uncertain demand in agile manufacturing. Computers & Operations Research 37(4): 668–683.

Pankaj Raj, S., Larry, E. W., Don, M., Pankaj Raj, S., Larry, E. W. and Don, M. 2004. Methodology to mitigate supplier risk in an aerospace supply chain. Supply Chain Management: An International Journal 9(2): 154–168.

Park, M., Jung, K. M. and Park, D. H. 2013. Optimal post-warranty maintenance policy with repair time threshold for minimal repair. Reliability Engineering & System Safety 111: 147–153.

Peng, M., Liu, L. and Jiang, C. 2012. A review on the economic dispatch and risk management of the large-scale plug-in electric vehicles (PHEVs)-penetrated power systems. Renewable and Sustainable Energy Reviews 16(3): 1508–1515.

Peng, P., Snyder, L. V., Lim, A. and Liu, Z. 2011. Reliable logistics networks design with facility disruptions. Transportation Research Part B: Methodological 45(8): 1190–1211.

Ponomarov, S. Y. and Holcomb, M. C. 2009. Understanding the concept of supply chain resilience. The International Journal of Logistics Management 20(1): 124–143.

Shahidehpour, M., Yamin, H. and Li, Z. 2002. Market Operations in Electric Power Systems: Forecasting, Scheduling, and Risk Management: Wiley-IEEE Press. New York : Institute of Electrical and Electronics Engineers : Wiley-Interscience.

Sheffi, Y. and Rice, J. B., Jr. 2005. A supply chain view of the resilient enterprise: an organization's ability to recover from disruption quickly can be improved by building redundancy and flexibility into its supply chain. While investing in redundancy represents a pure cost increase, investing in flexibility yields many additional benefits for day-to-day operations. MIT Sloan Management Review 47(1): 41.

Shepherd, C. and Günter, H. 2006. Measuring supply chain performance: current research and future directions. International Journal of Productivity and Performance Management 55(3/4): 242–258.

Stevenson, M. and Spring, M. 2007. Flexibility from a supply chain perspective: definition and review. International Journal of Operations & Production Management 27(7): 685–713.

Sun, H. J., Zhao, H. and Wu, J. J. 2008. A robust matching model of capacity to defense cascading failure on complex networks. Physica A: Statistical Mechanics and its Applications 387(25): 6431–6435.

Tachizawa, E. M. and Thomsen, C. G. 2007. Drivers and sources of supply flexibility: an exploratory study. International Journal of Operations & Production Management 27(10): 1115–1136.

Tang, C. S. 2006. Robust Strategies for Mitigating Supply Chain Disruptions. UCLA: Decisions, Operations, and Technology Management. International Journal of Logistics: Research and Applications 9(1): 33–45.

Tomlin, B. 2006. On the value of mitigation and contingency strategies for managing supply chain disruption risks. Management Science 52(5): 639–657.

Trec. Annual and monthly reports. Available at < http://www.trec.co.ir > Retrieved May 31, 2013. 2010]. Available from www.trec.co.ir.

Ucte. 2007. Final report: System disturbance on 4 November 2006, Brussels.

Van Der Vleuten, E. and Lagendijk, V. 2010. Transnational infrastructure vulnerability: The historical shaping of the 2006 European "Blackout". Energy Policy 38(4): 2042–2052.

Wang, J.-W. and Rong, L.-L. 2011. Robustness of the western United States power grid under edge attack strategies due to cascading failures. Safety Science 49(6): 807–812.

Xing, W. and Wu, F. F. 2002. Genetic algorithm based unit commitment with energy contracts. International Journal of Electrical Power & Energy Systems 24(5): 329–336.

Xu, N., Nozick, L., Xu, N. and Nozick, L. 2009. Modeling supplier selection and the use of option contracts for global supply chain design. Computers and Operations Research 36(10): 2786–2800.

You, A. D., Chen, B. Q., Yin, C. X. and Wang, D. B. 2011. A study of electrical security risk assessment system based on electricity regulation. Energy Policy 39(4): 2062–2074.

Yu, C.-S. and Li, H.-L. 2000. A robust optimization model for stochastic logistic problems. International Journal of Production Economics 64(1–3): 385–397.

Zio, E. and Aven, T. 2011. Uncertainties in smart grids behavior and modeling: What are the risks and vulnerabilities? How to analyze them? Energy Policy 39(10): 6308–6320.

CHAPTER 7

Structural Controllability in Managing Disruptions in Supply Networks

In Chapter 7, we explain the role of structural controllability as a primary element in managing disruptions in supply networks (see Chapter 1, Figure 1.9). We discuss structural controllability in networks, the distinction between controllability and structural controllability, and the integration of structural controllability in designing supply networks. Several examples in this chapter demonstrate methods of testing the controllability of a network. We identify the minimum number of driver nodes or driver facilities required for a network and demonstrate the inherent importance of those driver or transportation nodes. We will go on to use the concepts above and illustrate them with an example from the petroleum industry. Finally, we illustrate the connection between structural controllability and resilience using a three-stage design method we introduce in this chapter.

7.1 Introduction: Structural Controllability in Supply Networks

A supply network comprises of different entities that are connected by the flow of materials, products, information or electricity. As we explain in Chapter 6, networks are vulnerable to disruptions from many sources. General examples of disruptions include extreme weather, terrorism, or changes in the business or regulatory landscape. However, when a disruption occurs, access to every node, especially a market or client node, is critical to manage the effects of that disruption. Structural controllability is an effective means of managing disruptions that allows managers to maintain the supply network function and flow of resources to customers.

Structural controllability provides access to all nodes using routes that begin at driver nodes (i.e., controllers). It is possible to apply the concept of structural controllability to self-organized complex engineered networks (Liu et al. 2011). According to Liu et al. (2011), "an engineered network is structurally controllable if, with a suitable choice of inputs, it can be driven from any initial state to any desired final state within finite time." Simply stated, a supply network can be controlled through the appropriate manipulation of driver nodes (i.e., driver facility, control nodes or controllers), and all other nodes in the network are accessible through these driver nodes. The access provided by structural control allows a network to allocate resources to affected nodes, thus increasing network resilience.

In the context of an architecture for fail-safe networks, as introduced in Section 1.3, we explain the use of structural controllability for risk management in supply networks (see Figure 1-4). The connector is the supply network, as it contains the variables used in this method. We express the form of our architecture in this chapter as mathematical constructs, algorithms and theorems that capture the weights, properties and relationships between the structural controllability and risk management. The elements and their inter-relationships are captured using properties like minimum number of driver nodes. We use the requirements of managing the type(s) of risk to guide the selection of elements and form, along with user assumptions and system constraints, establishing the rationale of the architecture. We summarize the constituents of this architecture and our interpretation for structural controllability in risk management in Table 7-1.

This chapter is organized into two parts: Sections 7.2 to 7.6 explain the concept and its practical implementation in disruption management; Section 7.7 employs the three-stage method to illustrate the relationship between the resilience of a network and structural controllability. In the following section, we briefly review the literature relevant to structural controllability.

7.2 Structural Controllability in the Literature

Access to every node is critical to managing disruptions affecting a network. Structural controllability provides that essential access through driver nodes. This access is a key component to a network's resilience.

The various potential sources of disruption must be considered when planning supply network performance. The performance of supply networks is subject to the real-time dynamics of operations within a supply network (Ivanov and Sokolov 2012; Sarimveis et al. 2008; Vahdani

Table 7-1. Summary of architecture for structural controllability in risk management.

Architecture Constituents	Summary Interpretation for Fail-Safe Networks
Elements	**What?**
Components	Structural controllability
Connectors	Supply network
Form	**How?**
Component weights	Structural controllability: 1
Properties	Open/close nodes, active links between nodes, etc.
Relationship	Minimum Input Theorem to minimize number of driver nodes/facilities
Rationale	**Why?**
Motivation	Disruption management
Assumptions	Forward supply network, possibility of adding redundant links between nodes to span cacti
Constraints	Spanning cacti in network structure
Interpretation	Understanding of the solution; may provide motivation for further study

et al. 2011). We can, therefore, conclude that decisions in network planning and control are interconnected.

Ruths and Ruths (2014) study control properties to offer insights into the methods of manipulation that can allow designers to achieve the desired behavior from complex networks. It has been shown that specific control properties have a significant correlation to the topology of a network. The *control profile* was developed to quantify the proportions of control-inducing structures statistically within a given network. Jia and Barabási (2013) demonstrate that a fundamental challenge in designing networks is establishing control over them. They suggest the possible existence of multiple Minimum Driver Node Sets (MDS) in networks and demonstrate that nodes are not equal participants in network control. Jia and Barabasi also develop the concept of control capacity, a method that can measure the probability that a node is also a driver node. A random sampling algorithm was developed as an efficient means of measuring this probability.

The simplicity of the links between network nodes plays a crucial role in establishing dynamical processes (Wang and Lin 2013). Basing their views on recent studies investigating global controllability and connectivity, they conceive of a control robustness index. Through the work of Wang and Lin the problem of control robustness transforms from a computationally infeasible problem in a large-scale network into the problem of transitivity maximization for control routes and presents an efficient greedy algorithm to solve this very problem. From the linear structured systems viewpoint, Blackhall and Hill (2010) study the joint, or global, controllability of networks of interconnected linear systems. They go on to establish criteria, with only the local structural controllability properties and the interconnection topology, to assess the joint structural controllability of a dynamical network (Blackhall and Hill 2010).

Pasqualetti et al. (2014) study the means of controlling complex networks, including the dual task of selecting a set of driver nodes and of designing control interfaces to manipulate a network into a desired state. They achieve the proper selection of driver nodes through network partitioning and design the control input by leveraging optimal and distributed control techniques.

Chen et al. (2005) describe using a backward dynamic programming method to achieve the limited goal of matching chilling capacity with tank size in an ice storage system. Controllability in the design of small energy systems has also been the subject of some investigation. Diaz-Dorado et al. (2003) focus on the issues affecting the design of an unbalanced low-voltage distribution network for a small community, provide a method for its design, but do little more than ensure that the configurations provide an acceptable output. Ipsakis et al. (2009) use simulated annealing to address the design of a stand-alone power system that is based on renewable energy. Giannakoudis et al. (2010) implement this approach and adapt it to address uncertainty in the design of renewable energy generation systems. Stochastic annealing, a computationally intensive approach, emerges as their recommended method for resolving these problems and they propose parallel computing for problems that may surface in the future. The researchers above do not include variable demand in their respective investigations.

A relatively small amount of work has been done in this field despite the significant potential economic benefits of applying the concept of structural controllability to large, complex engineered networks. The limited work may be due to the dual barriers of computational and mathematical barriers to the problem. Dynamic programming is an oft used method for studying system controllability; this method is known to be afflicted by what is called the *curse of dimensionality*, which may limit its utility and appeal. Additional challenges posed by modeling uncertainty and the often nonlinear nature of system behavior can easily discourage researchers from approaching this topic.

In Section 7.3, we consider the current state of knowledge concerning structural controllability in the available research and explain the distinction between structural controllability and controllability. In Section 7.4, details regarding the functionality of structural controllability in managing disruptions in supply networks are described.

7.3 Controllability vs. Structural Controllability in Supply Networks

If with an appropriate choice of inputs a dynamical system can be modified or reshaped from any baseline state to a different targeted state within a finite period, it is by the definition offered in control theory, controllable. To control a system, we must first identify the set of nodes that, when driven by specific signals, can provide full control over that system. The value of all parameters in the network must be determined to establish if a network is controllable. It is, however, extremely difficult to know the exact value of all parameters due to the possible occurrence of variations and disruptions. This measurement is unnecessary, however, if it is possible to choose the nonzero values for parameters such that the system satisfies equation $\dot{X}(t) = A.X(t) + B.u(t)$, which is the general, canonical, time-invariant, linear control theory equation (see Section 7.3.1 for more detail). In this manner, structural controllability aids us in overcoming our otherwise incomplete knowledge of parameter values.

7.3.1 Structural Controllability in Supply Networks: Theorem

We begin our discussion of the concept of controllability using its related theorems and some examples. We will then move onto the benefit of structural controllability as compared to controllability alone. Finally, we provide our rationale for choosing structural controllability in our approach to designing supply networks.

Controllability is a quantitative property of control systems; it also occupies the position of being a fundamental concept in modern mathematical control theory. The study of this concept began in the early half of the 1960s. The theory of controllability itself is built on the mathematical interpretation of the dynamical system. Controllability refers to the ability to use a limited number of permissible manipulations to move a system around its entire configuration space.

Most natural and technological systems are organized into networks of components and these networks are governed by underlying dynamical processes. The metabolic process of living cells serves as an example. In this process, cells exchange energy and may control, so to speak, its metabolism by regulating the concentration of the enzymes which catalyze the transformation of metabolites. These reactions form a scale-free metabolic network.

The controllability of a real system is subject to the effects of two factors:

1) The system's architecture, represented by the network description of the connections between system components.

2) The dynamical rules that frame the time-dependent interactions of components.

Consider the linear dynamic system: $\dot{X}(t) = A.X(t) + B.u(t)$
where $\dot{X}(t) = (x_1(t), \ldots, x_N(t))^T$ presents the status of the system of N nodes at time t.

$u(t) = (u_1(t), \ldots, u_M(t))^T$ is the input vector.

A is the N*N matrix which describes the system's wiring and the strength of the described interaction between components (for example, matrix A is representative of the level of traffic on individual communication links or the depth and breadth of the impact of regulatory interactions within a regulatory network).

B is the N*M matrix which is the input that describes the nodes controlled by external controllers.

R.E. Kalman gave an algebraic criterion, known as the *Kalman Rank Condition*, which is dependent solely upon matrices A and B, which can be used to assess the controllability of this system.

The Kalman Rank Condition:

A necessary and sufficient condition for a system to be controllable is

Rank(c) = rank $[B, AB, A^2B, \ldots, A^{N-1}B] = N$

C is called Kalman's controllable matrix of size N*NM.

We can offer two examples of controllable and uncontrollable systems shown in Figures 7-1 and 7-2 (Liu et al. 2011).
The linear dynamics shown in Figure 7-1 can be written as:

$$\begin{bmatrix} \dot{x}_1(t) \\ \dot{x}_2(t) \\ \dot{x}_3(t) \end{bmatrix} = \begin{bmatrix} 0 & 0 & 0 \\ a_{21} & 0 & 0 \\ a_{31} & 0 & 0 \end{bmatrix} \cdot \begin{bmatrix} x_1(t) \\ x_2(t) \\ x_3(t) \end{bmatrix} + \begin{bmatrix} b_1 \\ 0 \\ 0 \end{bmatrix} u(t)$$

The controllability matrix is given by:

$$C = [B, A.B, A^2.B] = b_1 \begin{bmatrix} 1 & 0 & 0 \\ 0 & a_{21} & 0 \\ 0 & a_{31} & 0 \end{bmatrix}$$

Since rank C = 2 < N, the system shown in Figure 7-1 is not controllable. The linear dynamics shown in Figure 7-2 can be written as:

$$\begin{bmatrix} \dot{x}_1(t) \\ \dot{x}_2(t) \\ \dot{x}_3(t) \end{bmatrix} = \begin{bmatrix} 0 & 0 & 0 \\ a_{21} & 0 & 0 \\ a_{31} & 0 & a_{33} \end{bmatrix} \cdot \begin{bmatrix} x_1(t) \\ x_2(t) \\ x_3(t) \end{bmatrix} + \begin{bmatrix} b_1 \\ 0 \\ 0 \end{bmatrix} u(t)$$

The controllability matrix is given by:

$$C = [B, A.B, A^2.B] = b_1 \begin{bmatrix} 1 & 0 & 0 \\ 0 & a_{21} & 0 \\ 0 & a_{31} & a_{33}a_{31} \end{bmatrix}$$

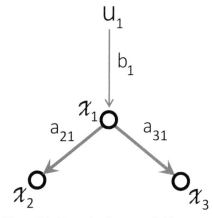

Figure 7-1. Example of uncontrollable system.

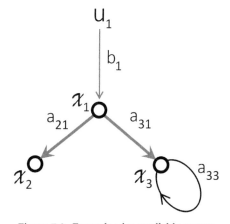

Figure 7-2. Example of controllable system.

Since rank $C = 3 = N$, the system shown in Figure 7-2 is controllable.

The Kalman rank condition can be used to test the controllability of networks as illustrated in the previous two examples. However, there are two factors that render testing for the controllability of a network extremely difficult:

a) All the values of matrices A and B must be determined. For most supply networks the exact values of all entries of A are frequently indeterminable. These unknown values can create a situation where a given network is controllable under some parameter values but not for others.

b) Determining the rank of C is computationally difficult for networks of any size and scale. Applying the filtering method to high-dimensional problems poses a high degree of challenge that stems from both propagating the distribution of the high-dimensional state forward temporally and from solving the high-dimensional problem when new data is observed.

Lin addresses these challenges by introducing the concept of structural controllability discussed as follows.

"A system is said to be strongly structurally controllable if its controllability is independent of the system parameters, as long as they are non-zero."

Lin's Theorem on Structural Controllability:

The following three statements are equivalent:

1. A linear control system (A, B) is structurally controllable.
2. i) The digraph $G(A, B)$ contains no inaccessible nodes.

    ii) The digraph $G(A, B)$ contains no dilation.
3. The digraph $G(A, B)$ is spanned by cacti.

Lin's Theorem on structural controllability leads us to the conclusion that there is no need to know the value of all parameters in a network to calculate the ranking of C through the application of Kalman's rank condition; however, if a cactus graph can be spanned throughout a supply network, or there is at least one link from each supplier node to each demand node, then the network fits the definition of structurally controllable. The practical function of structural controllability in a supply network is further explained in Section 7.4.

We address two topics in this section: the difference between controllability and structural controllability, and the importance of structural controllability using Lin's Theorem instead of controllability.

In the next section, the basic parameters for using Lin's Theorem are presented.

7.3.2 Structural Controllability in Supply Networks: Background

Lin's Theorem can be harnessed to achieve the design of a structurally controllable network. Lin's Theorem is built on a framework of graph theory and spanning cacti structures. In this section, we explain the methodology for applying Lin's Theorem.

Graphs are mathematical structures that are used to model the pairing oriented relations between objects of a certain collection. The study of graphs began in the 18th century and graph theory is now an important area of study within the discipline of discrete mathematics. Furthermore, graph theory has emerged as a particularly useful method for solving practical problems. Network theory is a segment of study within graph theory that scrutinizes the networks of real systems. Networks permeate a multitude of disciplines. Thus its applications range from the internet to biological systems. This discipline also introduces the foundational definitions and theorems of structural controllability. Thulasiraman and Swamy (1992) elucidate the concepts and fundamental definitions of graph theory itself.

Undirected Cactus Graph: An undirected cactus is an undirected connected simple graph if any two simple cycles have at most one vertex in common. Of equivalent importance, every edge of such a graph belongs a maximum of one cycle (see Figure 7-3).

Stem: An elementary path.

Root or Top: The initial, or terminal vertex, of a stem.

Bud Cycle: A bud cycle, or bud in shorthand, is an elementary cycle plus an additional edge, referred to as a distinguished edge, that ends, but does not begin, at a vertex within the cycle.

Directed Cactus Graph: A digraph (directed graph) that is defined as: Given a stem (a stem is a cactus) S_0 and buds $B_1, B_2, \ldots, B_l$ then $S_0 \cup B_1 \cup B_2 \ldots \cup B_l$ is a cactus if for every I ($1 <= i <= l$) the initial vertex of the distinguished edge of B_i is not the top of S_0 and the only vertex that belongs simultaneously to B_i and $S_0 \cup B_1 \cup B_2 \ldots \cup B_{i-1}$ (see Figure 7-4).

Driver nodes: The vertices directly connected to input vertices (or origins) are controlled nodes in the context of a controlled network. A controlled node is called a driver node if it does not share an input vertex with any other vertices (see Figure 7-6).

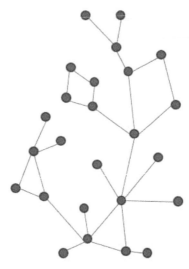

Figure 7-3. Example of an undirected cactus graph (Anh 2012).

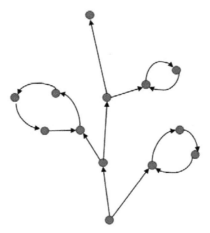

Figure 7-4. Example of a directed cactus graph (Anh 2012).

Inaccessibility: If there are no directed edges connecting the vertex to the driver node, the vertex is referred to as inaccessible.

Matching: In graph theory matching is the term applied to a set of edges that do not share common vertices. The concept of matching is fundamental to the understanding of the Minimum Input Theorem.

Matched and unmatched in undirected graphs: In an undirected graph, a matching M is an independent edge set or a set of edges without common vertices. If it is incidental to an edge in the matching, then a vertex is referred to as matched. Otherwise, the vertex is unmatched. Similarly, an edge is matched if it is in *M*; otherwise, it is unmatched.

Matched and unmatched in directed graphs: For a digraph, or directed graph, a matching *M* is a subset of edges where no two edges have a common vertex. A vertex is matched if it is the ending vertex of an edge in the matching *M* only; otherwise, it is unmatched. Similarly, an edge is matched if it is only in *M*.

Alternating path: An alternating path is a path in which the edges alternate between belonging or not belonging to the matching.

Maximum Matching Theorem: If there is no augmenting path concerning M, a matching M in a graph is a maximum matching, but not so under any other circumstance.

Minimum Input Theorem: If there is a perfect matching, the minimum number of inputs or driver nodes required to control a network completely is no more than one. Stated simply: any single node could be the driver node. Otherwise, the minimum is equal to the number of unmatched nodes with respect to any maximum matching. Simply stated, the driver nodes are simply the unmatched nodes.

Graph Dilation: Let the nodes of graph *G* be numbered with distinct integers 1 to $|G|$. The dilation of *G* is the maximum (absolute) difference between integers assigned to adjacent vertices. Stated simply, it is the maximum value of $|i\text{-}j|$ over all nonzero elements of the adjacency matrix (a_{ij}).

The definitions we provide in this section help to understand Lin's Theorem regarding the implementation of structurally controllable design in supply networks. Before explaining the algorithms required to design a structurally controllable network, we discuss the basic functions and benefits of structural controllability in supply networks in Section 7.4.

7.4 Functions of Structural Controllability in Supply Networks

As we mention in Section 7.1, "an engineered network is structurally controllable if, with a suitable choice of inputs, it can be driven from any initial state to any desired final state within finite time" (Liu et al. 2011). In this study, we employ Lin's theorem to assess whether a network is structurally controllable. Lin's theorem asserts that a network is structurally controllable if a cactus can span across it (Lin 1974). Simply put, if a cactus structure can be identified in a network, that network is controllable. Four illustrations are shown in Figures 7-5 to 7-8 that demonstrate the difference

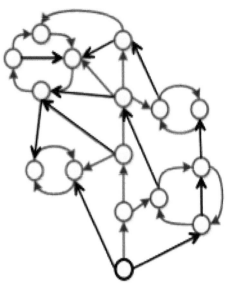

Figure 7-5. A supply network structure sample.

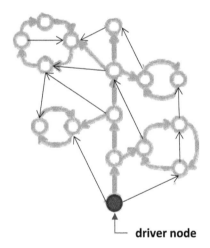

Figure 7-6. A structurally controllable network structure.

between a structurally controllable network and one that is not. In Figure 7-5, a network is shown with various cycles and routes that connect all nodes.

We explain in detail the algorithms required for spanning cacti in a network to determine whether the network is structurally controllable in Section 7-5. By following the steps laid out in Section 7-4, the spanned cactus is shown as highlighted links and nodes in the network example in Figure 7-7.

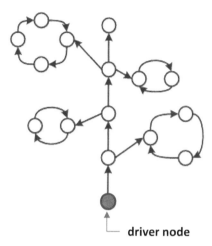

Figure 7-7. The spanned cactus in the network example.

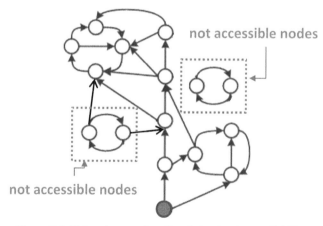

Figure 7-8. Network example without structural controllability.

In this figure, the cactus structure is formed by the links and nodes highlighted in green; the driver node is indicated in black. Structural controllability in this network example means that there is at least one link from the driver node to each of the remaining nodes in the cactus structure associated with it. The spanned cactus is shown separately in Figure 7-8.

In a structurally controllable network, each driver node is associated with one cactus structure and there may be more than one driver node required in such a network. As an example, the network structure illustrated in Figure 7-8 is not structurally controllable using the driver node is shown in black.

The example that is shown in Figure 7-8 is not a structurally controllable network since there is not any feasible path from the driver node (shown in black) to all other nodes. Not accessible nodes are shown in dotted areas.

Various restoration strategies are available to manage network disruptions whenever they occur. Some examples of restoration strategies are backup inventory, facility fortification, flexible inventory capacity, transportation reconfiguration and flexible production capacities. Since disruptions may happen in any facility with varying probabilities, it would be very expensive to apply every restoration strategy at every vulnerable facility. Driver nodes are unique in that they provide access to all other nodes. Structural controllability in a supply network is achieved by identifying or establishing driver nodes and leveraging their positions to implement restoration strategies. The cost of managing disruptions in this can be significantly lower, the efficiency of using the restoration strategies can be increased through the application of structural controllability to design supply networks.

In Section 7.5, the principle of designing structurally controllable networks with the minimum number of driver nodes is addressed.

7.5 Implementation of Structural Controllability in Supply Networks

The concept of structural controllability is developed, based on Lin's theorem (see Section 7.3.1). Furthermore, we must identify the set of driver nodes available to control a supply network completely, in particular, the minimum number of driver nodes necessary for that control.

When we apply the minimum input theorem, we find that the minimum number of driver nodes is equal to the minimum number of unmatched nodes (see Section 7.3.2). We, therefore, conclude that the maximum matching and minimum input theorems are fundamental to the concept of structural controllability.

We can outline in four steps the algorithm required for applying structural controllability. We elucidate each step in detail and illustrate each with an example.

Step a: Find or design the structure of the planned supply network and represent it as $G(A) = (V, E)$, where $V = \{v_1, v_2, ...,v_N\}$ as its facilities (nodes) and E as its set of routes (links). A small digraph is an example of a planned supply network, shown in Figure 7-9.

Step b: Find a bipartite representation of the considered supply network in Step (*a*). For the given $G(V, E)$, the bipartite representation is a graph such as $BP(A) = (V^+$ and $V^-, £)$. In $BP(A) = (V^+$ and $V^-, £)$:

V^+ is the set of N facilities (nodes) $V^+ = \{v+1, v+2, \ldots, v+N\}$

V^- is the set of N facilities (nodes) $V^- = \{v-1, v-2, \ldots, v-N\}$

£ is the set of routes (links) $£ = \{(v_i^+, v_j^-) \mid (v_i, v_j) \in E\}$

Each link of the bipartite representation of the supply network contains both a plus and minus node. In Figure 7-10, we show the bipartite representation of the network example for Step (*a*).

Step c: Here we apply the maximum matching theory to find unmatched nodes within the digraph. For the given $G(A) = (V, E)$ from Step (*a*), and the given BP(A) from Step (*b*), a matching is only a subset of links where no two links share a common starting node or an ending node. The maximum matching is a matching containing the maximum number of matched facilities.

In Figure 7-11, both links from x_1^+ to x_2^- and x_3^+ to x_3^- do not share any starting or ending nodes, the unique maximum matching is therefore shown in green. In Figure 7-12, we indicate the unique matched links. In Figure 7-13, we highlight the matched nodes in blue in the bipartite representation of the network.

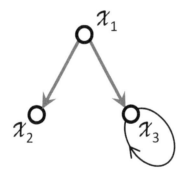

Figure 7-9. Example of a simple digraph.

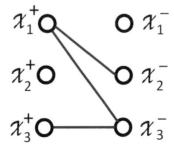

Figure 7-10. Bipartite representation of a simple digraph example.

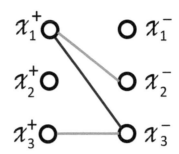

Figure 7-11. Matched links in the bipartite network representation.

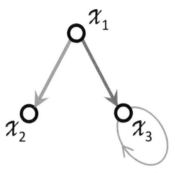

Figure 7-12. Matched links in the network example.

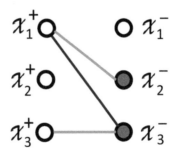

Figure 7-13. Matched nodes in the bipartite network representation.

Step d: The last step is the identification of driver nodes. Unmatched facilities in each layer are chosen as driver nodes in accordance with the minimum input theorem. In Figure 7-14, unmatched nodes are selected as driver nodes and shown in red.

In this section, we present four steps for identifying the minimum number of driver nodes to have structurally controllable supply networks. Within the network structure, there is at least one route from the driver nodes to all remaining nodes. Identification is the first step in recruiting

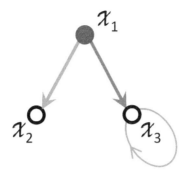

Figure 7-14. Unmatched nodes (driver nodes) in the network example.

driver nodes in the implementation of restoration strategies. Identifying the minimum viable number of driver nodes minimizes the cost of managing disruptions. In the following section, we present an example from the petroleum industry, which we will employ both in Chapters 7 and 8 to illustrate the use of the four-step process we describe in this section.

7.6 Computational Results of the Proposed Model

While preserving generality, we consider a simple supply network example which addresses operations within the petroleum industry. In this supply network, the first layer is a representation of the production process carried out in refineries (*R1:R3 for i ∈ I* with capacity $capr_i$). Hubs form the second layer of the network (*H1:H3 for j ∈ J* with capacity $caph_j$), where products (*p*) are produced from the material supplied by refineries. Warehouses form the third layer (*W1:W3 for k ∈ K* with capacity $capw_k$) where products may be stored or shipped to distribution centers (*DC1:DC4 for l ∈ L* with capacity $capd_l$) that form the fourth layer. The distribution centers (DC) are then charged with distributing product demands (*D*) to the fifth layer formed by markets (*M1:M8 for m ∈ M* with capacity $capd_l$); note that time activity is not a consideration for DCs in this example. We offer a schematic view of this five-layered forward supply network in Figure 7-15.

For the network example in Figure 7-15, the four-step process of structurally controllable design can be followed. With the use of this process, we can deduce the minimum viable number of driver nodes for each layer.

Step a: All nodes are numbered from v_1 to v_{19} as illustrated in Figure 7-16. Our objective in this phase is to identify driver nodes for Layers 2 and 3.

Step b: The bipartite representation of nodes needs to be indicated. In the bipartite representation thus produced, each node will be indicated by two representations, v⁺ and v⁻, in which v⁺ shows the output links from node v and v⁻ shows the input links to node v. The bipartite representation for layers 2 and 3, complete with five nodes and four links, is illustrated in Figure 7-17.

Step c: In this step, we apply the maximum matching theory to determine unmatched nodes in the network. For the given network example from Step (*a*) and the given bipartite representation from Step (*b*), a matching is a subset of links only where no two links have a common starting node nor an ending node. As is indicated in Figure 7-18, matched links are red, the nodes so linked are also matched. The maximum number of matched nodes is the maximum matched. The diagrams in Figure 7-18 illustrate two

Refinery   Hub   Warehouse   DC   Market

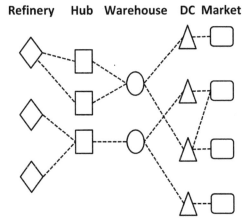

Figure 7-15. The schematic view of the petroleum supply network problem.

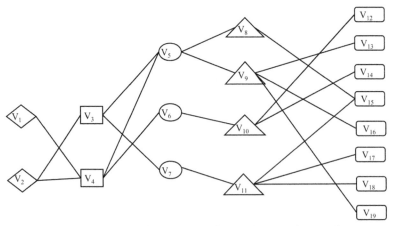

Figure 7-16. Designed structure for the supply network example.

sets of nodes, (v_3, v_4, v_5, v_6) and (v_3, v_4, v_5, v_7), with maximum matching. Therefore, the driver node is an unmatched node, which in this example can be either node 7 or node 6 highlighted in green in Figure 7-19.

By utilizing the four-step process, all unmatched nodes and by logical extension all driver nodes, can be identified. These driver nodes have at least one path to the customers and markets in the fifth layer. Driver nodes thus revealed in the supply network example, are shown in Figure 7-20. In Figure 7-20, four nodes V = (v_1, v_2, v_7, v_9) are identified as driver nodes in the example. The minimum number of required driver nodes to fully control this network is four, as determined by our use of the minimum input theorem. Stated simply, less than four driver nodes will result in a loss of control over the network and having more than four nodes results in a redundant and unnecessarily expensive design in terms of structural

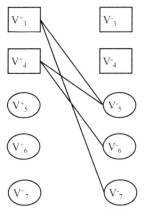

Figure 7-17. Bipartite representation for layers two and three.

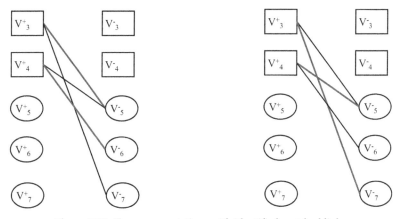

Figure 7-18. Two representations with identified matched links.

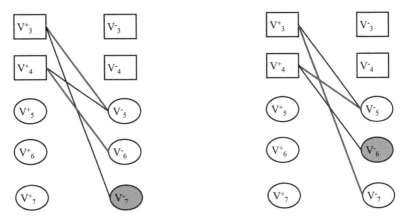

Figure 7-19. Two representations with identified driver nodes.

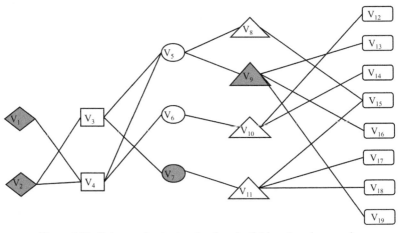

Figure 7-20. Driver nodes in structural controllable network example.

controllability. In Chapter 8, we will discuss different control protocols where a designer can include more driver nodes in the network; however, in all control protocols (see discussions in Chapter 8) the currently identified driver nodes $V = (v_1, v_2, v_7, v_9)$ should still be considered as such.

In Figure 7-21, four available paths from the identified driver nodes to the nodes in the last layer are shown. Each of these paths emerges from a driver node (v_1, v_2, v_7, v_9) and ends at a node in the final layer of the network. As dictated by the definition of structural controllability, all nodes in the network can be accessed by these four driver nodes. This access ensures that not every node in the network requires the implementation of restoration strategies at its location, such as safety stock. This access inevitably reduces the cost of managing disruptions and control in general.

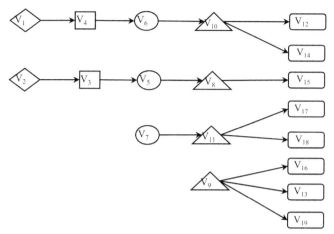

Figure 7-21. Driver nodes in structural controllable network example.

From the vantage point provided by Lin's theorem, each path shown in Figure 7-21 is a cactus with only stems. To adhere to Lin's theorem mathematically and gain full control of a network, self-cycled links must be included in some of the nodes in the final layer. However, for business, self-cycled links are not a mandated design feature in the final layer of the network.

Another important step is establishing the relationship between the structural controllability of a network and its resilience in managing disruptions.

7.7 Three-stage Proposed Model for Managing Disruptions

As we establish in previous sections, a supply network is structurally controllable if there is at least one path from at least one driver node to all remaining nodes in the network. Driver nodes occupy the critical role of providing access throughout structurally controllable networks; the three-stage model is based on this role. Structural controllability is integral in managing disruptions and increasing the resilience of supply networks. Since disruptions can occur at any facility in a network, driver nodes are essential to the maintenance of restoration strategies and resources. The cost of managing disruptions can be significantly lower and the efficiency of operating restoration strategies can be higher, using structural controllability principles to design resilient supply networks.

To increase the resilience of a supply network (see Chapter 8 for a discussion of resilience) driver nodes should be identified in it. Identified driver nodes can be strengthened against disruptions and will be used as special nodes with back up inventory that can be leveraged through their complete access to the rest of the network; this is a fundamental concept to increase the resilience of a given network.

The problem that we approach using the three-stage method is formulated thus:

How can structural controllability be applied to design a supply network that is resilient in the face of disruptions through the selection of appropriate restoration strategies and consideration of effectiveness and redundancy as measures for resilience analysis?

The problem thus stated includes three main parts: structural controllability, restoration strategies and resilience analysis. Structural controllability is discussed in Sections 7.1 through 7.7. Restoration strategies refer to any strategy that can be applied proactively or reactively when disruptions happen in a network. Storing backup inventory at a facility is an example of a pre-disruption or proactive restoration strategy and the reconfiguration of product flow is an example of a post-disruption or reactive restoration strategy. Resilience analysis refers to any quantitative measures for analyzing resilience while evaluating the trade-off between redundancy and effectiveness. The proposed three-stage method is described in Figure 7-22.

The three-stage method we offer is comprised of (1) Strategic Stage, (2) Control Stage and (3) Operational Stage. As we illustrate in Figure 7-22, the focus in the first stage is on capturing the existing network structure, designing a new structure, or redesigning a current network structure. Since the focus of this stage is on location and allocation decisions, which lead to locating nodes and links, we name it the strategic stage.

The objective of the second stage of the method is to render the network structurally controllable. The output of the first stage, the location of nodes and links to each of them, is used as the input for stage two. In stage two, the location and number of driver nodes are identified and the network will be rendered structurally controllable.

The resulting structurally controllable network with the minimum viable number of identified driver nodes, the outcome of stage two, is the input for stage three. In stage three, we identify and define all possible disruption scenarios and consider countermeasures for each specific disruption. In stage three, our purpose is to conduct resilience analysis of the structurally controllable network under the pressure of disruptions. In Figure 7-23, the three-stage method is shown in more detail.

Two types of restoration strategies can be applied once stage three is reached: pre-disruption and post-disruption strategies. Examples of pre-disruption strategies include facility fortification or backup inventory.

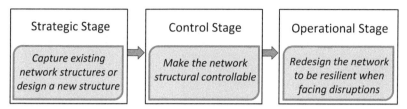

Figure 7-22. Resilient and structurally controllable supply network method (RCSN).

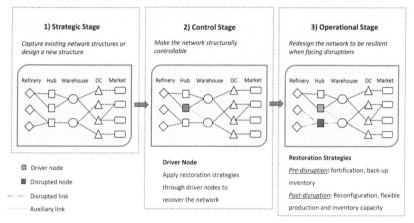

Figure 7-23. Stages of the RCSN proposed method.

Examples of post-disruption strategies are reconfigurations and flexible production and inventory capacities.

7.8 Closing Remarks

In this chapter, we explain the concepts related to structural controllability, as well as the fundamental differences between controllability and structural controllability. We address the functionality of structural controllability in designing supply networks. We go on to explain in detail the implementation of structural controllability within a supply network and define the method for identifying the minimum viable number of driver nodes. We combine those concepts in a petroleum industry example to illustrate their functions and importance. Furthermore, we illustrate the role of structural controllability in the context of architecture for fail-safe networks as explained in Chapter 1. We summarize the constituents of this architecture and our interpretation for structural controllability in risk management in Table 7-1. Finally, we employ a three-stage method to illustrate the connection between structural controllability and resilience.

While we introduce and elucidate the three-stage method in this chapter, we will apply and reiterate it in a petroleum industry example in Chapter 8.

References

Anh, N. T. T. 2012. Spanning Cacti for Structurally Controllable Networks, Department of Mathematics, National University of Singapore.

Blackhall, L. and Hill, D. J. 2010. On the structural controllability of networks of linear systems. IFAC Proceedings Volumes 43(19): 245–250.

Chen, H.-J., Wang, D. W. P. and Chen, S.-L. 2005. Optimization of an ice-storage air conditioning system using dynamic programming method. Applied Thermal Engineering 25(2): 461–472.

Diaz-Dorado, E., Pidre, J. C. and Garcia, E. M. 2003. Planning of large rural low-voltage networks using evolution strategies. IEEE Transactions on Power Systems 18(4): 1594–1600.

Giannakoudis, G., Papadopoulos, A. I., Seferlis, P. and Voutetakis, S. 2010. Optimum design and operation under uncertainty of power systems using renewable energy sources and hydrogen storage. International Journal of Hydrogen Energy 35(3): 872–891.

Ipsakis, D., Voutetakis, S., Seferlis, P., Stergiopoulos, F. and Elmasides, C. 2009. Power management strategies for a stand-alone power system using renewable energy sources and hydrogen storage. International Journal of Hydrogen Energy 34(16): 7081–7095.

Ivanov, D. and Sokolov, B. 2012. The inter-disciplinary modelling of supply chains in the context of collaborative multi-structural cyber-physical networks. Journal of Manufacturing Technology Management 23(8): 976–997.

Jia, T. and Barabási, A.-L. 2013. Control capacity and a random sampling method in exploring controllability of complex networks. Scientific Reports 3(2354).

Lin, C.-T. 1974. Structural controllability. IEEE Transactions on Automatic Control 19(3): 201–208.

Liu, Y.-Y., Slotine, J.-J. and Barabási, A.-L. 2011. Controllability of complex networks. Nature 473(7346): 167–73.

Pasqualetti, F., Zampieri, S. and Bullo, F. 2014. Controllability metrics, limitations and algorithms for complex networks. IEEE Transactions on Control of Network Systems 1(1): 40–52.

Ruths, J. and Ruths, D. 2014. Control profiles of complex networks. Science 343(6177): 1373–1376.

Sarimveis, H., Patrinos, P., Tarantilis, C. D. and Kiranoudis, C. T. 2008. Dynamic modeling and control of supply chain systems: A review. Computers & Operations Research 35(11): 3530–3561.

Thulasiraman, K. and Swamy, M. N. S. 1992. Graphs: Theory and Algorithms. 6th Edition ed: New York: Wiley.

Vahdani, B., Zandieh, M. and Roshanaei, V. 2011. A hybrid multi-stage predictive model for supply chain network collapse recovery analysis: a practical framework for effective supply chain network continuity management. International Journal of Production Research 49(7): 2035–2060.

Wang, Y.-W. and Lin, C.-C. 2013. Locating multiple types of recharging stations for battery-powered electric vehicle transport. Transportation Research Part E: Logistics and Transportation Review 58: 76–87.

Chapter 8

Disruption Management
Resilience Design of Structurally Controllable Supply Networks

In Chapter 8, resilience as another main element in managing disruptions in supply networks is introduced (see Chapter 1, Figure 1.9). In this chapter, we explain the importance of disruption management in supply networks using resilience and structural controllability. We present resilience analysis in supply networks to manage disruptions and explain the benefits of having both pre-disruption and post-disruption restoration scenarios in supply networks under disruptions. We explain the three-stage method we introduced in Chapter 7 in greater detail in this chapter. In this approach, structural controllability is incorporated as a key element for resilience design as discussed in Chapter 7. We discuss different aspects of the method through an example of the petroleum industry. We initiate the expansion of disruption management to disruption and variation management in this chapter using a scenario-based approach and expand it further in Chapter 9.

8.1 Introduction: Disruption Management in Supply Networks

A supply network is comprised of connections between separate entities communicating through the flow of materials, products, information or electricity. Disruptions could take place at any portion of the network for many reasons. Some examples are mergers (e.g., Halliburton's impending purchase of Baker Hughes), union strikes (e.g., labor strike on the west coast of the United States in 2002), the application or removal of sanctions (e.g., economic sanctions against Iran being lifted by the UN in July 2015), the destruction of crops (Hurricane Mitch destroyed banana plantations in 1998), the suspension of air traffic due to weather or terrorism, and principal suppliers being shut down by natural disasters (e.g., the 1999 earthquake in Taiwan disrupted semiconductor fabrication facilities).

Many sources of disruptions are involved in supply networks that render the networks vulnerable to various disruptions (see Chapter 7). Companies are exposed to operational and financial disruptions within infrastructure networks (Stauffer 2003). According to Sarkar et al. (2002), during the labor strike in 2002, 29 ports on the West Coast of the United States were shut down which led to the closure of the New United Motor Manufacturing production factory. Because of the devastating earthquake in Japan in 2011, Toyota Motor Company suspended operations at its twelve assembly plants. This suspension of operations led to a production loss of 140,000 automobiles. In March 2000, the lightning that struck a Philips semiconductor plant in Albuquerque, New Mexico, generated a 10-minute fire that ruined millions of radio-frequency chips (RFCs) which delayed shipments to its two primary customers, Nokia of Finland and the Swedish Ericsson. Although facing the same situation, two companies responded differently and thus ended up with two endings: Nokia survived from the disruption while Ericsson ultimately exited from the business (Gong et al. 2014).

We can classify disruptions as random events and accidents or intentional disruptions, where estimating the likelihood of each class differs (Sheffi 2005). Mulani and Lee (2002) show that disruption managers spend about 40–60% of their working time handling disruptions in infrastructure networks (Ivanov and Sokolov 2013). Therefore, a system is designed not only with disruptive events and their attendant likelihoods in mind, but also the system's resistance to and recovery from these events; managing disruptions through restoration scenarios is critical.

Supply network design defines resilience as the capability of effectively absorbing, adapting to or recovering from disruptive events and returning to an acceptable level of performance after being disrupted. The importance of resilience is in the face of disruptions when the ability to restore the planned execution along with the achievement of the planned or acceptable performance is the objective using appropriate pre-disruption and post-disruption restoration strategies.

In the context of an architecture for fail-safe networks, as introduced in Section 1.3, we explain the use of resilience and structural controllability for risk management in supply networks (see Figure 1-4). The connector is the supply network, as it contains the variables used in this method. We express the form of our architecture in this chapter as a three-step method including mathematical models that capture the weights, properties and relationships between the resilience, structural controllability and risk management. The elements and their inter-relationships are captured using properties such as minimize cost and maximize service level.

Table 8-1. Summary of architecture for resilience and structural controllability in risk management.

Architecture Constituents	Summary Interpretation for Fail-Safe Networks
Elements	**What?**
Components	Resilience and structural controllability
Connectors	Supply network
Form	**How?**
Component weights	Resilience: 1, Structural controllability: 1
Properties	Demand, cost, capacity, etc.
Relationship	Compromise Decision Support Problem - Minimize deviation from goals such as cost service level and the number of driver nodes
Rationale	**Why?**
Motivation	Disruption management
Assumptions	Linear relation between variables, forward supply network
Constraints	Production and transportation capacity, demand fulfillment, etc.
Interpretation	Understanding of the solution; may provide motivation for further study

We use the requirements of managing the type(s) of risk to guide the selection of elements and form, along with user assumptions and system constraints, establishing the rationale of the architecture. We summarize the constituents of this architecture and our interpretation for resilience and structural controllability in risk management in Table 8-1.

In the next chapter, we describe the significance of resilience in designing structurally controllable supply networks.

8.2 Significance of Resilience in Designing Structurally Controllable Supply Networks

To manage disruptions, utilizing preventive and proactive strategies increase the resilience in supply networks. Also, structural controllability is an important characteristic of a network that impacts the resilience significantly.

1) Disruption management using Restoration Strategies: Considering the impact of recovery strategies, we show that the resilience of a disrupted supply network depends on a combination of both pre-disruption and post-disruption restoration strategies. Given that a supply network's resilience indicates how rapidly its performance can

return to an acceptable performance after disruptions, we show that the resilience of a supply network depends on the best combination of preventive and proactive restoration strategies with having cost-redundancy trade-offs. In this chapter, the compromise Decision Support Construct to select the best restoration strategies for supply networks is presented and discussed (see Section 8.6).

2) Disruption management using Structural Controllability: Considering the impact of structural controllability in determining **driver nodes/ facilities** in a network and critical transportation routes from driver nodes/facilities to customers (see Chapter 7), we show that resilience of a disrupted supply network depends on applying structural controllability in supply networks. Therefore, our proposed method constructed upon structural controllability is important toward resilience design of supply networks.

8.3 Resilience Analysis and Restoration Strategies

When a disruption occurs in a supply network, it deactivates a part of the network (number of facilities or transportation links). Therefore, a sudden reduction happens in the performance (e.g., supply quantity) as is shown in Figure 8-1. It usually takes some time for supply network managers to start to recover the network from disruptions. This period is called the recovery lead-time, and restoration strategies used after a disruption are called post-disruption restoration strategies.

When the recovery process starts, the supply network performance gradually improves until it reaches its pre-disruption performance level or a new acceptable performance level. The time required to complete the recovery process is called recovery time (RT). A resilient supply network is one that can recover quickly from disruptions and ensure that customers are affected minimally. Resilience analysis consists of the trade-off analysis among recovery lead-time, recovery time, and recovered performance. Not

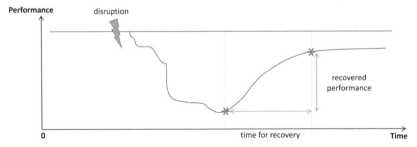

Figure 8-1. Pre-disruption and post-disruption states of a supply network.

only efficiency measures (recovery lead-time, recovery time and recovered performance), but also redundancy measure (e.g., the cost of recovery or restoration strategies) can be considered in the resilience analysis.

To reduce the total loss in managing disruptions, not only post-disruption strategies should be employed, but also pre-disruption strategies should be incorporated as well. Taking this action will help supply network managers to be more prepared in the face of disruptions and to decrease recovery lead-time tremendously. Fortifying driver nodes and storing backup inventory are examples of pre-disruption restoration strategies and reconfiguration of flow planning and operating facilities and utilizing flexible production and inventory capacity are examples of post-disruption restoration strategies.

In the next section, we discuss the three-stage method in detail.

8.4 Three-stage Model for Managing Disruptions

As we discussed in Chapter 7, a supply network is said to be structurally controllable if there is at least one path from drive nodes to all other nodes in the network. Driver nodes have a critical role in providing accessibility in structurally controllable networks. An organization can use structural controllability for managing disruptions and increasing resilience in supply networks. This new concept is based on the unique role of driver nodes in controllable networks. Since disruptions can occur at any facility in a network, driver nodes can be considered as nodes with backup inventory or with flexible production/inventory capacities to provide fortification against disruptions. *The cost of managing disruptions can be significantly lower and the efficiency of operating restoration strategies can be higher using structural controllability in designing resilient supply networks.*

The main concept that we address here is *applying structural controllability to design a resilient supply network facing disruptions with a selection of suitable restoration strategies and the consideration of effectiveness and redundancy as measures for resilience analysis.*

This concept includes three main parts: structural controllability, restoration strategies and resilience analysis. We explain structural controllability in detail in Sections 7.1 to 7.7. Restoration strategies refer to any strategy that can be applied proactively (pre-disruption) or reactively (post-disruption) when disruptions occur in networks. Having backup inventory in facilities is an example of a pre-disruption or proactive restoration strategy and product flow reconfiguration is a case of a post-disruption or reactive restoration strategy. Resilience analysis refers to any quantitative measures for analyzing resilience while evaluating the trade-off between redundancy and effectiveness that we explain in Section 8.4. To

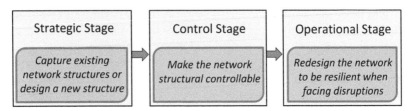

Figure 8-2. Resilient and structurally controllable supply network method (RCSN).

address the new concept of utilizing structural controllability in designing resilient supply networks with restoration strategies, we propose a three-stage method that is shown in Figure 8-2.

The proposed three-stage method includes the following stages: (1) Strategic Stage, (2) Control Stage, and (3) Operational Stage. The focus in Stage One is on capturing the existing network structure, or designing/ redesigning a new one; in Stage Two the emphasis is on constructing a structurally controllable network; and in Stage Three, the focus is on managing disruptions using restoration strategies.

In the following sections, we explain the connection between the three stages in detail. Since mathematical models in stages one and three are built on the compromise Decision Support Problem (cDSP) construct, we briefly discuss the cDSP in Section 8.4.1. In Section 8.4.2, we present the construct for three stages in the context of cDSP.

8.4.1 Compromise Decision Support Problem (cDSP) Construct

The mathematical models in the three-stage method are shown in the construct of cDSP. The compromise Decision Support Problem (cDSP) (Mistree et al. 1992) is utilized in the three-stage method to design mathematical models in stages one and three. The cDSP is a mathematical construct for determining design solutions while considering multiple conflicting goals. The cDSP is a hybrid formulation that incorporates concepts from both traditional mathematical programming and goal programming. The cDSP and mathematical programming are similar to the extent that they refer to system constraints that must be satisfied for feasibility.

They differ in the way the deviation or objective function is modeled. In the cDSP, as in goal programming, multiple objectives are formulated as system goals involving deviation variables and the deviation function is modeled using deviation variables rather than system or decision variables. The cDSP differs from goal programming, however, because it is tailored to address common engineering design situations in which physical limitations are manifested as system constraints (mostly

Table 8-2. The mathematical construct of the compromise Decision Support Problem (Mistree et al. 1992).

Given

    n, number of system variables
    p, number of equality constraints
    q, number of inequality constraints
    m, number of system goals
    $g_i(\mathbf{x})$, constraint functions
    G_{i}, system goals
    $A_i(\mathbf{x})$, performance functions

Find

    $\mathbf{x}$ (system variables)
    d_i^-, d_i^+ (deviation variables)

Satisfy

    System constraints:
      $g_i(\mathbf{x}) \leq 0 \qquad i = p+1,..., p+q$
      $g_i(\mathbf{x}) = 0 \qquad i = 1,..., p$
    System goals:
      $A_i(\mathbf{x})/G_i + d_i^- - d_i^+ = 1 \qquad i = 1,...,m$
    Bounds:
      $x_i^{min} \leq x_i \leq x_i^{max}$
      $d_i^-, d_i^+ \geq 0$ and $d_i^- \cdot d_i^+ = 0 \qquad i = 1,..., n$

Minimize

    $Z = [f_1(d_i^-, d_i^+), ..., f_k(d_i^-, d_i^+)]$ *Preemptive*
    $Z = \Sigma\, W_i(d_i^- + d_i^+)\ \Sigma\, W_i = 1,\ W_i >\, = 0$ *Archimedean*

---

inequalities) and bounds on the system variables. We illustrate the cDSP construct in Table 8-2.

The conceptual basis of the compromise DSP is to minimize the difference between that which is desired (the goal, G_j) and that which can be achieved ($A_i(\mathbf{x})$) for multiple goals. We accomplish this goal by minimizing the deviation function, Z, expressed in terms of deviation variables. The deviation function provides a measure of the extent to which multiple goals are achieved. In the compromise DSP, multiple goals are considered conventionally by formulating the deviation function either with Archimedean weightings or preemptively (lexicographically) (Mistree et al. 1992).

8.4.2 Three-Stage Method for Resilience Design of Supply Network

In this section, we discuss details on each stage of the method. The general example that we consider in this section is a supply network in the petroleum industry with five different layers considering different transportation modes, components and products.

Strategic stage of the three-stage method

As is shown in Figure 8-2, the focus in the first stage is on capturing the existing network structure, designing a new structure, or redesigning a current network structure. Since the output at this stage is on location and allocation decisions, which results in locating nodes and links, this is named the strategic stage.

In this section, we present the first stage of the method in the context of supply networks using the cDSP construct. In this construct, as explained in Section 8.4.1, we have four parts named Given, Find, Satisfy, and Minimize.

Given (Parameters): Given includes all required parameters in the example to be considered in the model. In the example of the petroleum supply network, the *Given* part includes the following:

- Potential locations of facilities
- Potential transportation modes with transportation time
- Capacity of facilities, Bills of Materials, costs, and demands

Find (Variables): Find includes all variables in the model. In other words, in this part, all variables that must be found are determined. In the considered example of the supply network, the *Find* step includes the following:

- Structural variables
  - ○ Location of selected facilities
  - ○ Transportation links between facilities
- Production, flow and transportation planning

Satisfy: Satisfy includes all constraints in the model. In other words, in this part, all constraints that need to be satisfied in the model are determined. In addition to constraints, goals also need to be addressed in *Satisfy*. In the considered example of the supply network, the *Satisfy* part includes the following:

Constraints:

- Demand and capacity constraints
- Network flow and structural constraints

Goals:

- Minimize the total tardiness
- Minimize the total cost
- Maximize the total service level

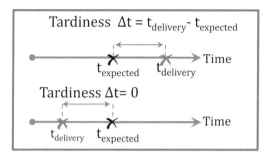

$$\text{Tardiness } \Delta t = t_{delivery} - t_{expected}$$

$$\text{Tardiness } \Delta t = 0$$

Figure 8-3. Tardiness as a result of actual and expected delivery times.

Tardiness in this example is defined as the difference between the expected delivery time and the actual delivery time as is shown in Figure 8-3.

Minimize: *Minimize* includes minimizing the deviation of goals from the targeted values that are set by designers.

We present the mathematical model for the example considered in Section 8.5 in Appendix 8-A. Section 8.6 presents the results of stage one (see Appendix 8-A) for further discussion and analysis.

Control stage of the three-stage method

The focus of the second stage of the method is on making the network structurally controllable. The output of the first stage, which is the location of nodes and connections between them (structural variables), is used as the input for stage two. In stage two, we identify the location and number of driver nodes to make the network structurally controllable. We present details on structural controllability as in Chapter 7. Although there is no mathematical model for designing a structurally controllable network, we can present the structure of the second stage as follows:

Given (Parameters): We consider the value of structural variables from the strategic stage (stage one) of the method as the input for stage two.

Find (Variables): We set the number and location of driver nodes in the second stage of the method.

Satisfy: Maximum matching theorem, minimum input theorem, and Lin's theorem are three important theorems that need to be satisfied in this section to determine the minimum number of driver nodes in structurally controllable supply networks.

Minimize: We minimize the number of driver nodes in the structurally controllable network in this step.

To demonstrate details of this stage, in Section 8.6 the results of implementing this stage for the considered example in Section 8.5 are presented and discussed.

Operational stage of the three-stage method

The designed structurally controllable network with a minimum number of identified driver nodes, which is the output of stage two, is the input for stage three wherein we define all possible disruption scenarios. Further, we identify the restoration strategies that need to be applied when different disruption scenarios occur. The focus in stage three is on resilience analysis of structurally controllable networks while disruption scenarios may occur.

In stage three, we can apply two types of restoration strategies: pre-disruption and post-disruption strategies. Examples of pre-disruption strategies are facility fortification or backup inventory and examples of post-disruption strategies are reconfigurations, and flexible production and inventory capacities.

Given (Parameters): Given includes all required parameters to be considered in the model. In the considered example of the supply network, the *Given* part includes the following:

- Designed network structure from stage one
- Location of driver nodes and controllable structure from stage two
- Disruption scenarios

Find (Variables)

- Select appropriate restoration strategies:
  - Pre-disruption strategies: Facility fortification and backup inventory strategies
  - Post-disruptions strategies: Reconfiguration, flexible production and inventory capacity

Satisfy: *Satisfy* includes all constraints in the model. In other words, in this part, all constraints that need to be satisfied in the model are determined. In addition to constraints, goals also need to be addressed in *Satisfy*. In the considered example of the supply network, the *Satisfy* part includes the following:

Constraints:

- Demand and capacity constraints
- Network flow and structural constraints

Goals:

- Minimize deviation in the service level
- Minimize control cost deviation

Minimize: Minimize includes minimizing the deviation of goals from the targeted values that are set by designers.

To demonstrate details of this stage, in Appendix 8-B, the mathematical model for the considered example in Section 8.5 is presented. Section 8.6 presents the results of stage three (see Appendix 8-B) for further discussion and analysis.

8.5 Petroleum Industry Example of Supply Networks under Disruptions

Without loss of generality, we consider a simple supply network that is dealing with producing and supplying products to target markets in the petroleum industry. In this supply network, we have petroleum components produced in refineries (*R1:R3 for i* ∈ *I* with capacity *capr$_i$*) from crude oil through the distillation and refining processes in the first layer. In hubs (*H1:H3 for j* ∈ *J* with capacity *caph$_j$*), the petroleum products (*p*) are produced from the petroleum components (*β*). In the third layer, warehouses (*W1:W3 for k* ∈ *K* with capacity *capw$_k$*) may store (if necessary) products and ship them to distribution centers (*DC1:DC4 for l* ∈ *L* with capacity *capd$_l$*) in the fourth layer. The function of distribution centers (DC) is to distribute product demands (*D*) to markets (*M1:M8 for m* ∈ *M* with capacity *capd$_l$*) in the fifth layer; no time activity is considered for DCs. In Figure 8-4, a schematic view of this forward supply network with five layers is shown.

Each set of simultaneously disrupted facilities is called a disruption scenario (*S*) and is assigned a finite probability of occurrence (*P$_s$*). Each disruption scenario occurs independently. Two types of states in the network are considered: the steady state where no disruptions occur and the disrupted state when a disruption(s) occurs within a network. We assume that after a disruption, the network returns to a steady state before the occurrence of another disruption. As we show in Figure 8-5, a (possible) disruption happens in a warehouse in the third echelon and products cannot be shipped from the disrupted warehouse to DCs.

We assume that the transportation time between echelons and production time in refineries and hubs are greater than zero. Stated simply, we consider the transportation time between echelons, production time in production facilities and expected inventory time (expected time

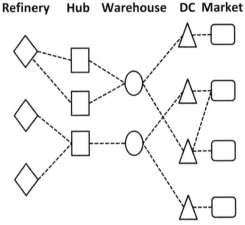

Figure 8-4. Schematic view of the petroleum supply network problem.

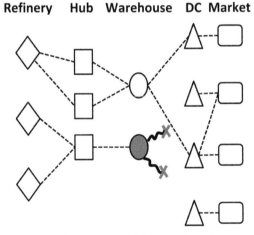

Figure 8-5. A schematic view of disrupted supply network.

required for load and reload in warehouses) in warehouses. We consider three refineries in the first echelon, three hubs in the second echelon, three warehouses in the third echelon, four distribution centers in the fourth echelon and eight markets in the last echelon of the supply network. We address the production capacity, production time, unit cost of production and the setup cost of the production line for different echelons in Tables 8-3 to 8-6.

Table 8-7 illustrates various weight sets for the multi-goal mathematical model in stage one. We use these weights for the weight of three goals in stage one (see Appendix 8-A).

Table 8-3. Characteristics of refineries in the petroleum supply network.

	Refinery 1 (Sweden)	Refinery 2 (Sweden)	Refinery 3 (Sweden)
Production capacity (parts)	12000	12000	12000
Production time (*hr*)	10	10	10
Setup cost of production lines ($)	1000	1000	1000
Production cost per component ($)	0.15	0.15	0.15

Table 8-4. Characteristics of hubs in the petroleum supply network.

	Hub 1 (USA)	Hub 2 (Belgium)	Refinery 3 (Germany)
Production capacity (parts)	4000	3500	4500
Production time (*hr*)	4	6	4
Setup cost of production lines ($)	750	750	750
Production cost per product ($)	0.4	0.4	0.4

Table 8-5. Characteristics of warehouses in the petroleum supply network.

	Warehouse 1 (Germany)	Warehouse 2 (Turkey)	Warehouse 3 (USA)
Inventory capacity (parts)	4000	3500	4500
Average inventory time for a product (*hr*)	4	6	4
Cost of operating a warehouse ($)	500	500	500

Table 8-6. Characteristics of distribution center in the petroleum network.

	Distribution Center 1 (Brazil)	Distribution Center 2 (France)	Distribution Center 3 (UAE)	Distribution Center 4 (USA)
Capacity (parts)	2000	4000	3000	4000
Cost of operating a distribution center ($)	200	200	200	200

In the next section, we describe and discuss the results of applying the three-stage method for the considered example.

Table 8-7. Weight set for conflicting goals.

Weight Set	Conflicts between Goals	W_1	W_2	W_3	$\sum_{i=1}^{3} W_i = 1$
WS_1	Lower tardiness (G_1)	1	0	0	1
WS_2	Lower cost (G_2)	0	1	0	1
WS_3	Higher service level (G_3)	0	0	1	1
WS_4	All goals, G_3 emphasized	0.1	0.1	0.8	1
WS_5	All goals, G_2 emphasized	0.1	0.8	0.1	1
WS_6	All goals, G_1 emphasized	0.8	0.1	0.1	1
WS_7	All goals, G_3 emphasized	0.2	0.2	0.6	1
WS_8	All goals, G_2 emphasized	0.2	0.6	0.2	1
WS_9	All goals, G_1 emphasized	0.6	0.2	0.2	1
WS_{10}	All goals	0.33	0.33	0.33	~ 1
WS_{11}	All goals, G_3 emphasized	0.25	0.25	0.5	1
WS_{12}	All goals, G_2 emphasized	0.25	0.5	0.25	1
WS_{13}	All goals, G_1 emphasized	0.5	0.25	0.25	1

8.6 Computational Results for Resilient Design of Structural Controllable Supply Networks

In this section, we present results in the context of the three-stage method.

Strategic stage of the three-stage method

According to the 13 weight-sets defined in Table 8-6, we show the normalized values for three goals in Figure 8-6.

As is shown in Figure 8-6 the normalized values of total cost and tardiness goals increase when the weight of the third goal (i.e., service level) increases. When the normalized value of the service level is more than 75%, there will be tardiness in meeting the demand of customers. We can conclude that the method is sensitive to the changing of weights of these goals. Considering the sensitivity of goals, exploration of the solution space is required.

In Figure 8-7, as an example, the normalized value of the three goals for the seventh weight set is presented. As is shown in Figure 8-7, since the weight of the service level is more than the two other goals, it meets more than 83% of the demand in the markets, while there is lateness in delivering the demand to the market.

For this weight set, we show the flow of products on the infrastructure network in Figure 8-8. As is shown in this figure, we include in the network two refineries and two hubs for meeting 83% of the demand. The

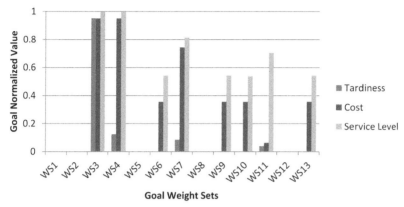

Figure 8-6. Normalized value of three goals of Stage 1.

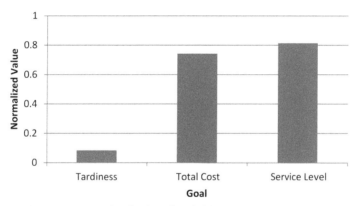

Figure 8-7. Normalized value of goals (W1 = 0.2, W2 = 0.2, W3 = 0.6).

network does not meet the demand in Market M7 fully because of the transportation consideration in delivering the products to customers (i.e., increase in the tardiness).

The maximum delivery time to the market is five days. Results are sensitive to this parameter. Therefore, the tardiness when the maximum delivery time is changing, is analyzed. As is shown in Figure 8-9, there is no tardiness in meeting the current demand of the markets when delivery time is six days and tardiness takes its highest value when we consider their real-time delivery or shortest delivery time.

When four days is the delivery time, the normalized value of the service level is 0.545 and we include only one refinery. However, assuming five days as the maximum delivery time, while satisfying both goals of the model, two refineries operate, the service level increases up to 83% and tardiness increases by 11%. Therefore, the optimum value for the maximum delivery time is four days.

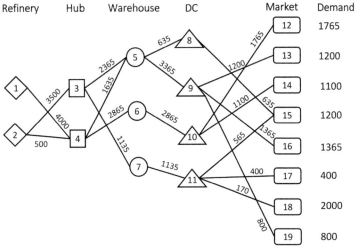

Figure 8-8. Product flow in the infrastructure network (W1 = 0.2, W2 = 0.2, W3 = 0.6).

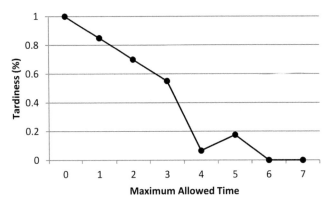

Figure 8-9. Analyzing the normalized value of the tardiness by changing the maximum delivery time.

We analyze the designed structure as the output of the modeling design (i.e., strategic design) from the perspective of the network. Figure 8-10 is an illustration of the designed infrastructure network.

The diameter of this network structure (the length of the longest of all the computed shortest paths between all pairs of facilities in the network) is four facilities and it has three connected components. The thickness of each link represents the volume of the flow of products. The modularity of this structure is 0.495 and demonstrated by four different colors. The modularity measures the strength of division of a network into modules (also called groups, clusters or communities). Networks with high modularity have dense connections between the facilities within modules

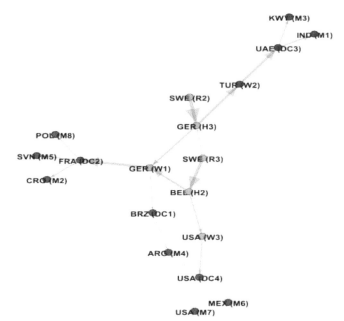

Figure 8-10. Illustration of the designed infrastructure network (W1 = 0.2, W2 = 0.2, W3 = 0.6).

but sparse connections between facilities in different modules. In general, the value of the modularity lies in the range [−1/2, 1).

We conduct an exploration of the solution space in this chapter to complete the result analysis and managerial insights. Especially because models are incomplete and inaccurate, exploration of the solution is required. Therefore, the ternary plot is used to explore the solution space through considering the trade-off among three goals, namely, tardiness, cost and service level. Ternary plots are created to show the interdependence among goals and to understand possible compromises among individual goals. These plots can help a policy maker or designer visually explore potential opportunities for the resilient and structurally controllable design of supply networks under disruption. Using ternary plots contributes to a reduction in the time required to provide results of all possible weights in the decision-making process for policy makers/designers and allows the rapid, convenient exploration of various alternative configurations. In other words, instead of solving the proposed method for all possible weight sets which require high computational cost and time, ternary plots can be created with a few sample points.

Figure 8-11 is a visualization of the normalized value of the service level for the considered supply network. As indicated in Figure 8-11, the red color indicates the highest normalized value of the service level (the value equal to one) and the blue color shows the lowest normalized value

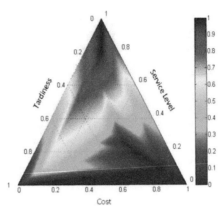

Figure 8-11. Visualization of the normalized value of the service level.

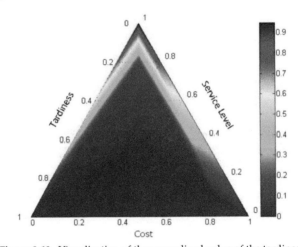

Figure 8-12. Visualization of the normalized value of the tardiness.

of the service level (the value equals zero). The intent for the service level in designing supply networks is maximizing the service level or equivalently the red area in the triangle. Each side of the triangle and numbers on it show one of the goals and its weights. As is shown in Figure 8-11, at any point in the interior of the triangle, we determine the value of the weights for each goal by finding the intersection of lines drawn parallel to the grid lines.

Figure 8-12 is a visualization of the normalized value of the tardiness for the considered supply network. As indicated in Figure 8-12, the red color indicates the highest normalized value of the tardiness (the value equal to one) and the blue color shows the lowest normalized value of the tardiness (the value equals zero). The intent for the tardiness in designing supply networks is minimizing the tardiness or equivalently maximizing

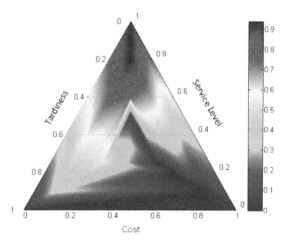

Figure 8-13. Visualization of the normalized value of cost.

the blue area in the triangle. Each side of the triangle and numbers on it show one of the goals and its weights. As is shown in Figure 8-12, at any point in the interior of the triangle, we determine the value of the weights for each goal by finding the intersection of lines drawn parallel to the grid lines.

Figure 8-13 is a visualization of the normalized value of the cost for the considered supply network. As indicated in Figure 8-13, the red color indicates the highest normalized value of the cost (the value equal to one) and the blue color shows the lowest normalized value of the cost (the value equals zero). The justification for the expense in designing supply networks is minimizing the cost or equivalently maximizing the blue area in the triangle. Each side of the triangle and numbers on it show one of the goals and its weights. As is shown in Figure 8-13, at any point in the interior of the triangle, we determine the value of the weights for each goal by finding the intersection of lines drawn parallel to the grid lines.

In this section, we perform the exploration of the solution space using ternary plots. The next section addresses the empirical performance validation of the work.

Control stage of the three-stage method

The purpose of the control stage of the three-stage method is determining the minimum number of driver nodes. We show identified driver nodes in the supply network example in Figure 8-14. As is shown in Figure 8-14, we identify four nodes $V = (v_1, v_2, v_7, v_9)$ as driver nodes in the supply network example. Since we base the proposed steps for identifying driver nodes on the minimum input theorem, the minimum number of driver nodes required to control this network fully is four. In other words, having less

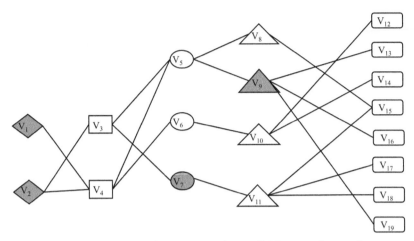

Figure 8-14. Driver nodes in structural controllable network example.

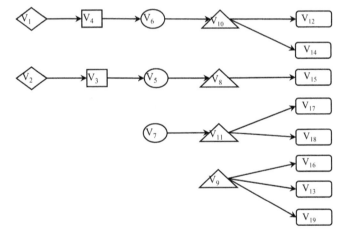

Figure 8-15. Path from driver nodes to markets in structurally controllable network.

than four driver nodes will result in not being able to control this network fully, and having more than four driver nodes will result in redundancy and higher control cost in designing the supply network. In Chapter 7, we discuss details of determining driver nodes in this supply network example.

In a structurally controllable network, there is at least one path from each driver node to other nodes in the network. Figure 8-15 shows four paths from identified driver nodes to other nodes in the last layer.

Each of these four paths initiates from a driver node (v_1, v_2, v_7, v_9) and ends at a node in the last layer of the network. As stated by the structural controllability definition, all nodes in the network are accessible from these four driver nodes. Therefore, there is no need to have safety stock or flexible production or inventory capacity in all nodes of the network. Freedom from this requirement will minimize the disruption management and control cost in the network. These driver nodes will be used in the third stage of the method to operate restoration strategies.

Operational stage of the three-stage method

We consider the occurrence of disruptions to be disruption scenarios. Each set of simultaneously disrupted facilities is a disruption scenario and is assigned a finite probability of occurrence. Each disruption scenario is an independent occurrence. In other words, we do not address dependence among disruption scenarios.

The two resilience measures considered in evaluating the control policies are the control cost and the deviation in the service level. In the control cost goal, minimizing the cost of fortifying driver nodes and having additional transportation arcs is considered. In the deviation goal, minimizing the deviation in the service level with and without disruptions is considered.

As is shown in Figure 8-16, we compare three different cases to each other:

I) No disruption occurred

II) Disruptions happen, but no structural controllability is considered

III) Disruptions happen, and structural controllability is considered

In Figure 8-16, two goals, service level, and tardiness are compared with each other. As is shown, when there is no disruption, the service level is 0.83 and tardiness is 0.06 (Case I). Service level decreases and tardiness increases when disruption scenarios happen (Case II). With considering structural controllability, the service level increases and tardiness converges to zero (Case III). Although we do not consider the cost of controllability in this analysis, from service level and tardiness perspective, Case III (with structural controllability) provides a better design for a network under disruption.

Another analysis was performed to consider the control cost. In this analysis, we describe three assumptions in the example as follows:

I) Consider a set of disruption scenarios

II) Time for recovering the disrupted network is 148 hours

III) Time for setting up post-disruptions strategies (for structural controllability) is 24 hours

In Figure 8-17, states of the network when it is in the steady state (before the disruption), disrupted state and recovered state (after recovery) are

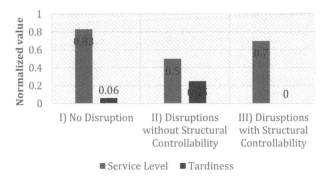

Figure 8-16. Service level and tardiness trade-off.

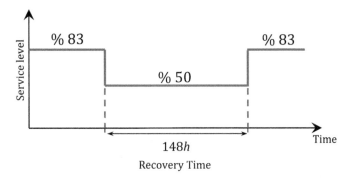

Figure 8-17. Changing of service level in a disrupted supply network.

shown. The service level in an undisrupted network is 83%, and during the recovery time, the service level is 50%. The total cost of operating the network example with and without disruptions is calculated as well and shown in Table 8-8.

Figure 8-18 shows the states of the network regarding service level for the supply network example. In this example, after the occurrence of disruptions the service level dropped to 50%; however, because of utilizing structural controllability and restoration strategies, after 24 hours the service level increased by 20% and reached as much as 70% for the remaining 124 hours of recovery. This shift decreases the total cost of the supply network example as is explained in Table 8-7. Utilizing structural controllability increases the control cost of networks, but it can decrease the full cost of designing and operating networks when disruptions happen.

In addition to the service level, tardiness and control cost analysis in this stage, we consider several control policies to improve the operational stage output. Although the main purpose of stage two is in minimizing the number of driver nodes, in some scenarios designers may decide to have more driver nodes in a network or increase the number of redundant

Table 8-8. Total cost of the supply network example.

Cases	Total Cost Calculation
No disruption	Strategic and operational cost + Lost sales cost = $1,847,530
Disruptions without structural controllability	Strategic and operational cost + Lost sales cost = $3,050,496
Disruptions with structural controllability	Strategic and operational cost + Lost sales cost + Control cost = $2,489,300

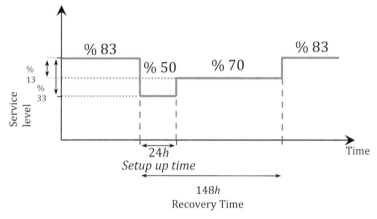

Figure 8-18. Changing of the service level in a structurally controllable supply network.

transportation routes. Here five control policies are presented and analyzed as is shown in Figure 8-18.

Control Policy 1: locate driver nodes on all unmatched nodes (same as determined driver nodes in Figure 8-14).

Control Policy 2: locate driver nodes on all unmatched nodes and use auxiliary transportation links if required.

Control Policy 3: locate driver nodes on all unmatched nodes. Make sure each layer of the network has at least one driver node by adding an arbitrary node to each layer without a driver node.

Control Policy 4: locate one arbitrary driver node on each layer of the network.

Control Policy 5: locate one driver node on each layer of the network and add auxiliary transportation arcs.

These control policies, which determine the location and number of driver nodes, are possible control alternatives that designers may apply in designing structurally controllable supply networks. In Figure 8-19 the comparison between the total control cost and the difference between the service level is shown. As indicated in Figure 8-19, there is a trade-off between the service level and cost of control when increasing the number of driver nodes. Control policies 2 and five could increase the service level although disruptions happen on the supply network. As the service level improves for both control policies 2 and 5, the control cost increases as well. Based on the preferences of the supply network designers, either improving the service level (or keeping the same service level before disruptions happen) or decreasing the control cost, can be emphasized in recovering disrupted supply networks.

In addition, one may want to consider variation management in addition to managing disruptions. We discuss the details regarding integrating disruption and variation management in Chapter 9. However, to expand the scope of the proposed model from disruption management to both disruption and variation management, occurrence of variations can also be considered as a scenario-based stochastic programming expansion approach. For this purpose, five variation scenarios are defined as follows with the same occurrence probabilities.

Variation Scenario 1: supply-side variation in Refinery 2 that decreases its production capacity to 50%.

Variation Scenario 2: supply-side variation in Hub 2 that decreases its output capacity to 50%.

Variation Scenario 3: demand-side variation in markets that increase the demand by 10%.

Variation Scenario 4: demand-side variation in markets that increase the demand by 20%.

Variation Scenario 5: demand-side variation in markets that decrease the demand by 10%.

The probability of occurrence of these five variation scenarios is considered equal to 20%. We discuss two situations: when we consider the first control policy (i.e., see for Control Policy 1) as the recovery scenario and when we do not apply any of the control policies. Figure 8-20 shows results for the service level.

As is shown in Figure 8-20, if Variation Scenario 1 occurs on Refinery 2, the production capacity of the supply network will decrease to 6000 products and the service level will decrease to 61%. However, using the Control Policy 1 will help in reaching to the initial service level (i.e., 81%), especially because Refinery 2 is a driver facility. On the other hand,

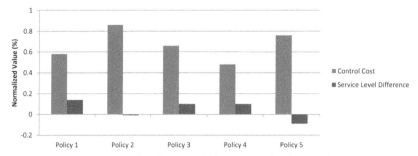

Figure 8-19. Trade-off among different control policies in Stage 3.

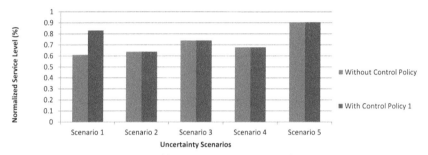

Figure 8-20. Impact of five variation scenarios in the service level.

because no driver facility is selected in the second, as is shown in Variation Scenario 2, using the Control Policy 1 cannot make any difference in managing the supply variation on Hub 2.

From the cost perspective, we arrive at two conclusions. First, regarding the value of control cost for these five variation scenarios, as is shown in Figure 8-20, the control cost is same for all variation scenarios. In other words, from the structural perspective, to make a network structurally controllable, the network should incur a one-time cost. Therefore, the control cost for all these five variation scenarios is same (see Figure 8-20 for the result). Second, the only factor, which may cause a difference in the value of total cost function, is the operating cost of the network. The ratio of the control cost in comparison with the operating cost can be much higher. Therefore, considering the cost with and without the Control policy 1 for these five variation scenarios, demonstrates that using control policies for a short-term decision-making time frame are usually not economically acceptable. The reason for this conclusion is that the cost when control policies are in use, is much higher than the time when control policies have not been used. Therefore, analyzing the cost of control policies in the decision-making process should be considered as a strategic decision (long-term decision-making).

8.7 Closing Remarks

In this chapter, we explain different examples of disruptions and disruption scenarios. We introduced resilience analysis in supply networks to manage disruptions and we explained the benefits of having both pre-disruption and post-disruption restoration scenarios in supply networks under disruptions. We illustrate the role of resilience and structural controllability in the context of architecture for fail-safe networks as explained in Chapter 1. We summarize the constituents of this architecture and our interpretation for resilience and structural controllability in risk management in Table 8-1. In addition, a three-stage method, based on the compromise DSP construct is proposed in this chapter to manage disruptions for having resilient and structurally controllable supply networks. In this model, we incorporate the structural controllability as a major factor for resilience design. In Section 8.5, we explained different aspects of the model through an example problem and we expand the model from disruption management to both disruption and variation management by considering a scenario-based approach for variation scenarios in the proposed model.

In Chapters 6 to 8, we discussed different aspects of disruption management: in Chapter 6, we addressed robustness; in Chapter 7, we discussed structural controllability; and, finally in Chapter 8, we introduce a new method for managing resilience through an example of the petroleum industry. We initiate the expansion of disruption management to disruption and variation management in Chapter 8 using a scenario-based approach, but will expand it further to combine both disruption and variation management in Chapter 9.

References

Gong, J., Mitchell, J. E., Krishnamurthy, A. and Wallace, W. A. 2014. An interdependent layered network model for a resilient supply chain. Omega 46: 104–116.

Ivanov, D. and Sokolov, B. 2013. Control and system-theoretic identification of the supply chain dynamics somain for planning, analysis and adaptation of performance under uncertainty. European Journal of Operational Research 224(2): 313–323.

Mistree, F., Hughes, O. F. and Bras, B. A. 1992. The compromise decision support problem and the adaptive linear programming algorithm. *In*: Kamat, M. P. (ed.). Structural Optimization: Status and Promise. Washington, D.C.: AIAA.

Mulani, N. and Lee, H. 2002. New business models for supply chain excellence. Journal—Achieving Supply Chain Excellence Through Technology. 4: 1–13. Publisher Montgomery Research San Francisco.

Sarkar, P., Armstrong, C. and Hua, V. 2002. Idling time: the West Coast shutdown is beginning to hurt workers, industries dependent on imports. San Francisco Chronicle:B1.

Sheffi, Y. 2005. A supply chain view of the resilient enterprise. MIT Sloan Management Review 47(1): 41–48.

Stauffer, D. 2003. Risk: The weak link in your supply chain. Harvard Management Update 8(3): 3–5.

Appendices

Appendix 8-A Stage One Mathematical Formulation

In Section 8.4.2, we discuss details on each stage of the method. The general example that we consider in this section is a supply network in the petroleum industry with five different layers considering different transportation modes, components and products. The first stage of the method is strategic design. The mathematical model to support the strategic design is developed based on the CDSP construct as follows.

Given

Indices

$i \in I$: set of potential locations for refineries
$j \in J$: set of potential locations for hubs
$k \in K$: set of potential location for warehouses
$l \in L$: set of potential locations for distribution centers
$m \in M$: set of markets
$p \in P$: set of products
$q \in Q$: set of components used in different products
$h \in H$: set of transportation modes (truck, train, ship, etc.) between facility layers

Parameters

D_{pm} : demand of product p at market m
β_{qp} : number of component q is required for product p
τ : the maximum allowed delivery time for demanded products at markets
t_{ij}^h : transportation time between refinery i and hub j with transportation mode h
t_{jk}^h : transportation time between hub j and warehouse k with transportation mode h
t_{kl}^h : transportation time between warehouse k and distribution center l with transportation mode h
t_{lm}^h : transportation time between distribution center l and market m with transportation mode h
t_{pj} : time required for producing product p in hub j

t_{qi} : time required for blending component q in refinery i

t_k : the average time a product can be stored in warehouse k

$capr_i$: capacity of refinery i

$caph_j$: capacity of hub j

$capw_k$: capacity of warehouse k

$capd_l$: capacity of distribution center l

c_{qi} : cost of blending component q at refinery i

c_{pj} : cost of producing product p at hub j

c_i : fixed cost of opening a refinery in candidate location i

c_j : fixed cost of opening a hub in candidate location j

c_k : fixed cost of opening a warehouse in candidate location k

c_l : fixed cost of opening a distribution center in candidate location l

w_1, w_2, w_3 : weight for goals one to three, respectively ($> = 0$)

Find

Continuous Variables

X_{ij}^{ph} : amount of product p flows from refinery i to hub j using transportation mode h

Y_{jk}^{ph} : amount of product p flows from hub j to warehouse k using transportation mode h

W_{kl}^{ph} : amount of product p flows from warehouse k to distribution center l using transportation mode h

V_{lm}^{ph} : amount of product p flows from distribution center l to market m using transportation mode h

d_1^+, d_1^- : the deviation of the actual value of goal one (tardiness) from the target goal value

d_2^+, d_2^- : the deviation of the actual value of goal two (cost) from the target goal value

d_3^+, d_3^- : the deviation of the actual value of goal three (service level) from the target goal value

Structural Variables

μ_{ij} : binary variable equal to 1 if there is a transportation arc between refinery i and hub j and 0 otherwise

γ_{jk} : binary variable equal to 1 if there is a transportation arc between hub j and warehouse k and 0 otherwise

β_{kl} : binary variable equal to 1 if there is a transportation arc between warehouse k and distribution center l and 0 otherwise

α_{lm} : binary variable equal to 1 if there is a transportation arc between distribution center l and market m and 0 otherwise

U_i : binary variable equal to 1 if a refinery is opened at location i and 0 otherwise

O_j : binary variable equal to 1 if a hub is opened at location j and 0 otherwise

G_k : binary variable equal to 1 if a warehouse is opened at location k and 0 otherwise

F_l : binary variable equal to 1 if a distribution center is opened at location l and 0 otherwise

Satisfy (Constraints)

$$\sum_{l=1}^{L} \sum_{h=1}^{H} V_{lm}^{ph} \leq D_{pm} \qquad\qquad \forall m \in M, p \in P \qquad\qquad (8\text{-}1)$$

$$\sum_{k=1}^{K} \sum_{h=1}^{H} W_{kl}^{ph} = \sum_{m=1}^{M} \sum_{h=1}^{H} V_{lm}^{ph} \qquad\qquad \forall l \in L, p \in P \qquad\qquad (8\text{-}2)$$

$$\sum_{j=1}^{J} \sum_{h=1}^{H} Y_{jk}^{ph} = \sum_{l=1}^{L} \sum_{h=1}^{H} W_{kl}^{ph} \qquad\qquad \forall k \in K, p \in P \qquad\qquad (8\text{-}3)$$

$$\sum_{i=1}^{I} \sum_{h=1}^{H} X_{ij}^{ph} = \sum_{k=1}^{K} \sum_{h=1}^{H} Y_{jk}^{ph} \qquad\qquad \forall j \in J, p \in P \qquad\qquad (8\text{-}4)$$

$$\sum_{j=1}^{J} \sum_{h=1}^{H} \sum_{q=1}^{Q} \sum_{p=1}^{P} \beta_{qp} X_{ij}^{ph} \leq capr_i U_i \qquad \forall i \in I \qquad\qquad (8\text{-}5)$$

$$\sum_{k=1}^{K} \sum_{h=1}^{H} \sum_{p=1}^{P} Y_{jk}^{ph} \leq caph_j O_j \qquad\qquad \forall j \in J \qquad\qquad (8\text{-}6)$$

$$\sum_{l=1}^{L} \sum_{h=1}^{H} \sum_{p=1}^{P} W_{kl}^{ph} \leq capw_k G_k \qquad\qquad \forall k \in K \qquad\qquad (8\text{-}7)$$

$$\sum_{m=1}^{M} \sum_{h=1}^{H} \sum_{p=1}^{P} V_{lm}^{ph} \leq capd_l F_l \qquad\qquad \forall l \in L \qquad\qquad (8\text{-}8)$$

$$\sum_{h=1}^{H} \sum_{p=1}^{P} X_{ij}^{ph} \leq N\mu_{ij} \qquad\qquad \forall i \in I, j \in J \qquad\qquad (8\text{-}9)$$

$$\sum_{h=1}^{H} \sum_{p=1}^{P} Y_{jk}^{ph} \leq N\gamma_{jk} \qquad\qquad \forall j \in J, c \qquad\qquad (8\text{-}10)$$

$$\sum_{h=1}^{H} \sum_{p=1}^{P} W_{kl}^{ph} \leq N\beta_{kl} \qquad\qquad \forall k \in K, l \in L \qquad\qquad (8\text{-}11)$$

$$\sum_{h=1}^{H} \sum_{p=1}^{P} V_{lm}^{ph} \leq N\alpha_{lm} \qquad\qquad \forall l \in L, m \in M \qquad\qquad (8\text{-}12)$$

$$X_{ij}^{ph}, Y_{jk}^{ph}, W_{kl}^{ph}, V_{lm}^{ph} \geq 0 \qquad \forall i \in I, j \in J, k \in K, l \in L, m \in M, p \in P, h \in H \quad (8\text{-}13)$$

$$\mu_{ij}, \gamma_{jk}, \beta_{kl}, \alpha_{lm}, U_i, O_j, G_k, F_l \in \{0,1\} \qquad \forall i \in I, j \in J, k \in K, l \in L, m \in M \quad (8\text{-}14)$$

$$d_1^+ . d_1^- = 0, d_2^+ . d_2^- = 0, d_3^+ . d_3^- = 0 \qquad\qquad (8\text{-}15)$$

Satisfy (Goals)

$$G_1 = \sum_{i=1}^{I} \sum_{j=1}^{J} \sum_{k=1}^{K} \sum_{l=1}^{L} \sum_{m=1}^{M} \sum_{p=1}^{P} \sum_{h=1}^{H} \max\Big[\big((t_{qi}\beta_{qp} X_{ij}^{ph}) + (t_{qj} Y_{jk}^{ph}) +$$

$$(t_k W_{kl}^{ph}) + (t_{ij}^h X_{ij}^{ph}) + (t_{jk}^h Y_{jk}^{ph}) + (t_{kl}^h W_{kl}^{ph}) + (t_{lm}^h V_{lm}^{ph})\big) - \tau V_{lm}^{ph},\, 0\Big] + d_1^- - d_1^+ \qquad (8\text{-}16)$$

$$G_2 = \sum_{i=1}^{I} \sum_{j=1}^{J} \sum_{q=1}^{Q} \sum_{p=1}^{P} \sum_{h=1}^{H} c_{qi}\beta_{qp} X_{ij}^{ph} + \sum_{j=1}^{J} \sum_{k=1}^{K} \sum_{p=1}^{P} \sum_{h=1}^{H} c_{pj} Y_{jk}^{ph} +$$

$$\sum_{i=1}^{I} c_i U_i + \sum_{j=1}^{J} c_j O_j + \sum_{k=1}^{K} c_k G_k + \sum_{l=1}^{L} c_l F_l + d_2^- - d_2^+ \qquad (8\text{-}17)$$

$$G_3 = \sum_{m=1}^{M} \sum_{p=1}^{P} \sum_{l=1}^{L} \sum_{h=1}^{H} \frac{V_{lm}^{ph}}{D_{pm}} + d_3^+ - d_3^- \qquad (8\text{-}18)$$

Minimize

$$\text{Minimize } w_1(d_1^+ + d_1^-) + w_2(d_2^+ + d_2^-) + w_3(d_3^+ + d_3^-) \qquad (8\text{-}19)$$

$$w_1 + w_2 + w_3 = 1 \qquad (8\text{-}20)$$

Appendix 8-B Stage Two Mathematical Formulation

In Section 8.4.2, we discuss details at each stage of the method. The general example that we consider in this section is a supply network in the petroleum industry with five different layers considering different transportation modes, components, and products. The third stage of the method is operational design. The mathematical model to support the operational design is developed based on the CDSP construct as follows.

Given

The flow parameters

$\overline{x_{ij}^{ph}}$: amount of product p flowed from refinery i to hub j using transportation mode h

$\overline{y_{jk}^{ph}}$: amount of product p flowed from hub j to warehouse k using transportation mode h

$\overline{w_{kl}^{ph}}$: amount of product p flowed from warehouse k to distribution center l using transportation mode h

$\overline{v_{lm}^{ph}}$: amount of product p flowed from distribution center l to market m using transportation mode h

The structural parameters

$\overline{\mu_{ij}}$: binary parameter equal to 1 if there was a transportation arc between refinery i and hub j and 0 otherwise

$\overline{\gamma_{jk}}$: binary parameter equal to 1 if there was a transportation arc between hub j and warehouse k and 0 otherwise

$\overline{\beta_{kl}}$	:	binary parameter equal to 1 if there was a transportation arc between warehouse k and distribution center l and 0 otherwise
$\overline{\alpha_{lm}}$	:	binary parameter equal to 1 if there was a transportation arc between distribution center l and market m and 0 otherwise
$\overline{u_l}$	:	binary parameter equal to 1 if refinery i was opened and 0 otherwise
$\overline{o_j}$	:	binary parameter equal to 1 if hub j was opened and 0 otherwise
$\overline{g_k}$	:	binary parameter equal to 1 if warehouse k was opened and 0 otherwise
$\overline{f_l}$	:	binary parameter equal to 1 if distribution center l was opened and 0 otherwise
$cap\varphi_i^n$	:	level n of flexible production capacity at refinery I
$cap\omega_j^n$	:	level n of flexible production capacity at hub j
$cap\theta_k^n$	:	level n of flexible inventory capacity at warehouse k
$cap\alpha_l^n$	:	level n of extra inventory at distribution center l
$c\varphi_i$	:	cost of flexible production capacity at refinery i
$c\omega_j$	:	cost of flexible production capacity at hub j
$c\theta_k$	:	cost of flexible inventory capacity at warehouse k
$c\alpha_l$	:	cost of keeping inventory at distribution center l
cfr_i	:	cost of driver facility fortification at refinery i
cfh_j	:	cost of driver facility fortification at hub j
cfw_k	:	cost of driver facility fortification at warehouse k
cfd_l	:	cost of driver facility fortification at distribution center l
$ca\mu_{ij}$	:	cost of auxiliary transportation arc between refinery i and hub j
$ca\gamma_{jk}$	:	cost of auxiliary transportation arc between hub j and warehouse k
$ca\beta_{kl}$	:	cost of auxiliary transportation arc between warehouse k and distribution center l
$ca\alpha_{lm}$	:	cost of auxiliary transportation arc between distribution center l and market m

Control parameters

$c\mu_{ij}$	:	binary parameter equal to 1 if a control (auxiliary) extra transportation arc is added for the controllability purpose between refinery i and hub j and 0 otherwise
$c\gamma_{jk}$	:	binary parameter equal to 1 if a control (auxiliary) extra transportation arc is added for the controllability purpose between hub j and warehouse k and 0 otherwise
$c\beta_{kl}$	:	binary parameter equal to 1 if a control (auxiliary) extra transportation arc is added for the controllability purpose between warehouse k and distribution center l and 0 otherwise

ca_{lm} : binary parameter equal to 1 if a control (auxiliary) extra transportation arc is added for the controllability purpose between distribution center l and market m and 0 otherwise

cu_i : binary parameter equal to 1 if refinery i is selected as the driver refinery and 0 otherwise

co_j : binary parameter equal to 1 if hub j is selected as the refinery hub and 0 otherwise

cg_k : binary parameter equal to 1 if warehouse k is selected as the driver warehouse and 0 otherwise

cz_l : binary parameter equal to 1 if distribution center l is selected as the driver distribution center and 0 otherwise

Disruption parameters

P_s : probability of occurrence Scenario s

dr_i^s : binary parameter equal to 1 if refinery i is disrupted in scenario s and 0 otherwise

dh_j^s : binary parameter equal to 1 if hub j is disrupted in scenario s and 0 otherwise

dw_k^s : binary parameter equal to 1 if warehouse k is disrupted in scenario s and 0 otherwise

Find

$X_{ijph}^{s\ +}$: over flow of product p from refinery i to hub j using transportation mode h

$X_{ijph}^{s\ -}$: lower flow of product p from refinery i to hub j using transportation mode h

$Y_{jkph}^{s\ +}$: over flow of product p from hub j to warehouse k using transportation mode h

$Y_{jkph}^{s\ -}$: lower flow of product p from hub j to warehouse k using transportation mode h

$W_{klph}^{s\ +}$: over flow of product p from warehouse k to distribution center l using transportation mode h

$W_{klph}^{s\ -}$: lower flow of product p from warehouse k to distribution center l using transportation mode h

$V_{lmph}^{s\ +}$: over flow of product p from distribution center l to market m using transportation mode h

$V_{lmph}^{s\ -}$: lower flow of product p from distribution center l to market m using transportation mode h

φ_i^n : binary variable equal to 1 if driver refinery (driver facility) i is opened for blending components with flexible production capacity n

ω_j^n : binary variable equal to 1 if driver hub (driver facility) j is opened for producing products with flexible production capacity n

θ_k^n : binary variable equal to 1 if driver warehouse (driver facility) k is opened for inventorying products with flexible inventory capacity n

α_l^n : binary variable equal to 1 if driver distribution center (driver facility) l is opened for keeping extra inventory capacity n

Satisfy

Constraints

$$\sum_{l=1}^{L} \sum_{h=1}^{H} (\overline{v_{lm}^{ph}} + V_{lmph}^{s}{}^{+} - V_{lmph}^{s}{}^{-}) \le D_{pm} \qquad\qquad \forall m \in M, p \in P, s \in S \qquad (8\text{-}21)$$

$$\sum_{l=1}^{L} \sum_{h=1}^{H} (\overline{v_{lm}^{ph}} + V_{lmph}^{s}{}^{+} - V_{lmph}^{s}{}^{-}) \ge \sum_{l=1}^{L} \sum_{h=1}^{H} \overline{v_{lm}^{ph}} \qquad \forall m \in M, p \in P, s \in S \qquad (8\text{-}22)$$

$$\sum_{k=1}^{K} \sum_{h=1}^{H} (\overline{w_{kl}^{ph}} + W_{klph}^{s}{}^{+} - W_{klph}^{s}{}^{-}) = \sum_{m=1}^{M} \sum_{h=1}^{H} (\overline{v_{lm}^{ph}} + V_{lmph}^{s}{}^{+} - V_{lmph}^{s}{}^{-})$$
$$\forall l \in L, p \in P, s \in S \qquad (8\text{-}23)$$

$$\sum_{j=1}^{J} \sum_{h=1}^{H} (\overline{y_{jk}^{ph}} + Y_{jkph}^{s}{}^{+} - Y_{jkph}^{s}{}^{-}) = \sum_{l=1}^{L} \sum_{h=1}^{H} (\overline{w_{kl}^{ph}} + W_{klph}^{s}{}^{+} - W_{klph}^{s}{}^{-})$$
$$\forall k \in K, p \in P, s \in S \qquad (8\text{-}24)$$

$$\sum_{i=1}^{I} \sum_{h=1}^{H} (\overline{x_{ij}^{ph}} + X_{ijph}^{s}{}^{+} - X_{ijph}^{s}{}^{-}) = \sum_{j=1}^{J} \sum_{h=1}^{H} (\overline{y_{jk}^{ph}} + Y_{jkph}^{s}{}^{+} - Y_{jkph}^{s}{}^{-})$$
$$\forall j \in J, p \in P, s \in S \qquad (8\text{-}25)$$

$$\sum_{j=1}^{J} \sum_{h=1}^{H} \sum_{q=1}^{Q} \sum_{p=1}^{P} \beta_{qp} (\overline{x_{ij}^{ph}} + X_{ijph}^{s}{}^{+} - X_{ijph}^{s}{}^{-}) \le [capr_i \, \overline{u}_i + \sum_{n=1}^{N} cap\varphi_i^n \, \varphi_i^n](1 - dr_i^s)$$
$$\forall i \in I, s \in S \qquad (8\text{-}26)$$

$$\sum_{k=1}^{K} \sum_{h=1}^{H} \sum_{p=1}^{P} (\overline{y_{jk}^{ph}} + Y_{jkph}^{s}{}^{+} - Y_{jkph}^{s}{}^{-}) \le [caph_j \, \overline{o}_j + \sum_{n=1}^{N} cap\omega_j^n \, \omega_j^n](1 - dh_j^s)$$
$$\forall j \in J, s \in S \qquad (8\text{-}27)$$

$$\sum_{l=1}^{L} \sum_{h=1}^{H} \sum_{p=1}^{P} (\overline{w_{kl}^{ph}} + W_{klph}^{s}{}^{+} - W_{klph}^{s}{}^{-}) \le [capw_k \, \overline{g}_k + \sum_{n=1}^{N} cap\theta_k^n \, \theta_k^n](1 - dw_k^s)$$
$$\forall k \in K, s \in S \qquad (8\text{-}28)$$

$$\sum_{m=1}^{M} \sum_{h=1}^{H} \sum_{p=1}^{P} (\overline{v_{lm}^{ph}} + V_{lmph}^{s}{}^{+} - V_{lmph}^{s}{}^{-}) \le capd_l \overline{f}_l + \sum_{n=1}^{N} cap\alpha_l^n \, \alpha_l^n$$
$$\forall l \in L, s \in S \qquad (8\text{-}29)$$

$$\sum_{h=1}^{H} \sum_{p=1}^{P} X_{ijph}^{s}{}^{+} \le N \left(\overline{\mu_{ij}} + c\mu_{ij} \right) \left(1 - dr_{i}^{s} \right) \left(1 - dr_{j}^{s} \right) \quad \forall i \in I, j \in J, s \in S \qquad (8\text{-}30)$$

$$\sum_{h=1}^{H} \sum_{p=1}^{P} X_{ijph}^{s}{}^{-} \le N \, \overline{\mu_{ij}} \left(1 - dr_{i}^{s} \right) \left(1 - dr_{j}^{s} \right) \qquad\qquad \forall i \in I, j \in J, s \in S \qquad (8\text{-}31)$$

$$\sum_{h=1}^{H} \sum_{p=1}^{P} Y_{jkph}^{s}{}^{+} \le N \left(\overline{\gamma_{jk}} + c\gamma_{jk} \right) \left(1 - dh_{j}^{s} \right) \left(1 - dh_{j}^{s} \right) \quad \forall j \in J, c \in C, s \in S \qquad (8\text{-}32)$$

$$\sum_{h=1}^{H} \sum_{p=1}^{P} Y_{jkph}^{s}{}^{-} \le N \left(\overline{\gamma_{jk}} \right) \left(1 - dh_{j}^{s} \right) \left(1 - dw_{k}^{s} \right) \qquad \forall j \in J, c \in C, s \in S \qquad (8\text{-}33)$$

$$\sum_{h=1}^{H} \sum_{p=1}^{P} W_{klph}^{s}{}^{+} \le N \left(\overline{\beta_{kl}} + c\beta_{kl} \right) \left(1 - dw_{k}^{s} \right) \qquad \forall k \in K, l \in L, s \in S \qquad (8\text{-}34)$$

$$\sum_{h=1}^{H} \sum_{p=1}^{P} W_{klph}^{s}{}^{-} \le NN \left(\overline{\beta_{kl}} \right) \left(1 - dw_{k}^{s} \right) \qquad \forall k \in K, l \in L, s \in S \qquad (8\text{-}35)$$

$$\sum_{h=1}^{H} \sum_{p=1}^{P} V_{lmph}^{s}{}^{+} \le N \left(\overline{\alpha_{lm}} + c\alpha_{lm} \right) \qquad \forall l \in L, m \in M, s \in S \qquad (8\text{-}36)$$

$$\sum_{h=1}^{H} \sum_{p=1}^{P} V_{lmph}^{s}{}^{-} \le N \overline{\alpha_{lm}} \qquad\qquad \forall l \in L, m \in M, s \in S \qquad (8\text{-}37)$$

$$\sum_{n=2}^{N} \varphi_{i}^{n} \le cu_{i} \qquad\qquad \forall i \in I \qquad (8\text{-}38)$$

$$\sum_{n=2}^{N} \omega_{j}^{n} \le co_{j} \qquad\qquad \forall j \in J \qquad (8\text{-}39)$$

$$\sum_{n=2}^{N} \theta_{k}^{n} \le cg_{k} \qquad\qquad \forall k \in K \qquad (8\text{-}40)$$

$$\sum_{n=2}^{N} \alpha_{l}^{n} \le cz_{l} \qquad\qquad \forall k \in K \qquad (8\text{-}41)$$

$$\sum_{n=1}^{N} \varphi_{i}^{n} = 1 \qquad\qquad \forall i \in I \qquad (8\text{-}42)$$

$$\sum_{n=1}^{N} \omega_{j}^{n} = 1 \qquad\qquad \forall j \in J \qquad (8\text{-}43)$$

$$\sum_{n=1}^{N} \theta_{k}^{n} = 1 \qquad\qquad \forall k \in K \qquad (8\text{-}44)$$

$$\sum_{n=1}^{N} \alpha_{l}^{n} = 1 \qquad\qquad \forall k \in K \qquad (8\text{-}45)$$

$$X_{ijph}^{s}{}^{+} X_{ijph}^{s}{}^{-} = 0 \qquad\qquad \forall i \in I, j \in J, p \in P, h \in H, s \in S \qquad (8\text{-}46)$$

$$Y_{jkph}^{s}{}^{+} Y_{jkph}^{s}{}^{-} = 0 \qquad\qquad \forall j \in J, k \in K, p \in P, h \in H, s \in S \qquad (8\text{-}47)$$

$$W_{klph}^{s}{}^{+} W_{klph}^{s}{}^{-} = 0 \qquad\qquad \forall k \in K, l \in L, p \in P, h \in H, s \in S \qquad (8\text{-}48)$$

$$V_{lmph}^{s}{}^{+} V_{lmph}^{s}{}^{-} = 0 \qquad\qquad \forall l \in L, m \in M, p \in P, h \in H, s \in S \quad (8\text{-}49)$$

$$X_{ijph}^{s}{}^{+}, X_{ijph}^{s}{}^{-}, Y_{jkph}^{s}{}^{+}, Y_{jkph}^{s}{}^{-}, W_{klph}^{s}{}^{+}, W_{klph}^{s}{}^{-}, V_{lmph}^{s}{}^{+}, V_{lmph}^{s}{}^{-} \geq 0$$

$$\forall i \in I, j \in J, k \in K, l \in L, m \in M, p \in P, h \in H, s \in S \quad (8\text{-}50)$$

$$\varphi_{i}^{n}, \omega_{j}^{n}, \theta_{k}^{n}, \alpha_{l}^{n} \in \{0,1\} \qquad\qquad \forall i \in I, j \in J, k \in K, l \in L \quad (8\text{-}51)$$

Minimize

$$Z_4 = \sum_{s=1}^{S} \sum_{m=1}^{M} P_s \left[\sum_{p=1}^{P} \sum_{h=1}^{H} \sum_{l=1}^{L} \frac{V_{lm}^{ph}}{D_{pm}} - \sum_{p=1}^{P} \sum_{h=1}^{H} \sum_{l=1}^{L} \frac{V_{lmph}^{s}{}^{+} + V_{lmph}^{s}{}^{-}}{D_{pm}} \right] Z_4 =$$

$$\sum_{s=1}^{S} \sum_{i=1}^{I} \sum_{j=1}^{J} \sum_{k=1}^{K} \sum_{l=1}^{L} \sum_{m=1}^{M} \sum_{p=1}^{P} \sum_{h=1}^{H} P_s [X_{ijph}^{s}{}^{+} + X_{ijph}^{s}{}^{-} + Y_{jkph}^{s}{}^{+} + Y_{jkph}^{s}{}^{-} +$$

$$W_{klph}^{s}{}^{+} + W_{klph}^{s}{}^{-} + V_{lmph}^{s}{}^{+} + V_{lmph}^{s}{}^{-}] \qquad\qquad (8\text{-}52)$$

$$Z_5 = \left[\sum_{i=1}^{I} \sum_{n=1}^{N} c\varphi_i \, cap\varphi_i^n \, \varphi_i^n + \sum_{j=1}^{J} \sum_{n=1}^{N} c\omega_j \, cap\omega_j^n \, \omega_j^n + \right.$$

$$\sum_{k=1}^{K} \sum_{n=1}^{N} c\theta_k \, cap\theta_k^n \, \theta_k^n + \sum_{k=1}^{K} \sum_{n=1}^{N} c\alpha_l \, cap\alpha_l^n \, \alpha_l^n \right] + \left[\sum_{i=1}^{I} cfr_i \, cu_i + \right.$$

$$\sum_{j=1}^{J} cfh_j \, co_j + \sum_{k=1}^{K} cfw_k \, cg_k + \sum_{l=1}^{L} cf \, d_l \, cz_l \right] + \left[\sum_{i=1}^{I} \sum_{j=1}^{J} ca\mu_{ij} \, c\mu_{ij} + \right.$$

$$\left. \sum_{j=1}^{J} \sum_{k=1}^{K} ca\gamma_{jk} \, c\gamma_{jk} + \sum_{k=1}^{K} \sum_{l=1}^{L} ca\beta_{kl} \, c\beta_{kl} + \sum_{l=1}^{L} \sum_{m=1}^{M} ca\alpha_{lm} \, c\alpha_{lm} \right] \qquad (8\text{-}53)$$

CHAPTER 9

Concurrent Management of Disruptions and Variations

A fail-safe SN is able to handle both (1) variations modifying its planned flow and (2) disruptions distorting its network structure. In Chapter 9, we investigate how risk management decisions made to handle variations in SNs (Chapters 2, 3, 4, and 5) affect or are affected by risk management decisions made to handle disruptions in SNs (see Chapter 1, Figure 1-9). In this chapter, we develop a model to make these decisions concurrently. Numerical analysis of results helps to determine the interactions existing between these two groups of risk management decisions.

9.1 Variations and Disruptions in Supply Networks

Supply networks (SNs) are crucial components of competitive and globalized markets. Companies improve their competitive advantage by working as parts of a SN, which results in lower production costs, higher product quality and greater responsiveness with respect to customers' rapidly changing needs and expectations (Chopra and Sodhi 2004). Conversely, because SNs are globally distributed, they are vulnerable to risks in business and working environments (Schmitt et al. 2010; Peng et al. 2011; Baghalian et al. 2013; Farahani et al. 2014). Therefore, risk management is critical for successful SNs because many different types of risks exist.

According to Sarkar et al. (2002), during the labor strike in 2002, 29 ports on the west coast of the United States were shut down which led to the closure of the new United Motor manufacturing production factory (disruption in transportation facilities). During the destructive earthquake in Japan in 2011, the Toyota Motor Company ceased production in twelve assembly plants to repair production facilities, which resulted in a production loss of 140,000 automobiles (disruption in production facilities). In another instance, Ericsson lost 400 million Euros after their supplier's semiconductor plant was damaged due to a fire in 2000 (disruption in production facilities). The Taiwan earthquake of 1999 resulted in a supply shortage of DRAM chips for Apple that culminated in numerous order losses (variation in supply process). This supply variation has a cascading effect in multi-echelon SNs. For example,[1] consider an apparel supply network: a small variation in machine performance at a thread manufacturing plant in India can cause a four-day delivery delay to a knitter in Malaysia, which can result in a seven-day delivery delay to a dyer in Hong Kong and finally lead to a 10-day delivery delay of trendy, new apparel at a clothing manufacturer in Europe and a loss of sales worth millions of dollars (variation propagation in supply process). Hendricks and Singhal (2005) quantify negative effects of risks in SNs through empirical analysis. Their results demonstrate that risks result in 33 to 40% lower stock returns, a 107% drop in operating income, 7% lower sales growth, and 11% increase in cost.

Clearly, there are numerous sources of risk in SNs. In this chapter, we demonstrate that risk mitigation strategies used by SNs for different risk sources (disruptions and variations) are not independent and important correlations exist among them. Therefore, compartmentalized decision making for the mitigation of variations and disruptions, as done in prior studies, results in sub-optimal solutions.

9.2 Disruption and Variation Management in Supply Networks Literature

Scholars have suggested numerous methods to classify the risks of SNs. Waters (2011) divides SN risk sources into *internal risks* and *external risks* based on their controllability. Internal risks are controllable and appear during normal operations, such as late deliveries, excess stock, poor forecasting, human error and faults in IT systems. External risks are uncontrollable and come from outside a supply network, such as earthquakes, hurricanes, industrial actions, wars, terrorist attacks, price increases, problems with trading partners, shortages of raw materials and crime. Furthermore, Chopra and Sodhi (2004) categorize potential supply chain risks into nine categories: (a) Disruptions (e.g., natural disasters, terrorism, war, etc.), (b) Delays (e.g., inflexibility of supply source), (c) Systems (e.g., information infrastructure breakdown), (d) Forecast (e.g., inaccurate forecast, bullwhip effect, etc.), (e) Intellectual property (e.g., vertical integration), (f) Procurement (e.g., exchange

---

[1]   http://www.decisioncraft.com/dmdirect/variability.htm.

rate risk), (g) Receivables (e.g., number of customers), (h) Inventory (e.g., inventory holding cost, demand and supply uncertainty, etc.) and (i) Capacity (e.g., cost of capacity). These classification schemes are not adequate to analyze correlations among SNs' different risk mitigation strategies. Therefore, we identify and use a different classification. For this classification, risks are categorized into two groups based on the nature of the SNs' decisions that are affected:

- *Disruptions in a SN*: Disruptions refer to rare and unexpected events that have significant impact and distort the topology of a SN by rendering certain facilities or connecting inoperative links. A SN's topology is determined by strategic level network design decisions (see Figure 9-1). Network design decisions are related to determine the number, location and capacity of the facilities (Schmidt and Wilhelm 2010). We summarize certain recent studies that have been conducted in this domain. Tomlin (2006) investigates the unavailability of a supplier in a two echelon SN that includes one manufacturer and two suppliers. Chopra et al. (2007) analyze the appropriate selection of mitigation strategies for a two echelon SN that includes one buyer that is serviced by two suppliers. One of these suppliers is reliable and the other is unreliable but less expensive. Peng et al. (2011) develop a model to design a SN topology that performs well under normal conditions and performs relatively well when unreliable facilities are disrupted. Baghalian et al. (2013) and Mohammaddust et al. (2017) propose a path-based approach to design a robust SN topology for which there is a possibility of disruption in facilities and connecting links. These studies focus only on employing risk mitigation strategies to preserve the performance of SNs or communities against disruptions. Risk mitigation strategies that are utilized to address disruptions are referred to as "Strategic Risk Mitigation (SRM)" strategies in this chapter because they include strategic network design decisions (see Figure 9-1).

- *Variations in a SN*: Variations refer to frequent and expected events with less significant impacts that reduce only the efficiency of flow planning in SNs (see Figure 9-1). Flow planning in a SN refers to production quantities in the SNs' facilities and quantities that are transported among the facilities (Schmidt and Wilhelm 2010). Variations that occur in the performance of upstream facilities in a SN lead to changes in the quantities that flow from these facilities. This type of upstream variation is important because, the perfect

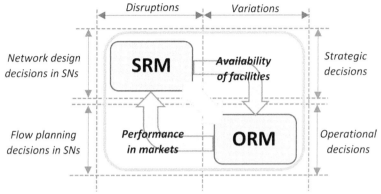

Figure 9-1. Disruptions and variations in SNs.

production system does not exist. Furthermore, increasing the rate of production increases the likelihood of machinery and labor failures, which results in a higher rate of defective items that are produced (Sana 2010). To the best of our knowledge, prior studies generally ignore variations in the performance of multi-echelon SNs (Rezapour et al. 2015).

Downstream variations also occur for market demands; these can be modeled by defining scenarios (Pan and Nagi 2010; Georgiadis et al. 2011; Leung et al. 2007; Lin and Wang 2011; Hasani and Khosrojerdi 2016) or considering demand as a random variable (Shen and Daskin 2005; Santoso et al. 2005; Dada et al. 2007; Schmitt et al. 2010; Baghalian et al. 2013). This type of variation is critical for managing flow and service level estimation in a SN. Prior studies focus only on downstream variations in demand and assume that the performance of the SNs' facilities is perfect. In this study, we demonstrate how upstream variations in the performance of facilities and their propagated impact should be managed in multi-echelon SNs. Prior studies address only variations and their corresponding risk mitigation strategies. Risk mitigation strategies that are utilized to address variations are referred to as "Operational Risk Mitigation (ORM)" strategies in this study because they include operational flow planning decisions (see Figure 9-1).

As illustrated in Figure 9-1, SRM and ORM strategies are not independent. SRM strategies preserve the availability of facilities in a SN's topology. Flow planning is conducted for SNs' available facilities. In addition, ORM strategies increase the efficiency of flow planning in a SN and improve its performance in markets; this performance is used for economic evaluation of SRM strategies. The existing literature mostly ignores this mutual impact between ORM and SRM approaches. Therefore, we contribute to SN risk management literature by answering the following question: What correlations exist between SRM and ORM strategies? Risk mitigation that includes either redundancy or flexibility ensures that SNs are robust, resilient and reliable. The standard use of redundancy includes holding safety stock of material and finished goods (You and Grossmann 2008; Park et al. 2010; Schmitt 2011) or multi-sourcing (Yu et al. 2009; Li et al. 2010; Schmitt and Snyder 2010; Peng et al. 2011; Schmitt 2011). Flexibility implies that facilities have adaptable capacities (Tomlin 2006). In this study, we focus on redundancy in ORM strategies and flexibility in SRM strategies.

9.3 Our Contributions to the Supply Network Literature

This study makes multi-fold contributions to SN risk management literature as follows:

1) **Variation management:** For a multi-echelon SN's flow planning, we consider upstream variations in the performance of facilities in addition to downstream variations in market demands. We demonstrate that local reliability as an ORM strategy should be assigned to each facility to control redundancy (extra production) in production systems against variation. In addition, we demonstrate that a SN's service level is a function of these local reliabilities. Finally, we develop a mathematical model to determine the optimal local reliabilities (ORM strategies) and service levels for the SN (in Section 9.5). Prior studies have ignored upstream variations in flow planning for SNs.

2) **Disruption management:** Considering flexibility as a SRM strategy, we demonstrate that the robustness of a SN's topology for maintaining acceptable performance during and after a disruption depends on its facilities' flexibility levels. The flexibility level of a facility indicates to what extent the capacity of that facility can be increased during a disruption. A SN's resilience is how quickly its performance can be returned to an acceptable level after a disruption; hence we demonstrate that the resilience of a SN depends on the speed of flexibility in its facilities. The flexibility speed of a facility is how rapidly the capacity of that facility can be increased during a disruption. Finally, we develop a mathematical model to determine the optimal flexibility levels and speeds (SRM strategies) to ensure that a SN's facilities are robust and resilient against disruptions (in Section 9.6). In prior studies, the robustness and resilience of SNs against disruptions have been investigated separately.

3) **Integrated decision making for ORM and SRM strategies:** The final model we develop in Section 9.6 facilitates concurrent decision making about reliability (and the facilities' local reliabilities as ORM

strategies), robustness and resilience (and the facilities' flexibility levels and speeds as SRM strategies). Therefore, a sensitivity analysis of this integrated model helps us to determine if correlations exist between ORM and SRM strategies and their corresponding reliability, robustness, and resilience (in Section 9.6.4). In prior studies, decisions regarding SRM and ORM strategies are made independently.

This chapter is organized as follows. In Section 9.4, the details of the problem under normal (without disruption) and disrupted conditions are presented. The mathematical model, solution approach and computational results for the operation of the SN under normal (without disruption) conditions are presented in Section 9.5. In Section 9.6, mathematical modeling, solution approach and computational results for the SN under disrupted conditions are discussed. The chapter is concluded in Section 9.7.

In the context of an architecture for fail-safe networks, as introduced in Section 9.3, we explain the use of reliability, robustness, and resilience for risk management in a SN (see Figure 1-4). The connector is a SN. We express the form of our architecture as an optimization model that determines the best local reliabilities, flexibility levels, and flexibility speeds (properties) for the network's facilities in a way to maximize the total profit (relationship). This model helps us to understand the relationship between the risk management components (reliability, robustness, and resilience). A summary of the problem investigated in Chapter 9 is as follows:

Table 9-1. A summary of the problem investigated in Chapter 9.

Elements	What?
Components	Reliability, Robustness and Resilience
Connectors	Forward supply network
Form	**How?**
Component importance	Reliability: 1, Robustness: 1 and Resilience: 1
Properties	Local reliabilities, Flexibility levels and Flexibility speeds
Relationship	Profit optimization in markets
Rationale	**Why?**
Motivation	Variation and disruption management
Assumptions	There is enough information to quantify variations and disruptions
Constraints	✓ Order amplification in echelons due to variations ✓ Capacity constraints ✓ Market demand depends on service levels, pre-sales market price and after-sales market warranty
Interpretation	Relationship between risk management components (reliability, robustness and resilience)

9.4 Problem Description

Without loss of generality, we consider a simple SN dealing with producing and supplying a product to target markets. This SN has two manufacturers, *M1* and *M2*, manufacturing products and four target markets which are serviced by these two manufacturers through retailers. *M1* fulfills the demands of the first and second markets through the first retailer, *R1*. The third and fourth markets' demands are fulfilled by *M2* through the second retailer, *R2*. The components required by these two manufacturers, *M1* and *M2*, are provided by two suppliers, *S1* and *S2*, respectively. In Figure 9-2, the existing network structure of the SN is shown. Product demand in the markets is a stochastic function of the SN's marketing factors, e.g., price and service level (downstream variations in the SN's markets). Before the beginning of each sales period, retailers determine the quantities of product required and then issue the orders to the corresponding manufacturers. The manufacturers receive the orders from the retailers and plan to produce the ordered products.

We assume that the performance of the manufacturers' production systems are imperfect and they produce a stochastic percentage of defective units in their batches (upstream variations in the SN's manufacturers). To compensate for these defective units, the manufacturers plan to make extra products. To assemble the products, the manufacturers order the required components from their corresponding suppliers. The suppliers' production systems (after initial setup), start producing components in an in-control state with almost zero defects. After a stochastic time, the suppliers' production systems deteriorate to an out-of-control state in which γ percent of output is non-conforming (upstream variations in the SN's suppliers). Similarly, the suppliers plan to produce some surplus components for the manufacturers, to compensate for the non-conforming output of their systems.

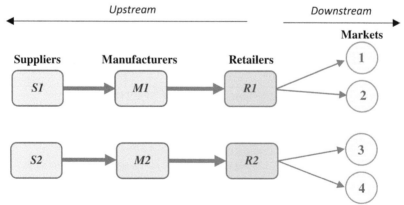

Figure 9-2. The network structure of the SN.

In a SN with multiple imperfect production facilities (multiple types of upstream variation), the conforming component/product quantity is reduced by moving from upstream to downstream in the SN. Modeling this flow reduction is necessary to quantify the conforming product volumes that can be supplied in the last echelon and to determine the best service level which balances the stochastic product demand (downstream variation) and product supply (upstream variation) in the most economical way. To preserve an appropriate service level in the markets, reliable flow planning throughout the SN is required to mitigate upstream and downstream variations. Increasing reliability of facilities is an ORM strategy used to neutralize impacts of variations in flow planning. In Section 9.5, we develop a mathematical model to plan the most profitable reliable flow through the SN. In this chapter, reliability in SNs' flow planning is defined as follows (see Figure 9-3):

Definition 1: Reliable flow planning in SNs employs appropriate ORM strategies to mitigate upstream and downstream variations and their propagation and preserves appropriate service levels for customers in markets.

In addition to variations that affect flow planning in a SN, we also consider the possibility that disruptions affect the availability of facilities in the SN. For the SN model in this study, *M1* is always available, but *M2* is prone to disruption. *M2* may be unavailable to fulfill *R2*'s orders. There may be several reasons which explain why this occurs, e.g., the failure of its machinery or the inability of its supplier (*S2*) to fulfill its order on time. In the event that *M2* is unavailable, the third and fourth markets cannot be served and their sales are lost, which leads to a large loss in the SN's profitability and brand reputation. To avoid this possible loss, we redesign the SN's network (by adding extra capacity to its facilities) to simultaneously provide:

- **Robustness** against disruptions: A robust SN can manage disruptions and maintain service continuity appropriately. To have a robust SN, we must modify the production capabilities of its undisrupted facilities (*M1* and *S1*) to compensate for the unavailability of its disrupted facilities (*M2* and *S2*). For this purpose, the production capacities of *M1* and *S1* must be flexible enough to increase production, when needed, to compensate for the unavailability of disrupted facilities and decrease production when those facilities become available again. For this problem, we seek to determine the flexibility level that is required for the undisrupted facilities, *M1* and *S1*, to have a robust network. The flexibility level of a facility refers to the extent its capacity can be increased when it is needed.

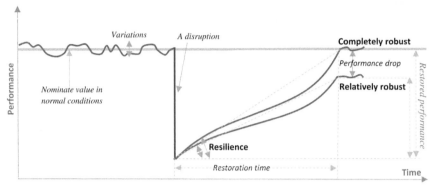

Figure 9-3. Reliability, robustness and resilience in SNs.

- **Resilience** against disruptions: Resilience of a SN is shown by how quickly disruptions can be managed by that SN and depends on the speed of its facilities to increase their capacities after disruptions. This is their flexibility speed. The flexibility speed of a facility is shown by how quickly its capacity can be increased when needed. Therefore, another important decision that must be made is to determine the optimal flexibility speed for the undisrupted facilities, $M1$ and $S1$, to maintain the SN's resilience.

Because numerous definitions exist for SNs' robustness and resilience in risk management literature, the definitions for these terms used in this study are as follows (see Figure 9-3):

Definition 2: A robust SN has appropriate SRM strategies to reduce it's drop in performance when it is affected by disruptions. In Figure 9-3, we show how a SN's robustness can be measured using this definition. After employing SRM strategies, if a SN's performance returns to its nominal value (and the performance drop is zero), it means that the SN is completely robust. Since complete robustness can be very costly for SNs, a relatively robust SN is sometimes preferred, wherein the performance returns to an acceptable level with a finite performance drop.

Definition 3: A resilient SN can use SRM strategies rapidly after disruptions to reduce the restoration time during which the SN's performance returns to the acceptable level that is defined by its robustness. In Figure 9-3, it is shown that a SN's resilience can be measured based on this definition. A SN's resilience is measured by its average restoration rate (ratio of restored performance to restoration time).

Flexibility (including flexibility levels and speed) in facilities is a SRM strategy that is used in this study to neutralize the impacts of disruptions and to design a robust and resilient SN. Our definition for a facility's flexibility is as follows:

Definition 4: A flexible facility can increase its processing capacity when needed. The flexibility level of the facility is the maximum level to which its capacity can be increased. The flexibility speed of a facility is how quickly the capacity can be increased when needed.

The problem of managing a SN's variations and disruptions is done in two steps: (i) use an ORM strategy: in the first step, we ignore disruptions in the SN, focus solely on flow planning and use an ORM strategy against variations (Section 9.5); and (ii) use a SRM strategy: in the second step, we add disruptions to the problem and use a SRM strategy to alleviate these disruptions (Section 9.6).

In this study, we consider a very simple SN that with two supply paths: [$S1 \rightarrow M1 \rightarrow R1$] and [$S2 \rightarrow M2 \rightarrow R2$] (see Figure 9-2). We demonstrate what changes are needed in the first supply path, [$S1 \rightarrow M1 \rightarrow R1$], to substitute for the second supply path, [$S2 \rightarrow M2 \rightarrow R2$], when the latter is unavailable. We consider only two supply paths to simplify this analysis, but the problem is generalizable to more complicated SNs with more supply paths. For a SN with more supply paths, a subset of paths is unavailable during each disruption. To continue servicing customers, each unavailable path must be substituted by an available path and changes similar to those proposed in this study will need to be made in the available path.

9.5 Variation Management

In conditions without disruption, all the facilities ($M1$, $M2$, $S1$ and $S2$) are available. This SN case includes two product supply paths (Figure 9-2):

I) [$S1 \rightarrow M1 \rightarrow R1$] represents the "first supply path", in which the flow of components begins with the first supplier, $S1$. These components then pass through the SN and become finished products at the first manufacturer $M1$ and are transported to the first retailer $R1$, to supply the first and second markets and fulfill their demands.

II) [$S2 \rightarrow M2 \rightarrow R2$] represents the "second supply path", in which the flow of components begins with the second supplier $S2$. These components then pass through the SN and become finished products at the second manufacturer, $M2$ and are transported to the second retailer $R2$, to supply the third and fourth markets and fulfill their demands.

In this section, we discuss reliable flow planning of the first path against variations, in conditions without a disruption (in the second path, it is conducted in the same manner). In Section 9.6, we discuss how this flow planning changes during a disruption, when the second supply path is unavailable.

The first path includes three types of facilities: the supplier (*S1*), the manufacturer (*M1*) and the retailer (*R1*). Each of these facilities faces a specific type of variation. The retailer faces a stochastic demand in the markets. The supplier and manufacturer encounter stochastic non-conforming units in their production batches. For each of these facilities, a desired local reliability must be determined to manage its corresponding variation. As will be demonstrated later, the service level provided by the supply path in the first and second markets is a function of these local reliabilities. We assume that rl_{S1}^{WD}, rl_{M1}^{WD} and rl_{R1}^{WD} represent the local reliabilities of the first supply path's supplier, manufacturer and retailer, respectively, in conditions without any disruptions. In the remainder of this section, the performance of each facility when confronted with its corresponding variation is investigated from downstream to upstream along the supply path (for notation, refer to Appendix 9.A).

9.5.1 Retailer in the First Supply Path R1

The first supply path services the first and second markets. The most important marketing factors in these markets are price, *p*, and service level, *sl*. The service level refers to the probability of fulfilling the realized demand from the retailer's on-hand product inventory. Therefore, the expected demand during each sale period of Market *k* (*k* = 1 and 2), $D_k(p, sl^{WD})$, is a function of these two factors. sl^{WD} represents the service level that is provided by the SN during normal conditions without disruptions. The retailer of the first supply path (*R1*) fulfills the total demand for the first and second markets. Therefore, the average demand for *R1* is $\sum_{k=1}^{2} D_k(p, sl^{WD})$. However, the actual demand is stochastic and varies around this mean value. This variation is treated as a random variable, ε, with a cumulative distribution function $G_{R1}(\varepsilon)$ (variation in *R1*'s demand). The actual demand of *R1* is $\sum_{k=1}^{2} D_k(p, sl^{WD}) \times \varepsilon$. Without loss of generality, we assume $E(\varepsilon) = 1$, which implies $E[\sum_{k=1}^{2} D_k(p, sl^{WD}) \times \varepsilon] = \sum_{k=1}^{2} D_k(p, sl^{WD})$ (Bernstein and Federgruen 2004, 2007).

Prior to the beginning of each sales period, a decision must be made about the quantity of *R1*'s product stock, which is represented by x^{WD} and an order must be issued to the corresponding manufacturer *M1*. After realizing the actual demand, the unit holding cost h^+, and unit shortage cost h^-, are paid by the retailers for each unit of the end-of-the period for inventory and lost sales. Therefore, the expected total cost of *R1*, Π_{R1}^{WD}, should be minimized as in Eq. (9-1):

$$MIN \ \Pi_{R1}^{WD} = h^+ \cdot E\left[x^{WD} - \sum_{k=1}^{2} D_k(p, sl^{WD}) \times \varepsilon\right]^+ + h^- \cdot E\left[\sum_{k=1}^{2} D_k(p, sl^{WD}) \times \varepsilon - x^{WD}\right]^+$$

$$(9\text{-}1)$$

$$S.T. \quad Pr\left[\sum_{k=1}^{2} D_k(p, sl^{WD}) \times \varepsilon \leq x^{WD}\right] \geq rl_{R1}^{WD} \tag{9-2}$$

The constraint in Eq. (9-2) preserves *R1*'s local reliability, which guarantees that in rl_{R1}^{WD} percentage of time, *R1*'s product stock can fulfill the actual demand. The first term in the objective function, Eq. (9-1), represents the expected end-of-period inventory holding cost for *R1* ($[]^+$ is used to compute the expected value of $x^{WD} - \sum_{k=1}^{2} D_k(p, sl^{WD}) \times \varepsilon$ when it is positive). The second term in (1) is the expected cost of lost sales. $x^{WD} = \left[\sum_{k=1}^{2} D_k(p, sl^{WD})\right] . G_{R1}^{-1} \left(\frac{h^-}{h^- + h^+}\right)$ minimizes Π_{R1}^{WD} (see Appendix 9.D for further evidence). Conversely, to satisfy the constraint in Eq. (9-2), we must have $x^{WD} \geq \left[\sum_{k=1}^{2} D_k(p, sl^{WD})\right] . G_{R1}^{-1} (rl_{R1}^{WD})$ (see Appendix 9.D for evidence). Accordingly, the quantity of product that must be ordered for *R1* is calculated as follows:

$$x^{WD} = \left[\sum_{k=1}^{2} D_k(p, sl^{WD})\right] . G_{R1}^{-1} \left(Max\left\{rl_{R1}^{WD}, \frac{h^-}{h^- + h^+}\right\}\right) \tag{9-3}$$

By substituting Eq. (9-3) into (9-1), the least total cost for *R1*, Π_{R1}^{WD*}, is:

$$\Pi_{R1}^{WD*} = \left(h^+ . E\left[G_{R1}^{-1}\left(Max\left\{rl_{R1}^{WD}, \frac{h^-}{h^- + h^+}\right\}\right) - \varepsilon\right]^+ + h^- . E\left[\varepsilon - G_{R1}^{-1}\left(Max\left\{rl_{R1}^{WD}, \frac{h^-}{h^- + h^+}\right\}\right)\right]^+\right) \times \left[\sum_{k=1}^{2} D_k(p, sl^{WD})\right] \tag{9-4}$$

Ordering x^{WD} product units from *M1* enables *R1* to fulfill the product demand for the next sales period with a probability of rl_{R1}^{WD}. Maintaining local reliability, rl_{R1}^{WD} is an ORM strategy that is used by *R1* to manage demand variation. In Section 9.5.2, we demonstrate how *R1*'s order must be increased by moving backward to *M1*.

We assume that each facility either fulfills the order from its downstream facility completely, or misses the order and sends nothing. This assumption is used widely in prior studies in the yield-uncertainty literature and is referred to as the Bernoulli supply process (Parlar et al. 1995; Swaminathan et al. 1999; Dada et al. 2003; Tomlin and Wang 2005).

9.5.2 Manufacturer in the First Supply Path, M1

M1 receives an order for x^{WD} product units from *R1*. *R1*'s order is produced by *M1* in O_{M1} production runs and includes y^{WD} items for each production batch (Figure 9-4). *M1*'s production system is not perfect and always includes an amount of waste. *M1*'s wastage ratio, α_{M1}, depends on the general condition of its machinery and the skills of its labor force and is a

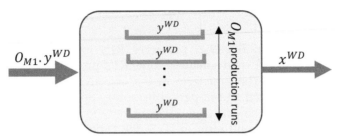

Figure 9-4. Production runs in M1.

random variable with cumulative distribution function G'_{M1} (a variation in M1's production system).

To compensate for waste in its production system *M1*, more products must be produced than *R1*'s order quantity (x^{WD}). This implies that *M1*'s extra production, represented by $O_{M1} \cdot y^{WD} - x^{WD}$, should be positive. The batch size of each production run y^{WD}, must be determined to preserve *M1*'s local reliability, rl_{M1}^{WD} (α_{M1}^i represents the value of random variable α_{M1} realized in production run $i = 1, 2, ..., O_{M1}$) as follows:

$$rl_{M1}^{WD} = \text{PR}(\alpha_{M1}^1 \cdot y^{WD} + \alpha_{M1}^2 \cdot y^{WD} + \alpha_{M1}^3 \cdot y^{WD} + \cdots + \alpha_{M1}^{O_{M1}} \cdot y^{WD} \leq O_{M1} \cdot y^{WD} - x^{WD})$$
(9-5)

To preserve rl_{M1}^{WD} local reliability for *M1*, the number of defective items in all production runs ($\alpha_{M1}^1 \cdot y^{WD} + \alpha_{M1}^2 \cdot y^{WD} + \alpha_{M1}^3 \cdot y^{WD} + \cdots + \alpha_{M1}^{O_{M1}} \cdot y^{WD}$) must be less than the extra production volume ($O_{M1} \cdot y^{WD} - x^{WD}$) with rl_{M1}^{WD} probability, as noted in Eq. (9-5). Without loss of generality, we assume that to manufacture one unit of product, one unit of component is required. Because *M1* will produce $O_{M1} \cdot y^{WD}$ product units, *M1* will issue an order for $O_{M1} \cdot y^{WD}$ component units from it supplier *S1*. This implies that *R1*'s order is increased to $O_{M1} \cdot y^{WD} - x^{WD}$ units in *M1*. Maintaining local reliability, rl_{M1}^{WD}, is an ORM strategy that is used in *M1* to manage variations in its production system. In Section 9.5.3 it is shown that *M1*'s order is further amplified by moving backward to the supplier.

9.5.3 Supplier in the First Supply Path, S1

In the first supply path, *S1* receives an order for $O_{M1} \cdot y^{WD}$ units of component from *M1*. To fulfill this order, O_{S1} production runs are performed by *S1* with z^{WD} items in each production batch. After setting up *S1*'s machines to produce z^{WD} items, all machines work in an in-control state and all the produced components are in perfect condition. Gradually, the machines deteriorate and after a stochastic time, they shift to an out-of-control state. γ_{S1} is the percentage of the produced components which are defective. The deterioration time of the machines, is represented by t, and is a random variable with a G''_{S1} cumulative distribution function. When the production system shifts to an out-of-control state, it remains in that state until the end of the batch production because interrupting the machines is prohibitively expensive (Rosenblatt and Lee 1986; Lee and Rosenblatt 1987). Cap_{S1}^{WD} represents the production capacity of *S1* during each production run with *T* time units. Therefore, the production rate of *S1* is Cap_{S1}^{WD}/T and it requires $T \cdot z^{WD}/Cap_{S1}^{WD}$ time units to produce each production batch. Before the production system deteriorates, all output units are sound, but after the production system deteriorates, γ_{S1} percent are defective. Therefore, the total number of defective units in the product batch *i* (*i* = 1, 2, ..., O_{S1}) is equal to $\left(T \cdot z^{WD}/Cap_{S1}^{WD} - t_i\right) \cdot (\gamma_{S1} \cdot Cap_{S1}^{WD})$. t_i represents the value of random variable *t* in production run *i* (*i* = 1, 2,..., O_{S1}). To preserve the local reliability of *S1*, the following constraint is needed:

$$rl_{S1}^{WD} = \Pr\left(\sum_{i=1}^{O_{S1}} \left(T.z^{WD}/Cap_{S1}^{WD} - t_i\right) \cdot (\gamma_{S1} \cdot Cap_{S1}^{WD}) \leq (O_{S1} \cdot z^{WD}) - (O_{M1} \cdot y^{WD})\right)$$

$$= \Pr\left((T \cdot \gamma_{S1} - 1) \cdot O_{S1} \cdot z^{WD} + O_{M1} \cdot y^{WD} \leq \gamma_{S1} \cdot Cap_{S1}^{WD} \cdot \sum_{i=1}^{O_{S1}} t_i\right) \quad (9\text{-}6)$$

Constraint (6) ensures that with rl_{M1}^{WD} probability, the total number of defective components produced by *S1* will be less than its surplus production quantity, $O_{S1} \cdot z^{WD} - O_{M1} \cdot y^{WD}$. The value of the z^{WD} variable must ensure that the local reliability of *S1* is preserved. Maintaining local reliability rl_{S1}^{WD} is an ORM strategy that is used to manage variations in *S1*'s production system.

The component production batch size (z^{WD}) satisfies Constraint (6) and ensures the ability of *S1* to fulfill *M1*'s entire order with rl_{S1}^{WD} probability. The production batch size (y^{WD}) satisfies Constraint (5) and guarantees the ability of *M1* to fulfill *R1*'s order with rl_{M1}^{WD} probability. The product stock quantity (x^{WD}) satisfies Constraint (3) and assures the ability of *R1* to fulfill the demand of the market during the next sale period with rl_{R1}^{WD} probability. In this case, the first supply path has a guaranteed probability of $rl_{S1}^{WD} \cdot rl_{M1}^{WD} \cdot rl_{R1}^{WD}$ to fulfill the markets' demand. In this problem, this probability of demand fulfillment is referred to as the service level:

$$sl^{WD} = rl_{S1}^{WD} \cdot rl_{M1}^{WD} \cdot rl_{R1}^{WD} \quad (9\text{-}7)$$

The relationship among the local reliabilities of the facilities in the first supply path and the SN's service level in the markets that are serviced by that path is shown in Eq. (9-7).

In this problem, we assume that all variations (in *R1*'s demand, *M1*'s waste ratio, and *S1*'s deterioration time) are random variables with known distribution functions. Because these variations are related to the SNs' short term operational decisions (either weekly or monthly), in practice it is possible to gather historical data to fit an appropriate distribution function. Several statistical methods, e.g., goodness-of-fit, can be used to analyze historical data and fit an appropriate distribution function for variations.

9.5.4 Mathematical Model for ORM Strategy Selection Under without Disruption Conditions

In this section, a mathematical model is presented for planning reliable flow in the SN's first supply path by using the analysis and the relationships presented in Sections 9.5.1–9.5.3:

Max

$$\Psi^{WD} = \left(p - h^+. E\left[G_{R1}^{-1}\left(Max\left\{sl^{WD}, \frac{h^-}{h^- + h^+}\right\}\right) - \varepsilon\right]^+ - h^-. E\left[\varepsilon - G_{R1}^{-1}\left(Max\left\{sl^{WD}, \right.\right.\right.$$

$$\left.\left.\left.\frac{h^-}{h^- + h^+}\right\}\right)\right]^+\right) \times \left[\sum_{k=1}^2 D_k(p, sl^{WD})\right] - c_{S1}.(O_{S1}. z^{WD}) - c_{S1,M1}.(O_{M1}. y^{WD}) - c_{M1}.(O_{M1}. y^{WD}) -$$

$$c_{M1,R1}.(x^{WD}) \tag{9-8}$$

Subject to:

$$O_{S1}. z^{WD} \geq O_{M1}. y^{WD} \tag{9-9}$$

$$O_{M1}. y^{WD} \geq x^{WD} \tag{9-10}$$

$$x^{WD} = \left[\sum_{k=1}^2 D_k(p, sl^{WD})\right]. G_{R1}^{-1}\left(Max\left\{rl_{R1}^{WD}, \frac{h^-}{h^- + h^+}\right\}\right) \tag{9-11}$$

$$rl_{M1}^{WD} = PR(\alpha_{M1}^1. y^{WD} + \alpha_{M1}^2. y^{WD} + \alpha_{M1}^3. y^{WD} + \cdots + \alpha_{M1}^{O_{M1}}. y^{WD} \leq O_{M1}. y^{WD} - x^{WD}) \tag{9-12}$$

$$rl_{S1}^{WD} = Pr\left(\sum_{i=1}^{O_{S1}}\left(T.z^{WD}\Big/_{Cap_{S1}^{WD}} - t_i\right).(\gamma_{S1}. Cap_{S1}^{WD}) \leq (O_{S1}. z^{WD}) - (O_{M1}. y^{WD})\right) \tag{9-13}$$

$$sl^{WD} = rl_{S1}^{WD}. rl_{M1}^{WD}. rl_{R1}^{WD} \tag{9-14}$$

$$y^{WD} \leq Cap_{M1}^{WD} \tag{9-15}$$

$$z^{WD} \leq Cap_{S1}^{WD} \tag{9-16}$$

$$0 \leq rl_{S1}^{WD}, rl_{M1}^{WD} \text{ and } rl_{R1}^{WD} \leq 1 \text{ and } x^{WD}, y^{WD} \text{ and } z^{WD} \geq 0 \tag{9-17}$$

The objective function, Eq. (9-8), is used to maximize total profit during conditions without disruptions. The first term of Eq. (9-8) is used to compute the capturable income after discarding the inventory holding cost for the end-of-period extra inventory and the shortage cost for end-of-period lost sales. The second term is the procurement and production cost of components for *S1*. The third term is the cost of transporting components from *S1* to *M1*. The fourth term is the cost of manufacturing products in *M1*. The fifth term represents the cost of transporting products from *M1* to *R1*. Based on the constraint in Eq. (9-9), the number of components that are planned to be produced by *S1* should be more than *M1*'s order quantity. According to the constraint in Eq. (9-10), the product production quantity in *M1* must be more than *R1*'s order quantity. The constraints in Eqs. (9-11), (9-12) and (9-13) represent the relationship between the order and production quantities in *R1*, *M1* and *S1* and their corresponding local reliabilities. The relationships between the service level during conditions without any disruptions and the local reliabilities of stochastic facilities are illustrated in Eq. (9-14). Equations (9-15) and (9-16) and are used to ensure that the production quantity for each run of *M1* and *S1* is less than its capacity, Cap_{M1}^{WD} and Cap_{S1}^{WD}, respectively. Equations (9-17) is used to ensure that facilities' local reliabilities are selected from the [0, 1] interval.

9.5.5 Solution Procedure for ORM Strategy Selection Under without Disruption Conditions

The mathematical model proposed in Section 9.5.4 is nonlinear. The objective function and certain constraints in this model (such as Eqs. (9-11) and (9-14)) are highly nonlinear. In addition, this model includes two chance constraints, Eqs. (9-12) and (9-13). Because of these chance constraints, our model belongs to the category of Chance Constrained Problem (CCP). CCPs were first introduced by Charnes et al. (1958). For the theoretical background of CCPs, please refer to Prékopa (1995). From an application perspective, CCPs have been used for water management (Dupačová et al. 1991), chemical process optimization (Henrion et al. 2001; Henrion and Möller 2003), and others. Although CCPs were introduced almost 50 years ago, little progress has been made to date. A CCP is extremely difficult to solve even in its linear form because it requires multi-dimensional integration (Pagnoncelli et al. 2009).

In prior studies, two approaches are used to solve CCPs: (1) in the first approach, the probability distribution of the chance constraints is discretized and the combinatorial problem thus obtained, is solved sequentially (Dentcheva et al. 2000; Luedtke and Ahmed 2008); and (2) in the second approach, the chance constraints are substituted by convex approximations (Nemirovski and Shapiro 2006). A well-known approximation approach used to address the CCP is the sample average approximation (SAA). SAA is also referred to as the Monte Carlo method, the Sample Path Optimization (SPO) method and the Stochastic Counterpart (Robinson 1996; Pagnoncelli et al. 2009; Atlason et al. 2008; Luedtke and Ahmed 2008). The SAA approach replaces the actual distribution in chance constraints by an empirical distribution that corresponds to a random sample. Refer to Ruszczynski and Shapiro (2003) for a comprehensive review of this approach. We use SAA to approximate chance constraints. Then, we linearize the model by discretizing reliability variables. The final model is a Mixed Integer Linear Programming (MILP) that is solved by using CPLEX software (for details about linearizing the model, please refer to Appendix 9.B).

9.5.6 *Computational Result: Test Problem*

In this section, we assume that in the first supply path, [S1 → M1 → R1], the performance of production systems for *M1* and *S1* is imperfect. After the equipment is set up in *S1*, the machinery works in an in-control state and all the produced components are in perfect condition. After a stochastic time that follows an exponential distribution with $\mu = 2$, the machinery shifts to an out-of-control state and $\gamma_{S1} = 10\%$ of the output is defective. For *M1*, the product assembly process always includes a stochastic percentage of defective products. This percentage is a random variable with a uniform distribution in the interval $[0, \beta = 0.15]$. The total demand for the first and second markets that should be fulfilled by *R1* is a stochastic linear function of price, $p = \$14$, and service level, sl^{WD}: $\sum_{k=1}^{2} D_k(p, sl^{WD})$. $\varepsilon = [1000 - 150 \times (p - 14) + 1000 \times (sl^{WD} - 0.85)]$. ε. ε is a normally distributed random variable with a mean of 1 and a variance of 1. Prior regression studies that used historical sales data demonstrated that a linear demand function fits very well for ($\sum_{k=1}^{2} D_k, p, sl^{WD}$) triples recorded for past sales periods. Biases of the real and estimated mean demand in these triples are analyzed by conducting a goodness-of-fit statistical test to determine the optimal distribution that represents these biases. The unit production cost for *S1* is \$1.40. The unit transportation cost for moving a component unit from *S1* to *M1* is \$0.50. The unit assembly cost for *M1* and the unit transportation cost from *M1* to *R1* is \$1.00 and \$0.60, respectively. The unit extra inventory and unit shortage costs for *R1* are \$0.10 and \$0.30, respectively. Demand for each period is fulfilled by $O_{S1} = 3$ and $O_{M1} = 4$ production runs.

 Formulating and solving the mathematical model for this problem leads to the following results: the optimal service level for conditions without any disruptions is 80 percent (corresponding to the highest profit in Figure 9-5). In Figure 9-5, each point on Line AB corresponds to a service level $sl^{WD} = rl^{WD}_{S1} \cdot rl^{WD}_{M1} \cdot rl^{WD}_{R1} = 0.8$. Point A (red point) is the optimal (rl^{WD}_{S1},

rl_{M1}^{WD}, rl_{R1}^{WD}) combination that maximizes the Model (Eqs. (9-8)–(9-17)). Other points on Line AB (gray points) are feasible (rl_{S1}^{WD}, rl_{M1}^{WD}, rl_{R1}^{WD}) combinations in the Model (Eqs. (9-8) to (9-17)) that would result in a less than optimal profit for the SN. As illustrated in Figure 9-5, different combinations of local reliabilities for facilities can lead to the same service level, $sl^{WD} = rl_{S1}^{WD} \cdot rl_{M1}^{WD} \cdot rl_{R1}^{WD}$. For all points on line AB, the service level is 0.8, but these correspond to different local reliability combinations and significantly different profit levels. Therefore, for a supply path with multiple stochastic facilities, determining the optimal service level is not sufficient. We must also determine the least costly local reliability combination that supports the required service level. The mathematical model of this problem helps us to determine the optimal local reliability combination, which is calculated as $rl_{S1}^{WD} = 1$, $rl_{M1}^{WD} = 1$ and $rl_{R1}^{WD} = 0.8$. To preserve the local reliability of R1, its product order quantity from M1 must equal $x^{WD} = 1748$. The optimal production quantity for each production run of M1 is 496.15 which implies that M1 produces 236.6 extra units (4. $y^{WD} - x^{WD} = 236.6$). This extra production preserves its local reliability, which is equal to 1. The optimal component production quantity for each production run of S1 is 684.78. This production quantity leads to the extra production of 70 units for S1 ($3.z^{WD} - 4.y^{WD} = 70$). This extra production assures local reliability of 1 for S1.

In the remainder of this section, we analyze the relationships between the local reliabilities of facilities in the supply path and the SN's profitability. For this purpose, we solve the model for different values of local reliabilities. The results are illustrated in the graphs of Figure 9-6. Based on these graphs, we conclude the following:

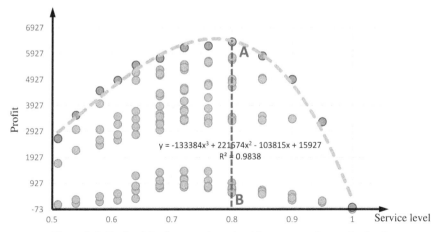

Figure 9-5. Profit of the first supply path with respect to the service level.

- For a given local reliability of *R1*, the patterns that determine the profit change with respect to *S1*'s local reliability, are similar for all local reliabilities of *M1*. This implies that for a given quantity of ordered product, the most profitable local reliabilities for *S1* and *M1* are almost independent. Therefore, separate local reliability determination for these facilities leads to a workable and near optimal solution. This feature decreases the size and computational burden of the mathematical model significantly. Therefore, it is necessary to check this feature for large scale problems to reduce their computational time.

- For a given local reliability of *R1*, the effects of the local reliabilities for *M1* and *S1* on the path's profit are similar. For instance, if reductions

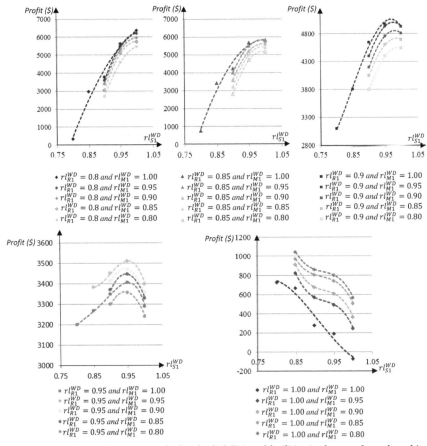

Figure 9-6. Relationships among the local reliabilities of facilities in the supply path and its profitability.

in $S1$'s local reliability lead to profit reductions for the path, reductions in $M1$'s local reliability also lead to profit reductions for the path and vice versa (see $rl_{R1}^{WD} = 1.00$ case in Figure 9-6). If reductions in $S1$'s local reliability first increment the path's profit and then reduce it, reductions in $M1$'s local reliability impose a similar pattern of changes on the path's profit (see $rl_{R1}^{WD} = 0.95$ case in Figure 9-6). Therefore, determining the optimal local reliability for one of these facilities provides a good estimate for the tentative local reliability of another facility. Using this feature significantly reduces the search interval for the local reliability of the other facility. Therefore, it is necessary that we check this feature for large scale problems to reduce the computational time.

In this section, we developed a mathematical model to determine the most profitable local reliability (ORM strategy) for the SN's facilities against their variations. In Section 9.6, we consider the possibility of disruption and demonstrate how the model should be extended to incorporate SRM strategies.

9.6 Disruption Management

The SN is disrupted when $M2$ or $S2$ is unavailable. In this case, the second supply path, $[S2 \rightarrow M2 \rightarrow R2]$, is inoperative and unable to fulfill the demands of the third and fourth markets. Therefore, the only active supply path is $[S1 \rightarrow M1 \rightarrow R1]$ which can be used to fulfill the demands of all markets (Figure 9-7).

To address this disruption, the first supply path must not only service the first and second markets but must also fulfill the demands of the third and fourth markets. For this purpose, its facilities, $S1$ and $M1$, need flexible capacities. Following the onset of a disruption, the capacities of these

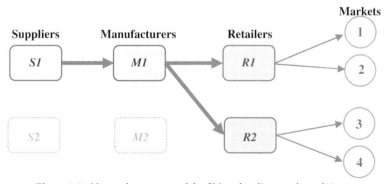

Figure 9-7. Network structure of the SN under disrupted conditions.

facilities should increase to service both retailers and after the duration of the disruption, they should decrease to only service *R1*. The measurement of the extent to which the capacity of a facility can be increased during disruptions is its flexibility level and the length of time that it takes to increase that capacity is its flexibility speed. The robustness of a SN is determined by its flexibility levels and the resilience of a SN is determined by its flexibility speeds. Determining the capacity of a production system is a strategic design problem and depends on factors like the layout of its machinery. Adding capacity is generally a discrete process that involves adding machines to the system (Koren and Shpitalni 2010). Figure 9-8 provides examples of *M1*'s flexibility speed. In this figure, it is assumed that one period that includes four production runs, $O_{M1} = 4$, is the maximum time that is available to increase capacity and the flexibility level of *M1* is equal to Δ_{M1}. These flexibility speed options imply the following:

- **For the first flexibility speed option that is indicated by r^1_{M1} in Figure 9-8:** an amount of time that is equal to three production runs is provided to *M1* to generate the extra capacity. In this extreme case, all of *M1*'s extra capacity Δ_{M1}, is added at the beginning of the last (fourth) production run. The time pattern for this flexibility speed option is $r^1_{M1} = (r1^1_{M1} = 0, r2^1_{M1} = 0, r3^1_{M1} = 0, r4^1_{M1} = \Delta_{M1})$, which implies that capacity increases during the first $(r1^1_{M1})$ second $(r2^1_{M1})$ and third $(r3^1_{M1})$ production runs which are equal to 0 and for the last run $(r4^1_{M1})$ is equal to Δ_{M1};

- **For the second flexibility speed option that is indicated by r^2_{M1} in Figure 9-8:** $r^2_{M1} = (r1^2_{M1} = 0, r2^2_{M1} = 0, r3^2_{M1} = \Delta_{M1}/2, r4^2_{M1} = \Delta_{M1}/2)$;

- **For the third flexibility speed option indicated by r^3_{M1} in Figure 9-8:** $r^3_{M1} = (r1^3_{M1} = \Delta_{M1}/4, r2^3_{M1} = \Delta_{M1}/4, r3^3_{M1} = \Delta_{M1}/4, r4^3_{M1} = \Delta_{M1}/4)$;

- **For the fourth flexibility speed option indicated by r^4_{M1} in Figure 9-8:** $r^4_{M1} = (r1^4_{M1} = \Delta_{M1}/2, r2^4_{M1} = \Delta_{M1}/2, r3^4_{M1} = 0, r4^4_{M1} = 0)$;

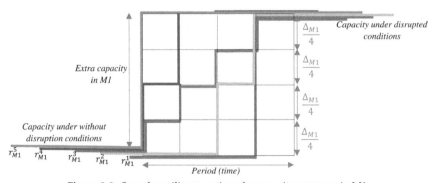

Figure 9-8. Sample resilience options for capacity ramp up in M1.

- **For the fifth flexibility speed option indicated by r_{M1}^5 in Figure 9-8:**
  $r_{M1}^5 = (r1_{M1}^5 = \Delta_{M1}, r2_{M1}^5 = 0, r3_{M1}^5 = 0, r4_{M1}^5 = 0)$;

Therefore, we define a new set, $RO_{M1} = \{r_{M1}\}$, which includes all flexibility speed options that are available for *M1*. Providing extra production capacity costs more during early production runs, following a disruption. Acquiring additional machinery and labor to increase the capacity over a short time can be difficult and costly. Conversely, an early increment in capacity leads to the availability of increased capacity during future production runs and subsequently, more feasible production plans will be available to select from and more uniform production quantities during future production runs are possible. Therefore, we assume that the unit capacity increment cost is higher for early production runs. This assumption is consistent with observations in manufacturing systems (Koren and Shpitalni 2010).

Assuming that parameter cap_{M1}^i ($i = 1, 2, ..., O_{M1}$) represents the unit extra capacity cost for *M1's* production run i, we have $cap_{M1}^1 \geq cap_{M1}^2 \geq cap_{M1}^3 \geq \cdots \geq cap_{M1}^{O_{M1}}$. To determine the flexibility speed option, the binary variables, $w_{M1}^{r_{M1}}$ ($r_{M1} \in RO_{M1}$), are used. Variable $w_{M1}^{r_{M1}}$ is 1 if the flexibility speed option r_{M1} is selected for *M1* and 0 otherwise. In the same manner, Δ_{S1} represents the flexibility level of *S1* and different flexibility speed options are available that are included in the set, $RO_{S1} = \{r_{S1}\}$. Assuming that parameter cap_{S1}^j ($j = 1, 2, ..., O_{S1}$) represents the unit extra capacity cost for *S1's* production run j, we have $cap_{S1}^1 \geq cap_{S1}^2 \geq cap_{S1}^3 \geq \cdots \geq cap_{S1}^{O_{S1}}$. To select the resilience option for *S1*, the binary variables, $w_{S1}^{r_{S1}}$ ($r_{S1} \in RO_{S1}$), are used. Variable $w_{S1}^{r_{S1}}$ is 1 if the resilience option r_{S1} is selected for *S1* and 0 otherwise.

When a disruption occurs in the second supply path, the capacities of the first supply path's facilities, *M1* and *S1*, shift from their without disruption values, Cap_{M1}^{WD} and Cap_{S1}^{WD}, to capacity values that are suitable for the disrupted condition, Cap_{M1}^D and Cap_{S1}^D, based on the flexibility speed options that are selected. The time period in which the undisrupted capacity of a facility, Cap_{M1}^{WD} or Cap_{S1}^{WD}, shifts to its disrupted condition capacity, Cap_{M1}^D or Cap_{S1}^D, is referred to here as the ramp-up disruption period. The production capacities of *M1* and *S1* are not fixed during this ramp-up disruption period and may change for each production run. In Section 9.6.1, we elaborate on the production plan in the first supply path's facilities in the ramp-up disruption period. After the ramp-up period, capacity Cap_{M1}^D and Cap_{S1}^D are available for *M1* and *S1* for all production runs until the disruption dissipates. The disrupted periods that occur after ramp-up period are referred to as normal-disruption periods. In Section 9.6.2, we elaborate on the production plan in the first supply path's facilities for a normal-disruption period. When the disruption

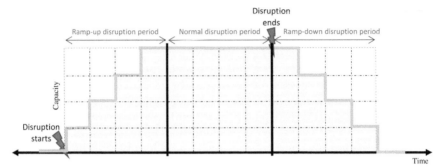

Figure 9-9. Ramp-up, normal disruption and ramp-down periods for a disruption lasting for two periods.

ends, the extra capacity is not needed in the facilities of the first supply path. Therefore, the capacities of M1 and S1 must be reduced from Cap_{M1}^D and Cap_{S1}^D to Cap_{M1}^{WD} and Cap_{S1}^{WD}, respectively. The time period after the disruption is referred to as the ramp-down disruption period. The ramp-down disruption period is also the without disruption period; the only difference is that extra capacity is available. In Section 9.6.3, we elaborate on the production plan in the first supply path's facilities for a ramp-down disruption period. In Figure 9-9, we illustrate these periods for r_{M1}^3 (one of the flexibility speed options illustrated in Figure 9-8) when the disruption lasts for only two periods. In this case, there is one ramp-up, one normal and one ramp-down disruption period. For longer disruptions, more than one normal disruption period would occur.

9.6.1 Ramp-up Disruption Period (see Figure 9-9)

The capacity of facilities in the first supply path (S1 and M1) in each production run of the ramp-up disruption period depends on their selected flexibility speed options. Assume that y_i^{RUD} and z_i^{RUD} variables represent the production quantity in the ramp-up disruption period's production run i of M1 and S1 respectively.

During the ramp-up disruption period, each facility's production quantity in each production run must be less than its available capacity. Hence the following restrictions are required for these facilities:

$$y_i^{RUD} \leq Cap_{M1}^{WD} + \sum_{r_{M1}=1}^{|RO_{M1}|} \left(\sum_{j=1}^{i} rj_{M1}^{r_{M1}} \right). w_{M1}^{r_{M1}} \quad (i = 1, 2, \ldots, O_{M1}) \quad (9\text{-}18)$$

$$z_i^{RUD} \leq Cap_{S1}^{WD} + \sum_{r_{S1}=1}^{|RO_{S1}|} \left(\sum_{j=1}^{i} rj_{S1}^{r_{S1}} \right). w_{S1}^{r_{S1}} \quad (i = 1, 2, \ldots, O_{S1}) \quad (9\text{-}19)$$

Only one of the available options for the flexibility speed of each facility can be selected. Hence:

$$\sum_{r_{M1}=1}^{|RO_{M1}|} w_{M1}^{r_{M1}} = 1 \qquad (9\text{-}20)$$

$$\sum_{r_{S1}=1}^{|RO_{S1}|} w_{S1}^{r_{S1}} = 1 \qquad (9\text{-}21)$$

In the disrupted periods, the total product order received by *M1*, x^D, is as follows:

$$x^D = x_1^D + x_2^D \qquad (9\text{-}22)$$

$$x_1^D = [\Sigma_{k=1}^2 \, D_k(p, \, sl^D)]. \, G_{R1}^{-1}\left(Max\left\{rl_{R1}^D, \frac{h^-}{h^- + h^+}\right\}\right) \qquad (9\text{-}23)$$

$$x_2^D = [\Sigma_{k=3}^4 \, D_k(p, \, sl^D)]. \, G_{R2}^{-1}\left(Max\left\{rl_{R2}^D, \frac{h^-}{h^- + h^+}\right\}\right) \qquad (9\text{-}24)$$

In these equations, x_1^D and x_2^D represent the orders issued by *R1* and *R2* respectively. As explained in Section 9.5, Eqs. (9-23) and (9-24) determine the ordering quantities of the retailers in a way so as to preserve their local reliabilities under disrupted conditions, rl_{R1}^D and rl_{R2}^D.

sl^D represents the service level that is provided by the SN during disruptions. To preserve the local reliabilities of *M1* and *S1* during a disruption, rl_{M1}^D and rl_{S1}^D, the following equations are necessary:

$$rl_{M1}^D = \Pr(\Sigma_{i=1}^{O_{M1}} \alpha_{M1}^i. \, y_i^{RUD} \leq \Sigma_{i=1}^{O_{M1}} y_i^{RUD} - x^D) \qquad (9\text{-}25)$$

$$rl_{S1}^D = \Pr\left((\gamma_{S1}.T - 1). \, \Sigma_{i=1}^{O_{S1}} z_i^{RUD} + \Sigma_{j=1}^{O_{M1}} y_j^{RUD} \leq \Sigma_{k=1}^{O_{S1}} \gamma_{S1}. \, t_k. \left(Cap_{S1}^{WD} + \right.\right.$$
$$\left.\left. \Sigma_{r_{S1}=1}^{|RO_{S1}|} \left(\Sigma_{j=1}^i rj_{S1}^{r_{S1}}\right). \, w_{S1}^{r_{S1}}\right)\right) \qquad (9\text{-}26)$$

Based on Eq. (9-25), the sum of defective products for all production runs in the ramp-up disruption period is less than the added manufacturing quantity, $\Sigma_{i=1}^{O_{M1}} y_i^{RUD} - x^D$, with a probability of rl_{M1}^D. Equation (9-26) is used to ensure that the number of defective components for all production runs of *S1* during the ramp-up disruption period is less than the added production quantity with a probability of rl_{S1}^D. Equation (9-26) is a simplified version of the following equation, which is the modified version of Eq. (9-13):

$$rl_{S1}^D = \Pr\left(\Sigma_{k=1}^{O_{S1}}\left(\frac{T.z_k^{RUD}}{Cap_{S1}^{WD} + \Sigma_{r_{S1}=1}^{|RO_{S1}|}\left(\Sigma_{j=1}^k rj_{S1}^{r_{S1}}\right). \, w_{S1}^{r_{S1}}} - t_k\right). \, \gamma_{S1}. \left(Cap_{S1}^{WD} + \right.\right.$$
$$\left.\left. \Sigma_{r_{S1}=1}^{|RO_{S1}|} \left(\Sigma_{j=1}^k rj_{S1}^{r_{S1}}\right). \, w_{S1}^{r_{S1}}\right) \leq \left(\Sigma_{i=1}^{O_{S1}} z_i^{RUD}\right) - \left(\Sigma_{j=1}^{O_{M1}} y_j^{RUD}\right)\right) \qquad (9\text{-}27)$$

Similarly, to the service level in conditions without disruption shown in Eq. (9-14), the service levels provided by *R1* and *R2* to their markets during the ramp-up disruption period are rl^D_{S1}, rl^D_{M1}, rl^D_{R1} and rl^D_{S1}, rl^D_{M1}, $rl^D_{R2'}$ respectively. Without loss of generality, we assume that identical service levels are provided for all markets, which implies that $rl^D_{R1} = rl^D_{R2}$. Therefore, rl^D_R represents the local reliability of both retail facilities. Using a model that assumes similar service levels makes it easier to analyze the relationship between a SN's ORM and SRM strategies. Using this assumption, the service level for all markets under disrupted conditions is as follows:

$$sl^D = rl^D_{S1} \cdot rl^D_{M1} \cdot rl^D_R \tag{9-28}$$

The total profit that can be captured in the ramp-up disruption period is as follows:

$$\Psi^{RUD} =$$

$$\left\{ \left[\left(p - h^+ \cdot E\left[G^{-1}_{R1}\left(Max\left\{sl^D, \frac{h^-}{h^- + h^+}\right\}\right) \right] - \varepsilon \right]^+ - h^- \cdot E\left[\varepsilon - G^{-1}_{R1}\left(Max\left\{sl^D, \frac{h^-}{h^- + h^+}\right\}\right) \right]^+ \right) \times \right.$$

$$[\Sigma^2_{k=1} D_k(p, sl^D)] + \left(p - h^+ \cdot E\left[G^{-1}_{R2}\left(Max\left\{sl^D, \frac{h^-}{h^- + h^+}\right\}\right) \right] - \varepsilon \right]^+ - h^- \cdot E\left[\varepsilon - \right.$$

$$\left. G^{-1}_{R2}\left(Max\left\{sl^D, \frac{h^-}{h^- + h^+}\right\}\right) \right] \times [\Sigma^4_{k=3} D_k(p, sl^D)] \right\}$$

$$-c_{S1} \cdot \left(\Sigma^{O_{S1}}_{i=1} z^{RUD}_i\right) - c_{S1,M1} \cdot \left(\Sigma^{O_{M1}}_{i=1} y^{RUD}_i\right) - c_{M1} \cdot \left(\Sigma^{O_{M1}}_{i=1} y^{RUD}_i\right)$$

$$- c_{M1,R1} \cdot x^D_1 - c_{M1,R2} \cdot x^D_2$$

$$- \Sigma^{O_{M1}}_{i=1} Cap^i_{M1} \cdot \left(\Sigma^{|RO_{M1}|}_{r_{M1}=1} ri^{r_{M1}}_{M1} \cdot w^{r_{M1}}_{M1}\right) - \Sigma^{O_{S1}}_{j=1} Cap^j_{S1} \cdot \left(\Sigma^{|RO_{S1}|}_{r_{S1}=1} rj^{r_{S1}}_{S1} \cdot w^{r_{S1}}_{S1}\right)$$

$$- \Sigma^{O_{M1}}_{i=1} h^i_{M1} \cdot \left(Cap^{WD}_{M1} + \Sigma^{|RO_{M1}|}_{r_{M1}=1} (\Sigma^i_{j=1} rj^{r_{M1}}_{M1}) \cdot w^{r_{M1}}_{M1} - y^{RUD}_i\right)$$

$$- \Sigma^{O_{S1}}_{i=1} h^i_{S1} \cdot \left(Cap^{WD}_{S1} + \Sigma^{|RO_{S1}|}_{r_{S1}=1} (\Sigma^i_{j=1} rj^{r_{S1}}_{S1}) \cdot w^{r_{S1}}_{S1} - z^{RUD}_i\right) \tag{9-29}$$

Most of the terms in this function were explained in Section 9.5. However, the last four terms are new. The first two new terms represent the cost of adding capacity to the production runs of *M1* and *S1*, respectively. The last two new terms are related to the unused capacity costs for *M1* and *S1*, respectively.

9.6.2 The Normal Disruption Period (see Figure 9-9)

A disruption that continues after the ramp-up disruption period results in at least one normal disruption period. The capacities of $M1$ and $S1$ for all production runs during a normal disruption period are calculated as $Cap_{M1}^D = Cap_{M1}^{WD} + \Delta_{M1}$ and $Cap_{S1}^D = Cap_{S1}^{WD} + \Delta_{S1}$, respectively. The total product order received by $M1$ during a normal disruption period is similar to the ramp-up period:

$$x^D = x_1^D + x_2^D \tag{9-30}$$

$$x_1^D = [\Sigma_{k=1}^2 \, D_k \, (p, \, sl^D)]. \, G_{R1}^{-1}\left(Max\left\{rl_R^D, \frac{h^-}{h^- + h^+}\right\}\right) \tag{9-31}$$

$$x_2^D = [\Sigma_{k=3}^4 \, D_k \, (p, \, sl^D)]. \, G_{R2}^{-1}\left(Max\left\{rl_R^D, \frac{h^-}{h^- + h^+}\right\}\right) \tag{9-32}$$

Variables y^{ND} and z^{ND} represent the production quantities for the production runs during a normal disruption period for $M1$ and $S1$, respectively. The amount of production for each run of these facilities must be less than their available capacities. Therefore, the following restrictions are imposed on the facilities:

$$y^{ND} \leq Cap_{M1}^{WD} + \Delta_{M1} \tag{9-33}$$

$$z^{ND} \leq Cap_{S1}^{WD} + \Delta_{S1} \tag{9-34}$$

It is assumed that rl_{S1}^D, rl_{M1}^D and rl_R^D represent the local reliabilities of the first supply path's supplier, manufacturer and retailers, respectively, during disruptions. To preserve these local reliabilities during normal disruption periods, the following equations become necessary:

$$rl_{M1}^D = \Pr(\Sigma_{i=1}^{O_{M1}} \alpha_{M1}^i \cdot y^{ND} \leq O_{M1} \cdot y^{ND} - x^D) \tag{9-35}$$

$$rl_{S1}^D = \Pr\left(\Sigma_{i=1}^{O_{S1}}\left(\frac{T.z^{ND}}{Cap_{S1}^{WD} + \Delta_{S1}} - t_i\right). \, \gamma_{S1}. \, \left(Cap_{S1}^{WD} + \Delta_{S1}\right) \leq (O_{S1}. \, z^{ND}) - (O_{M1}. \, y^{ND})\right)$$

$$= \Pr\left((T.\gamma_{S1} - 1). \, O_{S1}. \, z^{ND} + O_{M1}. \, y^{ND} \leq \gamma_{S1}. \, (Cap_{S1}^{WD} + \Delta_{S1}). \, \Sigma_{i=1}^{O_{S1}} t_i\right) \tag{9-36}$$

The total profit that can be captured during the normal disruption period is calculated as follows:

$$\Psi^{ND} =$$

$$\left\{ \left(\left[p - h^+ . E\left[G_{R1}^{-1}\left(Max\left\{ sl^D, \frac{h^-}{h^- + h^+} \right\} \right) - \varepsilon \right]^+ - h^- . E\left[\varepsilon - G_{R1}^{-1}\left(Max\left\{ sl^D, \frac{h^-}{h^- + h^+} \right\} \right) \right]^+ \right) \times \right.$$

$$[\Sigma_{k=1}^2 D_k(p, sl^D)] + \left(p - h^+ . E\left[G_{R2}^{-1}\left(Max\left\{ sl^D, \frac{h^-}{h^- + h^+} \right\} \right) - \varepsilon \right]^+ - h^- . E\left[\varepsilon - \right. \right.$$

$$\left. \left. G_{R2}^{-1}\left(Max\left\{ sl^D, \frac{h^-}{h^- + h^+} \right\} \right) \right]^+ \right) \times [\Sigma_{k=3}^4 D_k(p, sl^D)] \right\}$$

$$- c_{S1}. (O_{S1}. z^{ND}) - c_{S1,M1}. (O_{M1}. y^{ND}) - c_{M1}. (O_{M1}. y^{ND})$$

$$- c_{M1,R1}. x_1^D - c_{M1,R2}. x_2^D$$

$$- \Sigma_{i=1}^{O_{M1}} h_M^i. \left(Cap_{M1}^{WD} + \Delta_{M1} - y^{ND} \right)$$

$$- \Sigma_{i=1}^{O_{S1}} h_{S1}^i. \left(Cap_{S1}^{WD} + \Delta_{S1} - z^{ND} \right) \tag{9-37}$$

9.6.3 The Ramp-down Disruption Period (see Figure 9-9)

During the ramp-down disruption period, the disruption is terminated and the second supply path is available again to service its corresponding markets. During this period, the production plan is similar to normal periods that do not have a disruption as discussed in Section 9.5. The only difference is that certain extra production capacities have been added to the non-disrupted facilities, M1 and S1. Therefore, the total profit during the ramp-down disruption period is calculated as follows:

$$\Psi^{RD} = \Psi^{WD*} - \sum_{i=1}^{O_{M1}} h_{M1}^i. \left[\sum_{r_{M1}=1}^{|RO_{M1}|} \left(\sum_{j=1}^{O_{M1}-(i-1)} rj_{M1}^{r_{M1}} \right). w_{M1}^{r_{M1}} \right]$$

$$- \sum_{i=1}^{O_{S1}} h_{S1}^i. \left[\sum_{r_{S1}=1}^{|RO_{S1}|} \left(\sum_{j=1}^{O_{M1}-(i-1)} rj_{S1}^{r_{S1}} \right). w_{S1}^{r_{S1}} \right] \tag{9-38}$$

Ψ^{WD*} is the solution of the model without disruption that is given in Eqs. (9-8) to (9-17) and represents the highest profit that can be achieved during each period that does not have a disruption. The second and third terms of Eq. (9-38) represent the unused capacity costs for M1 and S1, respectively.

9.6.4 Mathematical Model for ORM and SRM Strategy Selection under Disrupted Conditions

We define different scenarios by the length of the disruptions. The number of normal disruption periods is different for each scenario. Set $SCE = \{s\}$

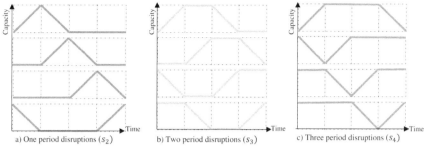

Figure 9-10. Sample scenarios for the length of disruption.

includes all possible scenarios. In Figure 9-10, set *SCE* is assumed to include four scenarios, i.e., $\{s_1, s_2, s_3, s_4\}$. Scenario s_1 represents the without disruption case. The remaining scenarios are described below.

✓ **In Scenario s_2:** the disruption continues for only one period. Therefore, there is no normal disruption period. In this case, the planning horizon spanning four sales periods has one ramp-up disruption, one ramp-down disruption and two without disruption sales periods.

✓ **In Scenario s_3:** the disruption continues for two periods. Therefore, there is only one normal disruption period. In this case, the planning horizon includes one ramp-up disruption, one ramp-down disruption, one normal disruption and one without disruption period.

✓ **In Scenario s_4:** the disruption continues for three periods and there are two normal disruption periods. In this case, the planning horizon includes one ramp-up disruption, one ramp-down disruption, and two normal disruption periods.

Each of these disruption scenarios, $s \in SCE$, occurs with a probability of pr_s. It is clear that:

$$\sum_{s=1}^{|SCE|} pr_s = 1 \qquad (9\text{-}39)$$

Parameters num_s^{WD}, num_s^{RUD}, num_s^{ND} and num_3^{RD} respectively show the number of without disruption, ramp-up disruption, normal disruption and ramp-down disruption periods in scenario $s \in SCE$. Flexibility level decisions (represented by Δ_{M1} and Δ_{S1} variables) and flexibility speed decisions (represented by $w_{M1}^{r_{M1}}$ and $w_{S1}^{r_{S1}}$) for the first supply path's facilities should be made in a manner that maximizes the expected profit for all possible disruption scenarios. Therefore, the objective function of the SN under disrupted conditions is as follows:

$$Max \quad \Psi = \sum_{S=1}^{|SCE|} pr_s \cdot [num_s^{WD} \cdot \Psi^{WD*} + num_s^{RUD} \cdot \Psi^{RUD} + num_s^{ND} \cdot \Psi^{ND} + num_s^{RD} \cdot \Psi^{RD}]$$
$$(9\text{-}40)$$

Subject to: (18-26), (28) and (33-36)   (9-41)

$$\Delta_{M1}, \Delta_{S1}, y_i^{RUD}, z_j^{RUD}, y^{ND}, z^{ND}, x^D, x_1^D, x_2^D, sl^D, rl_{S1}^D, rl_{M1}^D, rl_R^D \geq 0$$

$$(i = 1, 2,..., O_{M1} \text{ and } j = 1, 2, ..., O_{S1})$$ (9-42)

$$w_{M1}^{r_{M1}}, w_{S1}^{r_{S1}} \in \{0,1\} \qquad (\forall r_{M1} \in RO_{M1}, \forall r_{S1} \in RO_{S1})$$ (9-43)

The mathematical model of disrupted conditions is a CCP similar to the model that was developed in Section 9.5 for normal conditions without any disruptions (the model in Eqs. (9-8) to (9-17)). The objective function of the model and the constraints that are presented in Eqs. (9-23), (9-24) and (9-41) are non-linear. The constraints in Eqs. (9-25), (9-26), (9-35) and (9-36) are chance constraints. This model can be linearized using the approach described in Section 9.5. Appendix 9.C provides more information about the size of the problems that can be solved by this model.

This model is used simultaneously to determine the most profitable: (1) local reliabilities for the SN's facilities against their corresponding variations (ORM strategies) and (2) flexibility levels and speed for its non-disrupted facilities that can compensate for the unavailability of its disrupted facilities and ensure the SN remains robust and resilient (SRM strategies). This concurrent determination makes it possible to determine what correlations exist between optimal ORM and SRM strategies in SNs. These correlations are investigated in Section 9.6.5.

9.6.5 Computational Result: Extension of Test Problem

In this section, we extend the test problem that was investigated in Section 9.5.6. We assume that disruption is possible in the second supply path, for which the total demand of the third and fourth markets is calculated as $\sum_{k=3}^4 D_k(p, sl^D)$. $\varepsilon = [850 - 150 \times (p - 14) + 900 \times (sl^D - 0.85)]$. ε and should be fulfilled by the first supply path. ε is a normal random variable with mean of 1 and variance of 1. Four different scenarios for the length of disruption are possible in this problem, $SCE = \{s_1, s_2, s_3, s_4\}$. There is no disruption in Scenario s_1. Scenarios s_2, s_3 and s_4 represent disruptions with zero, one and two normal disruption periods. The probabilities of these scenarios are as follows: $p_{s1} = .83$, $p_{s2} = .04$, $p_{s3} = .10$ and $p_{s4} = .03$.

The cost of adding extra capacity for each production run of *M1* is $Cap_{M1}^1 = \$1$, $Cap_{M1}^2 = \$0.8$, $Cap_{M1}^3 = \$0.65$, and $Cap_{M1}^4 = \$0.55$, respectively. The cost of adding extra capacity for the first, second and third production runs of *S1* is $Cap_{S1}^1 = \$1$, $Cap_{S1}^2 = \$0.7$, and $Cap_{S1}^3 = \$0.5$. The extra capacity cost for *S1* and *M1* in all production runs is $h_{S1}^i = h_{M1}^j = 0.10$ $(i = 1, ..., O_{S1}$ and $j = 1, ..., O_{M1})$. The production and transportation cost components are similar to those in Section 9.5.6. The only new cost component is $c_{M1,R2}$ = \$0.70 (the cost of transporting a unit of product from $M1$ to $R2$). Based on the optimal production quantities that were determined for the production runs of the test problem in Section 9.5.6, we assume Cap^{WD}_{S1} = 800 and Cap^{WD}_{M1} = 500. Five different options for $M1$'s flexibility speed are assumed:

$$r^1_{M1} = (r1^1_{M1} = 0, r2^1_{M1} = 0, r3^1_{M1} = 0, r4^1_{M1} = \Delta_{M1}), r^2_{M1} = \left(r1^2_{M1} = 0, r2^2_{M1} = 0, r3^2_{M1} = \frac{\Delta_{M1}}{2},\right.$$

$$r4^2_{M1} = \frac{\Delta_{M1}}{2}\right), r^3_{M1} = \left(r1^3_{M1} = \frac{\Delta_{M1}}{4}, r2^3_{M1} = \frac{\Delta_{M1}}{4}, r3^3_{M1} = \frac{\Delta_{M1}}{4}, r4^3_{M1} = \frac{\Delta_{M1}}{4}\right), r^4_{M1} =$$

$$\left(r1^4_{M1} = \frac{\Delta_{M1}}{2}, r2^4_{M1} = \frac{\Delta_{M1}}{2}, r3^4_{M1} = 0, r4^4_{M1} = 0\right), \text{ and } r^5_{M1} = (r1^5_{M1} = \Delta_{M1}, r2^5_{M1} = 0,$$

$$r3^5_{M1} = 0, r4^5_{M1} = 0).$$

In addition, for $S1$, five flexibility speed options are considered:

$$r^1_{S1} = (r1^1_{S1} = 0, r2^1_{S1} = 0, r3^1_{S1} = \Delta_{S1}), r^2_{S1} = \left(r1^2_{S1} = 0, r2^2_{S1} = \frac{\Delta_{S1}}{3},\right.$$

$$r3^2_{S1} = 2\frac{\Delta_{S1}}{3}\right), r^3_{S1} = \left(r1^3_{S1} = \frac{\Delta_{S1}}{3}, r2^3_{S1} = \frac{\Delta_{S1}}{3}, r3^3_{S1} = \frac{\Delta_{S1}}{3}\right), r^4_{S1} = \left(r1^4_{S1} = 2\frac{\Delta_{S1}}{3}, r2^4_{S1} = \frac{\Delta_{S1}}{3},\right.$$

$$r3^4_{S1} = 0\right) \text{ and } r^5_{S1} = (r1^5_{S1} = \Delta_{S1}, r2^5_{S1} = 0, r3^5_{S1} = 0). \text{ We solved this model using}$$
CPLEX Concert Technology on a Dell laptop computer with Windows 10, an Intel i7 processor, and 8 GB of installed RAM. The computational time was less than 6 minutes.

Solving the model of this problem leads to the following results. The optimal service level for the disrupted condition is 80 percent and the best supporting local reliability combination is $rl^D_{S1} = 1$, $rl^D_{M1} = 1$ and $rl^D_R = 0.8$. To preserve these local reliabilities, the required flexibility levels of $S1$ and $M1$ are $\Delta_{S1} = 555.2$ and $\Delta_{M1} = 634.9$, respectively. The optimal flexibility speed for $M1$ is $w^3_{M1} = 1$, which implies that uniform capacity scalability is preferred for this facility. The optimal flexibility speed for $S1$ is $w^5_{S1} = 1$, which implies that all extra capacity is added at the beginning of the first production run after disruption. Ordering and production quantities for the production runs of the first supply path's facilities during the ramp-up and normal disruption periods are represented in Figures 9-11 and 9-12, respectively.

The average profit of the first supply path, with respect to the disrupted condition's service level, is displayed in Figure 9-13. When comparing Figures 9-5 and 9-13, it can be noted that the profit reduction on both sides of the most profitable service level is less during the disrupted condition than for the condition without disruption. This gentler reduction is due to: (1) the higher potential demand that is assigned to this path during the disrupted condition in which the first supply path services the first, second, third and fourth markets and (2) decreased sensitivity of the third

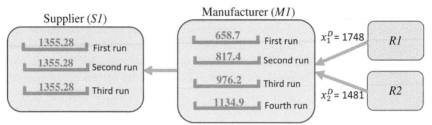

Figure 9-11. Flow dynamics in the first supply path during the ramp-up disruption period.

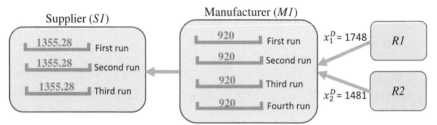

Figure 9-12. Flow dynamics in the first supply path during the normal disruption period.

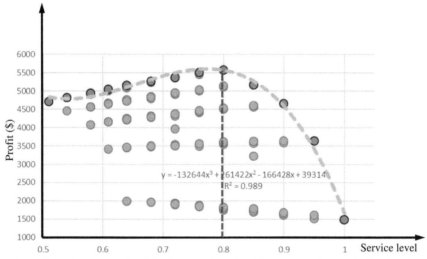

Figure 9-13. Average profit of the first supply path with respect to the service level under disruption.

and fourth markets with respect to the service level (the service level sensitivity parameter in these markets is 900).

This study's example was constructed using assumptions that are often used in prior studies regarding SNs. We tried to be as comprehensive as possible by considering different common options. Here, we summarize assumptions (and their references) and options that were considered in our example:

- *Density function for variations:* we consider three different density functions for variations in the SN
  - Normal distribution for the market's demands (Bernstein and Federgruen 2007; Bernstein and Federgruen 2004; Santoso et al. 2005; Shen and Daskin 2005; Baghalian et al. 2013; Rezapour et al. 2016a; Rezapour et al. 2016b; Mohammaddust et al. 2017)
  - Uniform distribution for the manufacturers' wastage ratio (Rezapour et al. 2015; Rezapour et al. 2016a; Rezapour et al. 2016b)
  - Exponential distribution for the suppliers' deterioration time (Rosenblatt and Lee 1986; Lee and Rosenblatt 1987)
- *Demand functions:* we assume that the markets' demand is a linearly decreasing function of price and a linearly increasing function of service level. This assumption is widely used in prior studies regarding SNs such as Bernstein and Federgruen (2004, 2007), Carr and Karmarkar (2005), Ha et al. (2003), Jiang and Wang (2010), Zhang and Rushton (2008), Rezapour and Farahani (2014), and Rezapour et al. (2017, 2016a, 2016b).
- *Duration of the disruption:* we consider different scenarios for the duration of the disruption in the SN (Schmitt 2011; Klibi and Martel 2012).
- *Extra capacity costs:* we assume that providing extra production capacity is costlier during the early production runs following a disruption. This assumption is consistent with observations in manufacturing systems (Koren and Shpitalni 2010).

In this problem, there are three important risk mitigation strategies (one ORM and two SRM strategies) that determine the behavior of the SN when faced with variations and disruptions:

I) **Robustness** of the SN's structure/topology against disruptions: this feature of the SN's structure/topology depends on the levels of flexibility that are assigned to its facilities (SRM),

II) **Resilience** of the SN's structure/topology against disruptions: this feature of the SN's structure/topology depends on the flexibility speeds assigned to its facilities (SRM),

III) **Reliability** of the SN's flow planning against variations: this feature of the SN's flow dynamics depends on the local reliabilities assigned to its facilities (ORM).

In the remainder of this section, the correlations among the ORM and SRM strategies are investigated. For this purpose, we solve the model for our example and conduct a sensitivity analysis to analyze the correlations.

Correlation between robustness and resilience

First, we analyze the relationship between the two SRM strategies: the flexibility levels and flexibility speeds that are assigned to the SN's facilities (*M1* and *S1*). We solve the mathematical model (Model Eqs. (9-53) to (9-56)) for 3 scenarios for the disruption duration and use 5 different values for the retailer's local reliability to change order quantities in the SN, 5 different values for the local reliability of *M1*, and 5 different values for the local reliability of *S1* to provide more variety in the markets' service levels. We solved 375 problems and summarize their results in Figures 9-14, 9-15 and 9-16. By increasing the local reliability of the retailer in the model, more products are ordered from the first supply path and consequently, greater extra capacity or more flexibility level, is needed in its facilities to address the disruptions. Therefore, the flexibility levels that are assigned to the facilities increase in the model's solution. In addition, we follow the trend of changes in the flexibility speeds that are assigned to the facilities to determine whether there is a correlation between the flexibility levels and flexibility speeds. These results are summarized in Figure 9-14.

In Figure 9-14, the changes in the flexibility speeds of *S1* and *M1* with respect to their flexibility levels are shown for different values of rl_R^D. For instance, in $rl_R^D = 0.80$, when the flexibility level of *S1*, Δ_{S1}, is less than 70 (capacity units), the flexibility speed assigned by the model to this facility is rl_{S1}^5. This implies that the most rapid increase, or the highest flexibility speed, is selected for this facility. However, in the case that $70 \leq$

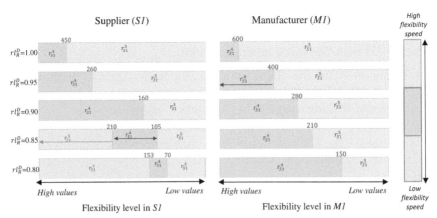

Figure 9-14. Correlation between flexibility levels and speeds.
(Each color is corresponding to one flexibility speed option).

$\Delta_{S1} < 153$, the flexibility speed of this facility reduces to rl_{S1}^4. By increasing Δ_{S1} to more than 153, the flexibility speed reduces further to rl_{S1}^3. The other bars of this figure can be interpreted similarly. Based on the results that are summarized in Figure 9-14, we conclude the following:

- For a given product order quantity (rl_R^D), when a facility's flexibility level is low, a high flexibility speed is generally preferred for that facility. This implies that when a low extra capacity is needed in a facility, it is primarily added during the early production runs after disruptions. However, when the required extra capacity increases, part of this increase should be postponed to later production runs to avoid high costs. Therefore, a negative correlation exists between the flexibility level and flexibility speed of each facility. For all the facilities in the SN, higher robustness leads to lower resilience in profit-based SNs. This tradeoff between robustness and resilience should be considered when designing/redesigning profit-based SNs.

- By increasing the product order quantity (caused by increasing rl_R^D), the flexibility level values differentiate two subsequent pairs of flexibility speed options increment. The red numbers in Figure 9-14 represent these differentiating flexibility level values. As an example, for $rl_R^D = 0.80$, the flexibility level value of *S1* that differentiates rl_{S1}^5 and rl_{S1}^4, flexibility speed option is equal to 70 (capacity units). However, by increasing rl_R^D to 0.85, this differentiating flexibility level value increases to 105 (capacity units). This implies that high production rates stabilize the facilities' flexibility speeds against changes in their flexibility levels. To clarify, to reduce the flexibility speed of facilities, a greater increase in the flexibility level is required. For all the facilities in the SN, larger SNs with higher production rates can absorb greater levels of flexibility in their facilities without reducing their flexibility speeds. Greater flexibility levels and lower flexibility speeds in facilities result in higher robustness and lower resilience in the SN. Therefore, the tradeoff between robustness and resilience is more stable in large SNs with high production rates. This tradeoff is more fragile for low production rates.

Correlations between Robustness, Resilience, and Reliability

Figures 9-15 and 9-16 represent the flexibility levels of *M1* and *S1*, respectively, with respect to the local reliabilities of the first supply path's facilities. Analyzing Figures 9-15 and 9-16 leads to insights that are summarized below.

- Based on Figures 9-15 and 9-16, increasing the retailers' local reliabilities leads to higher flexibility levels in *M1* and *S1*. The retailers' increased reliabilities lead to an increase in the product ordering quantities in

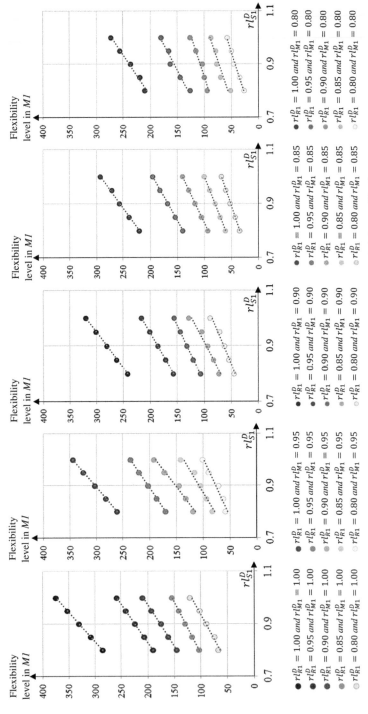

Figure 9-15. Flexibility level in M1 with respect to the local reliabilities of facilities.

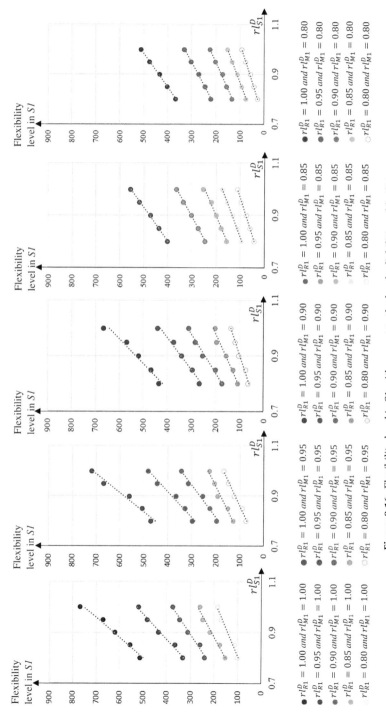

Figure 9-16. Flexibility level in S1 with respect to the local reliabilities of facilities.

the first supply path. To fulfill these larger orders, greater capacities are needed in the supply path's facilities.

- Based on Figures 9-15 and 9-16, increasing the local reliabilities in *S1* and *M1* leads to higher flexibility levels for *M1* and *S1*. This implies that there is a positive correlation among the local reliability of each facility and the flexibility level of other factories.

Based on these results, we conclude that for SNs, there is a positive correlation between the flow reliability against variations (ORM) and the structural robustness against disruptions (SRM). We have presented evidence for a negative correlation between robustness and resilience; therefore, a negative correlation exists between the flow reliability against variations (ORM) and structural resilience against disruptions (SRM).

9.7 Closing Remarks

In this study, we classify SN risks into two groups: (1) variations that affect flow planning decisions and (2) disruptions that affect topology design decisions of the SN. We develop a model in Section 9.5 to plan a reliable flow for SNs to manage downstream and upstream variations by assigning the optimal local reliabilities to facilities (ORM strategies). We extend the model constructed in Section 9.5 in Section 9.6 by considering the possibility of disruptions. This model redesigns a robust and resilient network structure by adding flexibility levels and flexibility speeds to facilities (SRM strategies). Finally, we analyze the correlations among reliability, robustness and resilience. Our results demonstrate that in profit-based SNs: (1) the correlation between robustness and resilience is negative, (2) the correlation between robustness and reliability is positive and (3) the correlation between resilience and reliability is negative.

In the context of an architecture for fail-safe networks, the focus of this chapter is on concurrent managing of variations and disruptions in SNs. In Chapter 10, we discuss that the framework and techniques in this monograph are applicable beyond the SC/SN domain for architecting fail safe networks in other industries such as manufacturing systems and power networks.

References

Atlason, J., Epelman, M. A. and Henderson, S. G. 2008. Optimizing call center staffing using simulation and analytic center cutting-plane methods. Management Science 54(2): 295–309. doi:10.1287/mnsc.1070.0774.

Baghalian, A., Rezapour, S. and Farahani, R. Z. 2013. Robust supply chain network design with service level against disruptions and demand uncertainties: A real-life case. European Journal of Operational Research 227(1): 199–215.

Bernstein, F. and Federgruen, A. 2004. A general equilibrium model for industries with price and service competition. Operations Research 52(6): 868–86.

Bernstein, F. and Federgruen, A. 2007. Coordination mechanisms for supply chains under price and service competition. Manufacturing & Service Operations Management 9(3): 242–62.

Carr, S. M. and Karmarkar, U. S. 2005. Competition in multiechelon assembly supply chains. Management Science 51(1). INFORMS : 45–59. doi:10.1287/mnsc.1040.0216.

Charnes, A., Cooper, W. W. and Symonds, G. H. 1958. Cost horizons and certainty equivalents: An approach to stochastic programming of heating oil. Management Science. INFORMS. doi:10.2307/2627328.

Chopra, S. and Sodhi, M. S. 2004. Managing Risk to Avoid Supply-Chain Breakdown. MIT Sloan Management Review 46(1): 53.

Chopra, S., Reinhardt, G. and Mohan, U. 2007. The importance of decoupling recurrent and disruption risks in a supply chain. Naval Research Logistics (NRL) 54(5): 544–55.

Dada, M., Petruzzi, N. C., Schwarz, L. B., Dada, M., Petruzzi, N. C. and Schwarz, L. B. 2003. A Newsvendor Model with Unreliable Suppliers. University of Illinois at Urbana-Champaign, College of Business. https://econpapers.repec.org/paper/eclillbus/03-0112.htm.

Dada, M., Petruzzi, N. C. and Schwarz, L. B. 2007. Newsvendor's procurement problem when suppliers are unreliable. Manufacturing & Service Operations Management 9(1): 9–32.

Dentcheva, D., Prékopa, A. and Ruszczynski, A. 2000. Concavity and efficient points of discrete distributions in probabilistic programming. Mathematical Programming 89(1). Springer-Verlag: 55–77. doi:10.1007/PL00011393.

Dupačová, J., Gaivoronski, A., Kos, Z. and Szántai, T. 1991. Stochastic programming in water management: A case study and a comparison of solution techniques. European Journal of Operational Research 52(1). North-Holland: 28–44. doi:10.1016/0377-2217(91)90333-Q.

Farahani, R. Z., Rezapour, S., Drezner, T. and Fallah, S. 2014. Competitive supply chain network design: An overview of classifications, models, solution techniques and applications. Omega 45 (June). Pergamon: 92–118. doi:10.1016/J.OMEGA.2013.08.006.

Georgiadis, M. C., Tsiakis, P., Longinidis, P. and Sofioglou, M. K. 2011. Optimal design of supply chain networks under uncertain transient demand variations. Omega 39: 254–272.

Ha, A. Y., Li, L. and Ng, S.-M. 2003. Price and delivery logistics competition in a supply chain. Management Science 49(9): 1139–53. doi:10.1287/mnsc.49.9.1139.16567.

Hasani, A. and Khosrojerdi, A. 2016. HYPERLINK "http://www.sciencedirect.com/science/article/pii/S1366554515002343" Robust global supply chain network design under disruption and uncertainty considering resilience strategies: A parallel memetic algorithm for a real-life case study. Transportation Research Part E: Logistics and Transportation Review 87: 20–52.

Hendricks, K. B. and Singhal, V. R. 2005. An empirical analysis of the effect of supply chain disruptions on long-run stock price performance and equity risk of the firm. Production and Operations Management 14(1): 35–52.

Henrion, R., Li, P., Möller, A., Steinbach, M. C., Wendt, M. and Wozny, G. 2001. Stochastic optimization for operating chemical processes under uncertainty. *In*: Online Optimization of Large Scale Systems, 457–78. Berlin, Heidelberg: Springer Berlin Heidelberg. doi:10.1007/978-3-662-04331-8_24.

Henrion, R. and Möller, A. 2003. Optimization of a continuous distillation process under random inflow rate. Computers & Mathematics with Applications 45 (1–3). Pergamon: 247–62. doi:10.1016/S0898-1221(03)80017-2.

Jiang, L. and Y. Wang. 2010. Supplier competition in decentralized assembly systems with price-sensitive and uncertain demand. Manufacturing & Service Operations Management 12(1). INFORMS : 93–101. doi:10.1287/msom.1090.0259.

Klibi, W. and Martel, A. 2012. Modeling approaches for the design of resilient supply networks under disruptions. International Journal of Production Economics 135(2). Elsevier: 882–98. doi:10.1016/J.IJPE.2011.10.028.

Koren, Y. and Shpitalni, M. 2010. Design of reconfigurable manufacturing systems. Journal of Manufacturing Systems 29(4). Elsevier: 130–41. doi:10.1016/J.JMSY.2011.01.001.

Lee, H. L. and Rosenblatt, M. J. 1987. Simultaneous determination of production cycle and inspection schedules in a production system. Management Science 33(9): 1125–36.

Leung, S. C. H., Tsang, S. O. S., Ng, W. L. and Wu, Y. 2007. A robust optimization model for multi-site production planning problem in an uncertain environment. European Journal of Operational Research. 181: 224–238.

Li, J., Wang, S. and Cheng, T. C. E. 2010. Competition and cooperation in a single-retailer two-supplier supply chain with supply disruption. International Journal of Production Economics 124: 137–150.

Lin, C. C. and Wang, T. H. 2011. Build-to-order supply chain network design under supply and demand uncertainties. Transportation Research: Part B 45(8): 1–15.

Luedtke, J. and Ahmed, S. 2008. A sample approximation approach for optimization with probabilistic constraints. SIAM Journal on Optimization 19(2). Society for Industrial and Applied Mathematics: 674–99. doi:10.1137/070702928.

Mohammaddust, F., Rezapour, S., Farahani, R. Z., Mofidfar, M. and Hill, A. 2017. Developing lean and responsive supply chains: a robust model for alternative risk mitigation strategies in supply chain designs. International Journal of Production Economics 183 (January). Elsevier: 632–53. doi:10.1016/J.IJPE.2015.09.012.

Nemirovski, A. and Shapiro, A. 2006. Convex approximations of chance constrained programs. SIAM Journal on Optimization 17(4). Society for Industrial and Applied Mathematics: 969–96. doi:10.1137/050622328.

Pan, F. and Nagi, R. 2010. Robust supply chain design under uncertain demand in agile manufacturing. Computers and Operations Research 37: 668–683.

Pagnoncelli, B. K., Ahmed, S. and Shapiro, A. 2009. Sample average approximation method for chance constrained programming: theory and applications. Journal of Optimization Theory and Applications 142(2). Springer US: 399–416. doi:10.1007/s10957-009-9523-6.

Park, S., Lee, T. E. and Sung, C. S. 2010. A three level supply chain network design model with risk pooling and lead times. Transportation Research Part E 46: 563–581.

Parlar, M., Wang, Y. and Gerchak, Y. 1995. A periodic review inventory model with markovian supply availability. International Journal of Production Economics 42(2). Elsevier: 131–36. doi:10.1016/0925-5273(95)00115-8.

Peng, P., Snyder, L. V., Lim, A. and Liu, Z. 2011. Reliable logistics networks design with facility disruptions. Transportation Research Part B: Methodological 45(8): 1190–1211. doi:http://dx.doi.org/10.1016/j.trb.2011.05.022.

Prékopa, A. 1995. Stochastic Programming. Kluwer Academic, Dordrecht.

Rezapour, S. and Zanjirani Farahani, R. 2014. Supply Chain Network Design under Oligopolistic Price and Service Level Competition with Foresight. Vol. 72. doi:10.1016/j.cie.2014.03.005.

Rezapour, S., Singh, Allen, J. K. and Mistree, F. 2015. Stochastic Supply Networks Servicing Pre- and After-Sales Markets, no. 57175: V007T06A021. doi:10.1115/DETC2015-46749.

Rezapour, S., Allen, J. K. and Mistree, F. 2016a. Reliable flow in forward and after-sales supply chains considering propagated uncertainty. Transportation Research Part E: Logistics and Transportation Review 93 (September). Pergamon: 409–36. doi:10.1016/J.TRE.2016.04.016.

Rezapour, S., Allen, J. K. and Mistree, F. 2016b. Reliable product-service supply chains for repairable products. Transportation Research Part E: Logistics and Transportation Review 95 (November). Pergamon: 299–321. doi:10.1016/J.TRE.2016.07.016.

Rezapour, S., Farahani, R. Z. and Pourakbar, M. 2017. Resilient supply chain network design under competition: a case study. European Journal of Operational Research 259(3). North-Holland: 1017–35. doi:10.1016/J.EJOR.2016.11.041.

Robinson, S. M. 1996. Analysis of sample-path optimization. Mathematics of Operations Research 21(3). INFORMS : 513–28. doi:10.1287/moor.21.3.513.

Rosenblatt, M. J. and Lee, H. L. 1986. Economic production cycles with imperfect production processes. IIE Transactions 18(1): 48–55.

Ruszczyński, A. and Shapiro, A. 2003. Stochastic programming models. Handbooks in Operations Research and Management Science 10 (January). Elsevier: 1–64. doi:10.1016/S0927-0507(03)10001-1.

Sana, S. S. 2010. An economic production lot size model in an imperfect production system. European Journal of Operational Research 201: 158–170.

Santoso, T., Ahmed, S., Goetschalckx, M. and Shapiro, A. 2005. A stochastic programming approach for supply chain network design under uncertainty. European Journal of Operational Research 167(1): 96–115.

Sarkar, P., Armstrong, C. and Hua, V. 2002. Idling Time: The West Coast Shutdown Is Beginning to Hurt Workers, Industries Dependent on Imports. San Francisco Chronicle, B1.

Schmitt, A. J. and Snyder, L. V. 2010. Infinite-horizon models for inventory control under yield uncertainty and disruptions. Computers & Operations Research 39(4): 850–862.

Schmidt, G. and Wilhelm, W. E. 2010. Strategic, tactical and operational decisions in multi-national logistics networks: a review and discussion of modelling issues. International Journal of Production Research 38(7). Taylor & Francis Group: 1501–23. doi:10.1080/002075400188690.

Schmitt, A. J., Snyder, L. V. and Shen, Z.-J. M. 2010. Inventory systems with stochastic demand and supply: properties and approximations. European Journal of Operational Research 206(2): 313–28.

Schmitt, A. J. 2011. Strategies for customer service level protection under multi-echelon supply chain disruption risk. Transportation Research Part B: Methodological 45(8): 1266–83.

Shen, Z.-J. M. and Daskin, M. S. 2005. Trade-offs between customer service and cost in integrated supply chain design. Manufacturing & Service Operations Management 7(3): 188–207.

Swaminathan, J. M., Shanthikumar, J. G. and Haas, W. A. 1999. Supplier diversification: effect of discrete demand. Operations Research Letters 24(5): 213–21. www.elsevier.com/locate/orms.

Tomlin, B. and Wang, Y. 2005. On the value of mix flexibility and dual sourcing in unreliable newsvendor networks. Manufacturing & Service Operations Management 7(1). INFORMS : 37–57. doi:10.1287/msom.1040.0063.

Tomlin, B. 2006. On the value of mitigation and contingency strategies for managing supply chain disruption risks. Management Science 52(5): 639–57.

Waters, D. 2011. Supply Chain Risk Management: Vulnerability and Resilience in Logistics. Kogan Page Publishers.

You, F. and Grossmann, I. E. 2008. Design of responsive supply chains under demand uncertainty. Computers and Chemical Engineering 32: 3090–3111.

Yu, H., Zeng, A. Z. and Zhao, L. 2009. Single or dual sourcing: decision-making in the presence of supply chain disruption risks. Omega 37: 788–800.

Zhang, L. and Rushton, G. 2008. Optimizing the size and locations of facilities in competitive multi-site service systems. Computers & Operations Research 35(2). Pergamon: 327–38. doi:10.1016/J.COR.2006.03.002.

Appendices

Appendix 9.A: Notation of the Model

Nomenclature

Sets	
$J = \{j\}$	Set of samples used in SAA
$RL = \{rl\}$	Set of discretized values that can be taken by reliability variables
$RO_{M1} = \{r_{M1}\}$	Set of all flexibility speed options available for $M1$
$RO_{S1} = \{r_{S1}\}$	Set of all flexibility speed options available for $S1$
$SCE = \{s\}$	Set of all possible scenarios for the length of disruptions
Parameters	
p	Price
ε	Random deviation of the actual demand from its mean value
G_{R1}	Cumulative distribution function for ε in $R1$
h^+	Unit holding cost paid by the retailers for each unit of end-of-period extra inventory
h^-	Unit shortage cost paid by the retailers for each unit of lost sales
O_{M1}	Number of production runs in $M1$
α_{M1}	$M1$'s random wastage ratio
G'_{M1}	Cumulative distribution function for α_{M1}
α^i_{M1}	Value of random variable α_{M1} realized in production run $i = 1, 2, ..., O_{M1}$
O_{S1}	Number of production runs in $S1$
γ_{S1}	Nonconforming production rate when $S1$'s machinery is in an out-of-control state
t	Random deterioration time in $S1$'s machinery
G''_{S1}	Cumulative distribution function for t
Cap^{WD}_{S1}	Production capacity of $S1$ in each production run
Cap^{WD}_{M1}	Production capacity of $M1$ in each production run
T	Number of time units in each production run
t_i	Value of random variable t realized in production run $i = 1, 2, ..., O_{S1}$
c_{S1}	Cost of procuring and producing a component unit in $S1$
$c_{S1,M1}$	Cost of transporting a component unit from $S1$ to $M1$

c_{M1}	Cost of manufacturing a product unit in *M1*
$c_{M1,R1}$	Cost of transporting a product unit from *M1* to *R1*
cap^i_{M1}	Unit extra capacity cost in *M1*'s production run $i = 1, 2, ..., O_{M1}$
cap^j_{S1}	Unit extra capacity cost in *S1*'s production run $j = 1, 2, ..., O_{S1}$
$rj^{r_{M1}}_{M1}$	Capacity ramp-up quantity in production run j of *M1* if flexibility speed option r_{M1} is selected for it ($\forall r_{M1} \in RO_{M1}$ and $j = 1, 2,..., O_{M1}$)
$rj^{r_{S1}}_{S1}$	Capacity ramp-up quantity in production run j of *S1* if flexibility speed option r_{S1} is selected for it ($\forall r_{S1} \in RO_{S1}$ and $j = 1, 2,..., O_{S1}$)
h^i_{M1}	Unused capacity cost in *M1*'s production run $i = 1, 2, ..., O_{M1}$
h^i_{S1}	Unused capacity cost in *S1*'s production run $i = 1, 2, ..., O_{S1}$
pr_s	Occurrence probability of scenario $s \in SCE$
num^{WD}_s	Number of without disruption periods in scenario $s \in SCE$
num^{RUD}_s	Number of ramp-up disruption periods in scenario $s \in SCE$
num^{ND}_s	Number of normal disruption periods in scenario $s \in SCE$
num^{RD}_s	Number of ramp-down disruption periods in scenario $s \in SCE$
Variables	
sl	Service level
sl^{WD}	Service level provided by the SN under without disruption conditions
x^{WD}	Number of products ordered by *R1* from *M1*
rl^{WD}_{R1}	Local reliability for *R1* under without disruption conditions
y^{WD}	Number of products produced by *M1* in each production run
rl^{WD}_{M1}	Local reliability for *M1* under without disruption conditions
z^{WD}	Number of components produced by *S1* in each production run
rl^{WD}_{S1}	Local reliability for *S1* under without disruption conditions
$rl^{WD}_{M1,j}$	1 if the term $(O_{M1} \cdot y^{WD} - x^{WD}) - y^{WD} \cdot \sum_{i=1}^{O_{M1}} \alpha^i_{M1}$ is positive based on the realized values of α^i_{M1} ($\forall i = 1, 2, ..., O_{M1}$) in sample $j \in J$ and 0 otherwise
$rl^{WD}_{S1,j}$	1 if the term $\gamma_{S1} \cdot Cap^{WD}_{S1} \cdot (\sum_{i=1}^{O_{S1}} t_i) - O_{S1} \cdot (\gamma_{S1} - 1) \cdot z^{WD} - O_{M1} \cdot y^{WD}$ is positive based on the realized values of t_i ($\forall i = 1, ..., O_{M1}$) in sample $j \in J$ and 0 otherwise
$\theta^{WD,rl}_{S1}$	1 if reliability option $rl \in RL$ is selected for *S1* and 0 otherwise
$\theta^{WD,rl'}_{M1}$	1 if reliability option $rl' \in RL$ is selected for *M1* and 0 otherwise
$\theta^{WD,rl''}_{R1}$	1 if reliability option $rl'' \in RL$ is selected for *R1* and 0 otherwise
$\Theta^{WD,rl,rl',rl''}_{S1,M1,R1}$	1 if all three variables $\theta^{WD,rl}_{S1}$, $\theta^{WD,rl'}_{M1}$ and $\theta^{WD,rl''}_{R1}$ are equal to 1 and 0 otherwise
$w^{r_{M1}}_{M1}$	1 if flexibility speed option r_{M1} is selected for *M1* and 0 otherwise ($r_{M1} \in RO_{M1}$)
$w^{r_{S1}}_{S1}$	1 if flexibility speed option r_{S1} is selected for *S1* and 0 otherwise ($r_{S1} \in RO_{S1}$)
Δ_{M1}	Flexibility level in *M1*

Δ_{S1}	Flexibility level in *S1*
y_i^{RUD}	Production quantity in the ramp-up disruption period's production run *i* of *M1* ($i = 1, 2, ..., O_{M1}$)
z_i^{RUD}	Production quantity in the ramp-up disruption period's production run *i* of *S1* ($i = 1, 2, ..., O_{S1}$)
x^D	Total product order received by *M1* in disrupted periods
x_1^D	Order issued by *R1* from *M1* in disrupted periods
x_2^D	Order issued by *R2* from *M1* in disrupted periods
rl_{R1}^D	Local reliability for *R1* under disrupted conditions
rl_{R2}^D	Local reliability for *R2* under disrupted conditions
sl^D	Service level provided by the SN under disrupted conditions
rl_{M1}^D	Local reliability for *M1* under disrupted conditions
rl_{S1}^D	Local reliability for *S1* under disrupted conditions
rl_R^D	Local reliability for *R1* and *R2* if a same service level is provided to all markets under disrupted conditions
y^{ND}	Production quantity in the production runs of normal disruption period in *M1*
z^{ND}	Production quantity in the production runs of normal disruption period in *S1*

Functions	
$D_k(p, sl^{WD})$	Expected demand in each sale period in market *k* (*k* = 1 and 2) under without disruption conditions
$\sum_{k=1}^2 D_k(p, sl^{WD})$	Average demand in *R1* under without disruption conditions
$\sum_{k=1}^2 D_k(p, sl^{WD}) \times \varepsilon$	Actual demand in *R1* under without disruption conditions
Π_{R1}^{WD}	Expected total cost in *R1* under without disruption conditions
Ψ^{WD}	Total profit in the first supply path under without disruption conditions
$D_k(p, sl^D)$	Expected demand in each sale period in market *k* (*k* = 1 and 2) under disrupted conditions
$\sum_{k=1}^2 D_k(p, sl^D)$	Average demand in *R1* under disrupted conditions
$\sum_{k=1}^2 D_k(p, sl^D) \times \varepsilon$	Actual demand in *R1* under disrupted conditions
Ψ^{RUD}	Total profit that can be captured in the ramp-up disruption period
Ψ^{ND}	Total profit that can be captured in the normal disruption period
Ψ^{RD}	Total profit that can be captured in the ramp-down disruption period
Cap_{M1}^D	Capacity needed by *M1* in disrupted conditions
Cap_{S1}^D	Capacity needed by *S1* in disrupted conditions
Ψ	Expected profit of the SN under disrupted conditions

Appendix 9.B: Linearizing Approach

The model (Eqs. (5-8) to (5-17)) is linearized in three steps as follows:

- First, the chance constraints, Eqs. (5-12) and (5-13), are linearized by using the SAA approach,
- Second, the nonlinear constraints, Eqs. (5-11) and (5-14), and the objective functions, Eq. (5-8), are linearized by discretizing reliability variables,
- Third, the multiplication of binary variables is linearized by defining a new variable.

The steps are explained in detail below.

Step 1: Chance constraints linearization

In this step, we explain how the SAA approach is used to approximate the chance constraints in the model (Eqs. (5-8) to (5-17)). The SAA for Eq. (5-12) is as follows:

$$rl_{M1}^{WD} = \Pr(\sum_{i=1}^{O_{M1}} \alpha_{M1}^i \cdot y^{WD} \leq O_{M1} \cdot y^{WD} - x^{WD}) = \frac{\sum_{j=1}^{J} rl_{M1,j}^{WD}}{j} \tag{9-57}$$

In Eq. (5-57), the probability of the event that is defined as the *"left hand side of the inequality in Eq. (5-57) is less than equal to its right hand side* $(\sum_{i=1}^{O_{M1}} \alpha_{M1}^i \cdot y^{WD} \leq O_{M1} \cdot y^{WD} - x^{WD})$*"* is replaced by the ratio of its occurrence in a sample that includes $J = \{j\}$ observations. Increasing the size of the sample, $|J|$, increases the accuracy of this statistical approximation. To determine the number of times in which terms $(O_{M1} \cdot y^{WD} - x^{WD}) - y^{WD} \cdot \sum_{i=1}^{O_{M1}} \alpha_{M1}^i$ are positive, a new binary variable $rl_{M1,j}^{WD}$ is defined and the following constraints are added to the model:

$$BM. (rl_{M1,j}^{WD} - 1) \leq (O_{M1} \cdot y^{WD} - x^{WD}) - y^{WD} \cdot \sum_{i=1}^{O_{M1}} \alpha_{M1}^i \leq BM. rl_{M1,j}^{WD}$$

$$(\forall j = 1, ..., J \text{ and } \forall i = 1, ..., O_{M1}) (\alpha_{M1}^i \sim G'_{M1}) \tag{9-58}$$

$$rl_{M1,j}^{WD} \in \{0,1\} \qquad (\forall j = 1, ..., J) \tag{9-59}$$

According to Constraint (5-58), variable $rl_{M1,j}^{WD}$ is 1 if the term $(O_{M1} \cdot y^{WD} - x^{WD}) - y^{WD} \cdot \sum_{i=1}^{O_{M1}} \alpha_{M1}^i$ is positive based on the realized values of α_{M1}^i $(\forall i = 1, ..., O_{M1})$ in sample $j \in J$ and 0 otherwise (*BM* is a large constant value; refer to Appendix 9.E for information about the *BM* value). Increasing the accuracy of this approximation increases the number of these new variables. Therefore, selecting the smallest $|J|$ that ensures an acceptable accuracy is necessary.

The chance constraint in Eq. (5-13) is approximated in the same manner. First it is simplified algebraically and rewritten as follows:

$$rl^{WD}_{S1} = \Pr\left(\gamma_{S1}.\ Cap^{WD}_{S1}.\ \left(\textstyle\sum_{i=1}^{O_{S1}} t_i\right) \geq O_{S1}.\ (\gamma_{S1} - 1).\ z^{WD} + O_{M1}.\ y^{WD}\right) \tag{9-60}$$

Then, it is approximated with the following constraints:

$$rl^{WD}_{S1} = \Pr\left(\gamma_{S1}.\ Cap^{WD}_{S1}.\ \left(\textstyle\sum_{i=1}^{O_{S1}} t_i\right) \geq O_{S1}.\ (\gamma_{S1} - 1).\ z^{WD} + O_{M1}.\ y^{WD}\right) = \frac{\sum_{j=1}^{J} y_i.rl^{WD}_{S1,j}}{j} \tag{9-61}$$

To determine the number of times in which term $\gamma_{S1}.\ Cap^{WD}_{S1}.\ \left(\sum_{i=1}^{O_{S1}} t_i\right) - O_{S1}.\ (\gamma_{S1} - 1).z^{WD} - O_{M1}.\ y^{WD}$ is positive, a new binary variable $rl^{WD}_{S1,j}$ is defined and the following constraints should be added to the model:

$$BM.\ (rl^{WD}_{S1,j} - 1) \leq \gamma_{S1}.\ Cap^{WD}_{S1}.\ \left(\textstyle\sum_{i=1}^{O_{S1}} t_i\right) - O_{S1}.\ (\gamma_{S1} - 1).\ z^{WD} - O_{M1}.\ y^{WD} \leq BM.\ rl^{WD}_{S1,j}$$

$$(\forall j = 1, \dots, J \text{ and } \forall i = 1, \dots, O_{S1})\ (t_i \sim G''_{S1}) \tag{9-62}$$

$$rl^{N}_{S1,j} \in \{0,1\} \qquad\qquad (\forall j = 1, \dots, J) \tag{9-63}$$

Variable $rl^{WD}_{S1,j}$ is 1 if the term $\gamma_{S1}.\ Cap^{WD}_{S1}.\ \left(\sum_{i=1}^{O_{S1}} t_i\right) - O_{S1}.\ (\gamma_{S1} - 1).\ z^{WD} - O_{M1}.\ y^{WD}$ is positive based on the realized values of t_i $(\forall i = 1, \dots, O_{M1})$ in sample $j \in J$ and 0 otherwise. To verify the accuracy of this approximation and suggest appropriate values for the sample size, $|J|$, we conducted a numerical analysis and compute the average error of this approximation for different density functions. The results are summarized in Table 9-1.

Table 9-2. Average error for different density functions.

Normal Density Function				Uniform Density Function				Exponential Density Function			
J	*Average error*	*J*	*Average error*	*J*	*Average error*	*J*	*Average error*	*J*	*Average error*	*J*	*Average error*
1	0.220	60	0.034	1	0.230	60	0.033	1	0.210	60	0.032
5	0.129	65	0.033	5	0.134	65	0.031	5	0.131	65	0.030
10	0.084	70	0.031	10	0.082	70	0.029	10	0.085	70	0.030
15	0.065	75	0.029	15	0.067	75	0.028	15	0.064	75	0.029
20	0.061	80	0.028	20	0.061	80	0.028	20	0.060	80	0.028
25	0.051	85	0.028	25	0.050	85	0.027	25	0.050	85	0.027
30	0.048	90	0.026	30	0.049	90	0.025	30	0.048	90	0.026
35	0.045	95	0.025	35	0.043	95	0.025	35	0.043	95	0.026
40	0.041	100	0.025	40	0.041	100	0.024	40	0.039	100	0.025
45	0.039	120	0.023	45	0.039	120	0.022	45	0.037	120	0.023
50	0.038	140	0.020	50	0.036	140	0.019	50	0.036	140	0.022
55	0.035	150	0.019	55	0.034	150	0.018	55	0.034	150	0.019

Based on these results, when $|J|$ is in the [25, 30] interval, the average error of the approximations is less than or equal to 5 percent. To reduce the error to less than 4, 3, and 2 percent, $|J|$ should be selected from the [40, 45], [65, 70], and [140, 150] intervals.

Step 2: Nonlinear objective function and constraints linearization

To linearize the objective function in Eq. (9-8) and the constraints in Eqs. (9-11) and (9-14), we discretize the facilities' local reliability variables, rl^{WD}_{S1}, rl^{WD}_{M1} and rl^{WD}_{R1}. These variables only assume values in the [0, 1] interval. Service level, a function of these local reliabilities, generally assumes a value that is greater than or equal to 50 percent. By restricting the feasibility range of local reliabilities to [0.8, 1], we ensure that the SN's service level for the markets is greater than 50 percent ($0.8^3 \geq 0.5$). This very restricted feasible range justifies the feasibility of their discretization (Rezapour et al. 2015). Set $RL = \{rl\}$ includes all discrete values that can be assumed by these variables. For example, if we use step size 0.05 to discretize the [0.8, 1] interval, we obtain $RL = \{0.80, 0.85, 0.90, 0.95, 1\}$ (the notation rl is used to represent the discretized values in Set RL). In this case, the variables rl^{WD}_{S1}, rl^{WD}_{M1} and rl^{WD}_{R1} can only assume a value from Set $RL = \{0.80, 0.85, 0.90, 0.95, 1\}$ rather than assuming any value from [0.8, 1]. To select one of these reliability options for each facility, we define new binary variables, $\theta^{WD,rl}_{S1}$, $\theta^{WD,rl}_{M1}$ and $\theta^{WD,rl}_{R1}$. Variable $\theta^{WD,rl}_{S1}$ is 1 if the reliability option $rl \in RL$ is selected for $S1$ and 0 otherwise. Only one of the options available in RL can be selected for $S1$:

$$\sum_{rl=1}^{|RL|} \theta^{WD,rl}_{S1} = 1 \qquad (9\text{-}64)$$

Variable $\theta^{WD,rl'}_{M1}$ is 1 if the reliability option $rl' \in RL$ is selected for $M1$ and 0 otherwise. Only one of the options available in RL can be selected for $M1$:

$$\sum_{rl'=1}^{|RL|} \theta^{WD,rl'}_{M1} = 1 \qquad (9\text{-}65)$$

Variable $\theta^{WD,rl''}_{R1}$ is 1 if the reliability option $rl'' \in RL$ is selected for $R1$ and 0 otherwise. Only one of the options available in RL can be selected for $R1$:

$$\sum_{rl''=1}^{|RL|} \theta^{WD,rl''}_{R1} = 1 \qquad (9\text{-}66)$$

By defining these new variables, the objective function, Eq. (9-8), is rewritten as:

$$Max\ \Psi^{WD} = \sum_{rl=1}^{|RL|} \sum_{rl'=1}^{|RL|} \sum_{rl''=1}^{|RL|} \cdot \theta_{S1}^{WD,rl} \cdot \theta_{M1}^{WD,rl'} \cdot \theta_{R1}^{WD,rl''} \cdot \left[\left(p - h^+ \cdot E \left[G_{R1}^{-1} \left(Max \left\{ rl.\,rl'.\,rl'', \right. \right. \right. \right. \right.$$

$$\left. \left. \left. \left. \frac{h^-}{h^- + h^+} \right\} \right) \right] - \varepsilon \right]^+ - h^- \cdot E \left[\varepsilon - G_{R1}^{-1} \left(Max \left\{ rl.\,rl'.\,rl'', \frac{h^-}{h^- + h^+} \right\} \right) \right]^+ \right) \times \left[\sum_{k=1}^{2} D_k(p, rl.\,rl'.\,rl'') \right]$$

$$(9\text{-}67)$$

After defining these new binary variables, the constraint in Eq. (9-11) can be rewritten as:

$$x^{WD} = \sum_{rl=1}^{|RL|} \sum_{rl'=1}^{|RL|} \sum_{rl''=1}^{|RL|} \cdot \theta_{S1}^{WD,rl} \cdot \theta_{M1}^{WD,rl'} \cdot \theta_{R1}^{WD,rl''} \cdot \left[\left(\sum_{k=1}^{2} D_k(p, rl.\,rl'.\,rl'') \right) \cdot G_{R1}^{-1} \left(Max \left\{ rl'', \right. \right. \right.$$

$$\left. \left. \frac{h^-}{h^- + h^+} \right\} \right) \right]$$

$$(9\text{-}68)$$

The constraint in Eq. (9-14) is rewritten:

$$sl^{WD} = \sum_{rl=1}^{|RL|} \sum_{rl'=1}^{|RL|} \sum_{rl''=1}^{|RL|} \cdot \theta_{S1}^{WD,rl} \cdot \theta_{M1}^{WD,rl'} \cdot \theta_{R1}^{WD,rl''} \cdot [rl.\,rl'.\,rl''] \qquad (9\text{-}69)$$

The accuracy of this linearization depends on the discretizing step of the reliability variables. To reduce complexity, we begin with a large step to determine a rough approximation of the optimal solution. Then, we can make the steps finer around the rough approximation to improve the solution's accuracy.

Step 3: Linearizing multiplication of binary variables

The objective function in Eq. (9-67) and the constraints in Eqs. (9-68) and (9-69) are still nonlinear because there is a multiplication of binary variables in these equations. These multiplications can be easily linearized by defining a new binary variable, $\Theta_{S1,M1,R1}^{WD,rl,rl',rl''}$ and substituting as follows:

$$\Theta_{S1,M1,R1}^{WD,rl,rl',rl''} = \theta_{S1}^{WD,rl} \cdot \theta_{M1}^{WD,rl'} \cdot \theta_{R1}^{WD,rl''} \qquad (9\text{-}70)$$

We must add the following constraints to the model to ensure that variable $\Theta_{S1,M1,R1}^{WD,rl,rl',rl''}$ is equal to 1, only if all three variables $\theta_{S1}^{WD,rl}$, $\theta_{M1}^{WD,rl'}$, and $\theta_{R1}^{WD,rl''}$ are equal to 1:

$$\theta_{S1}^{WD,rl} + \theta_{M1}^{WD,rl'} + \theta_{R1}^{WD,rl''} - 2 \leq \Theta_{S1,M1,R1}^{WD,rl,rl',rl''} \leq \frac{\theta_{S1}^{WD,rl} + \theta_{M1}^{WD,rl'} + \theta_{R1}^{WD,rl''}}{3} \qquad (9\text{-}71)$$

$$\Theta_{S1,M1,R1}^{WD,rl,rl',rl''} \leq BM. \theta_{S1}^{WD,rl} \qquad (9\text{-}72)$$

$$\Theta_{S1,M1,R1}^{WD,rl,rl',rl''} \leq BM. \theta_{M1}^{WD,rl'} \qquad (9\text{-}73)$$

$$\Theta_{S1,M1,R1}^{WD,rl,rl',rl''} \leq BM. \theta_{R1}^{WD,rl''} \qquad (9\text{-}74)$$

$\Theta_{S1,M1,R1}^{WD,rl,rl',rl''} \in \{0,1\}$ (9-75)

After these steps, our model becomes a MILP. The solution time of a MILP depends primarily on the number of binary variables that are equal to $|RL|^3 + 3.|RL| + 2.|J|$. We solve this model using CPLEX Concert Technology on a Dell laptop computer with Windows 10, an Intel i7 processor, and 8 GB of installed RAM. The computational time for the Test Problem (in Section 9.5.6) is less than 4 minutes.

Given that the test problem is not complicated, we verify the computational capability of the solution method by solving more complicated SNs with larger numbers of suppliers, manufacturers, and retailers. Features of these SNs and their computational times are summarized in Table 9-2. In these problems, we assume that the local reliability of the facilities in each echelon is selected from set $RL = \{0.8, 0.85, 0.90, 0.95, 1\}$ and the sample size used in SAA is $|J| = 25$.

Table 9-3. Computational capability for the model developed for without disruption conditions.

Problem	Features of SN				Computational time
	Number of suppliers	Number of manufacturers	Number of retailers	Number of paths	
1	2	2	2	2	3':47"
2	2	3	6	8	10':12"
3	2	4	9	12	49':50"
4	2	5	12	16	2:53':31"
5	3	6	15	21	7:12':45"
6	3	7	18	26	15:55':23"
7	4	8	22	32	29:05:11"
8	4	9	26	38	> 48

Decisions about SN's risk mitigation strategies are types of strategic level decisions. These decisions are not made daily and do not need short computation times. As noted in Table 9-2, for Problem 8 and problems larger than Problem 8, the computational time is more than 48 hours. Therefore, for this type of problem, we can use meta-heuristic approaches to solve the MILP and determine a good suboptimal solution in a rational computational time rather than the global optimum.

Appendix 9.C: Computational Times

The model developed in Section 9.6.4 is a MILP. The solution time of a MILP depends primarily on the number of binary variables that are equal to $|RL|^3 + 3.|RL| + 2.|J| + |RO_{M1}| + |RO_{S1}|$. The computational time for the test problem (in Section 9.6.5) is less than 6 minutes. Given that the test problem is not complicated, we verify the computational capability of the model and solution method by solving the first 7 problems that are summarized in Table 9-2. The number of disrupted paths considered in these SNs and their computational times are summarized in Table 9-3. In these problems, we assume that the numbers of flexibility speed options available for undisrupted suppliers and manufactures are 3 and 4, respectively. In addition, the facilities' local reliability in each echelon is selected from set $RL = \{0.8, 0.85, 0.90, 0.95, 1\}$ and the sample size used in the SAA is $|J| = 25$.

As noted in Table 9-3, for Problem 7 and problems larger than Problem 7, the computational time is more than 48 hours. Therefore, for this type of problems we suggest using meta-heuristic approaches to solve the MILP and determine a good suboptimal solution in a rational computational time rather than the global optimum.

Table 9-4. Computational capability for the model developed for disrupted conditions.

Problem	Features of SN					Computational time
	Number of suppliers	Number of manufacturers	Number of retailers	Number of paths	Number of disrupted paths	
1	2	2	2	2	1	5':14"
2	2	3	6	8	3	40':39"
3	2	4	9	12	4	1:38':57"
4	2	5	12	16	6	7:21':02"
5	3	6	15	21	8	16:13':33"
6	3	7	18	26	8	28:50':47"
7	4	8	22	32	9	> 48

Appendix 9.D: Fubini's Theorem

In Section 9.5.1 we referred to Fubini's Theorem. According to Fubini's Theorem, it is possible to calculate the mean of a random function, such as $x^{WD} - \Sigma_{k=1}^{2} D_k(p, sl^{WD}) \times \varepsilon$, using its cumulative distribution function (for more information about this relationship refer to Hajek (2015) – Eq. (1.11)):

$$E[x^{WD} - \Sigma_{k=1}^{2} D_k(p, sl^{WD}) \times \varepsilon]^+ = \int_{0}^{\frac{x^{WD}}{\Sigma_{k=1}^{2} D_k(p, sl^{WD})}} G_{R1}(\varepsilon).\, d\varepsilon \qquad (9\text{-}76)$$

$$E[x^{WD} - \Sigma_{k=1}^{2} D_k(p, sl^{WD}) \times \varepsilon]^+ - E(\Sigma_{k=1}^{2} D_k(p, sl^{WD}) \times \varepsilon - x^{WD})^+ = x^{WD} - \Sigma_{k=1}^{2} D_k(p, sl^{WD}) \qquad (9\text{-}77)$$

Therefore, we can manipulate the objective function (1) as follows:

$$MIN\ \Pi_{R1}^{WD} = h^+ \cdot E\left[x^{WD} - \sum_{k=1}^{2} D_k(p, sl^{WD}) \times \varepsilon\right]^+ + h^- \cdot E\left[\sum_{k=1}^{2} D_k(p, sl^{WD}) \times \varepsilon - x^{WD}\right]^+$$

$$= h^+ \cdot \frac{x^{WD}}{\int_0^{\frac{x^{WD}}{\sum_{k=1}^{2} D_k(p, sl^{WD})}}} G_{R1}(\varepsilon) \cdot d\varepsilon + h^-\left[\Sigma_{k=1}^2 D_k(p, sl^{WD}) - x^{WD} + \frac{x^{WD}}{\int_0^{\frac{x^{WD}}{\sum_{k=1}^{2} D_k(p, sl^{WD})}}} G_{R1}(\varepsilon) \cdot d\varepsilon\right]$$

$$(9\text{-}78)$$

Therefore, to compute the minimum x^{WD}, we should compute the derivative of Eq. (9-78) respect to x^{WD}:

$$\frac{\sigma \Pi_{R1}^{WD}}{\sigma x^{WD}} = h^+ \cdot G_{R1}\left(\frac{x^{WD}}{\Sigma_{k=1}^2 D_k(p, sl^{WD})}\right) + h^- \cdot \left(-1 + G_{R1}\left(\frac{x^{WD}}{\Sigma_{k=1}^2 D_k(p, sl^{WD})}\right)\right) = 0 \quad (9\text{-}79)$$

$$G_{R1}\left(\frac{x^{WD}}{\Sigma_{k=1}^2 D_k(p, sl^{WD})}\right) = \frac{h^-}{(h^- + h^+)} \rightarrow x^{WD} = \Sigma_{k=1}^2 D_k(p, sl^{WD}) \cdot G_{R1}^{-1}\left(\frac{h^-}{h^- + h^+}\right) \quad (9\text{-}80)$$

Furthermore, Constraint (2) can be simplified as follows:

$$Pr[\Sigma_{k=1}^2 D_k(p, sl^{WD}) \times \varepsilon \leq x^{WD}] \geq rl_{R1}^{WD} \rightarrow Pr[\varepsilon \leq \frac{x^{WD}}{\Sigma_{k=1}^2 D_k(p, sl^{WD})}] \geq rl_{R1}^{WD} \quad (9\text{-}81)$$

$$G_{R1}\left(\frac{x^{WD}}{\Sigma_{k=1}^2 D_k(p, sl^{WD})}\right) \geq rl_{R1}^{WD} \quad (9\text{-}82)$$

$$G_{R1}^{-1}(rl_{R1}^{WD}) \leq \frac{x^{WD}}{\Sigma_{k=1}^2 D_k(p, sl^{WD})} \rightarrow x^{WD} \geq [\Sigma_{k=1}^2 D_k(p, sl^{WD})] \cdot G_{R1}^{-1}(rl_{R1}^{WD}) \quad (9\text{-}83)$$

Appendix 9.E: BM Value

BM is a large constant in Eq. (9-58); see Appendix 9.B. Equation $(O_{M1} \cdot y^{WD} - x^{WD}) - y^{WD} \cdot \sum_{i=1}^{O_{M1}} \alpha_{M1}^i$ is used to demonstrate the difference between the extra production in M1 $(O_{M1} \cdot y^{WD} - x^{WD})$ and the total waste in its production runs $(y^{WD} \cdot \sum_{i=1}^{O_{M1}} \alpha_{M1}^i)$. Extra production in M1 cannot be greater than $O_{M1} \cdot y^{WD}$. $Max(\alpha_{M1})$ and the total waste in M1 cannot be less than $O_{M1} \cdot y^{WD} \cdot Min(\alpha_{M1})$. Therefore, we can claim that:

$$-1 \times \left(O_{M1} \cdot y^{WD} (Max(\alpha_{M1}) - Min(\alpha_{M1}))\right) \leq (O_{M1} \cdot y^{WD} - x^{WD}) - y^{WD} \cdot \sum_{i=1}^{O_{M1}} \alpha_{M1}^i$$

$$\leq O_{M1} \cdot y^{WD} (Max(\alpha_{M1}) - Min(\alpha_{M1})) \quad (9\text{-}84)$$

Furthermore, the maximum value that can be assumed by y^{WD} corresponds to a case for which $O_{M1} = 1$ and at most is equal to x^{WD}

$(Max(\alpha_{M1}) + 1)$. Because the maximum value for x^{WD} is $[\Sigma_{k=1}^{2} D_k(p, sl^{WD} = 1)]$.

$G_{R1}^{-1}\left(Max\left\{rl_{R1}^{WD} = 1, \dfrac{h^-}{h^- + h^+}\right\}\right)$, the BM in Eq. (9-58) must satisfy the following inequality:

$$BM \geq O_{M1}. [\Sigma_{k=1}^{2} D_k(p, 1)]. G_{R1}^{-1}\left(Max\left\{1, \dfrac{h^-}{h^- + h^+}\right\}\right). (Max(\alpha_{M1}) + 1). (Max(\alpha_{M1})$$

$$- Min(\alpha_{M1})) \tag{9-85}$$

CHAPTER 10

Emerging Technologies and Extension of the Fail-Safe Framework to Other Networks

We establish in Chapter 1 that networks are ubiquitous and permeate many aspects of human endeavor. Advancing technologies driven by the Digital Five Forces of Mobility and Pervasive Computing, Big Data and Analytics, Social Media, Cloud Computing, and Artificial Intelligence and Robotics are extending the reach of networks while simultaneously accelerating their real-time capabilities (Krishnan 2017). The "digital network business model" is a direct result of the convergence of these technologies, growing rapidly and providing excellent value (Libert et al. 2016). Emerging technologies enable users to acquire and disseminate information through extensive networks on web based and mobile platforms. Such opportunities are accompanied by challenges such as security and failure prevention in these networks. We will discuss how fail-safe designs can be implemented to harness these networks fully while minimizing or eliminating the risks involved in their use. Further, we argue that the framework and techniques in this monograph are applicable beyond the supply chain domain for architecting fail safe networks in other industries. In this chapter, we also discuss the implications in selected areas such as manufacturing and power networks.

10.1 Summary of Contributions

The function of a supply network is to ensure the flow of goods from supply nodes to demand nodes. The aim is to set objectives such as the minimization of flow cost, the maximization of service level, and the maximization of profits to select the optimal structure of the supply network. Every network is subject to variations in demand and supply and disruptions caused by disabled nodes or links. In this monograph we present techniques for addressing such variations and disruptions to enable the uninterrupted function of a given supply network.

The performance of a supply network depends on the availability of its facilities (nodes and links) in determining its structure and efficiency of flow planning throughout that network (flow of material, products, information, money). Extreme, unexpected and rare stochastic events called disruptions can distort a network's structure. Disruptions include natural disasters, bankruptcies, labor strikes and similar social unrest and governmental legislation. Minor, expected and frequent variations that occur in downstream demand nodes and upstream production facilities can affect the efficiency of a given network's flow planning. Effective risk management strategies to handle disruptions and variations are at the core of a fail-safe network. In this monograph, we present methods for designing fail-safe supply networks by achieving reliability, robustness, structural controllability, resilience and flexibility (see Figure 10-1). A summary of the contributions of the book is presented in Table 10-1.

Figure 10-1. Components of fail-safe supply networks.

Table 10-1. Contributions in the monograph.

Architecture Constituents	Interpretation for Fail-safe networks	Chapters 2–5	Chapters 6–9
Elements	**What?**	**What?**	**What?**
Components	Methods of network risk management (refer Figure 1-4)	Reliability	Structural Controllability (Chapters 7, 8) Robustness (Chapters 6, 9) Resilience (Chapters 8, 9)
Connectors	The media that links the selected components, typically the supply network	Forward supply chain (Chapters 2–5) After-sales supply chain (Chapters 3–5)	Supply networks (Chapters 6–9)
Form	**How?**	**How?**	**How?**
Component weights	Relative importance of the selected components	Reliability	Structural Controllability (Chapters 7, 8) Robustness (Chapters 6, 9) Resilience (Chapters 8, 9)
Properties	Attributes of the elements used to form the relationship, ex. Cost	Local Reliabilities	Demand, Cost, Capacity, etc. (Chapters 6, 8) Open/close nodes, active links between nodes, etc. (Chapter 7) Local Reliabilities, Flexibility levels and Flexibility speeds (Chapter 9)
Relationship	Links within and between components, expressed as a mathematical construct	Profit maximization	Cost minimization, maximization of service level, minimize number of driver nodes, local reliabilities and flexibility

Table 10-1 contd. ...

...Table 10-1 contd.

Architecture Constituents	Interpretation for Fail-safe networks	Chapters 2–5	Chapters 6–9
Rationale	Why?	Why?	Why?
Motivation	The underlying reason to use this model, driven by user requirements	Variation management	Disruption management (Chapters 6–8) Variation management (Chapter 9)
Assumptions	Generalizations or simplifications used to guide the selection of elements and form	No disruption. There is enough information to quantify variations	Linear relation between variables (Chapter 6) possibility of redundant links (Chapter 7) There is enough information to quantify variations (Chapter 9)
Constraints	Upper and lower limits on performance, utilization, etc.	Order amplification in echelons due to variations; Market demand depends on service levels, pre-sales market price and after-sales market warranty	Production and transportation capacity, demand fulfilment, etc. (Chapters 6, 8)
Interpretation	Understanding of the solution; may provide motivation for further study	Relationship between the chain's service levels in pre- and after-sales markets and the local reliabilities of its facilities. Relationship between pre- and after-sales marketing factors; Relationship between optimal service levels, price and warranty	Relationship between risk management components (reliability, robustness and resilience); Understanding of the solution

This monograph comprises two major parts: Variation Management and Disruption Management. The first part addresses the determination of optimum inventory levels per specific node. In Chapter 2, we describe two mathematical models to plan the most profitable flow for supply chains or networks by considering variations in the supply and demand of network facilities. Managers can exploit these models to select the best variation management strategies for their network. In Chapters 3 and 4, we show that the models available in Chapter 2 can be implemented in the complex after-sales segment of the supply chain for non-repairable and repairable products respectively. In Chapter 5, we focus on extending the models proposed in Chapters 3 and 4 to flow planning in forward and after-sales supply networks. In this case, the forward supply network is responsible for producing and supplying products to markets and the after-sales supply network provides spare parts to fulfill after-sales agreements. We developed mathematical models for both forward and after-sales supply networks.

Chapter 6 is the beginning of the second part of the monograph, where we address disruption management through the implementation of the principles of robustness. Disruption management using robust optimization modeling based on the flexible design of supply networks using scenario-based stochastic optimization modeling is the principal contribution to the relevant risk management literature. We study different disruption scenarios in this chapter and we show that targeted disruptions (e.g., terrorist attacks) have higher impacts on the robustness of infrastructure supply networks than random disruptions (e.g., random failures or natural disasters).

In Chapter 7, we describe disruption management using the principles of Structural Controllability. We discuss the impact of structural controllability in establishing transportation facilities in a network and critical transportation routes from said facilities to customers. We show that the resilience of a disrupted supply network can be managed using structural controllability through a three-stage method.

In Chapter 8, the focus is on disruption management using Restoration Strategies. Here we show that the resilience of a supply network is a function of the combined restoration strategies implemented before and after, a disruption. Therefore, we propose a mathematical model using the construct of Compromise Decision Support Problems to select the best restoration strategies to increase the resilience of supply networks.

When a disruption occurs in a supply network, various restoration strategies are available to manage the risk of disruptions. Some examples of restoration strategies are facility fortification, backup inventory, flexible production capacities, flexible inventory capacity and transportation route reconfiguration. Disruptions may happen in any facility with varying probabilities, making it far too costly to maintain measures such as redundant inventory in every facility, flexible capacities in all facilities, or the fortification of all facilities to defend against disruptions. Because they provide accessibility to all other nodes, transportation nodes occupy a unique position in structurally controllable networks. It follows that the true function of structural controllability in a supply network is establishing and designing transportation nodes by allowing the targeted implementation of restoration strategies. Strategies revolving around transportation nodes can lower the costs of managing disruptions significantly and increase the efficiency of restoration strategies significantly. Therefore, we propose a three-stage method using the Compromise Decision Support Construct to employ structural controllability in designing resilient supply networks.

In Chapter 9, we consider the potential of both disruptions and variations in supply networks. We develop a mathematical model that selects the best strategic risk mitigation strategies against disruptions and operational risk mitigation strategies against variations. We go on to show that these two groups of risk mitigation decisions are not independent. Therefore, there is a significant advantage in concurrent decision-making about risk in supply networks, in comparison to hierarchical decision-making used in the literature.

10.2 Emerging Technologies for Designing Fail-Safe Networked Systems

Several technological advances are reshaping the business landscape for numerous industries. The Digital Five Forces impact several aspects of an enterprise: business models, products and services, customer segments, channels and workplaces (Krishnan 2017). The digital network business model with its asset-light, connections-intensive approach is growing in almost all industries. Advances in automation and data exchange are leading to smart products manufactured in smart factories and delivered by smart supply chains. This trend is referred to as Industry 4.0. The prominent technologies that are defining the emerging industrial landscape are the Internet of Things (IoT), cyber-physical systems, and cloud computing (see Figure 10-2).

IoT is defined by IEEE as "a system consisting of networks of sensors, actuators, and smart objects whose purpose is to interconnect 'all' things, including everyday and industrial objects, in such a way as to make them intelligent, programmable and more capable of interacting with humans and each other" (IEEE-SA 2015). Networks, interconnectedness and interactions are key aspects of this definition that forms the conceptual bridge to our discussions of supply networks in preceding chapters. However, there are some differences. A supply network is predominantly static by design and can be reconfigured to deal with disruptions, but an IoT network is inherently dynamic due to the mobility of the devices and ad hoc connections with adjacent devices (Miorandi et al. 2012). Ramo (2016) estimates that ten thousand new devices are added to the Internet every minute; they range from smartphones and laptops to medical devices and aircraft diagnostic tools. Another key difference between other networks like supply networks and IoT lies in the network size as measured by the number of nodes. While some of the largest supply networks can have a few hundred or even a few thousand

Figure 10-2. Emerging technologies influencing the design of complex networked systems.

nodes, the size of IoT networks is usually measured in millions. This difference in size is because a supply network's nodes are its facilities, while an IoT network's nodes are the large number of "objects" in the Internet environment, such as mobile phones, sensors, and actuators, which interact to achieve common objectives.

According to the US National Intelligence Council (NIC 2008) "by 2025 Internet nodes may reside in everyday things—food packages, furniture, paper documents, and more" (National Intelligence Council 2008). This trend is referred to as the evolution of "smart connected products" and is fueled by advances in computing power, device miniaturization and widespread wireless connectivity (Porter and Heppelmann 2014). Such smart products have a physical structure, a unique identifier, some minimum computing capabilities and can act as sensors or actuators to produce and consume data respectively, using the Internet as a global platform for communication and coordination. A typical architecture for IoT has four layers: sensing layer, networking layer, service layer and interface layer (Xu et al. 2014). The sensing layer contains hardware such as sensors and actuators. The networking layer provides interconnections and networking support. The service layer manages services required by the user, e.g., security. Finally, the interface layer facilitates interactions with users and other applications. The interactions between these layers give rise to several applications, and the scope of these applications continues to evolve.

The interconnection of the physical devices, such as manufacturing equipment, along with software systems for modeling and controlling the state of physical devices form the foundation of cyber-physical systems. Cyber-physical systems have received significant attention from the research community during the past decade. Cyber-physical systems, such as smart grids, autonomous transportation systems and automatic health monitoring systems are characterized by systems that are controlled by software that communicates remotely over a network. The challenge in designing cyber-physical systems lies in bridging the gap between software engineering and physical systems design.

Finally, cloud-computing technologies provide shared computing resources such as data storage, applications, and services over a network. Cloud computing has five essential characteristics: (i) on-demand service, (ii) broad network access, (iii) resource pooling, (iv) rapid elasticity and (v) measured service (NIST). On-demand service allows consumers to access server time and network storage without human interaction from the service provider. Broad network access enables diverse client platforms to connect to the cloud services. Computing services are pooled to serve multiple clients. Elasticity refers to the ability to increase or decrease capabilities at the server side without affecting the customers. Measured service allows service providers to quantify service usage, which enables different business models.

10.2.1 Applications of Emerging Technologies within a Supply Network

The technological trends discussed above are likely to have a significant impact on our ability to analyze and design fail-safe network systems. Regarding supply networks, IoT devices "can monitor their environment, report their status, receive instructions, and even take action based on the information they receive" (Manyika et al. 2013). These devices are connected to individual items that are in turn connected to the cloud for asset and material tracking.

The assets can be rerouted automatically to overcome any anticipated delays with the aid of GPS trackers and real-time traffic and weather updates. Managers can monitor inventory and manage stock with RFID tags. Automatic restocking and instantaneous rerouting can help in reacting to changes in demand instantly. Managers can also track any supply chain contamination to its source, and take any corrective action necessary. Perishable items can be monitored for their condition and expected shelf life in real-time. Product in-use data helps in ensuring availability of replacement parts. The availability of real-time information enables informed decision making. Managers can benefit from end-to-end visibility, which allows them to use just-in-time and lean practices for appropriately balancing risk with cost.

All the information can be integrated throughout the value chain, ensuring efficiency while imbuing the network with robustness and resilience simultaneously. According to a Deloitte study, the resilience of a supply chain rests on visibility, flexibility, collaboration and control (Healy

2012). IoT enables visibility by providing the ability to monitor suppliers, material flow and consumption patterns. The rapid identification of alternate suppliers in case of disruption enables flexibility. IoT and cloud computing enable collaboration among different stakeholders in a supply network with secure data transfer among different suppliers. Finally, the availability of information enables real-time monitoring and control of operations within a supply network. This example extends beyond supply networks to other networked systems in other industries, as discussed in the following section.

10.2.2 Other Opportunities Created by the Emerging Technologies

The emerging industrial paradigm creates opportunities in a broad spectrum of industries. Tata Consultancy Services conducted a global study on IoT in 2015, spanning four geographical areas and 13 different industries ranging from industrial manufacturing to banking (TCS 2015). The study identified supply chain monitoring as one of the key application areas impacted by IoT. Installing digital devices in Source, Make and Deliver operations throughout a supply network enables real-time monitoring of operations. This area accounts for the second most widespread use of IoT, as evidenced by FedEx and other logistics providers' use of package tracking. In addition to supply chain monitoring, the study identified three other business areas for applying IoT technologies (see Figure 10-3).

- *Premises monitoring*: Installing sensors to monitor places of business like banks, retail stores and hotels. Companies with high product price points (> $1000) for their products or services use premises monitoring the most, making this a growth area.

- *Product monitoring*: Embedding devices into products such as refrigerators, automobiles, and aircraft engines. This area is also poised for growth and has the highest percentage of planned IoT expenditure.

- *Customer monitoring*: Tracking devices used by customers; for example, mobile phones, and wearables. With almost 2 billion smartphones in use worldwide and the growing popularity of wearables, this area is predominant in IoT applications.

Different industries showed significant differences in the adoption of IoT technologies, with the following important highlights (TCS 2015):

- Financial firms are investing greater amounts of capital on monitoring their premises compared to other sectors; industrial manufacturers on the other hand, are allocating more of their IoT budgets to product monitoring.

Figure 10-3. Four main business areas for IoT applications. Reproduced from "Internet of Things: The Complete Reimaginative Force. TCS Global Trend Study". 2015 by Tata Consultancy Services.

- Automotive companies, energy companies, and consumer packaged goods (CPG) companies have focused their IoT expenditure on supply chain monitoring, while compared to other industries, insurers are spending a significant portion of their IoT budget to monitor their customers.

- The smallest IoT spenders (as a percentage of revenue) are energy, CPG and insurance companies, while the biggest IoT spenders are travel, industrial manufacturing, media and telecom firms.

- Automotive manufacturers have the least IoT generated revenue, while industrial manufacturers have the highest revenue increase from IoT in 2014.

Despite these differences, all industries are optimistic and share the view that IoT programs will improve their business. We list the top five business impacts by 2020 recognized globally in Table 10-2.

These emerging technologies could help in addressing the challenges that face supply networks as listed in Table 10-3 (abstracted from Table 1-1).

Table 10-2. Top five business impacts of IoT by 2020.

1	More tailored or precise customer segmentation (for example, based on how customers use products or services)
2	Greater insights for salespeople on key aspects of company products (for example, product features) that customers use the most
3	More tailored products or services
4	Reduction in cost of sales through automated reordering for customers
5	Better service because of more informed service reps (they can view data on how customers are using the products)

Reproduced from "Internet of Things: The Complete Reimaginative Force. TCS Global Trend Study". 2015 by Tata Consultancy Services.

Table 10-3. Challenges facing supply networks.

Challenges/Needs/Priorities
Increasing complexity due to globalization of the supply chain*
Multiple channels of fulfillment
Shortening product lifecycles
Increasing customer expectations*
Volatile demand signals*
High capital investment drives need for high capacity utilization
Variable supplier commitments and delivery*
Escalating costs: inventory, transportation, penalties*
Complex and sluggish planning processes, needing frequent manual corrections
Lack of coordination between various facilities of the supply network*
Focus on Lean and JIT reduces margin of error*
Latency of information flow and lack of real-time visibility
Extracting knowledge or insight from data*
Stringent regulatory compliances
Natural disasters*
Lack of standard methods and frameworks for risk management*

* Addressed in this monograph

For example, IoT technologies can be used to track and fulfill demand from different channels of fulfillment in real time. Continuous information exchange among different aspects of the product lifecycle, such as product design, manufacturing, use and recycling, enables rapid reconfiguration of supply networks in response to any disruptions. The real-time availability of information through the network enhances coordination between various nodes in the supply chain.

10.3 Open Research Challenges

IoT must overcome several challenges, despite having made tremendous strides heretofore and holding great promise for the future. We summarize these challenges in Table 10.4. Some of these challenges have counterparts in supply networks as well.

First, the large number of devices imposes energy capacity and computational capacity limits (Atzori et al. 2010). Thus, resource utilization, resource efficiency and service level are key challenges. The methods described in this monograph can be leveraged to address some of these challenges.

Second, integration of the different functionalities of smart connected products, to provide an acceptable service level is another important challenge (Miorandi et al. 2012). As the number of devices continues to increase in both quantity and heterogeneity, scalability becomes an issue both at the network capacity and data analysis levels. The designers of IoT based systems should base their designs on certain core principles including interoperability, data exchange, and information availability to address the issues of heterogeneity. The success promised by IoT is heavily reliant on the information exchange between different devices that may be owned by different entities. The devices must be able to communicate with each other and the information gathered by the sensors must be available to distributed entities and decision makers throughout the network to achieve the full potential of IoT.

Table 10-4. Challenges in implementing IoT for supply networks.

	Challenges
1	Resource efficiency
2	Heterogeneity of information sources
3	Network security risks
4	Issues of trust among stakeholders
5	Decentralized decision making

Third and perhaps one of the greatest challenges posed to IoTs, is the network security risk. The U.S. National Intelligence Council issued the following warnings (NIC 2008):

- "… to the extent that everyday objects become information security risks, the IoT could distribute those risks far more widely than the Internet has to date."
- "The strong growth in interconnected, potentially adaptive devices implies a larger cyber security attack surface with potentially cascading adverse effects in both the cyber and physical domains."

These warnings highlight the risks inherent to IoT applications (O'Brien 2016). Similar to supply networks, risks can manifest in numerous ways, ranging from variations (e.g., interruptions in wireless service) to disruptions (e.g., targeted cyber-attacks on selected devices, such as those in a hospital or a car).

In addition to attacks from adversaries, the use of IoT within supply chains is also limited due to the concerns surrounding privacy and confidentiality. The optimization of the overall supply network compels entities to share their potentially confidential information with other entities within the supply network. These other entities may be current or future competitors. In such cases, entities may be unwilling to share their information on an IoT platform; this results in a need for technologies that can address trust issues within supply networks.

The techniques presented in the monograph are based on several assumptions; one such assumption is that one organization operates all of the nodes of a supply network and there is a single decision maker who can control the inventories and flow at each node. However, if different entities make the decisions and the entities are self-interested and profit maximizing in nature, then the interactions between these entities become important. In such cases, the models presented in this monograph can be updated to account for the interactions among the decision makers.

10.4 Beyond Supply Chains—Towards "Engineered Networks"—To Fail-safe Networks in Other Industries

Complex networks are at the core of many large-scale engineered systems. Examples of other networked systems include smart manufacturing, smart electricity grids and smart transportation systems. Electricity grids are special types of supply networks that transmit electricity from the source to the demand nodes. Similarly, transportation networks can also be viewed as supply networks. By identifying common traits across different classes of supply networks, the techniques developed in this monograph can apply to diverse applications.

10.4.1 Smart Manufacturing

While each network shares some similarities with supply networks discussed in the monograph, there are characteristics unique to each type of network that necessitate customization and development of new techniques. Consider, for example, the emerging manufacturing ecosystems. IoT technologies are also resulting in an ecosystem concept of manufacturing, also referred to as smart manufacturing, where data and information collected from sensors are used to reconfigure flexible manufacturing processes based on changes in demand and supply signals. A smart manufacturing ecosystem relies on IoT, big data and cloud for providing reconfigurability at low costs.

Another emerging paradigm related to smart manufacturing is the paradigm of Cloud-Based Design and Manufacturing (CBDM) (Wu et al. 2015). CBDM is a decentralized, service oriented design and manufacturing model where software and hardware are made available on-demand through the cloud. CBDM enables organizations to leverage the power of the crowd, as in crowd sourcing, by enabling large numbers of service providers to be connected to large numbers of service subscribers. The large numbers of providers enhance the robustness of the entire network because it is easier to find replacement providers from the large pool if any disruptions occur.

10.4.2 Smart Power Networks

One of the unique challenges confronting an electrical power network, or power grid, is the difficulty in storing electricity. The generation of electricity must be synchronized with distribution and its corresponding end use to lessen storage demands. The generation and distribution of electricity are governed by the laws of physics and by the characteristics of the generators and the transmission lines. Economic forces mediate supply and demand. The operation of an electric grid is highly dependent on price, which changes frequently. Therefore, both the laws of physics and economic principles govern the dynamics and function of the networked system, both of which require consideration in modeling.

The design of fail-safe power grids is further complicated by the fact that they are decentralized supply networks. There are multiple independent decision makers interacting with each other, each with a different set of objectives (see Figure 10-4). For example, the US power grid involves interactions among the following decision makers: consumers (residential

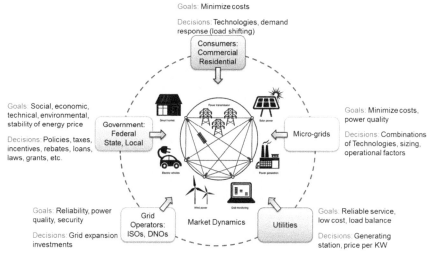

Figure 10-4. Decisions affecting the structure and function of a smart grid.

and commercial), grid operators, utilities, micro-grids, and governments (local, state & federal). Consumers make decisions about how to fulfill their energy needs at the lowest possible cost. Consumers can choose from different sources of energy or change their pattern of consumption. The goal of the grid operators is to ensure its reliable operation while maintaining power quality. They also make decisions about investments in grid expansion. Utility companies focus on providing reliable service at a low cost. Their decisions include operating different generating stations and determining prices. The government is interested in a wide range of social (e.g., employment), economic (e.g., lower prices) and environmental objectives. They make decisions regarding policies, taxes, incentives, rebates, grants and loans and legislate to ensure that the system is robust and sustainable.

10.4.3 Transportation Networks

In transportation networks, such as an air transportation network, the network is defined by nodes, such as airports and links, such as service between two airports. The interactive decisions made by passengers, airline companies, airports and federal agencies determine the structure and behavior of the air transportation system (see Figure 10-5). The passengers make ticket purchase decisions based on their preferences for cost and alternate routes. Airline companies make decisions about whether to serve an airport, the aircraft type to use and the ticket prices, all with the goal of maximizing their profit. Federal agencies make policy decisions and develop regulations to achieve the desired system-level performance.

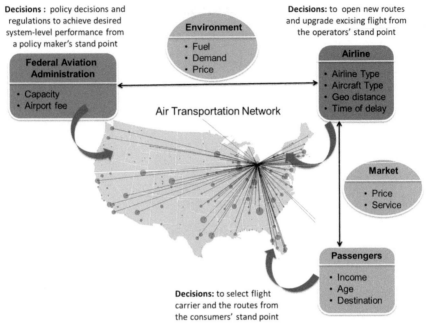

Decisions : policy decisions and regulations to achieve desired system-level performance from a policy maker's stand point

Federal Aviation Administration
• Capacity
• Airport fee

Environment
• Fuel
• Demand
• Price

Air Transportation Network

Decisions: to open new routes and upgrade excising flight from the operators' stand point

Airline
• Airline Type
• Aircraft Type
• Geo distance
• Time of delay

Market
• Price
• Service

Passengers
• Income
• Age
• Destination

Decisions: to select flight carrier and the routes from the consumers' stand point

Figure 10-5. Decision makers in the air transportation network.

Designing fail-safe transportation networks necessitates that the structure of the network that emerges from those decisions is reliable, robust, controllable, resilient and flexible. After the process described completes a cycle, policy makers can make decisions that influence stakeholder actions and lead to a modification of the network structure, which begins a new cycle of intersecting decisions.

10.4.4 Designing Fail-safe Decentralized Networks

All the complex networked systems discussed in this section, including smart manufacturing, smart power networks and smart transportation networks are decentralized in nature. Their structure is based on the decisions made by self-interested entities. With increasing trends towards autonomous systems, decentralized decision-making becomes more prevalent. Such decentralized systems are fundamentally different from traditional centrally designed networks in many ways (Sha and Panchal 2014). While centralized systems are designed as sets of interacting components forming integrated whole, complex-networked-systems evolve because of the decisions and behaviors of its constituents. To characterize the uniqueness of complex networked systems, Sha and Panchal (2014) present a framework with five levels: (i) node-level preferences, (ii) node-level behaviors, (iii) network structure, (iv) network properties and (v) system-level performance. They argue that the network structure emerges from node-level behaviors which are driven by node-level preferences. Therefore, to achieve desired structures for fail-safe networks, node-level behaviors must be influenced.

In such decentralized systems, the role of design in complex evolutionary systems is different from traditional complex systems (Sha and Panchal 2014). The focus shifts from designing network topology to designing incentives and interaction mechanisms for coordination between individual entities. Consider the example of an air transportation network. The failure of this type of network can be the result of the disruption of individual nodes, delays at an airport due to weather emergency for example, or the network overall, through disruptions such as congestion. Congestion is affected by the topology of the network, which is defined by the origin-destination pairs of flights. Managers can reduce congestion by re-routing flights within the network. However, routing decisions cannot be made centrally; they are made by individual airline companies whose primary goal is to maximize their profits. Furthermore, these decisions are made under the pressure of competition from other airline companies. Thus, the issue of congestion can be addressed only by providing appropriate incentives (or penalties) for airline companies that would lead them to make decisions in a manner that would improve the overall function of the air transportation network.

10.5 Closing Comments

Networks are pervading many spheres of business and society, accelerated by emerging technologies, such as the Digital Five Forces (Krishnan 2017). Mobility allows for data collection through sensors in smartphones, wearables and other devices, enabling the monitoring of product performance and customer preferences. Big data technologies enable businesses to connect data from various sources including databases, social media and the Internet to glean valuable insights about risks and opportunities. Social media facilitate the building of social networks enabling both business-to-consumer and consumer-to-consumer exchanges and improving customer experiences. Cloud computing allows users to store and retrieve data over the Internet, increasing cost-effectiveness and availability. Artificial Intelligence (AI) tools like neural networks in concert with robotics, form the foundational technologies for innovations such as driverless cars. The concept that underpins all the examples above is the use of networks, from providing a conduit for data flow between the provider and consumer to enabling communications between driverless cars. The implementation of fail-safe designs is crucial in this age of rapid network proliferation.

We present in this monograph various techniques for designing fail-safe networks. With an ever-increasing scientific understanding of physical phenomena, modeling and simulation (M&S) are becoming an integral part of designing complex engineered systems ranging from materials to manufacturing systems to healthcare. New research areas are emerging where the focus is on using simulation models to drive design decisions. One such example is Integrated Computational Materials Engineering (ICME), where the goal is to use scientific models to design new materials and to enable the concurrent design of products and materials. Scientific models are typically based on different levels of resolution within the system, ranging from atomistic levels to the system-wide level. These models are developed by different individuals, working on different geographically distributed teams that may belong to different organizations. The outputs of some models serve as inputs to other models. Some models can be executed in parallel, where the execution of other models may be exclusively sequential. The task of a systems integrator is to establish networks of simulation models, called workflows, linked together by the flow of information. These networks of simulation models have the characteristics of supply networks; but instead of the flow of material, there is a flow of information in such networks. With such a network of information flow, the techniques discussed in the monograph can be used to determine the characteristics of the modeling and simulation network, such as robustness and structural controllability. While the techniques described can be used to design fail-safe networks, there are also unique challenges associated with ensuring the quality of information and the propagation of uncertainty. Such unique challenges call for further research in this direction, both from the standpoint of the type of flow on the network and the specific domain of application.

References

Atzori, L., Iera, A. and Morabito, G. 2010. The internet of things: A survey. Computer Networks 54(15): 2787–2805.

Healy, E. 2012. Improving Supply Chain Resilience, Can You Afford Not To? 2012 [cited June 17 2017]. Available from https://www2.deloitte.com/ie/en/pages/deloitte-private/articles/improving-supply-chain-resilience.html.

IEEE-SA. 2015. Internet of Things (IoT) ecosystem study. In: IEEE Standards Association. New York, NY.

Krishnan, K. A. 2017. Digitally reimagining mobility. In: Tandon, M. C. and Ghosh, P. (eds.). Mobility Engineering: Proceedings of CAETS 2015 Convocation on Pathways to Sustainability. Singapore: Springer Singapore.

Libert, B., Beck, M. and Wind, J. 2016. The network imperative: How to survive and grow in the age of digital business models. Boston.: Harvard Business Review Press.

Manyika, J., Chui, M., Bughin, J., Dobbs, R., Bisson, P. and Marrs, A. 2013. Disruptive Technologies: Advances that will Transform Life, Business, and the Global Economy. San Francisco, CA: McKinsey Global Institute.

Miorandi, D., Sicari, S., De Pellegrini, F. and Chlamtac, I. 2012. Internet of things: Vision, applications and research challenges. Ad Hoc Networks 10(7): 1497–1516.

NIC. 2008. Disruptive Civil Technologies—Six Technologies with Potential Impacts on US Interests Out to 2025. National Intelligence Council.

O'brien, H. M. 2016. The Internet of things (data security and product liability collision). Journal of Internet Law 19(12): 1.

Porter, M. and Heppelmann, J. 2014. How smart, connected products are transforming competition. Harvard Business Review 92(11): 64–88.

Ramo, J. C. 2016. The Seventh Sense: Power, Fortune, and Survival in the Age of Networks. New York. Little, Brown and Company.

Sha, Z. and Panchal, J. H. 2014. Estimating local decision-making behavior in complex evolutionary systems. ASME Journal of Mechanical Design.

TCS. 2017. Internet of Things: The Complete Reimaginative Force. Tata Consultancy Services 2015 [cited June 13 2017]. http://sites.tcs.com/internet-of-things/.

Wu, D., Rosen, D. W., Wang, L. and Schaefer, D. 2015. Cloud-based design and manufacturing: A new paradigm in digital manufacturing and design innovation. Computer-Aided Design 59: 1–14.

Xu, L. D., He, W. and Li, S. 2014. Internet of things in industries: A survey. Industrial Informatics, IEEE Transactions on 10(4): 2233–2243.

Index